# CALIFORNIA
## Gardener's Guide

*Volume II*

09
———
111

IWO
1

±IWQ
1

Published by Cool Springs Press, 101 Forrest Crossing Boulevard, Suite 100, Franklin, Tennessee, 37064.

Library of Congress Cataloging-in-Publication Data is available.
ISBN: 978-1-59186-267-3

First printing 2007
Printed in the United States of America
10 9 8 7 6 5 4 3 2 1

Managing Editor: Ramona Wilkes
Designer: Sheri Ferguson, Ferguson Design
Horticulture Editor: Dee Maranhao
Production Design: S.E. Anderson

On the Cover: Matilija Poppy (*Romneya coulteri*), photographed by: Tom Eltzroth

# Photo Credits

Bruce Asakawa: Pages 156, 235

Liz Ball: Pages 39, 54, 131, 139, 143, 148, 241

Bamboo Headquarters (bamboheadquarters.com): Pages 102, 106

Pam Beck: Page 107

Paul Body (paulbodyphoto.com): Page 194

Diana Chapman, Telos Rare Bulbs: Page 61

John Cretti: Page 120

Dave Wilson Nursery: Pages 76, 78

Alan & Linda Detrick: Page 99

Mike Dirr: Page 179

Tom Eltzroth: Pages 33, 34, 35, 38, 40, 58, 48, 49, 50, 51, 55, 56 58, 60, 63, 68, 70, 71, 72, 73, 77, 80, 81, 96, 97, 101, 105, 108, 109, 126, 127, 129, 132, 134, 135, 149, 152, 161, 171, 175, 184, 193, 199, 200, 202, 207, 208, 209, 212, 214, 215, 217, 220, 222, 223, 231, 233, 236, 244

Lorenzo Gunn: Page 79

Dency Kane: Page 246

Peter Loewer: Pages 100, 110

Bob Lyons: Page 238

Charles Mann: Pages 21, 37, 41, 52, 83, 87, 90, 112, 114, 123, 128, 151, 170, 191

Mary McBride: Pages 234 (top), 247

Judy Mielke: Pages 230, 249

Linn Mills: Page 219

Monrovia: Pages 95, 121, 138, 150, 162, 165, 169, 173, 177, 178, 228

Mountain States Wholesale Nursery: Page 226

Jerry Pavia: Pages 43, 46, 57, 118, 137, 172, 176, 195, 211, 221

Rob Proctor: Pages 92, 94

Photos courtesy of Proven Winners (www.provenwinners.com): Pages 84, 163

Felder Rushing: Pages 44, 74, 98, 111, 125, 196, 227, 243

San Marcos Growers: 240

Renee Shepherd (reneesgardenseeds.com): Pages 30, 42

Nan Sterman, Plant Soup, Inc.: Pages 10, 11, 12, 15, 16, 20, 22, 23, 28, 29, 32, 36, 53, 59, 62, 64, 66, 67, 75, 82, 85, 86, 88, 89, 91, 103, 104, 113, 116, 117, 122, 124, 130, 133, 136, 140, 141, 142, 146, 147, 155, 157, 158, 159, 160, 164, 167, 168, 174, 180, 181, 182, 183, 185, 186, 187, 188, 189, 190, 192, 197, 198, 204, 205, 210, 203, 206, 213, 216, 218, 224, 229, 232, 234 (bottom), 237, 242, 245

Georgia Tasker: Page 65

Tree of Life Nursery: Page 248

Pete Veilleiux (eastbaywilds.com): Page 225, 239

**Thanks go to the owners of these gardens, and to these garden designers, for their contributions to this book:**

Pages 8, 10, 186: Designed by Dinah Grisdale, Serendipity Garden Design, San Diego

Pages 11, 103: Axelrod Garden, designed by Scott Spencer

Page 12: Garden of Richard and Britta Armstrong

Page 15: Designed by Jennifer Axelrod

Page 16: Martin Garden, designed by Debora Carl, Cardiff-by-the-Sea

Pages 20, 187: Garden of Debora Carl, designed by Deborah Carl, Cardiff-by-the-Sea

Page 22: Garden of Dinah Grisdale, designed by Dinah Grisdale, Serendipity Garden Design, San Diego

Pages 29, 64, 122, 140, 142, 147: Designed by Nan Sterman, Plant Soup, Inc.

Pages 104, 116, 136: Sterman/Wittenberg garden, designed by Scott Spencer

Page 117: Garden of Patrick Anderson

Page 185: Garden of Erik and Irina Gronborg

Page 186: Designed by Bishop Garden Design

Page 197: Garden of Jan Smithen

# CALIFORNIA
## Gardener's Guide
### Volume II

## Nan Sterman

## COOL SPRINGS PRESS
Franklin, Tennessee

# Acknowledgments

My deepest love and appreciation goes to my sweet husband Curt Wittenberg, for his unfailing support that allows me to follow my dreams. Thank you to my children Asher Wittenberg and Tamar Wittenberg, for tolerating years of visits to gardens, nurseries, and botanical gardens across the country. Thank you also to my stepson Gabriel, daughter-in-law Stephanie, and grandson River Zen Evaristo. My greatest wish for each of you is to always have dreams to pursue.

Thank you to friends and colleagues for their good humor and encouragement, for patiently answering my endless questions, and for being so generous with their expertise, photos, and knowledge: Jennifer Axelrod and Stephanie Evaristo, my fabulous research assistants; Bracey Tiede; Joe Seals; Debra Prinzing; Scott Spencer; Mary James; Jan Smithen; Paul Body; Katie Bloome, formerly of Monrovia; Richard Turner, Pacific Horticulture; Nicole Jackson and David Doolittle, Proven Winners; Deborah Lindsay; John C. Macgregor IV; Mary McBride; Bill Nelson; Lon Rombough; George Hull and Janet Rademacher, Mountain States Wholesale Nursery; Ed Laivo and Tom Spellman, Dave Wilson Nursery; Pete Veilleux, East Bay Wilds; Andy Maycen and Tom Piergrossi, Tom Piergrossi Landscape Nursery; Alessandra Vinciguerra; Jo O'Connell, Australian Native Plants Nursery; Diana Chapman, Telos Rare Bulbs; Ralph Evans, Bamboo Headquarters; Brent and Becky Heath, Brent and Becky's Bulbs; Ernie Wasson, Cabrillo College; Jim Threadgill, Easy to Grow Bulbs; John Schoustra, Greenwood Daylily Gardens; Whitney and Sui Lin Robinson, Multiflora; Mark and Cindy Pearson, Pearson's Gardens & Herb Farm; Renee Shepherd, Renee's Seeds; Randy Baldwin, San Marcos Growers; Jeff Moore, Solana Succulents; Barry Glick, Sunshine Farm and Gardens; Dan Heims, Terra Nova Nursery; Michael Buckner, The Plant Man; the ladies at Annie's Annuals and Perennials; and the staff at Theodore Payne Foundation and Tree of Life Nurseries.

My greatest appreciation also to the many other experts who answered questions, shared their expertise, and reviewed drafts: John Seeger, Four Winds Growers; Phil Bergman, Jungle Music; Marca Dickie, Marca Dickie Nursery; V.J. Billings, Mountain Valley Growers; Bob Hornback, Muchas Grasses; Barbara Eisenstein and Bart O'Brien, Rancho Santa Ana Botanic Garden; Saul Nadler, The Palm Broker; Jerry Parsons, UC Berkeley Botanical Garden; Kim Kaplan, USDA; Gary Bender, William Coates, Ben Faber, Pam Geisel, Mike Henry, Mario Moratorio, and Vincent Lazaneo, University of California Cooperative Extension; Jason DeWees; John Hazard; Doug Johnson, California Invasive Plant Council; Katherine Holmes; Lori Hubbart; Louise Lacey; and the many other people who offered their support during the process of writing this book.

A special thank you to fellow members of the Mediterranean Garden Society, Garden Writers, and Pacific Bulb Society listserv.

Finally, eternal thanks to Diana Maranhao for her meticulous horticulture and copy editing, and to the amazing team of Cindy Games, Ramona Wilkes, and Billie Brownell of Cool Springs Press.

# Table of Contents

# Featured Plants *for California*

# Welcome to Gardening
## *in California*

Have you recently purchased a new home without a bit of landscaping, or an older home with a worn-out garden? Or have you lived in the same home for a number of years and keep promising yourself to get to the garden "some day." Does your existing garden need a bit of freshening up? Or are you looking for some exciting and beautiful new plants that are easy to grow and take little water, little fertilizer, and little maintenance?

If you recognize any of these situations as your own, this book is for you. The plants described in these pages are all extremely well suited for California gardens. Not every plant will work in every region of the state, but there are plenty of plants for everyone.

Gardening in California is like gardening nowhere else in the world. While all gardening is wonderful, exciting, rewarding, and surprising, if you've come here from elsewhere, California gardening takes some getting used to. My goal for this introduction is to help you understand the big picture so you can create the garden of your dreams.

## Featured Plants

In each chapter of this book, plants are listed alphabetically by common name, followed by botanical name. Some gardeners, especially beginners, feel overwhelmed by botanical names, but they have a very important purpose. Common names differ by region or culture. What you call a daisy and what your best friend calls a daisy could be two very different plants with similarly shaped flowers. Or, you may refer to a plant as a daisy, but your friend calls it an aster. Botanical names, however, are unique. Each type of plant has a first name (that's the genus name) and a last name (that's the species name). When you shop for plants by their botanical names, you will get exactly what you are looking for. By the way, don't be afraid of mispronouncing botanical names. Say it phonetically, and when worse comes to worse, spell it.

In addition to the plant names, I've included interesting facts, observations, and descriptions of the plants themselves. I've included their estimated heights and spreads along with the minimum temperatures they can handle. In other regions of the country, gardeners need maximum temperatures as well, but in most of California, maximum temperature is not a concern.

## California's Mediterranean Climate

Most of California has a Mediterranean climate. California is one of five Mediterranean climate regions of the world, along with the Mediterranean basin, the west coast of Chile, southern and western Australia, and the southern tip of South Africa. These regions are all defined by hot, dry summers and mild winters with rainfall in winter.

California is an enormous state that includes deserts, coastlines, mountains, and valleys. The state measures 250 miles at its widest and 770 miles at its longest. To drive the 796 miles along Interstate 5 from the Mexican border to the Oregon border takes thirteen hours. The drive is 30 miles *longer* than the drive from Minneapolis to Columbus, Ohio, and 60 miles longer than Norfolk, Virginia to Portland, Maine. Imagine how much

Beautiful California landscapes use plants from Mediterranean climates

territory and how many different kinds of growing conditions you encounter in that distance! From north to south and east to west, there are dramatic differences in vegetation, geology, topography, and climate.

For example, in my San Diego County garden, average annual rainfall is only 10 inches. In San Francisco, about 475 miles to the north, annual rainfall averages 21 inches. Rainfall in Crescent City, just below the Oregon border, is a generous 75 inches annually, while El Centro, along the Mexican border, receives *less than 3 inches* of rain in an entire year!

Though rainfall differs widely, the state's unifying factor is its seasonal rainfall pattern. The tables in this introduction show average monthly and annual rainfall for communities throughout the state. Notice that our rainy season starts in November and ends in March—one of the key characteristics of a Mediterranean climate.

What else makes this a Mediterranean climate? Those hot, dry summer days when the sun shines bright. Those days are perfect for a trip to the beach, but for plants, they can mean overwhelming heat and water stress. Have you ever seen a limp plant whose leaves are soft and floppy in the middle of the day? If the surrounding soil is dry, then you are looking at a plant with water stress. The plant has lost more water to the atmosphere than its roots can take up from the soil. In addition, too much bright sunlight can wreak havoc with a plant's ability to regulate photosynthesis. Sunlight drives photosynthesis, the chemical process by which plants convert water and carbon dioxide from the air into carbohydrates (this is the beginning of the food chain).

## How Plants Adapt

Plants native to the world's five Mediterranean regions, much like those that grow in deserts, have evolved ways to conserve water and protect themselves from bright sunlight. Some are succulent. They accumulate water in stems and leaves to ensure a ready supply. Others have tough, leathery leaves that resist wilting. Still others have tiny, white or silvery hairs over their leaf surfaces. To us, the hairs are soft fuzz, but to a plant, they are shade from sunlight and a vapor barrier that keeps water from evaporating too quickly from the leaf surface. Though the leaf tissue itself may be green, the silvery hairs give it a characteristic gray-green tone that is typical of plants native to Mediterranean climates.

Another strategy has been to evolve narrow, needle-like leaves with little surface area. Less surface area means less area for water evaporation and exposure to the sun. Rosemary is a prime example. Many of the wonderful Australian plants also have narrow, leaves that at first glance look like pine needles.

Summer dormancy is yet another way native plants survive hot, dry summers. We all know of plants that go dormant to survive cold winters, but did you know that many Mediterranean climate plants go dormant to survive hot dry summers? A few, California buckeye being one example, drop their leaves and

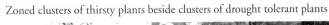

Zoned clusters of thirsty plants beside clusters of drought tolerant plants

remain bare until the rains of winter. Similarly, after spring bloom, South African bulbs let their leaves wither. By midsummer's intense heat, the bulbs have completely disappeared. Then, when the air cools in fall, the bulbs send their green leaves poking up out of the ground once again.

Summer dormancy is not always obvious. Many plants simply sit in a state of suspended animation through the heat of summer. Flowers fade, but leaves remain. Summer dormancy is why California's hillsides go brown in summer. It is also why most milder area gardens look their best from spring until early summer, and then again in fall. When the air cools, usually around October, they "wake up" and start what we gardeners refer to as our "second spring." They put on new growth and some flower for a second round. This is also the best planting time of the year. The soil is still warm enough to encourage good root establishment while the sun is less intense and cooler air means less heat stress.

## Just Go for It

Rather than fight the peculiarities of our climate, I encourage you to grow with them. These pages are filled with beautiful Mediterranean climate plants, many native to California and others native to other Mediterranean regions. These plants are so well adapted to our growing conditions that they thrive with little irrigation once established. They are also adapted to our poor soils and grow at a rate that won't overwhelm you with the need to prune (unless you plant them in too small a space).

European styling is one of many influences in California gardens

Better yet, pests tend to ignore them. In other words, if you are looking for great beauty with little maintenance, Mediterranean climate plants are the way to go.

In addition to water-wise Mediterranean climate plants, I've included some thirstier plants. Those plants fall into two categories: edible and ornamental. From my perspective, in order to "spend" water on thirsty plants, I need a significant return on my investment. Food is one such significant return. The other return is large, beautiful, and often fragrant flowers. If you choose any of these thirstier plants, site them nearest the house where you can best appreciate them and monitor their need for water.

## Smart Watering

We Californians chronically overwater our gardens. According to one estimate, Southern Californians water their gardens with the equivalent of 84 inches of rainfall each year. That is as much rain as falls in the Amazon jungle, two and a half times the rainfall of Seattle, and four times the rainfall of Honolulu! Few gardeners realize that they can especially reduce watering in spring and fall when the air is cool and sun less intense. In winter, gardens need little or no irrigation unless we have a long, dry spell. Overwatering isn't good for plants, it isn't good for your bank account, and it isn't good for our state's limited water resources.

When should you water? Any time a plant needs more water than the soil can supply. How much should you water? That is an age-old question.

In practical terms, there are three major factors that determine how much water soil holds at any point in time. Every part of the state, every neighborhood even, has a different combination of the three:

- **Texture:** Heavy soils, including clay soils, hold water longer than loamy soils, which hold water better than sandy soils.
- **Temperature and Humidity:** In the dry, hot air of desert gardens, water evaporates from both soil and plant leaves much faster than it does in the somewhat cooler and more humid conditions of valley gardens. In those valley gardens, water evaporates faster than in the cooler and more humid conditions of coastal gardens.
- **Regional Precipitation:** Gardens in the far north get much more rain (and snowfall) than those in the south. In addition, soils in those areas tend to have more organic matter that holds water. As a result, northern soils have more moisture naturally available to roots.

Over time, you'll learn how much water each plant needs in your garden. To help you along that learning curve, I've divided the plants in these chapters into three groups—those with low water needs, those with moderate water needs, and those with high water needs.

In general, the amount of water a plant needs changes from month to month and from season to season. Plants need the least irrigation from the time the weather cools in fall until the end of the winter rainy season. When the weather starts to warm in spring (and rains end), start watering a bit more often. Irrigate most often in the heat of summer.

**Low Water Plants** are those that need very little water *once they are established*, i.e. after the first year or two in the ground. Low water plants typically come from climates where rain and snowfall are about the same or less than what occurs naturally in your garden. Many (but not all) native plants will survive with little supplemental irrigation, as will many succulents and plants from southwest deserts and other Mediterranean climates of the world.

Remember that in that first year or two after planting, all low water plants need regular, deep watering to saturate the entire rootball and beyond. Watering deeply encourages roots to go deep, part of what helps plants survive on little water later on. Only after they are established can you cut back to watering once a month or once every few months or only in summertime—depending on the particular plant and your garden's growing conditions. Some experimentation will help you determine how frequently to water. When you *do* water, be sure to wet the soil slowly and deeply to saturate those deep roots.

**Medium (or Moderate) Water Plants** are those that fall in between low and high. Many flowering perennials, soft leaved plants, and culinary herbs fall into the moderate water category. In general, when the soil is dry 3 to 6 inches down from the surface, it is time to water. If you have heavy clay soils or if you are lucky enough to have rich loamy soil, moderate water plants may easily go a week or more between waterings, depending on your climate. If you have sandy soils that drain quickly and/or a very hot exposure, you may need to water twice that often, depending on the season. Moderate water plants might need water once a week in spring, twice a week in the heat of summer, and once a week again in fall, and not at all in winter except during long dry spells.

**High Water Plants** do best in soils that are constantly moist but not saturated. The soil should feel slightly damp, not muddy. Many tropical and subtropical plants fall into this "frequent water" category. These plants are best grown together in a single, high water zone. That way, you can give them enough water without overwatering the plants that prefer drier conditions. Unless you live in a higher rainfall area or have a natural source of water on your property, it is wise to limit the number of thirsty, high water plants in your garden.

When you do water, do it because your plants need it, not because you do. You may find hand watering to be a good way to unwind after work. It is great therapy, but it may not be the best thing for your plants. Before you turn the spigot on, know whether your plants are low, moderate, or high water plants. Then, go into the garden and dig down into the soil. How deep do you dig before encountering damp soil? Is the surface already moist? Is it dry 3 inches down? 6 inches? Match the soil moisture to your plant's needs.

Regardless of your soil type or plant type, your garden will benefit from a thick layer of mulch to seal in the water and improve soil texture, and it allows you to stretch out the intervals between waterings. The last step of any planting project should be a nice thick layer of mulch.

## The Online Watering Calculator

The amount of water your plants need depends on the type of plant you are watering, your garden soil, your growing region, microclimate, and type of watering system. With so many different variables, precise watering directions are impossible. There is, however, a great online tool to help you determine how often and how long to water each zone of your garden every month of the year. The online Watering Calculator uses your zip code, soil type, the kind of plants you grow, and the kind of watering system you use (drip, bubbler, sprinkler, etc.) to generate a customized monthly irrigation schedule for each of your garden watering zones.

The online Watering Calculator is available for all areas of Southern California. If you live in San Diego County, go to **http://apps.SanDiego. gov/landcalc/**. If you live in Santa Barbara County, go to **www.Santa Barbara.gov/WaterCalc/**. If you live in any other part of Southern California, go to **www. BeWaterWise.com/ calculator.html**. If you live north of Santa Barbara, contact your local water agency to see whether the online Watering Calculator is available for your area. If not, encourage them to adopt it.

A rustic copper birdbath set in a foliage border offers an oasis

Use the information from the Watering Calculator to run your sprinklers manually or to program an automatic irrigation clock. Keep in mind that if you don't program your automatic irrigation controller, it will water at the manufacturer's preset rate: usually every zone runs ten minutes every day (it also resets to that schedule after a power outage unless there is a backup battery). That is way, way too much water even in the heat of summer.

## Irrigation Controls

Managing your automatic irrigation controller is one of the most important ways to control water. Set your clock to go on between 4 and 6 a.m. on weekdays and between 4 and 8 a.m. on weekends. The air is still cool at that time, so little water is lost to evaporation. Any leaves that get wet will dry quickly in the morning sun. Equally important, the greatest demand on municipal water systems is between 6 and 8 a.m. weekdays. Watering in the off hours reduces the stress on the system.

With newer, "smart" irrigation controllers, you enter your zip code information, plant and soil types, and the time of day to water. The controller decides how often and how much to water based on information from on-board weather sensors, weather satellite data, or historical weather data.

By the same token, since plants take water directly from the ground, the best way to irrigate is to water the ground—not trunks, stems, or leaves. Wet leaves make plants vulnerable to fungi and disease. It is fine to rinse the dust off leaves occasionally, but unless you live in a very windy or dusty area, a shower once or twice a year should suffice.

My entire garden is watered by drip irrigation—my flowering perennials, shrubs, trees, herb garden, vegetable garden, native, and desert gardens. Only our former lawn (now a meadow) has been watered with overhead sprinklers. Despite the horror stories landscapers like to tell about drip irrigation, my garden is living proof that it works extremely well. The water I save is well worth my investment in some extra maintenance time.

## Principles of Water-efficient Gardening

In our water-poor climate, water-efficient gardening (sometimes referred to as "Xeriscape™") just makes sense. The basic principles of water-efficient gardening are simple and straightforward:

- Start with a plan based on a water-efficient approach. The concept of clustering plants based on water need, for example, means that low water plants are in one part of the garden and watered by one set (zone) of sprinklers, bubblers, or drip emitters. Plants with medium water needs should be in a different area and watered by a different zone. High water plants should have their own irrigation zone as well.

A soft, lush transition using low water plants with strong forms and a restrained color palette

- Install a good, efficient irrigation system with an irrigation controller. "Smart" weather based, irrigation controllers take the worry out of programming. If your controller is not weather based, it is your responsibility to update watering times monthly. Don't leave it to your gardener.

- Limit your lawn space to the amount needed by pets, small children, or for playing bocce. If you simply need a green carpet, skip the lawn and plant lower water, lower maintenance ground covers. Better yet, plant a meadow of low water grasses. I cover all of these choices later in this book.

- Choose low water plants and place them according to their need for sun, shade, and soil type. Always place a plant in a spot that will accommodate its ultimate size.

- Most California native plants and most Mediterranean climate plants prefer our native soils, but if you plan to grow edibles or the thirstier exotics, first amend the soil generously with compost. Compost improves drainage, helps the soil hold moisture, adds some nutrients, and encourages beneficial organisms.

- Cover your soil and surround your plants with composted organic mulches. Mulch impedes water loss, keeps weeds down, and improves the soil as it decays. Spread mulch everywhere, leaving no bare soil. If there is a silver bullet in the garden, composted organic mulch is it.

- Practice good maintenance. Keep the garden tidy by mulching, weeding, pruning, fertilizing when needed, and controlling pests.

## California's Growing Regions

Most California gardeners reside in one of five of the state's growing regions: the coast, inland valleys, the Central Valley, low deserts, and high deserts. Many plant descriptions include comments about which regions a plant is or is not particularly well suited to.

Coastal gardens are bathed in cool moist air, fog, and ocean breezes that flow inland along bays, estuaries, and lagoons. Because of the ocean's buffering capacity, coastal gardens have the mildest growing conditions; these frost-free gardens are warmer in winter and cooler in summer. The ocean influence can be felt three miles, five miles, and even ten miles from the beach, depending on air currents, the position of coastal mountain ranges, and other factors. Small-scale climatic variations like these are what gardeners call "microclimates."

Though the ocean is a huge reservoir of water, plants growing right along the beach are subject to significant stress from intense sun (which can alternate with summer fog and often a thick marine layer), constant wind, and salt spray. Wind and salt spray diminish quickly as you move away from the beach.

Coastal gardens are often divided geographically into north, central, and south. Point Conception in Santa Barbara County is the clear dividing line between southern and central coast gardens. The northern/central dividing line is not as clear. Some people place it at Santa Cruz, others at the Golden Gate Bridge in San Francisco, and some north of Marin County. Either way, coastal gardens are wettest and coolest in the north, and driest and warmest in the south.

## Examples of Rainfall and Warmest and Coolest Temperatures in California's Coastal Communities

| City | Average Annual Rainfall (Inches) | Average Maximum Temperature in August °F | Average Minimum Temperature in January °F |
|---|---|---|---|
| Crescent City | 75 | 66 | 41 |
| San Francisco | 20 | 64-72 | 42-46 |
| Santa Cruz | 31 | 75 | 39 |
| Monterey | 19 | 69-72 | 43 |
| San Luis Obispo | 23 | 79 | 42 |
| Santa Barbara | 17 | 74-76 | 40-43 |
| Santa Monica | 13 | 71 | 50 |
| Long Beach | 12 | 84 | 46 |
| San Diego | 10 | 76 | 48 |

Inland valleys (and associated foothills) have little ocean influence. Instead they are hot, sunny, and dry in all but the winter rainy season. Even then, valleys receive far less rain than the coast. Temperature variations are greater, with winter frost more common in northern valleys and less common in southern valleys.

## Examples of Rainfall and Warmest and Coolest Temperatures in California's Inland Valley Communities

| City | Average Annual Rainfall (Inches) | Average Maximum Temperature in August °F | Average Minimum Temperature in January °F |
|---|---|---|---|
| Ukiah | 37 | 92 | 36 |
| Santa Rosa | 30 | 83 | 37 |
| Livermore | 15 | 89 | 36 |
| San Jose | 15 | 82 | 42 |
| Napa Valley | 25 | 82 | 38 |
| King City | 11 | 85 | 36 |
| Santa Maria | 13 | 73 | 39 |
| Ojai | 21 | 91 | 37 |
| Santa Paula | 17 | 82 | 41 |
| Burbank | 16 | 89 | 42 |
| Pasadena | 20 | 90 | 43 |
| Riverside | 10 | 94-95 | 40-42 |
| Hemet | 11 | 100 | 38 |
| Escondido | 15.5 | 89 | 43 |
| El Cajon | 12 | 90 | 42 |

The Central Valley is actually two valleys, the San Joaquin Valley in the south and the Sacramento Valley in the north. Central Valley air is hot and dry in summer with average August temperatures well into the 90s. Winters are cool and damp with average January temperatures in the 30s. The Sacramento Valley gets more rain and frost than the drier San Joaquin Valley, where winter temperatures seldom dip below freezing. The Central Valley is known for dense, thick tule fog that blankets the ground in fall and winter.

## Examples of Rainfall and Warmest and Coolest Temperatures in California's Central Valley Communities

| City | Average Annual Rainfall (Inches) | Average Maximum Temperature in August °F | Average Minimum Temperature in January °F |
|---|---|---|---|
| Chico | 26 | 95 | 36 |
| Sacramento | 17-18 | 90-92 | 38-40 |
| Stockton | 14-16 | 93 | 37-38 |
| Merced | 12 | 95 | 37 |
| Fresno | 11 | 96 | 38 |
| Bakersfield | 6 | 96-97 | 36-38 |

Low desert regions are east of Southern California's mountains and include the Coachella Valley, Anza Borrego desert, and parts of the Imperial Valley. Desert air is dry and hot, peaking with average August temperatures over 100 degrees F and midwinter temperatures in the 40s. Annual rainfall is 6 inches or less.

## Examples of Rainfall and Warmest and Coolest Temperatures in California's Low Desert Communities

| City | Average Annual Rainfall (Inches) | Average Maximum Temperature in August °F | Average Minimum Temperature in January °F |
|---|---|---|---|
| Palm springs | 6 | 107 | 42 |
| Borrego Springs | 6 | 107 | 44 |
| Brawley | 3 | 108 | 39 |
| El Centro | 3 | 108 | 40 |

Intermediate and high deserts refer to the desert areas above 1,000 feet elevation, primarily those along Highway 395 down the backside of the Sierra Nevada Mountains, from north of Bishop, and south through the Mojave Desert to the vicinity of Twentynine Palms. Summers are cooler than those in low deserts and winters are much colder.

## Examples of Rainfall and Warmest and Coolest Temperatures in California Intermediate and High Desert Communities

| City | Average Annual Rainfall (Inches) | Average Maximum Temperature in August °F | Average Minimum Temperature in January °F |
|---|---|---|---|
| Bishop | 5 | 96 | 21-22 |
| Victorville | 6 | 98 | 30 |
| Barstow | 4 | 101 | 34 |
| Lancaster | 8 | 95 | 29 |
| Twentynine Palms | 4 | 104 | 35 |

## Soils

In this book, I use two basic terms to describe soils: heavy and well draining. Well draining soils allow water to run through freely. Heavy soils are harder to wet but hold water longer, sometimes too long.

As you design your garden, be sure to include places for sitting and contemplation

Soil's three components—non-living mineral, non-living organic, and living organisms—are essential to plant health and well being. No plant can stand upright unless it is firmly anchored in the soil. But the role of soil goes far beyond its function as a plant's foundation.

Soil's non-living mineral component includes three basic particles:

- Sand particles are large but irregularly round. They pack together loosely, leaving plenty of room for water and air to penetrate quickly and easily between particles. Sandy soils are low in plant nutrients.

- Clay particles are tiny and flattened. They pack close together, leaving little space for air and water to penetrate. Clay soils therefore take longer to wet and to dry, but clay soils are high nutrient soils.

- Silt particle sizes are in between sand and clay.

The optimal soil has all three types of particles in more or less equal portions and is referred to as loam.

Soil's complex, if nearly invisible, web of life includes fungi, bacteria and other microbes, insects, and other small beneficial organisms. Their complex and sophisticated relationship with plant roots facilitates the roots' ability to take up water, air, and nutrients from the soil.

Soil's non-living organic component is made up of dead and decaying roots, leaves, and stems, as well as decaying fungi, bacteria, and other tiny organisms. Organic mulch is made up of decaying organic matter as well. It suppresses weeds, feeds the soil food web, helps the soil hold more water, reduces evaporation, and generally improves the texture of your soil. Composted organic mulch is the best material to add to your soil whether it is clay, sand, or loam.

How do you know what kind of soil you have? Do a test. Saturate a small patch of soil from your garden then let it sit overnight. The next day, dig a handful and squeeze it together. Clay feels sticky and stays together in a tight ball once you open your hand. Sand feels gritty and crumbles when you let go. Dry silt feels soft and smooth, like cornstarch or baby powder. When wet, it crumbles a bit but still forms a loose ball.

To test your soil drainage, dig a hole about 2 feet deep and fill it with water. Let the water drain out, then fill the hole with water again. Monitor how long the water takes to drain. If it drains within an hour or two, your drainage is good. If it sits for more than that, it is poorly draining.

One more thing to be aware of regarding soils. At high elevation (above 5000 feet) and in the cool, far northern part of the state, higher precipitation and plentiful organic matter help create more acidic soils. Towards the south and at lower elevations, rain quickly diminishes, as does the production of organic matter, while temperatures increase. As a result, these soils tend to be more alkaline.

Plants that prefer acidic soils seldom perform very well in alkaline soils without considerable effort on the part of the gardener. But alkalinity and the accompanying reduction in iron availability are typical of most Mediterranean climate soils. Unless you live in the mountains, high deserts, or in far northern California, this is another reason you will have greater overall success with Mediterranean climate plants.

Winter chill allows for spectacular lilac displays in cooler foothills and northern regions

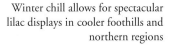

## Before You Begin Your Dream Garden

Creating your dream garden takes patience, time, and the willingness to experiment. There is no such thing as instant landscape, no matter what a salesperson tells you. So avoid the temptation to jump right in, especially if you have inherited someone else's garden. Live with it first.

Give yourself a full year to observe existing plants through the seasons. Notice how the sun moves through the space. Where is it shady in summer? Where in winter? Find the brightest spot and the warmest spot. The wettest spot, the driest spot. Notice where in the garden you most often gravitate and think about what draws you there. Notice where your family members (children, spouse, and pets) spends their time and what attracts them.

Make a list of how you want to use your garden space. Do you want a vegetable garden? Herb garden? Outdoor kitchen? Basketball court? Do you need a small lawn for children or pets? Do you need a large patio space for outdoor entertaining? How do you envision using the garden in the future? A child's sandbox, for example, can one day become a raised bed for vegetables, or be replaced with a spa. As you plan, remember to include pathways, lighting, hose spigots, places to sit, and garden art. Installing a water source or electricity now can make those eventual dreams come true quickly and easily.

A desert-inspired border of very low water plants edged in flagstone and gravel

Dragon trees at Lotusland in Santa Barbara include specimens planted in the late 1800s

Scan newspapers, magazines, and the Internet to find examples of gardens you like. Keep a file of the images so you can refer to them. Put a camera in the car and take snapshots of plants and gardens that appeal to you. You may find them in friends' gardens, in other neighborhoods, parks, botanical gardens, and nurseries. Add those images to your file.

Set some time aside to pull out your images and review them. Narrow the stack to the best of the best and decide what you like about each one. Do you like lots of colorful flowers, or are you more excited by the colors and textures of foliage? Do you prefer a more formal space or a more naturalistic one? Do you like to cut flowers for bouquets, or do you prefer to enjoy blooms out of doors (like me)?

Make sure that your garden's style complements the style of your home. An English garden simply does not fit a Southwest adobe style home. Nor does a Mediterranean garden fit a Tudor home. (Of course you can always create an English-style garden using Mediterranean climate plants.) What is the style of your home? What kind of garden will make it shine?

One more point—don't over plant. When plants are small, it is easy to put too many into the space to make it look full. The problem is, after three or four years it will be an overgrown jungle that requires too much maintenance to keep under control. Instead, plant with restraint. Plant sparsely and allow the plants time to fill in. Experienced gardeners have a saying: "The first year plants sleep, the second year they creep, the third year they leap." In other words, in the first year, a plant is overcoming transplant shock. The second year, roots become established. Once the roots are established, top growth kicks in. That third year is when you begin to see the final form of your garden and just how full it soon will be.

## Read the Label

How do you know how much space a plant needs? Most plant labels include a common name, scientific name, basic growing conditions (shade, sun, etc.), and most importantly, how large the plant will get.

A bit of experience will help you determine how much "truth in advertising" each label provides. Not that the grower or retailer is trying to be malicious or misleading in any way. The truth is, a plant that was evaluated several hundred (or even a thousand) miles away will grow differently in your garden than it does for the grower.

For example, years ago when I first planted my perennial garden (I've unplanted and replanted it several times since), I combed through mail-order catalogs and ordered dozens of plants chosen for year-round bloom and colorful and complex leaf textures. I mapped out the garden beds and knew where each plant would go before I made my orders. I ordered enough, I thought, to fill my beds without overfilling them. Most plants came from two wonderful nurseries, both about 600 miles to the north of my garden. One was near Chico in the northern Sacramento Valley, and the other along the cool northern coast of Mendocino.

The plants arrived, and we planted in fall. That first spring they looked great. By the third spring, however, they were a tangled mess. The plants had grown beautifully but a bit more vigorously than I expected. Some were two or three times larger than their descriptions. Had the nurseries deceived me? Not at all. It had more to do with the differences in soils, climate, and the fact that my growing season is two to three months longer than the nurseries'.

From that experience, I learned to check labels to see where the grower is located. Unless a plant comes from within 100 miles, I take size estimates as rule of thumb. I talk to friends who may have grown the plant and ask about its size in their gardens. I also research plants on the Internet. It doesn't take long to get a pretty good idea of how large a plant will grow in my garden.

By the way, while I am doing that research, I also make note of how much light or shade and water each plant prefers in my part of California. Plants that take full sun right along the beach often want some protection in my sunnier garden. The bottom line is, plant information is not written in stone, but it is important.

Just remember not to take all of this too seriously. Gardens are living, changing environments that should give you pleasure. Experimentation and experience are your best teachers. Have fun!

# USDA Cold Hardiness Zones

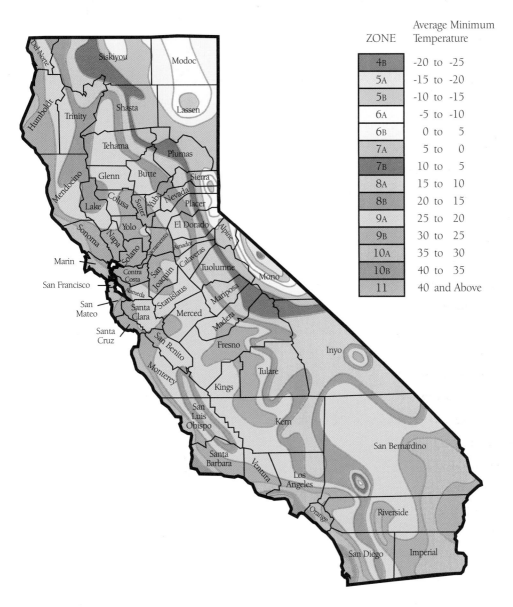

| ZONE | Average Minimum Temperature |
|------|------------------------------|
| 4B | -20 to -25 |
| 5A | -15 to -20 |
| 5B | -10 to -15 |
| 6A | -5 to -10 |
| 6B | 0 to 5 |
| 7A | 5 to 0 |
| 7B | 10 to 5 |
| 8A | 15 to 10 |
| 8B | 20 to 15 |
| 9A | 25 to 20 |
| 9B | 30 to 25 |
| 10A | 35 to 30 |
| 10B | 40 to 35 |
| 11 | 40 and Above |

## Preferred Zones

Cold-hardiness zone designations were developed by the United States Department of Agriculture (USDA) to indicate the minimum average temperature for an area. A zone assigned to an individual plant indicates the lowest temperature at which the plant can be expected to survive over the winter. California has an extremely wide zone range, from zone 4 to zone 11. The preferred zone range assigned to each plant in this book is based partly on the USDA cold-hardiness zone range, but mostly on our many years of experience. Our preferred zone recommendations take into account factors such as humidity, wind conditions, soil conditions, and salt tolerance. They represent the area in which a plant will grow *best*, not the *only* area in which the plant can grow.

www.digplantgrow.com

# How to Use the California Gardener's Guide

Each entry in this book includes specific information about each plant, including its botanical and common name, a description of the plant (along with some interesting facts and tidbits), when it blooms, how large it gets, and more. I've provided information about the best time to plant and the best spot for each plant, along with its long term care, including watering, pruning, fertilizing, and the pests you are most likely to deal with. Each entry suggest ways to use the plant in your garden, as well as a description of varieties that may be different sizes, or bloom in different colors or in different seasons.

Be sure to watch for the icons that tell you how much sun and water each plant needs, as well as some other interesting characteristics such as whether it is edible, attracts butterflies, or grows well along the coast.

## Sun Preferences

Full sun is six hours or more of direct sun per day. Part sun is four to six hours of direct sun, preferably in the morning with protection from hot afternoon sun. Part shade is two to four hours of direct sun per day, primarily in the morning, or all day bright, indirect light. Shade means all indirect light or dappled shade.

**Full Sun**    **Part Sun**    **Part Shade**    **Shade**

## Water Usage Requirements

High water plants do best in soils that are consistently damp but not saturated. Medium water plants need water when the soil is dry 3 to 6 inches down from the surface. Low water plants need very little water once they are established. See the book introduction for a detailed description of watering guidelines.

**High**        **Medium**        **Low**

## Companion Planting and Design

In this section, I make suggestions about ways to incorporate each plant into your garden's design to create a beautiful garden bed, form a lovely composition of potted plants, or solve a common gardening problem. I also suggest plant combinations based on similarity of cultural needs and the aesthetics of their combinations.

## Try These

In this section, you will find wonderful varieties of each plant, a related plant, or even an alternate plant to serve the same purpose in the garden. A note about using these plants: there simply is not enough room to include every variety, so use these lists as starting points. There are countless species and varieties that will perform beautifully in your garden. Don't be afraid to experiment.

## Additional Benefits

Many plants offer benefits that further enhance their appeal. The following symbols indicate some of the more interesting benefits:

 **Attracts butterflies and/or moths**

 **Attracts hummingbirds**

 **Some or all parts of this plant are edible**

 **Leaves or flowers are fragrant**

 **Plants make attractive fruits**

 **Flowers, leaves, branches, and/or fruits are suitable for bouquets or cut flower arrangements.**

 **Long blooming**

 **California native**

 **Supports bees**

 **Provides food or shelter for wildlife (including birds other than hummingbirds)**

 **Has colorful foliage**

 **Drought tolerant**

 **Grows well in a container**

 **Grows well in Mediterranean climate conditions**

 **Adds a tropical look to the garden**

 **Tolerates beach conditions (bright sun, wind, and/or salt spray)**

**Hardy to 8A**

**Min. Temp. 10° F**

## A Note About Zones

You may be familiar with the USDA growing zone schema which divides the country into 11 growing zones, each divided into two more subzones, all based on minimum winter temperatures.

While that system is quite popular, I find it too general to be helpful to home gardeners. So along with a zone map showing preferred zones, I have included the estimated minimum temperature that each plant is thought to survive. These temperatures (just like zones) are not written in stone. They are the accumulated experience of many professionals over a long period of time. Consider them estimates and don't be afraid to push the limit. Please note that if a plant is grown as an annual, or if there are many variables to determining minimum temperature, I did not include the zone map.

www.digplantgrow.com

# Annuals & Biennials *for California*

Flowering annuals mix with perennials and shrubs in an early springtime display

Springtime is prime time for annuals and biennials in California gardens. Annuals grow fast from seed and reward you with lots of big, beautiful blooms before they fade. Biennials sprout from seed one year, then flower and die the next year. Few other plants are as easy to grow and provide as much instant gardening gratification.

This chapter covers flowering annuals and biennials, all very well suited to California gardens.

Though annuals are extremely popular in colder winter parts of the country, Californians often overlook them in favor of longer lived flowering perennials, trees, and shrubs. Since we don't have long, bleak, colorless winters, we don't seem to need huge displays of colorful bedding plants to mark the transition from bitter winter to warm spring. Instead, we prefer to integrate annuals and biennials into flowerbeds, color bowls, and vegetable gardens (most vegetables are also annuals) year-round.

That said, it is best to designate spaces in the garden for growing annuals and biennials, especially if you set out seedlings instead of sprinkling seeds directly onto the ground. That way, you can avoid disturbing permanent plants whose roots resent the digging as you plant and replant.

## How to Buy Annuals and Biennials

Nurseries offer annuals and biennials as seedlings in 4-packs, 6-packs, 4-inch pots, and sometimes gallons. Many a plant lover has faced the dilemma of whether to buy these plants already in bloom or those not yet in bloom. If you buy them in bloom, you know the exact color, size, and shape of the flower. On the other hand, plants mature enough to flower in the pot, won't grow much larger once you plant them, nor will they live all that long. I prefer to purchase seedlings before they even begin to bud. Chances are, they will grow larger, live longer, and bloom longer.

If you aren't pressed to have immediate color, try this strategy. Look for plants already in bloom so you know what the flowers look like. Then, search through the pots for the youngest plants of the bunch— preferably ones that have yet to form flower buds. These plants haven't begun diverting their energy into making flowers, so once in the ground, they will put their energy into growing the sturdy roots, shoots and leaves needed to support a bigger bloom.

Sunny-orange California poppies

If your only choice is plants already in bud, pinch the buds off as soon as your purchase is complete. For many people—myself included— this is a real struggle. But in the long run, you'll have larger, healthier, longer lasting plants with more blooms.

## Try Them from Seed

While nursery seedlings give quick results, I encourage you to try your hand at growing annuals and biennials from seed. They are fun and easy, whether sown directly onto the ground or into pots and transplanted as seedlings. There is an enormous selection of seeds available in nurseries and by mail order. Try favorite heirloom varieties, new varieties in unusual colors, those bred for high nutrient content, and others bred to resist common pests and diseases. Whichever varieties you choose, purchase only top quality seed from well-known and reputable seed companies. The quality of seed determines how large a percentage of seeds sprout, as well as the health and vigor of those plants. Don't waste your money on the 50¢ or $1.00 packets. You may save some pennies but the seeds' poor performance will prove frustrating.

The better seed companies print their envelopes with directions that include planting time, preferred soils, soil type, and the amount of light and water each kind of seed needs. They also offer important tips, such as which seeds need to be planted directly into the ground ("direct seed") rather than started in pots. California poppies are a good example. Their long taproots are easily damaged and often don't survive transplanting, so it is best to seed them directly onto the ground. Again, better seed companies will offer that information on their envelopes.

**Direct seeding:** To direct seed, you first need to prepare the seedbed. Some seeds prefer well-amended soils while others prefer native, unamended soils. Either way, rake the seedbed smooth and saturate the soil 6 to 8 inches deep with water. Then, sprinkle the seeds evenly over the bed. Small seeds can be hard to spread evenly, so add them to a handful of fine sand (not silica sand) or dried coffee grounds, then sprinkle the mixture over the soil. Small seeds also need only a very thin layer of soil to cover them.

A container of bush-type annual sweet peas perfumes a patio

Simply rake the soil gently, leaving seeds near the surface. Larger seeds can be covered in a slightly thicker layer of soil. The rule of thumb is, look at how thick the seed is, then cover with a layer of soil three times that thickness.

Keep the seedbeds moist, using a gentle spray so seeds don't wash away. Thin your seedlings (the seed envelope will tell you when and how much). As seedlings develop, surround them with mulch to keep weeds down and soil moist.

**Growing in Pots:** Annuals and biennials that do transplant well can be seeded into pots or nursery flats filled with seed starting mix. Starting seeds in pots allows you to keep an eye on the seedlings and control how much water, sun, heat, or cold they get. Always plant a few more seeds per pot than you need. As the seedlings grow, sacrifice the weaker ones, leaving only a single plant per pot. For years, I resisted sacrificing weak seedlings. Reality is, however, that sacrificing the weaker seedlings allows the stronger ones to thrive.

You'll find more information about direct seeding and planting seeds in pots in my "Tips and Techniques" section in the back of this book. Whichever plants you chose and whichever method you choose to grow them by, remember annuals and biennials are not permanent, so enjoy them while you can!

# Breadseed Poppy

*Papaver somniferum*

*Annual breadseed poppies have enormous poppy flowers. Old-fashioned varieties have four petals that form an upward facing cup, 4 inches across in shades of lavender, pink, white, red, or raspberry. The bases of the petals have contrasting color spots that unite to form a large, dark "eye" in the flower center. Fancy varieties have multiple layers of petals that form pom-pom flowers. As flowers fade, they reveal blue-green, walnut-sized pods of tiny black seeds. Those seeds not only give rise to new poppies, but are also the poppy seeds used in cooking. Breadseed poppy flowers perch atop 3- to 4-foot-tall stems clothed in long, ice green leaves. As each bloom finishes, another appears for a long bloom time.*

## Other Common Name
Florist's Poppy

## Bloom Period and Seasonal Color
Spring flowers in lavender, pink, white, red, or raspberry, all with a large black eye.

## Mature Height × Spread
3 to 4 ft. × 1 ft.

## When, Where, and How to Plant
Poppies don't transplant well, so sow seeds directly onto a smooth, raked seedbed before winter rains arrive. If you amend the soil with compost, poppies will have more lush growth. Choose a spot in full sun. You can soak the soil before planting if you would like. See "Tips And Techniques" for suggestions for working with tiny seeds. Once seeds sprout and develop two or more sets of leaves, thin to 6 inches. Mulch well.

## Growing Tips
Water regularly through the growing season. No need to fertilize. *Note:* Aside from the seeds, all parts of this plant are poisonous.

## Care
No pruning is needed. To cut flowers, sever the flowering stem at its base as the bud begins to open. Cauterize the cut end of the stem over an open flame. Plants will develop more buds. Later in the season, allow pods to dry on the stalk. Cut stems with pods, turn upside down, and shake seeds through the holes at the top. Sprinkle onto the ground or collect in a cup or paper bag to save. Critters relish poppy flowers, but there is little you can do to protect them. Plant twice as many as you need so there are plenty to share.

## Companion Planting and Design
Sow breadseed poppies into a cutting garden, mixed border, or old-fashioned cottage garden. Scatter seed in among perennials or into the herb garden for the earliest wave of spring bloom. Dry seedpods to use in dried arrangements.

## Try These
'Danebrog Laced' (2 to 3 feet tall) has bright red flowers with white centers and fringe-edged petals. 'Hen and Chicks' (2 to 3 feet tall) flowers red or light pink. 'Peony Flowered' has pom-pom flowers formed by layers of white, pink, and red petals. The pale purple petals of 'Lavender Breadseed' (3 1/2 feet tall) have a dark purple spot at the base. 'Apple Green' (2 to 3 feet tall) has a pale green pom-pom style flower. 'Black Peony' (3 feet tall) has stunning, garnet color petals in a double, peony-like flower.

### When, Where, and How to Plant

California poppies' long, fleshy taproots make them poor candidates for transplanting. Instead, treat them as "sow and grow" seeds. In fall or winter, sprinkle over a sunny garden bed in nearly any type of soil. Rake smooth, water well, then scatter seeds (see "Tips and Techniques" for suggestions on spreading tiny seeds). Gently rake the bed to integrate seeds and soil. Water gently (take care not to wash seeds away).

### Growing Tips

Plant just as winter rains begin so that you don't need to water. California poppies need no fertilizer and very little water after they sprout. Occasional deep water (saturated the soil 6 to 8 inches deep) promotes longer bloom and lusher foliage. Wait until soil is dry several inches deep before watering again.

### Care

For a second bloom, cut leaves to the base once flowers fade and foliage turns dingy gray. Water well; in a few weeks a set of shorter leaves will sprout. Flowers will soon follow, though they too will be shorter. Though grown as annuals, California poppies are actually perennial. Once the dried seedpods release their seeds, cut leaves and flower stems back to the base. Plants are dormant through summer but sprout new leaves when rains come again in the winter. It has no pests.

### Companion Planting and Design

California poppies work in every garden, from a wild meadow to a Mediterranean border. Scatter seed on a steep hillside, ugly parking strip, or vacant lot. California poppy is also the perfect flower for a school garden. In areas where California poppies are native, plant locally grown seed only. Seeds from a garden center or other outside sources cross-pollinate with the local poppies, weakening and ultimately leading to the loss of native populations. So enjoy the poppies you see in the wild but leave them out of your garden.

### Try These

Try different color selections of California poppy: pale yellow 'Buttercream' and 'Mission Bells', soft pink 'Dusky Rose', magenta edged 'Carmine King', and lilac colored 'Purple Gleam'.

California poppy is one of California's most beautiful and easily recognized wildflowers. No wonder that back in 1903 California poppy was adopted as our state flower. California poppies have ferny, gray-green leaves that emerge from the base of the plant, forming a 12- to 18-inch mound. Flower stalks rise from the center, each with a pointed green bud at the tip. The green sepals split to reveal four furled, golden orange petals that open to the sun. California poppies were once pollinated exclusively by native beetles. But today, European honeybees also pollinate them. After a flower is pollinated, seeds start to develop. Petals fall away as long, narrow seedpods form. The pod dries out and splits, sending tiny black poppy seeds shooting out in all directions.

### Bloom Period and Seasonal Color

Cheery orange flowers over gray-green foliage in spring. Selections come in shades of creamy yellow to blood-red orange.

### Mature Height × Spread

12 to 18 in. × 12 to 18 in.

# Coleus

*Solenostemon scutellarioides*

*Their leaves are burgundy-velvet edged in chartreuse, fuchsia-blushed terracotta, raspberry-pink with burgundy, gold with green splashes, green netted in inky purple, and more. Some leaves are smooth edged, others are scalloped, lobed, or frilled. They are easy to grow both indoors and out. We are talking coleus here. New coleus. Sun coleus. Today's coleus are better, brighter, and easier to grow than ever. No longer relegated to brightly lit windowsills, coleus thrive where their leaves are exposed to six to eight hours of direct sun each day. Though technically perennials, Californians tend to grow coleus as annuals. They add billows of long season color to large, mixed container plantings (indoors and out), hanging baskets, and every kind of flower bed.*

### Bloom Period and Seasonal Color
Colorful leaves in combinations of cream, chartreuse, deep green, terracotta, raspberry, gold, burgundy, and purple.

### Mature Height × Spread
1 to 3 in. × 1 to 3 in.

### When, Where, and How to Plant
Set small plants (generally sold in 4-inch pots or larger) in the ground once the soil warms in spring. Choose a spot in full sun, part sun, or part shade. Amend soil well before planting. Follow planting directions in the Perennials introduction. Water well after planting and mulch generously. In containers, use a high quality potting mix to which you've added a handful of vermiculite for water retention, two handfuls of perlite for drainage, and a handful of worm castings. Water thoroughly after planting and top with a 1- to 2-inch layer of pebbles.

### Growing Tips
This is a high water plant. Keep soil (or potting mix) moist but not wet. Fertilize regularly with a balanced organic fertilizer. Follow directions on the label.

### Care
To keep coleus dense and full, regularly pinch out leaves and flowers at branch tips. Give leggy plants more sun. Watch for aphids, whitefly, and spider mites (especially indoors). See "Tips and Techniques" for more information on pests and pest control.

### Companion Planting and Design
Combine coleus with other high water plants in beds or pots placed for the greatest visual impact. For a stunning tropical bed, match variegated canna leaves to variegated coleus leaves and plant beneath a fragrant angel's trumpet. Combine coleus with green- and purple-leaved basils for an unexpected but effective foliage border. These same combinations work in large pots, but be sure to add a flowering nasturtium, Mexican flame vine, or other trailing vine to cascade over the edge.

### Try These
'Kong Red' (1½ to 2 feet × 1½ to 2 feet) has huge burgundy leaves with red center veins edged in bright green. 'Wizard Golden' (1 foot × 1 foot) has chartreuse leaves. The frilly foliage of 'Black Dragon' (1½ feet × 1½ feet) is velvet black with a garnet center. 'Chocolate Drop' (1 foot × 1 foot) has green leaves netted crimson. 'Sedona' (1½ feet × 1½ feet) is fuchsia-blushed terracotta.

## When, Where, and How to Plant

Sow seeds directly onto the ground starting in April. Choose a spot in full sun and almost any well-draining soil (see chapter introduction). Or sow seeds into pots as early as mid-February. Plant seedlings or nursery starts 10 inches apart and 1-gallon plants at 18 inches apart. Follow planting directions in the Perennials introduction. Add mulch.

## Growing Tips

Keep both seedbed and young seedlings moist. Once seedlings have several sets of leaves, allow the soil surface to dry out between waterings. Established cosmos are fairly drought tolerant. In pots, however, water regularly to keep potting mix moist but not wet. Fertilizer sparingly. Too much fertilizer promotes lots of foliage but few flowers.

## Care

Pinch out branch tips when cosmos reach about 18 inches tall. Pinching will keep plants bushy and full. Since blooms form at the tips of branches, more branches (fuller plants) make more flowers. Taller plants may need to be staked with a length of bamboo. Harvest flowers regularly to prolong bloom. Cut flower stalks at the base and don't leave stubs!

## Companion Planting and Design

Mix orange and gold-toned cosmos with blue and purple flowering perennials in the sage family, and with tall, orange-flowered annual Mexican sunflower. Add red and yellow flowering canna or brilliant leaved coleus for a one-two punch. Plant pale pink or white cosmos into a purple glazed pot with raspberry colored anise hyssop and cascading sweet peas for a soft welcoming spot on the patio.

## Try These

'Apricot' (3 feet × 3 feet) blooms apricot blushed with pink in late summer. *Cosmos bipinnatus* 'Harmony' (3 to 3$\frac{1}{2}$ feet × 3 to 3$\frac{1}{2}$ feet) flowers range from white to soft pink to deep rose. It's an early bloomer. 'Psyche Mix' (4 feet × 3 feet) has single and semi-double flowers in shades of pink through deep magenta. 'Snow Sonata' (2 feet × 2 feet) has white petals with golden centers. *Cosmos sulfureus* 'Bright Lights' (2 feet × 2 feet) has semi-double flowers in shades of yellow through amber and orange.

*If your vision of summer gardens includes daisy-shaped flowers for both the garden and for a vase, then cosmos are for you. These easy-to-grow annuals form 2- to 3-inch flowers with long, silky smooth petals that end in a slight ruffle. Cosmos come in a wide range of colors. Cosmos sulfureus varieties bloom in shades of golden orange to bright pumpkin. Cosmos bipinnatus varieties tend to be colors of white to pale pink, and deep magenta to rose. All summer long, dozens of blooms float above clouds of ferny green leaves. Cosmos are easy to start from seed and tolerate hot, dry conditions once they are established. Plant them in succession from spring through midsummer for ongoing flowers from midsummer into fall. They attract beneficial insects.*

### Bloom Period and Seasonal Color

Summer to fall blooms in white to pink, rose to deep magenta, golden orange to bright pumpkin.

### Mature Height × Spread

2 to 4 ft. × 2 ft.

# Madeira Cranesbill

## Geranium maderense

If Doctor Seuss had invented a plant, it would have been Madeira cranesbill. This large biennial is a true geranium but scarcely resembles its relatives. Its ferny green leaves are hand-sized, attached to the end of long, brick red stalks that reach 12 inches to the ground, making the plants look as if they stand on tall stalks of red licorice. In their second spring, Madeira cranesbill produces rounded heads of 1-inch flowers with silky, pale magenta petals and deep magenta throats, all on fuzzy red stems. Each flower head is as large as a hydrangea bloom. Flowers fade to seeds that spread throughout the garden. The mother plant dies, the seeds sprout, and the two-year cycle of leaf and bloom starts all over again.

**Bloom Period and Seasonal Color**
Spring flowers soft magenta pink with deep magenta throats.

**Mature Height × Spread**
3 to 4 ft. × 3 to 4 ft.

## When, Where, and How to Plant
Plant from 1-gallon nursery cans in spring, following planting directions in the Perennials introduction. Madeira cranesbill is perfect for dry, bright shade. In coastal gardens, it tolerates full sun. This plant also tolerates a wide range of soils but performs best in well-draining soils. Once Madeira cranesbill goes through its first round of flowering, it reseeds throughout the garden. That is not a warning but rather a "heads up," as seedlings should be thinned to at least 10 inches apart. Move thinnings to other parts of the garden or share with friends.

## Growing Tips
Keep soil moist until seedlings have two or more sets of leaves. Mature plants require very little water. No fertilizer is needed.

## Care
Pests seldom bother Madeira cranesbill. Plants need no pruning. Once they flower and finish dispersing their seed, remove the entire plant as it will soon die. Wear long sleeves and gloves to protect your skin from irritating fuzz along the flower stems.

## Companion Planting and Design
Plant Madeira cranesbill in the bright shade beneath a low water tree. Start with one plant and by year three (the year after the first bloom), you will have an impressive mass. For a dry, tropical looking garden, plant with pale pink bougainvillea, jelly or triangle palm, or even dragon tree. For a Mediterranean look, mix with gold flowering Jerusalem sage, sculptural agaves, and blue hibiscus. The thick, blue-gray succulent fingers of blue chalk sticks also make an excellent foil for Madeira cranesbill.

## Try These
Mullein (*Verbascum* sp.) is another group of garden biennials though some are short-lived perennials. These relatives of penstemon and monkey flower have flat rosettes of deep green leaves. Rose spikes appear of flat 5-petal flowers in shades of yellow to coral to mauve, usually with contrasting colored "eyes." *Verbascum bombyciferum* 'Arctic Summer' makes a 2-foot wide rosette of large, felty silver leaves with 4- to 6-foot tall felt-like stalks of lemon yellow flowers. *Verbascum boerhavii bicolor* makes 5-foot tall spires with yellow flowers and red eyes.

# Mexican Hat

## *Ratibida columnifera*

### When, Where, and How to Plant

Choose a spot in full sun and almost any kind of soil. In frost-free gardens, direct-seed in fall for sprouting in spring. In colder areas, start seeds once the ground warms in spring (see "Tips and Techniques" for planting). When seedlings have two sets of leaves, thin to 1 to 2 feet apart. Or start seeds in pots in spring and transplant later. Space seedlings 1 to 2 feet apart. Place a 2-foot-tall bamboo stake next to each plant. If the plant flops later in the season, simply tie it to the stake.

### Growing Tips

Keep the seedbed moist (not wet) until seedlings are several inches tall. Then ease back to let the soil dry out between waterings. Once established, these plants are tough and drought tolerant, requiring only occasional deep watering for a good flower show. Fertilize sparingly if at all.

### Care

Pests tend to ignore Mexican hat. No pruning is necessary though you might want to pinch the branch tips of young plants to make them full and bushy. Once flower bud forms, stop pinching. If they get too leggy or lax, gently tie plants to their stakes.

### Companion Planting and Design

Mexican hat is right at home in a planted meadow, wildflower, or other dry garden. Plants look best en masse. Add purple flowering penstemon, apricot flowering anise hyssop, grass like orange-leaved *Carex testacea* or its bronze leaved cousin, leather-leaved sedge. Native California fuchsia is a good companion as well. For texture, add taller grasses such as silver grass. Plan for flowering sequences by combining Mexican hat with California poppy. Soon after the poppies stop blooming, Mexican hat begins.

### Try These

'Buttons and Bows' (2 to 2½ feet × 2 to 2½ feet) has mahogany petals with golden edges and brown centers. Yellow cone flower (*Ratibida pinnata*) is Mexican hat's perennial cousin. Summer and fall flowers on 4-foot-tall plants have long, bright yellow petals that flex away from a deep gray, cone-like center. Hardy to -30 degrees F.

*Think Mexican hat is a strange name for a flower? You'll understand once you see this black-eyed-Susan relative whose rounded, gold, or gold-edged mahogany petals form a drooping "sombrero" brim around a tall, brown, central cone. We value these Great Plains native plants for the show they put on in late summer and early fall when their many flowers float above clouds of feathery green foliage. In times past, Cheyenne Indians valued a brew of Mexican hat leaves to draw the poison from rattlesnake bites. Birds eat their seeds. Though technically a perennial, Mexican hat is typically grown as a self-seeding annual. If you plant both gold flowering and mahogany flowering plants, the next generation may include all sorts of flower color and pattern variations.*

### Other Common Name

Upright Prairie Cone Flower

### Bloom Period and Seasonal Color

Summer blooms in gold, or gold-edged mahogany.

### Mature Height × Spread

1 to 3 ft. × 1 to 3 ft.

# Mexican Sunflower
*Tithonia rotundifolia*

*Late summer brings the brilliant bloom of Mexican sunflower, a 6-foot-tall annual in the sunflower family. Mexican sunflowers tall central stems are topped with 4- to 5-inch flowers with petals that are deep red-orange and centers that are bright orange. The flowers, which continue until frost, are actually made up of many, many small flowers that make seeds much beloved by goldfinches. Monarch butterflies seek out Mexican sunflowers for their nectar. Gardeners like them not just for their bright colored flowers but also for their velvety soft stems and leaves. Mexican sunflower is seldom available in the nursery as seedlings. Seeds are widely available, however, and starting these plants by seed is easy. At the end of the season, plants reseed themselves.*

**Bloom Period and Seasonal Color**
Brilliant deep orange flowers with bright orange centers, late summer to frost.

**Mature Height × Spread**
4 to 6 ft. × 3 to 4 ft.

## When, Where, and How to Plant
Start Mexican sunflower from seed in early spring. Smooth a plot of well-draining soil in full sun. Plant seeds 1/2 inch deep, 2 to 3 inches apart, and in rows 12 inches apart or simply sprinkle over an existing flower bed and cover with compost. Once seedlings have two sets of leaves, thin to 1 to 2 feet apart. If you start seeds in pots, they will be ready to transplant in about a month. Follow planting directions in the Perennials introduction.

## Growing Tips
Keep seedbed and seedlings moist but not wet. Once plants have several sets of leaves, reduce watering frequency to let the soil dry out more and more between waterings. Mature plants are very drought tolerant, especially in coastal gardens. No fertilizer is needed.

## Care
Pruning is not necessary, but pinch off fading flowers to prolong bloom. Pests are seldom a problem. Stake tall plants if they begin to lean.

## Companion Planting and Design
Mass plant Mexican sunflower with colorful zinnias, purple flowering Mexican bush sage or shrubby blue hibiscus, and yellow flowering Mexican marigold. To harvest flowers for bouquets, cut the stem well below the flower. The stalk at the base of the bloom is hollow; with too much handling it will collapse.

## Try These
'Aztec Sun' (4 to 6 feet × 3 feet) has yellow flowers. 'Torch' (4 to 6 feet × 3 feet) has deep red-orange blooms. Shorter varieties need no staking: bright orange flowered 'Fiesta del Sol' (2 to 3 feet × 2 to 3 feet), deep red-orange flowered 'Sundance' (3 feet × 3 feet), and mango-yellow flowered 'Yellow Torch'. Bolivian Sunflower (*Tithonia diversifolia*) is Mexican sunflower's perennial cousin. It grows as a loose shrub, 12 to 16 feet × 6 feet or more. Upright branches are covered in large green leaves lobed like huge mittens. Golden yellow daisy-like flowers, 6 to 7 inches across, appear in late summer. Cut back to 1 foot tall when flowers fade. Hardy to 30 degrees F.

## When, Where, and How to Plant

In frost-free winter areas, plant large nasturtium seeds directly into the ground, between fall and spring. In colder areas, plant seed in early spring. Set seeds ½ to 1 inch deep into amended, well-draining soil. After the second set of leaves appears, thin plants to 8 to 12 inches apart. Or plant seeds in pots and transplant when seedlings have several sets of leaves (see planting directions in the Perennials introduction). Water well and mulch.

## Growing Tips

Nasturtium thrives in well-watered flower beds but will grow just fine with only occasional water. No fertilizer is needed.

## Care

No pruning is necessary. Protect from the snails and slugs that hide amid nasturtium foliage, and watch for tiny black aphids and pale colored whiteflies on the leaves and flowers. Remove infected parts or spray with a sharp jet of water. See 'Tips and Techniques" for more on pest control.

## Companion Planting and Design

Large, easy sprouting nasturtium seeds and their bright, flavorful flowers make them ideal plants for children to grow. Plant dwarf nasturtium to cascade over a wall, the side of a container, or to edge an herb bed filled with dill and chives. Plant trailing nasturtiums into a cutting garden, or to climb (with help) a fence or trellis. Climbing nasturtium grown as a ground cover fills open spaces in beds waiting for spring plants. Or use their foliage to hide fading bulb leaves. Avoid planting nasturtium near moist, shady canyons and natural areas where they reseed too freely.

## Try These

Dwarf nasturtiums include 'Alaska Mix' with variegated cream and green leaves and yellow, orange, salmon, and red flowers. 'Dwarf Jewel Mix' has similar colored double flowers. 'Strawberries and Cream' has blooms in pale or clear yellow, or blushed apricot to strawberry, and a strawberry-red blotch at the base of each petal. Climbing nasturtium includes 'Empress of India' that has leaves of deep blue-green and cerise colored flowers. 'Amazon Jewel' (4- to 6-foot vine) is a climbing version of 'Alaska Mix'. 'Moonlight' (6 to 8 feet) has pale yellow flowers.

*Nasturtiums are old-fashioned flowers with round green leaves and colorful flowers from creamy yellow to bright yellow, soft apricot to brilliant orange, bright red to garnet, and combinations thereof. Nasturtiums come in two sizes: dwarf bush nasturtium make 8- to 18-inch rounded mounds, while climbing nasturtium form long stems that reach 8 feet or longer. In milder summer areas, nasturtiums bloom from spring until frost. In warmer summer areas, there are two crops of nasturtium each year. Spring plants bloom, go to seed, and die as the weather gets warm. Those seeds germinate in late summer and plants bloom again from fall to frost. Nasturtium leaves and flowers are deliciously peppery. They add color and zip to salads, soups, and so on. They also make a colorful garnish.*

### Bloom Period and Seasonal Color
Spring through fall blooms in shades of creamy yellow to bright yellow, soft apricot to brilliant orange, bright red to garnet and combinations.

### Mature Height × Spread
8 in. × 18 in. mounds, 8 ft. vines or longer

# Pot Marigold
## *Calendula officinalis*

Pot marigolds are one of the easiest and most reliable garden annuals. They come in many varieties with 3- to 4-inch-round flowers and multiple petal layers, some single, some double or more. Flowers are bright yellow, saffron yellow, bright peach, cream, or mixed colors. Pot marigolds often naturalize in irrigated gardens. Their long, curved seeds germinate early in spring, growing to 1- to 2-foot mounds with long, bright green, sticky leaves. Later in spring, buds open to cover the entire mound in flowers. Summer planted seeds bloom in winter, winter planted seeds (in mild climate gardens) bloom in early spring. Sprinkle petals into salads, rice, omelets, or onto soups for color. Calendula oil is a traditional ingredient in lotions and salves.

### Other Common Name
Poor Man's Saffron

### Bloom Period and Seasonal Color
Yellow, orange, peach, cream, mixed colored blooms in spring in cold winter areas, flowers most of the year in milder coastal gardens.

### Mature Height × Spread
1 to 2 ft. × 1 to 2 ft.

### When, Where, and How to Plant
For spring or summer flowers, sow seeds in early spring. In cold winter areas, start seeds in pots, six to eight weeks before the last frost. In frost-free areas, direct seed into well-amended soil (see directions in "Tips and Techniques"). In milder climates, direct seed again in fall for winter blooms. Thin seedlings to 8 inches apart. To transplant seedlings, space 8 to 12 inches apart. (Follow directions for transplanting in the Perennials introduction.) Water well after planting, and mulch.

### Growing Tips
Pot marigolds respond well to the same treatment as summer vegetables: deep water when soil is dry 2 to 3 inches below ground, with regular applications of all-purpose organic fertilizer. Follow directions on the label.

### Care
For fuller plants, pinch back branch tips before flower buds form. Deadhead to prolong bloom. Protect from slugs and snails (see "Tips and Techniques"). As plants age, leaves can develop a white blush called powdery mildew. Space plants for good air circulation and chose mildew resistant varieties.

### Companion Planting and Design
Grow pot marigold in flower borders, cottage gardens, or old-fashioned cutting gardens. Add them to vegetable beds or plant alongside chives, basil, and oregano. Plant in butterfly gardens with coreopsis, Mexican sunflower, and other annuals. For cut flowers, sever stems at the base just as buds begin to open. These sun lovers brighten the spring garden and hang around until frost.

### Try These
Mounding 2-foot pot marigolds include bright orange daisy-like 'Alpha', 'Pink Surprise' with peach pink-tinged flowers, or 'Indian Prince' whose deep orange blooms have red on the undersides and deep brown centers. 'Lashima' (1- to 2-foot mound) has deep orange, daisy-like flowers. 'Pacific Beauty' (1 to 2 feet) has daisy-like flowers in white, yellow, golden orange, and combinations. 'Flashback' (18- to 24-inch mound) has double and semi-double flowers in apricot, orange, red-blush peach, cream, and mixed colors with a red underside.

# Sunflower
## *Helianthus annus*

### When, Where, and How to Plant

Start sunflowers indoors in pots in early spring, or seed in the ground when the nighttime air reaches 50 degrees F. Choose a spot in full sun, amend the soil with compost and rake it smooth. Follow planting directions in the chapter introduction. Thin according to packet directions (different size sunflowers are thinned differently). Start a new batch of seed every few weeks through the summer for flowers into fall.

### Growing Tips

Sunflowers bloom best if watered whenever the top 2 inches of soil are dry. They tolerate drought but bloom better with regular water. Apply an organic fertilizer according to directions on the label.

### Care

No pruning is needed. Birds relish sunflowers seedlings and sunflower seeds. Cover seedbed with bird netting or hardware cloth. Once flower heads form, birds return for the seeds. If your goal is cut flowers or seeds, plant twice as many plants as you need—some for you and some for the birds. For cut flowers, harvest flower heads just as they start to open.

### Companion Planting and Design

Grown a sunflower house with 'Russian Mammoth' or other tall sunflower and annual vining morning glory. Sow the two seeds in a rectangle 9 feet × 6 feet and leave one side open for a doorway. Morning glory vines climb sunflower stalks as both reach for the sky. Once sunflower buds appear, gently weave twine back and forth overhead to form a "ceiling" for the vines to climb across.

### Try These

'Delta Sunflower' (to 6 feet) has 3-inch yellow blooms. 'Teddy Bear' (to 3 feet) has golden yellow 4-inch flowers that resemble chrysanthemums. 'Chocolate Cherry' (6 to 7 feet) has burgundy rays around chocolate centers with flowers 5 to 6 inches across. 'Music Box' (to 2½ feet) is multi-branching, with clear yellow flowers 4 to 5 inches across. 'Giant Sungold' (to 6 feet) has 7- to 8-inch golden pom-pom flowers. 'Russian Mammoth' (9 to 12 feet) is an heirloom with bright yellow 2-foot flowers producing edible seeds.

*Sunflowers are true American natives. Archeologists have found remains of these bright colored annuals dated from 3000 B.C. Native Americans grew them for food. Spanish explorers took them home to grow as ornamentals. Amazingly, the same sunflowers—and their modern relatives—remain a mainstay of our summer gardens. Sunflowers are popular in part because they are easy to grow. A spot in full sun, a bit of soft soil, and some water are about all it takes. Traditional sunflowers have a single row of large yellow ray petals surrounding a center made up of tiny disk flowers, each of which becomes an edible seed. Hybrids bloom in shades of bronze to chocolate, nearly red to cinnamon, and mixed colors. Some have multiple layers of petals.*

### Bloom Period and Seasonal Color

Summer blooms in shades of yellow, as well as bronze to chocolate, nearly red, cinnamon, and mixed colors.

### Mature Height × Spread

2 to 12 ft. × 2 ft.

# Sweet Pea
## *Lathyrus odoratus*

Fragrant flowering sweet peas started their journey into modern horticulture at the end of the 1600s, when a monk named Francisco Cupani sent wild seed from Sicily to a colleague in England. That single act sparked a long history of sweet pea crosses that have generated hundreds of varieties. Today's sweet peas are among the easiest and most rewarding early spring annuals. There are tall varieties and short varieties. Their two-lipped flowers come in a myriad of colors; shades of white to blue, pink to red and purple. Some are bi-colored, some speckled, some with colorful veins, and others banded in deep tones. Sweet peas flower in tandem with the equally easy-growing bright orange California poppy, making for an unbeatable early spring show.

### Bloom Period and Seasonal Color
Early spring flowers in shades of white to blue, pink to red and purple, with mixtures and patterns.

### Mature Height × Spread
8 in. to 8 ft. × 12 in. to 8 ft. depending on variety

### When, Where, and How to Plant
Sow the large sweet pea seeds directly into the ground fall through spring in mild winter gardens, in spring in cold winter gardens (see chapter introduction for directions). Soak seeds for up to eight hours to speed germination. Choose a spot in full sun and with well-amended soil. Plant tall sweet peas against a good support such as a chain link fence, trellis, wooden teepee, bamboo fence, or tomato cage. Short, bush sweet peas need no support. Set seed 1 inch deep, 3 to 4 inches apart, and thin to 6-inch spacing once seedlings have two sets of leaves. Alternatively, start seeds in flats or pots (or buy them at the nursery) and transplant 6 to 8 inches apart following directions in the Perennials introduction. Water well and mulch.

### Growing Tips
For longest bloom, start seeds in succession, a new crop every two or three weeks. Water regularly through the growing season. Keep the soil moist. Fertilize lightly.

### Care
Cut flowers for continuous flowering. Protect seedlings from hungry birds, slugs, and snails. Leaves can develop white blotches of powdery mildew, especially in coastal gardens. Grow resistant varieties, and space plants for good air circulation. For more on pest and disease control, see "Tips and Techniques."

### Companion Planting and Design
Grow tall, vining sweet peas in cutting gardens and along a fence line. Shorter, bush-type sweet peas are great cascading over the side of a hanging basket, container, or window box.

### Try These
Tall, vining sweet peas including heirlooms 'Mrs. Collier' (5 to 6 feet tall) with fragrant, creamy-white flowers, 'Lord Nelson' (to 6 feet) with fragrant deep blue/purple flowers, and 'Cupani's Original' (6 to 8 feet) with burgundy petals above and violet below with intense fragrance. 'Saltwater Taffy Swirls' (6 to 8 feet) has scented, multi-colored pastel flowers with colored veins in shades of blue, burgundy, red, purple, and orange. Among the bush-type sweet peas is 'Cupid' (8 to 10 inches) with fragrant rose flowers banded in deep tones.

# Zinnia
## *Zinnia elegans*

### When, Where, and How to Plant
Zinnias need full sun and well-amended garden soil. In spring, direct seed onto moist soil or start in pots, $1/2$ inch deep, 2 to 3 inches apart (see chapter introduction for details). Thin sprouted seeds to 1 foot apart. Start more seeds every few weeks for a long season of bloom. Transplant seedlings to 1 foot apart once they have several sets of leaves. Water well and mulch.

### Growing Tips
Water deeply when soil is dry 2 to 3 inches deep. Apply all-purpose organic fertilizer according to directions on the label.

### Care
Flower buds form at branch tips; the more branches, the more flowers. So before buds develop, pinch branch tips. Once flower buds appear, stop pinching. Cut faded flowers to extend bloom. Wet zinnia leaves can get powdery mildew (a fungus), so water the ground, not the leaves. Choose mildew resistant varieties.

### Companion Planting and Design
Create a cutting garden of colorful zinnias, purple flowering tall verbena, red, blue, or purple flowered sages, brilliant orange-flowered Mexican sunflower, tall yellow sunflowers, and bronze leaved fountain grass. Zinnias blooming alongside reed orchids bring color to the tropical garden long before the gingers and canna flowers kick in.

### Try These
'Benary's Giant' series are mildew resistant: 'Benary's Giant Coral' (3 to 4 feet tall) has luscious salmon colored flowers, 4 to 6 inches across. 'Benary's Giant Lime' (to 3 feet) has 4- to 5-inch double flowers in surprisingly beautiful lime green. 'Benary's Giant Orange' (to 3 feet) has double flowers in bright orange. 'Profusion Cherry' ($1^1/2$ feet × $1^1/2$ feet) has cherry colored single flowers and bright yellow centers. 'Purple Prince' (3 to 4 feet) has rose-purple double flowers and is mildew resistant. 'Scarlet Flame' (3 feet × 3 feet) has double, scarlet red flowers. 'Swizzle Cherry and Ivory' (1 foot × 1 foot) has 3- to 4-inch pom-pom blooms, with cherry towards the center and ivory towards the tip with a narrow edge of red.

*Few flowers shout "summer!" like bright colored zinnias. Remember zinnias from your childhood? In the heat of summer, their simple, daisy-like flowers bloomed in shades of papaya, lemon, and raspberry. But as the summer progressed, they inevitably succumbed to powdery mildew. Today's zinnias are taller and more floriferous than their predecessors, and even more exciting in the garden. Modern zinnia flowers come in double, pom-pom blooms in luscious shades of lemon, cream, melon, lime, raspberry, cherry, lilac, and bicolors. Breeders have created many wonderful mildew resistant varieties that bloom happily almost until frost. Start zinnias from seed (it's easy to do) and invite a child to help you. They'll love their quick germination, exuberant bloom, and colorful flowers. And so will you!*

### Bloom Period and Seasonal Color
Summer to frost blooms in lemon, cream, melon, lime, raspberry, cherry, lilac, and bicolors.

### Mature Height × Spread
1 to 4 ft. × 1 to 4 ft.

# Bulbs *for California*

Bulbs are the "ephemera" of the garden. They send up tall green shoots, put on a colorful display of flowers, often accompanied by fragrance, then wither and die, all within a short but glorious period of time. These garden jewels are like decorator's accessories, adding a touch of color here and there to delight our eyes.

Bulbs are also incredibly versatile. They grow as well in pots as in the ground. Tuck some in next to a big boulder, or sprinkle them among ornamental grasses in a meadow. Plant in masses for a big show, or scatter clusters of bulbs in perennial beds or cutting gardens.

This chapter includes twenty entries that describe close to 100 of the best bulbs, corms, tubers, and rhizomes for California gardens. What are the differences between a bulb, corm, tuber, or rhizome? Glad you asked. All four have underground plant parts that store energy, and from which leaves, stems, and roots emerge. Their differences are in their structures, but since those underground structures serve similar purposes, gardeners tend to simplify things by lumping them together under the single heading, "bulbs."

If you have gardened in parts of the country where winters are long and cold, you may miss those tulips and other fancy bulbs that require weeks of winter chill. Those bulbs will grow here, but not always

reliably, and not without six weeks or more in your refrigerator. But why go to all that work when so many gorgeous California native and South African bulbs thrive in our Mediterranean climate? These bulbs bloom from winter to early summer, with a major peak in spring. Through the hottest summer months, they go dormant, an adaptation to escape the intense heat and drought of their native habitats.

South African bulbs in particular are adapted to extremely poor but well-draining soils and no summer water. In fact, those planted in too-heavy soil can rot if watered in summer. Others tolerate summer water but don't require it. The South African bulbs included in this chapter are widely available and among the easiest to grow. In addition to native

Hot magenta *Gladiolus byzantius* thrives in California gardens

and South African bulbs, these pages include a selection bulbs from South America and other points around the globe. All are extremely well suited for our gardens.

Though the majority of the bulbs in this chapter can survive on little water, a few are thirstier plants whose that are worth growing for their showy flowers and/or fragrance. They are best sited nearest the house where they will have the biggest visual (and olfactory) impact. Always group plants according to their water needs; otherwise, you'll overwater some and deprive others.

One more advantage of these bulbs: in the vast majority of gardens up and down the state, none need to be lifted and stored at the end of the season.

## How to Select Bulbs

When it comes to bulbs, size matters. The larger the bulbs the stronger, healthier, and more vigorous the plants, and the more tolerant they are of challenging growing conditions. Perhaps most important though, larger size translates to more flowers.

Bulbs and corms (not tubers or rhizomes) are measured and graded by their circumference. The largest bulbs are 22/24, meaning that they are between 22 and 24 centimeters around. Corms, by comparison, typically max out at 6/8 (6 to 8 centimeters around).

A 16/18 Oriental lily, for example, will produce six to eight flowers per stem. The next size down, 14/16, will produce 4 to 5 flowers. Larger bulbs cost more but give you a better return on your investment. So when you buy bulbs in the nursery or order them online, pay attention to the size of the bulb. Look for the largest bulbs you can afford and make sure they come from a reliable source.

Largest bulb/corm circumferences commonly offered to home gardeners:

| | | |
|---|---|---|
| Asiatic lily | (*Lilium* hybrids) | 16/18 |
| Baboon flower | (*Babiana*) | 6/8 |
| Blazing star | (*Tritonia*) | 4/5 |
| Bugle lily | (*Watsonia*) | 6/8 or 8/10, depending on species and variety |
| Butterfly lily | (*Calochortus*) | 4/5 |
| Cuban lily | (*Scilla peruviana*) | 22/24 |
| Harlequin flower | (*Sparaxis*) | 4/5 |
| Naked lady | (*Amaryllis belladonna*) | 22/24 |
| Oriental lily | (*Lilium* hybrids) | 16/18 |
| Pineapple lily | (*Eucomis*) | 24/26 |
| Species gladiolus | (*Gladiolus*) | 4/5 |
| Spider lily | (*Hymenocallis*) | 20/22 |

Look for plump, fleshy bulbs with no obvious scars or holes. Nurseries mostly purchase their stock from just a few sources. The differences arise from both bulb size *and* how carefully each nursery cares for their bulbs.

Iris in a serene landscape

In case you wondered, those big beautiful lilies, gladiolus, and other flowers that florists sell come from even larger bulbs that are available to commercial cut-flower growers but not generally to home gardeners.

## How to Plant Dormant Bulbs

### Planting in the Ground

Plant dormant (leafless) bulbs in odd numbers (groups of 3, 5, 7, etc.). Dig individual holes to plant just a few bulbs. Planting depths are provided with each bulb description. Mix a handful or more of bone meal or other organic bulb fertilizer into the soil according to package directions.

To plant many bulbs over a large area, dig a long trench or a wide swath, the depth that each bulb requires. Set out bulbs individually based on their recommended spacing. Rather than line them up, create a more natural look by using a staggered or triangular arrangement. Some gardeners achieve a more natural, random look by simply tossing bulbs onto the prepared soil and then making slight adjustments to ensure they are not too close together.

Make sure that bulbs are root-side down, stem side up. The root side is usually curved while the stem side is usually pointed. With round corms, look carefully to find the flattened plate where the roots emerge, or for remnants of last year's roots.

Once bulbs are in place, cover them with soil. Set a hose-end sprinkler to slowly, thoroughly saturate the soil (it should be wet several inches deeper than the bulbs are planted). Apply a thick layer of mulch to insulate the soil from water loss and buffer it from temperature changes. Mulch also improves the soil, feeds beneficial microbes, and keeps weeds down.

## Planting in Pots

Bulbs don't need huge pots, nor do they require large pots, but the more bulbs in a pot, the more impressive the show. Start with a wide pot (that has a good sized hole in the bottom), good quality potting mix, some bone meal or organic bulb fertilizer, and a piece of fiberglass window screen to cover the pot's drain hole. Smaller bulbs such as harlequin flower are suited for shallow pots or even window boxes. Larger bulbs like pineapple lily and naked ladies need deeper pots.

Don't be afraid to mix bulbs that grow to different heights and/or bloom in sequence to extend the show. Simply plant them in layers—larger bulbs deeper than smaller bulbs, according to each type's depth requirement.

Determine how deep to plant (see each bulb entry in this chapter), then fill pots with potting mix up to that point. Sprinkle bone meal (or other organic fertilizer) onto the surface of the potting mix, set the bulbs a bit closer together than they would be if planted in the ground. Finish filling with potting soil. An inch or two of round gravel mulch on the surface of the soil will insulate the pot and keep soil from washing out when you water. Mulch also gives the pot a finished look.

Drip water into the pot until it runs out the hole in the bottom. The potting mix should be completely saturated. Place pots in full sun and wait. Soon, they will sprout, and in not too much time, they will grace your patio or outdoor dining table with gorgeous flowers.

Here's a tip. Large, planted pots can be heavy. To save your back, place larger pots in their permanent locations, then plant and water.

# Baboon Flower

*Babiana* spp.

*South African bulbs bring so many bright colors to the garden that they can sometimes become overwhelming. One group, however, blooms in deep tones that balance the others. These are baboon flowers, named because their underground corms are a favorite treat of wild baboons. The most common baboon flowers open in shades of blue or purple, magenta, or red. Less common (but no less beautiful) types bloom white or pale yellow. These are petite plants whose flower stalks (several per corm) reach only a foot tall, with five or more cup- or star-shaped blooms, each about 1½ inches across. Baboon flower's deep green, lance-shaped leaves are short and deeply grooved. In a dry garden, baboon flowers naturalize over a few years. A true garden gem!*

## Bloom Period and Seasonal Color

Spring flowers blue or purple, magenta, red, and occasionally white or pale yellow.

## Mature Height × Spread

6 to 12 in. and multiplying

Hardy to 9A

Min. Temp. 20° F

## When, Where, and How to Plant

Plant baboon flower in late summer or early fall, when corms are dormant. Choose a spot in full sun and in any soil. Amend the soil with organic compost and bonemeal. Set corms 3 to 4 inches deep and 4 to 6 inches apart. Water well after planting, and mulch. New leaves appear when the weather cools in fall. To grow in a container, add bonemeal to good quality potting mix. Plant corms at same depth and distance as in the ground. Water well and mulch.

## Growing Tips

Baboon flowers in the ground survive on rainfall in most coastal gardens. In hot inland and desert gardens, water deeply once or twice monthly in the growing season. Keep potted baboon flowers moist during growing season. Stop watering when bulbs go dormant in summer. Top-dress with bonemeal or organic bulb fertilizer when new leaves appear and growth begins.

## Care

Allow leaves to dry on the bulb after flowering. Cut (don't pull) leaves once they are completely brown and dry. Surround corms with hardware cloth or plant in gopher cages (see "Tips and Techniques") to deter hungry squirrels, rabbits, and rodents.

## Companion Planting and Design

Expect bulbs to naturalize, settling in tiny spaces between plants, sidewalk cracks, and other open spots within a few years. Add to a meadow planting, tucked in among tufts of ornamental grasses and sedges. Baboon flowers can fill a container after a few seasons, or mix with other summer dormant bulbs and plants such as tall bugle lilies, species *Gladiolus*, or annual California poppies.

## Try These

*Babiana angustifolia* has violet to blue flowers with maroon markings near base of petals; *Babiana nana* has rose-scented, pale purple, or blue flowers with white markings inside the petals. For magenta, purple, or blue blooms, try *Babiana stricta* or its variety 'Brilliant Blue', whose bright blue flowers are also fragrant. For fragrant white flowers, plant 'Pearly White' and 'Alba'. In a garden where you want magenta or wine-red flowers, try *Babiana villosa*, which also tolerates clay soil.

# Blazing Star
## *Tritonia crocata*

### When, Where, and How to Plant

Where winter temperatures stay above 20 degrees F, plant dormant corms in early fall. Otherwise wait until early spring. Choose a spot in full sun and well-draining soil where blazing star will get water in the growing season but not in winter. In the ground, plant 3 to 4 inches deep and 3 to 6 inches apart. Follow planting directions in the chapter introduction. After planting, water well and mulch. In higher rainfall areas, plant in containers and move to a dry place in winter. Or dig and store corms in a cool, dry location once they go dormant. For container culture, space corms 3 to 4 inches deep and 3 inches apart. Mulch with rounded gravel.

### Growing Tips

Water deeply during the growing season when the top several inches of soil dry out. Stop watering after May so bulbs go dormant. Store container-grown blazing star where they won't get winter water. If necessary, turn pots on their side so you remember to withhold water. Turn back up when fall rains begin. When new growth appears, top-dress with a layer of composted chicken manure, bonemeal, or composted mulch. If you dig dormant corms, brush off the dirt and store in a cool, dry location.

### Care

Watch for aphids, whitefly, slugs, and snails (see "Tips and Techniques"). Allow leaves to dry on the bulbs after bloom fades. Cut back leaves once they are completely dried out and brown.

### Companion Planting and Design

Create a low-water, all season orange flowering garden with California poppy, 'Salmon Run' blazing star, 'Seashell' bugle lily, 'Pumpkin Pie' African daisy, and 'Apricot Sunrise' anise hyssop. For texture, add succulent flapjack plant with its very round green leaves edged in burnt orange, and *Aloe marlothii* whose wintertime candelabra has bright orange flowers.

### Try These

'Princess Beatrix' has bright orange flowers. 'Salmon Run' has salmon colored flowers. 'Fruit Salad Mix' is a mixture of pale peach, apricot, lipstick red, and salmon colored flowers. *Tritonia crocata* 'Bermuda Sands' has pale pink flowers.

*One of the loveliest South African bulbs available in nurseries is blazing star, an iris relative that has many species. The blazing star most widely available are varieties of* Tritonia crocata, *with foot-tall, sword-shaped leaves forming fans. Each fan produces several tall, slender stems lined in 2-inch flowers that open from bottom to top. Flowers come in shades of pale pink, apricot, orange, lipstick red, or salmon. Each petal tends to be darkest towards the center, paler towards the edges. Contrasting yellow streaks are at the base, while stamens are tipped yellow. This perennial, summer deciduous bulb (technically a corm) is native to the drier areas of the country. Not surprisingly, blazing star tends to do best in drier winter parts of California.*

**Other Common Name**
Flame Freesia

**Bloom Period and Seasonal Color**
Spring to summer flowers in shades of pale pink, apricot, orange, lipstick red, and salmon.

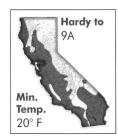
Hardy to 9A

Min. Temp. 20° F

**Mature Height × Spread**
1 to 2 ft. × 1 to 2 ft. and multiplying

# Blue-eyed Grass

*Sisyrinchium bellum*

Sometimes the smallest plant adds just the right touch to a garden. Our native blue-eyed grass is a case in point. Blue-eyed grass is a tiny member of the iris family that spreads by rhizomes, and has narrow grass-like leaves that form small tufts. The name "blue-eyed grass" comes from the many star-shaped flowers that rise from tufts in spring. Each little flower (about half an inch across) opens blue to purple with a yellow eye in the center. Blue-eyed grass is native to woodlands, chaparral, and sage scrub habitats across the state. Like so many other native plants, blue-eyed grass goes dormant briefly in the heat of summer. In a garden setting, they often naturalize, which is nice, especially in an informal garden.

**Bloom Period and Seasonal Color**
Periwinkle blue or purple flowers with yellow centers, early spring into early summer.

**Mature Height × Spread**
6 to 18 in. × 6 to 12 in.
(flower stems are 2 to 4 inches taller than foliage)

Hardy to 8A

Min. Temp. 10° F

## When, Where, and How to Plant
Plant fall through spring in a spot in full sun or bright shade. Blue–eyed grass is extremely adaptable to all soils without extensive soil preparation. Unamended soils are fine. Follow planting directions in the Perennials introduction. Water well after planting and mulch thickly. Blue-eyed grass can also be grown in containers with well-draining potting soil. Add mulch.

## Growing Tips
Blue-eyed grass is very easy to care for. These little iris cousins survive on rainfall alone along the coast, but in hot inland and valley gardens, they look better with twice weekly, deep water in summer. No fertilizer is needed.

## Care
Groom plants to remove spent flowers, brown leaves, and leaf litter. Dormant plants can be divided every few years if desired (see "Tips and Techniques"). Pests are not a problem.

## Companion Planting and Design
Diminutive plants like blue-eyed grass show best when used in small areas, such as tucked in among rocks or planted between pavers in a walkway. Blue-eyed grass tolerates a surprising amount of foot traffic. Alternatively, use blue-eyed grass as an accent or surprise element, i.e. as a bit of visual spice in a sedge meadow. In native gardens, use blue-eyed grass mixed with California poppy to underplant redbud, California lilac, and flannel bush (the blue/yellow combination is exceptional). In a container garden, mix with native *Penstemon*, monkey flowers, and native sage.

## Try These
'Rocky Point' has purple blue flowers; 'Raspberry' is 16 inches tall with purple flowers streaked raspberry pink. 'E.K. Balls' (also called 'Balls Mauve') is only 4 inches tall but has mauve colored flowers. Or try *Sisyrinchium californicum*, yellow-eyed grass. This tall relative to blue-eyed grass forms larger tufts with bright yellow flowers in late spring and early summer. As a native to marsh areas and coastal regions from Monterey north, it thrives in moist soils like those areas that drain poorly and in water gardens. 'Dwarf' is a selection that grows only 6 to 8 inches tall.

## When, Where, and How to Plant

Plant when bulbs (technically, corms) are dormant in fall. Any kind of well-draining soil in full sun is fine. Follow bulb planting directions in the chapter introduction, placing bulbs 4 inches deep and 4 to 6 inches apart. Water well after planting, and mulch. To grow bugle lily in containers, plant slightly closer together than they would be in the ground. Use a well-draining potting mix. Mulch with pebbles after planting.

## Growing Tips

Bugle lily in the ground survives on rainfall alone in coastal gardens. In hot inland and valley gardens, water weekly in summer. After May, stop watering. Store potted bugle lily where it won't get water through winter. If necessary, turn pots on their sides to remind you not to water. Turn them up when winter rains begin. When fall temperatures arrive, leaves emerge to begin the cycle once more. Top-dress with a layer of bonemeal and mulch.

## Care

Like other South African bulbs, allow leaves to turn completely brown before removing. Green leaves capture energy for the next year's leaves and flowers. That energy is stored in the dormant bulb. Bugle lilies multiply readily. When clumps get too wide, divide them (see "Tips and Techniques"). Few if any pests bother bugle lily.

## Companion Planting and Design

Plant in any low-water flower bed, against a background of broad green leaves like sweet bay. Try deep coral flowered *Watsonia aletroides* next to wispy-leaved *Grevillea* 'Long John'. Their leaf textures are complementary, while flower colors are nearly the same and peak simultaneously.

## Try These

*Watsonia aletroides* (1½ feet tall) has unusual narrow tubular flowers that are deep coral to scarlet. *Watsonia angusta* (to 5 feet) has tubular orange flower that flare at the mouth. For pink flowers on 4- to 6-foot stalks, try *Watsonia borbonica*. For pink flowers on 1-foot-tall flower stalks, try *Watsonia humilis*. *Watsonia pyramidata* (also called *Watsonia borbonica*) hybrids include the soft apricot flowers of 'Seashell', tangerine and raspberry flowered 'Ablaze', white flowers of 'Snow Queen', and rich rose-red of 'Flamboyant' (4 to 6 feet).

*Bugle lilies are among the easiest and showiest bulbs available to California gardeners. These gladiolus cousins have sword-like leaves that reach 4 feet or more (though a few are dwarfs), while flower stalks rise taller. Spring flowers are large, tubular or trumpet-shaped in orange, salmon, coral, clear pink, raspberry, or white and sometimes fragrant. Their size gives bugle lilies a commanding presence in the garden. They hold their weight better in the center of a flower bed rather than being right up front. They also multiply readily. I recently divided a large clump of white flowering bugle lilies that I planted only a few years ago. That single clump made six new clumps, some to replant in the garden and the rest to share.*

**Bloom Period and Seasonal Color**
Spring flowers in orange, salmon, coral, clear pink, raspberry, or white.

**Mature Height × Spread**
3 to 6 ft. × variable spread of clumps

**Minimum Temperature**
Depends on species

Hardy to 8B

Min. Temp. 15 to 20° F

# Canna
## *Canna* spp.

*Cannas are tropical perennials that bloom in hot colors. In early spring, canna stalks emerge from thick fleshy rhizomes and grow quickly to 3 to 8 feet or taller. Banana-like leaves unfurl from the stalks, some bronze (almost black), some olive, and some bright green. Others are green and yellow striped, red and green striped, even green, pink, and yellow striped. The colors and combinations of leaf and flower are almost endless. A cluster of flower buds tops each canna stalk. They open one by one, revealing a delicate bloom of petite petals, or an explosion of huge, floppy petals, which, depending on the species and variety, are reminiscent of iris flowers.*

### Bloom Period and Seasonal Color
Summer flowers in soft or hot yellow, tangerine, coral, electric pink, deep salmon, or bright red, multicolored or speckled.

### Mature Height × Spread
2 to 7 ft. × 2 to 8 ft. or under (depends on variety)

### Minimum Temperature
Perennial to 20 degrees F (Zone 9A), grown as annual in colder gardens

### When, Where, and How to Plant
Plant year-round in mild coastal and hot inland gardens. In cold winter areas, plant in spring. Buy bare-root canna in late winter and early spring, and plant according to directions in the chapter introduction. Nurseries carry potted canna in spring and summer. For best growth and bloom, choose a warm sunny location and amend soil generously with compost. Whether you plant dormant rhizomes or fully developed plants, set rhizomes just a few inches below the soil surface. Water and mulch after planting.

### Growing Tips
Thirsty canna wants constantly moist soil. Top-dress with organic fertilizer and compost. Mulch thickly to conserve moisture.

### Care
As each stalk finishes flowering, cut it to ground level. When clumps outgrow their spots, dig and divide rhizomes. Divide spring, summer, or fall. Share spares with other gardeners. Rows of ragged holes chewed in the center of leaves and flowers are signs of slugs and/or snails (see page "Tips and Techniques" for more care information).

### Companion Planting and Design
Mix canna with bamboo, palms, and gingers for a higher water tropical border. For an eclectic border with year-round interest, grow canna in a pot nestled among grasses, giant dracaena, dragon trees, sundrops, *Aloe*, and flapjack plant. Keep the pot well watered and allow surrounding plants to grow in the far drier conditions they prefer. Cut canna leaves for flower arrangements. Flowers fade too quickly to make them good cutting flowers.

### Try These
Dwarfs: 3-foot 'Pink Futurity' has coral pink flowers and burgundy striped leaves; 2-foot 'Pink Sunrise' has pale salmon flowers with spotted yellow and pink, green, and gold striped leaves; 3-foot 'Louis Cotton' has peach blush mango flowers and olive green leaves with reddish veins. Taller canna: 6- to 10-foot 'Stuttgart' has orange flowers and green leaves with white splotches; 5-foot 'Durban' has red/orange flowers and red/green/yellow striped leaves; 10- to 12-foot Ehemanni has magenta pink pendant flowers and green leaves.

# Caribbean Lily
## *Scilla peruviana*

### When, Where, and How to Plant

In late summer or early fall, plant dormant bulbs into well-draining soil amended with organic compost and organic bulb fertilizer or bonemeal (follow directions in chapter introduction). Plant bulbs 3 to 4 inches deep and 4 inches apart, with points up and rounded parts down. Cover, water well, and mulch. Or plant into a container large enough to accommodate several years' spreading growth without repotting. Space bulbs the same as in the ground.

### Growing Tips

Water regularly through the growing season, when soil is dry two inches deep. Err on the dry side if you are unsure about how much to water. Water occasionally when bulbs are dormant in summer. Top-dress with organic bulb fertilizer as winter/ spring growth begins. Follow package directions.

### Care

After a long bloom, flowers do a slow fade into summer. Like our native bulbs, leaves yellow as bulbs head into summer dormancy. Allow foliage to dry completely. Dead leaves loosen from the bulb and are easy to remove. After several years, if clumps grow too large, divide them (see "Tips and Techniques"). Bulbs may skip a bloom season after dividing. Pests are not problematic.

### Companion Planting and Design

Devote an entire large pot to Cuban lily, moving it to your garden's front stage when flowers are present, then backstage when flowers fade. A terracotta pot is a good choice both in terms of color and its ability to breathe and keep bulbs from becoming waterlogged. In a garden bed, mass Cuban lily bulbs and add a ground cover of ornamental oregano or other mounding, trailing plants that can distract from fading flowers and foliage.

### Try These

White squill (*Scilla tubergeniana* or *mischtschenkoana*) grows 6 to 8 inches tall with late winter/ early spring clusters of white to pale blue, star-shaped flowers with green centers. Amethyst meadow squill (*Scilla litardierei*) forms poker shaped clusters of starry, amethyst blue flowers from mid to late spring. Twin-leaf squill (*Scilla bifolia* 'Rosea') grows 12 inches tall and blooms from winter to spring.

*Spring is primary bulb season in the Mediterranean garden. In preparation for spring bloom, bulbs and corms send up their first leaves with the rains of winter. One of the most beautiful and unusual of these blooms belongs to the Caribbean lily. Caribbean lily bulbs produce strappy green leaves and green stalks topped by a fist-sized, dome-shaped flower cluster. Indigo blue buds open to tiny, starry purple flowers with blue and yellow centers. Flowers open in sequence, from outside to in, creating a contrast of color and texture. By the way, the name* Scilla peruviana *suggests origins in Peru, but in truth, this native of Spain and Portugal was named for the ship that first delivered it to England.*

**Other Common Name**
Cuban Lily

**Bloom Period and Seasonal Color**
Spring blooms in indigo blue, purple, and yellow.

**Mature Height × Spread**
12 to 16 in. × 12 to 16 in. or under

Hardy to 8A

Min. Temp. 10° F

# Clivia
## *Clivia miniata*

*Clivia are the shining lights of dry shade gardens. Their deep-green, tongue-shaped leaves grow 1- to 2-feet long, forming in fans. There are four (some say five) species of clivia, but most common clivia are hybrids of Clivia miniata. They have thick, fleshy, green flower stems that rise from the center of leaf fans. Each stalk is topped in a cluster of tubular flowers in shades of red-orange to coral, and even pale golden yellow from winter through spring. When flowers fade, the show continues with large colorful berries that start out green and ripen to red, orange, yellow, purple, and even pink. Their shallow roots don't mind being planted in shallow soils around the roots of trees and shrubs.*

**Bloom Period and Seasonal Color**
Orange, salmon, yellow, and red flowers in winter through spring followed by red, orange, yellow, purple, or pink berries.

**Mature Height × Spread**
1 to 2 ft. × 1 to 2 ft.
and multiplying

**Hardy to 9B**

**Min. Temp. 25° F**

### When, Where, and How to Plant
Plant clivia anytime during the year where soil is workable from 1 or 5-gallon pots. Choose a spot in shade or bright indirect light and well-draining soil. If your soil is heavy, plant into a mound of composted mulch or bark (follow raised bed planting directions in the Perennials introduction). Water well and mulch. For container culture, choose a large pot so plants can grow undisturbed for many years. Use a well-draining, organic mixture.

### Growing Tips
Once established, clivia are quite drought tolerant. Plants tolerate moist soils in the summer but prefer to be drier in the cool months. If you have a choice, then err on the dry side. Apply balanced organic fertilizer in early spring.

### Care
Groom to remove spent leaves and old fruit stalks. Clivia prefer to be crowded so don't be anxious to divide them. When you do divide them (see "Tips and Techniques"), replant new divisions in the ground, in a pot, or share with a friend. Avoid cultivating around or otherwise disturbing clivia roots and rhizomes. Remove snails from the crevices between leaves.

### Companion Planting and Design
Mass plant clivia in a shade garden, beneath Japanese maple, alongside flowering maple and giant dracaena, and king palms. Potted clivia is perfect for a shady spot on the patio or for adding architectural interest to a shady flower bed.

### Try These
Try hybrid clivia 'Arturo's Yellow' or 'Yellow Charm' that have butterscotch yellow flowers from mid to late winter and into early spring. Flowers are followed by yellow fruits. 'Orange Variegated' has lovely green and pale yellow striped leaves. *C. nobilis* is a slightly larger plant. Its long leaves are softly rounded or notched at the ends. This clivia makes hanging clusters of long tubular orange flowers with striking green tips. The leaves of *C. caulescens* end in a narrow point. Clusters of tubular flowers in paler orange or salmon with green tips hang from flower stalks.

## When, Where, and How to Plant

In mild winter climates, plant in full or part sun, any time of year. In colder winter climates, plant spring through fall. Plant bare root or from 1- or 5-gallon nursery cans. Provide well-amended, well-draining soils. In hottest climates or when growing deep color flowers, plant in part shade so colors don't fade. Follow planting directions in the Perennials introduction. For container culture, use large pots. Water thoroughly after planting, and mulch.

## Growing Tips

Water deeply to keep soil moist the first two years until plants are established. Then water when soil is dry several inches down from the surface. Unfertilized plants bloom, but organic fertilizer applied once in early spring makes for more blooms.

## Care

Divide daylily rhizomes when clumps get overly large (see "Tips and Techniques"). Remove spent leaves and flower stalks through the year. Protect from slugs and snails (also in "Tips and Techniques"). If older leaves turn yellow, check undersides for gold or rusty brown scabs of fungal daylily rust. Dispose of infected leaves (do not compost). Alternatively, cut all leaves to the ground. Check new leaves as they emerge. If rust returns, replace the plant with a rust resistant daylily.

## Companion Planting and Design

Plant daylily in just about any style garden, in traditional perennial beds, parking lot planters, tropical landscapes, or Mediterranean gardens. Combine with fine-leaved plants such as penstemon or with broad- or round-leaved plants such as sages and flowering maple. Tall daylilies fill that mid-border space against a background of shrubs such as lilac, butterfly bush, and 'Silver Sheen' pittosporum. Use sweeps of dwarf daylily to edge the front of flower beds.

## Try These

Rust resistant, reblooming daylilies: 'Bitsy' (to 2 feet) with yellow blooms 200 plus days a year. 'Buttered Popcorn' has larger yellow flowers for 150 days a year. Bright scarlet blooms of 'Frankly Scarlet' open in late season, each 4 inches across. Indigo flowered 'Plum Perfect' has golden throats, white ribs, and ruffled edges.

*Daylilies are easy-growing, long-blooming flowering perennials that are a mainstay in many gardens. Daylilies form clumps of strappy green leaves that arch from a center fan. From spring on, two or more (depending on the variety) lily-shaped flowers form at the tips of stalks that rise above the leaves. The topmost flower opens first, then those below in sequence, but only for a day each. Plants may make several stalks, so the overall effect is lots of flowers over a long period of time. Because daylilies are relatively easy to hybridize, there are countless hybrids available—tall, short, different flower colors, those that bloom in spring and rebloom in late summer into fall, those that go dormant in winter, and those that are evergreen (depending on your zone).*

**Bloom Period and Seasonal Color**

Spring to midsummer blooms in all shades of yellow, orange, raspberry, burgundy, nearly purple, and deepest blood red. Some are multicolored with distinct patterns.

Hardy to 5A

Min. Temp. -20° F

**Mature Height × Spread**

1 to 5 ft. × 1 to 5 ft. and multiplying

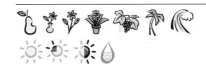

# Forest Lily
*Veltheimia bracteata*

*Beneath the tall pepper tree in my front garden are some of my favorite dry, bright shade bulbs—forest lilies. These winter and early spring bloomers look soft and somehow more sophisticated than their brightly colored springtime bulb buddies. They make lush rosettes of almost succulent leaves, 10 to 12 inches long with undulating edges. From the center of each rosette rise 1- to 2-foot tall flower stalks topped with cluster of tubular flowers, arranged almost like a poker shape, and opening in shades of pink rose, salmon, and occasionally pale yellow, all with an attractive green blush. After the flowers fade, leaves soon follow, allowing the bulbs to sleep through the hottest months of summer.*

### Bloom Period and Seasonal Color
Late winter to spring flowers, pale pink coral, deep rose, dusty pink, salmon, often with an attractive greenish caste, occasionally yellow-green.

### Mature Height × Spread
18 in. × 30 in. and multiplying

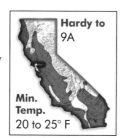

Hardy to 9A

Min. Temp. 20 to 25° F

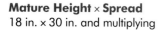

### When, Where, and How to Plant
Plant dormant bulbs in late summer to early fall in a shady spot with humusy well-draining soil. A tree with high branches and dense leaf litter is the ideal cover. Follow directions in the chapter introduction and set bulbs at or just below the surface of the soil. To grow in a container, start with a pot large enough to accommodate growth for several years. Set the pot where it will get a few hours of direct morning sun or in day-long indirect light. Indoors, choose a spot with medium light. Water pots during the growing season, and allow them to go dry when plants are dormant. Mulch in-ground bulbs with organic mulch, and containers with pebbles.

### Growing Tips
Use a general-purpose organic bulb fertilizer throughout the growing season (follow label directions). Provide an occasional deep drink when winter rains are sparse. Water to keep soil moist once rains end until plants go dormant, then stop watering until new leaves appear.

### Care
Remove leaves only when completely dry. Avoid digging around or otherwise disturbing bulbs and roots. Protect from slugs and snails (see page "Tips and Techniques"). Divide to propagate forest lily or cut a healthy growing leaf into pieces about two inches long. "Plant" each piece into a pot of sterile, sandy potting soil and cover loosely with a plastic bag to keep moist. Stand a chopstick upright in the pot so the bag doesn't touch leaves. Place in a shady spot and keep damp. Within a few months, little bulbs will develop at the base of each leaf.

### Companion Planting and Design
These bulbs are from the forests of South Africa and grow well in the shade of tall trees, alongside native currant and hellebore. While forest lily makes a great garden bulb, it can also be grown as a houseplant.

### Try These
'Lemon Flame' has pale or greenish yellow flowers. Sand lily (*Veltheimia capensis*) is similar to forest lily but takes full sun, a bit more water, and flowers earlier in the year. Sand lily leaves are shorter and blue-gray. Flowers are deeper pink and occasionally white.

# Gladiolus
## *Gladiolus* spp.

### When, Where, and How to Plant

Plant gladiolus corms in late summer or early fall, in full sun (or in a bit of shade in hot inland areas), and in a soil with excellent drainage. Follow basic directions in the chapter introduction. Set bulbs (technically corms) 4 inches deep and 5 inches apart. Or grow gladiolus in pots using a well-draining potting mix with added fertilizer. Space just as deep and a bit closer together. Water all bulbs well and mulch.

### Growing Tips

Plants bloom best with an application of organic bulb fertilizer when leaves first appear. Water when the top several inches of soil are dry, during the growing season only. Withhold summer water so corms dry out.

### Care

Allow leaves to dry on the corm after flowering. Cut (don't pull) leaves once they are completely brown and dry. Protect from hungry squirrels, rabbits, and rodents. Watch for whitefly (see "Tips and Techniques"). If you don't have a spot free from summer water, grow gladiolus in pots, nestled in the garden to look as if they are permanent. After one bloom fades, move the pot to a shaded spot and stop watering until new growth appears the next fall or winter. To help you remember not to water, turn the pot on its side in May and turn it back up when winter rains arrive.

### Companion Planting and Design

Species gladiolus flowers add a graceful touch to any low water flower bed. These early spring bloomers are beautiful when grown with lavenders, rosemary, ornamental grasses, and soft foliage ground covers such as ornamental oreganos.

### Try These

Yellow marsh Afrikaner (*Gladiolus tristis*) is one of the earliest blooming spring plants. It has tall narrow leaves and slender ivory flowers with a sweet afternoon/evening fragrance. Next blooming is sword lily (*Gladiolus byzantinus*) which is a bit beefier and flowers hot pink with white markings. Reed bell (*Gladiolus gracilis*) flowers are also fragrant but pale blue or lavender with magenta-purple streaks and speckles with a touch of yellow.

*Hybrid gladiolus that dominate the nurseries surely appeal to some gardeners, but I far prefer the delicate looking, tough growing species gladiolus. These are the wild gladiolus of Africa and southern Europe, and the ancient parents of those gaudy hybrids. "Gladiolus" is derived from the Latin term "gladius," meaning sword shaped, and refers to the sword shaped leaves that sprout in fall. Spring blooms follow with tall stalks of delicate 3- to 4-inch, star-shaped tubular flowers whose colors range from subtle tones to screaming hot. Flowers are speckled and streaked in contrasting colors, much like other members of the iris family. Some flowers are fragrant. After blooms fade, leaves persist for a time. Then species gladiolus corms sink into a deep summer sleep as suits our Mediterranean climate.*

### Bloom Period and Seasonal Color

Late winter or spring depending on species in orange, cream, mauve, purple, white, bright magenta, pale blue, coral, and yellow—marked with contrasting streaks and speckles on inner petal surfaces.

Hardy to 7A

Min. Temp. 0° F

### Mature Height × Spread

1 to 3 ft. × 6 in. and multiplying

# Harlequin Flower
*Sparaxis tricolor*

*Some of spring's most wonderful flowers are bright colored, star-shaped harlequin flowers. These South African perennial bulbs have foot-tall grass-like leaves, above which rise six-petal flowers, 2 to 3 inches across in three colors ("tricolor"), the dominant color being orange, coral, palest pink, or black cherry. At the base of each petal are burgundy-edged yellow flares that suggest a harlequin pattern, hence the bulb's common name. Harlequin flower is the busy gardener's best friend. It takes little water, little care, and multiplies happily. Bulbs increase, flowers make seed, and soon harlequin flower naturalizes throughout the garden. No problem though, because while individual flowers are short-lived, the more plants you have, the longer the bloom overall—and the more impressive.*

## Other Common Name
Wand Flower

## Bloom Period and Seasonal Color
Spring to early summer flowers in shades of orange, coral, palest pink, or black cherry with yellow and burgundy flares at the base of the petals.

Hardy to 8B

Min. Temp. 15° F

## Mature Height × Spread
12 in. × 4 in. and multiplying

## When, Where, and How to Plant
Plant into full sun when bulbs are dormant, late summer or early fall. Poor soil is fine, but amend the planting hole with a handful of organic compost and bulb fertilizer according to label directions. Follow planting directions in the chapter introduction, setting bulbs 2 inches deep and 4 inches apart. Place the bulb root side down (look for remnants of last year's roots). Water well after planting, and mulch. In a container, plant at same depth as in-ground plantings but slightly closer together. Water well after planting.

## Growing Tips
These bulbs can survive on rainfall alone (dry the rest of the year) but also tolerate garden beds that are watered in summer. In pots, water regularly during growing season. Little to no fertilizer is needed.

## Care
Cut (don't pull) leaves once they are completely brown and dry. To seed into a new area of the garden, simply grab a handful of seed capsules (you will see the little round seeds after the flowers fade) and shake the seed where you want them to grow. Pests are not a problem.

## Companion Planting and Design
Plant harlequin flower in clumps or swaths in a flower border but expect them to naturalize, settling in open spaces between plants, sidewalk cracks, among rocks, and other spots within a few years. Add to a meadow planting, tucked in among tufts of ornamental grasses, baboon flower, and sedges. Harlequin flowers can fill a container on their own after a few seasons. Mix with other summer dormant bulbs and plants such as purple baboon flower, blue-eyed grass, or yellow Mexican tulip poppies. In a flower bed, overplant harlequin flower with ornamental oregano or wooly thyme.

## Try These
While hybrids of *Sparaxis tricolor* are the most common harlequin flowers, there are a number of others to try. *Sparaxis grandiflora* 'Lady Buttercup' is 10 to 12 inches tall with bright yellow flowers, and *Sparaxis* 'Celebration Mix' that grows 10 to 12 inches tall and flowers in shades of apricot, yellow, cream, coral, or pink.

# Iris

## *Iris* spp.

### When, Where, and How to Plant

Plant dormant iris rhizomes or potted iris July through October into well-draining soil. Spuria and bearded iris prefer full sun. Amend the planting bed with organic matter and organic fertilizer. Set rhizomes horizontally, 1 inch below the surface with roots pointing down. Space 1 to 2 feet apart. For container-grown native iris, plant in shade, fall through early summer (see the Perennials chapter introduction). Water well. Mulch thickly. To grow iris from rhizomes in a pot, set rhizomes an inch below the surface, 6 to 8 inches apart. Soak, then mulch with pebbles or gravel.

### Growing Tips

Keep soil surrounding bearded iris damp (not wet) through the growing season. Water irises through the first summer, sparingly after that in coastal and far northern California, and water weekly in southern California. Spuria iris are drought tolerant and survive summer(though dormant) with monthly summer watering. Their leaves remain green if watered more frequently. Keep the soil of potted iris damp (not wet). In winter, let Mother Nature water iris. Fertilize once-blooming bearded, spuria, and PCH iris monthly through fall and spring. Feed rebloomers monthly through summer as well. Sprinkle organic fertilizer around the circumference of the rhizomes.

### Care

In fall, remove faded plant parts. Cut spuria leaves back to the ground (unless it dies back). Divide clumps of iris rhizomes when blooms decline; three to four years for bearded iris, eight to ten years for spuria, three to eight years for native iris. See "Tips and Techniques" for information on dividing and protection from snails and slugs.

### Companion Planting and Design

Plant native PCH iris for early season bloom, bearded iris for midseason bloom, spuria for late bloom. All three together make for a long blooming season.

### Try These

Spuria iris 'Vintage Year' has navy blue petals with gold splashes at the base. 'His Royal Highness' is the classic reblooming bearded iris with solid deep purple flowers. PCH 'Canyon Snow' has white flowers with yellow markings.

*Few plants are as diverse as irises, known for their colorful complex flowers, each with six petals: three curve upward and three curve downward. Of the many types of iris, three stand out as best suited for California's dry summers and mild winters. Tall bearded iris (Iris germanica) stands about 4 feet tall and has big, fancy, voluptuous flowers. Spuria iris (Iris spuria) tops out at 6 feet and has large flowers with more refined and streamlined petals; and the petite (8 to 24 inches tall) native Pacific Coast hybrid (PCH) irises have smaller, but no less beautiful, flowers. Iris flowers come in a huge range of colors, often with mixed colors, colored veins, and markings. They make a statement both in the garden and in a vase.*

### Bloom Period and Seasonal Color
Spring blooms in combinations of white, cream, pink, rose, violet, purple, blue, yellow, gold, bronze, mahogany, chocolate, maroon, and apricot.

### Mature Height × Spread
8 in. to 6 ft. and spreading

### Minimum Temperature
Depends on species

Hardy to 8B

Min. Temp. 15° F

59

# Lily
*Lilium* spp.

Lilies are famous for their huge gorgeous flowers and sweet fragrance. There are many kinds of lilies for California gardens. Oriental lilies and their close cousins, Asiatic lilies, are excellent in the garden and in bouquets. These two groups of hybrid lilies are a favorite of Dutch breeders whose crosses and re-crosses have created tall stemmed beauties topped with huge, six-petal trumpets. There are also native lilies, including the dry growing Humboldt lily and more moisture loving leopard lily. These two are distinguished by orange or gold to fire-engine-red petals, all freckled in deep maroon. Their petals curve back like graceful wings away from the flower center.

## Bloom Period and Seasonal Color
Summer blooms white to pink, deep rose to almost red, golden yellow, and pumpkin orange, many with blotches, colored edging, or freckles.

## Mature Height × Spread
3 to 4 ft. × 6 to 8 in. and spreading

## Minimum Temperature
Depends on species

Hardy to 7A

Min. Temp. 0° F

### When, Where, and How to Plant
With hybrid lilies, plant dormant bulbs in earliest spring into well-draining, well-amended soil in full sun (near the coast) or dappled shade (inland). Plant away from foot traffic (stems and flowers are fragile). Follow basic planting directions in the introduction. Dig holes 6 to 7 inches deep and 6 inches apart. Add amendments and place bulbs flat side down. Water thoroughly after planting. For container culture, start with a large pot. Plant bulbs at the same depth and distance as in the ground. Place the pot in full sun or dappled shade and soak until water runs out the hole in the bottom. Add mulch.

### Growing Tips
Water to keep soil moist and mulch to keep roots cool, except Humboldt lily, which should be dry in fall and winter. In early spring, top-dress with organic bulb fertilizer or a few inches of composted chicken manure. Native lilies need no fertilizer.

### Care
Once flowers fade, leave foliage in place until it dries completely. For cut flowers, harvest as the buds begin to crack open. Cut stems by no more than a third. Leave enough leaves to support the bulb and its bloom the following year. Watch for whiteflies (tiny white specks on the undersides of the leaves), and aphids (tiny black dots). See "Tips and Techniques" for treatment.

### Companion Planting and Design
Lily flowers can become top heavy. To keep them from flopping over, surround bulbs by 18-inch-tall plants such as penstemon, daylilies, or low shrubs like hebe. Or use plastic-covered metal supports, stakes or rings. Humboldt lily can be grown beneath oak trees. Mix hot-colored lilies with 'Flame' Peruvian lily whose red flowers have yellow throats or 'Casablanca', that has pink-blush to pale white flowers.

### Try These
'Starfighter' Oriental lily has dark, raspberry flowers with deeper raspberry freckles and white edges; 'Red Alert' Asiatic hybrid has straight, bright-red petals and white stamens and a gentle scent. 'Cancun', an Asiatic lily, adds pizzazz to a hot color scheme with its bright golden petals edged in bright orange.

# Mariposa Lily

## *Calochortus* spp.

### When, Where, and How to Plant

Plant bulbs in late fall, 2 inches deep and 4 to 6 inches apart, with the pointed side up. Follow basic planting directions in the chapter introduction. Choose a spot in full sun or bright shade and with no summer water. Well-draining soil is ideal (though some mariposa lilies tolerate clay). Mulch well after planting. Or grow in shallow containers with a good quality potting mix. Space as if planted in the ground.

### Growing Tips

Keep soil moist until they bloom. Following bloom, allow the bulbs to go dry through summer. The dry dormant period is an important stage of the mariposa lily lifecycle. One way to remember not to water potted bulbs is to turn pots on their sides once flowers fade. Turn them back up when winter rains start. No fertilizer is needed.

### Care

These plants require very little care. Remove leaves once they dry out completely. To protect in-ground bulbs from hungry critters, plant in a basket fashioned from hardware cloth. The basket acts as a barrier but won't hinder the roots.

### Companion Planting and Design

In the ground, grow mariposa lilies in an open meadow, rock garden, or as understory to native shrubs and trees. Grow mariposa lilies in containers to control watering and keep bulbs from predators. Display them as potted plants during the bloom season or nestle the pots amid foliage in the garden so they look potted. After bloom, lift the containers and store for the next year.

### Try These

One of the easiest mariposa lilies is yellow mariposa lily (*Calochortus luteus*). Its yellow petals are marked with burgundy deep inside the flower. Clay mariposa lily (*Calochortus argillosus*) stands 16 to 20 inches tall with flowers that are white, lavender, pink, deep rose purple, or pink and burgundy with yellow markings deep inside the cup. Desert mariposa lily (*Calochortus kennedyi*) takes part shade and has bright orange flowers (10 to 20 inches). Butterfly mariposa lily (*Calochortus venustus*) blooms white to bright pink, lavender, and burgundy. This bulb prefers bright shade.

Mariposa lilies are gorgeous flowering bulbs native to the West Coast from Baja to British Columbia. Forty species are California natives. The name Calochortus is Greek for "beautiful grass," evidently a reference to their narrow, green, grass-like leaves, topped in three petals that form cup-shaped, nodding, or star-like flowers, typically 3 to 4 inches across. The petals of cup-shaped mariposa (Spanish for "butterfly") lilies are often marked at their base with speckles, freckles, and mysterious looking "eyes." As a friend once commented, "their markings are like Mandalas, your mind sinks into them." Mariposa lilies sprout in spring, bloom from spring to early summer, and sleep through summer's heat and drought. Their short growing cycle is more than made up for, however, by the beauty of their flowers.

**Other Common Name**
Fairy Lantern

**Bloom Period and Seasonal Color**
Spring to early summer blooms in white, lavender, pale pink, bright pink, rose, burgundy, orange, and bright yellow with burgundy markings.

**Mature Height × Spread**
4 to 36 in. × 4 in.

Hardy to 4B

Min. Temp. -25° F

# Naked Lady
*Amaryllis belladonna*

When I mentioned that I was looking for naked ladies, a friend scaled the fence between her garden and the abandoned garden next door. She lobbed fist-sized bulbs over the fence, giggling as she recalled the antics of her youth. We took several dozen bulbs, leaving countless more behind. Naked ladies are tough showy South African bulbs. From fall through spring, they have tall, deep green leaves. In early summer, leaves die to the ground. In summer's heat, a 2- to 3- foot tall flower stalk rises, atop a cluster of up to twelve large, pink, trumpet-shaped flowers. Their fresh perfume fills the air. The name "naked lady" comes from the fact that without any foliage, the flower stalks look, well, naked.

## Bloom Period and Seasonal Color
Pink blooms in the heat of summer.

## Mature Height × Spread
24 in. × 6 in. and multiplying

Hardy to 8A

Min. Temp. 10° F

### When, Where, and How to Plant
Plant in summer when bulbs are dormant. Follow basic planting directions in the chapter introduction. Choose a spot in full sun or dry bright shade (especially in hot valley and inland gardens) with well-draining soil. In cool coastal gardens, blooms are deep pink, while in hot valley and desert gardens, blooms can be almost white. Set bulbs a foot apart, leaving their necks at or above soil level. In cold winter gardens, bury bulbs completely. Set bulbs slightly closer in containers. Water well and mulch. When growing naked ladies in a container, choose one large enough to accommodate several years of growth so as not to interrupt the bloom cycle.

### Growing Tips
Naked ladies thrive on neglect. They require little to no water and no fertilizer, yet reward you with fragrant blooms year after year. **Note:** This bulb is poisonous if ingested.

### Care
Allow leaves to dry completely once the bloom fades; leave in place as mulch or move to the compost pile. Very few pests are interested in these toxic bulbs. As bulbs age, they multiply. What were once few bulbs becomes a colony of a dozen, which means more flowers and more fragrance! If bulbs grow so crowded that they push up out of the soil, dig them up and separate them (see "Tips and Techniques"). Replant, add to a different area of the garden, or share the extras with a friend. Replanted bulbs may skip blooming for a year or two.

### Companion Planting and Design
Add to low water flower borders with perennial marigold, lavender, rosemary, blue hibiscus, honeybush, and bay. Combine with succulents for an interesting counterpoint. Use in an old- fashioned flower garden with lilac, iris, and geranium. For a classic California garden, plant naked ladies with bougainvillea, yucca, agave, and purple-flowering Mexican bush sage.

### Try These
Naked ladies hybridized with other bulbs in the Amaryllis family produce flowers in shades of deep pink to white and even red. In specialty nurseries, look for these bulbs labeled as × *Amarygia*, × *Amarine*, and × *Amacrinum*.

# Peruvian Lily
## *Alstroemeria* spp.

### When, Where, and How to Plant

Plant from gallon containers from fall through spring, taking care not to disturb fragile tubers too much. Site in full, part sun, or part shade (especially in hot desert and inland gardens) into well-draining amended soil. Follow planting directions in the Perennials introduction. Water well after planting, and mulch. Container-grown Peruvian lily needs a large pot to give tubers room to spread.

### Growing Tips

Fertilize with organic fertilizer, following label directions. Thanks to fleshy tubers, plants can survive on little water, especially in winter, but more water promotes lusher growth and flowers.

### Care

To maximize bloom, harvest flowers regularly by pulling up stalks with a sharp jerk (don't cut). Use the same technique to remove spent stalks. As tubers multiply, plants make a large patch that is easy to divide. Dig tubers and use your fingers to gently separate them into fist-sized clumps. Protect from snails and slugs (see "Tips and Techniques"). To support stems of taller varieties, set Peruvian lilies mid-border and support with other plants. Or use stakes and twine to suspend a square of wire mesh (with about 3-inch openings) horizontally, 12 to 20 inches above the soil, and guide stems up through the openings. For tallest plants, set a second layer, several inches above the first.

### Companion Planting and Design

Plant Peruvian lilies with iris, ornamental grasses, anise hyssop, naked ladies, and coneflower. Hotter colored varieties enhance the colors of tropical planting of gingers, butterfly weed, and flowering maples. Dwarf Peruvian lilies are ideal container plants.

### Try These

Evergreen varieties: 'Casablanca' (3 feet × 3 feet) has many pale white flowers and pink blush undersides, burgundy markings, and pale yellow throats. 'Tricolor' blooms in three shades of pink with a yellow throat. 'Flame' (1 to 1$^1$/$_2$ feet tall) has red flowers with yellow throats. 'Jupiter' blooms clear magenta and blush yellow in the throat. 'Zsa Zsa' is a dwarf (8 to 12 inches tall) with pink flowers.

*Peruvian lilies are prolific flowering perennials from South America that produce clusters of 2- to 3-inch azalea-shaped flowers. In the 1980s, Alstroemeria species were first hybridized for the cut-flower industry. Today, countless varieties are available for home gardens as well. All make long-lasting cut flowers. Peruvian lilies have thick tubers that send up fleshy, upright stems, covered in long, bright green leaves. Dwarf varieties grow 8 inches tall, while taller varieties can reach 5 to 6 feet. Stems are topped by clusters of six to twelve (or more) 2- to 4-inch flowers. Old style deciduous Peruvian lilies go dormant in summer. Newer varieties are evergreen and nearly everblooming.*

**Other Common Name**
Inca Lily

**Bloom Period and Seasonal Color**
Spring, early summer and/or fall blooms in shades of white, pink, red, orange, yellow, red-violet, and almost purple with yellow throats and burgundy or black speckles and markings.

Hardy to 8B

Min. Temp. 15° F

**Mature Height × Spread**
8 in. to 8 ft. × 5 ft. and multiplying

# Pineapple Lily
## *Eucomis* spp.

*If you love unusual looking plants, pineapple lily is for you. This deciduous bulb has strappy, upright leaves that are green, olive, or burgundy. Several thick-stemmed cylindrical flower stalks rise from the center of the leaves. Each 20-inch stalk is lined with rows of tiny of star-shaped flowers. Some are white, some pale green, yellow-green, deep cabernet, or pink colored. Topping every flower cluster is a flap of green or red leaf-like bracts that help give these flowers the look of a tall skinny pineapple. Pineapple lily flowers fade to tiny fruits that are every bit as attractive as the blooms. The combined display makes for season-long interest as well as a great cut flower—that is, if you can stand to cut them.*

**Bloom Period and Seasonal Color**
White, cabernet, pink, or yellow-green summer flowers followed by eye-catching seedheads.

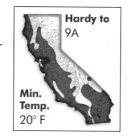

Hardy to 9A

Min. Temp. 20° F

**Mature Height × Spread**
1 to 2 ft. × 1½ to 2 ft. and multiplying

**Minimum Temperature**
Depends on species.

### When, Where, and How to Plant
Plant pineapple lily plants or bulbs in early spring, into a spot in full sun to dry bright shade (especially in hot inland and desert gardens). Plant in well-draining and amended soil, 4 to 6 inches deep and 12 inches apart. Follow basic planting directions in the chapter introduction. Soak after planting and mulch. To grow pineapple lily in a container, set bulbs about 2 inches below soil surface. Repot yearly into fresh soil and fertilizer. Add a layer of gravel or pebbles to keep soil moist.

### Growing Tips
Top-dress yearly with organic bulb fertilizer and water well while in active growth (spring and summer). Water only occasionally in winter when bulbs are dormant.

### Care
Remove spent plant parts once they are totally dry. Protect from slugs and snails (see "Tips and Techniques"). Directions for dividing bulbs—done only once every five to six years—are in "Tips and Techniques."

### Companion Planting and Design
Pineapple lily adds a touch of exotic to a tropical planting of ginger, canna, lemon grass, and angel trumpet. Like most bulbs, these look best if massed in odd numbers (3, 5, 7, etc.). For an ongoing bulb display, plant pineapple lily with earlier blooming bulbs such as gladiolus or their close relative, forest lily.

### Try These
*Eucomis bicolor* has pale green leaves (sometimes spotted burgundy) and star-shaped green flowers edged in burgundy/purple. Variety 'Alba' has white flowers. *Eucomis comosa* has green to burgundy leaves with undulating edges. Flowers are sweet scented (some of the other species smell faintly like rotting meat) and white tinged with pink or purple on purple freckled stalks. *Eucomis comosa* 'Rubrum', is one of the most beautiful pineapple lilies, with deep burgundy leaves and pink blush and white flowers topped in red bracts. The variety 'Sparkling Burgundy' has burgundy flower spikes and purplish flowers tipped in green. 'Striata', has purple striated leaves and 'Toffee', has purple flower spikes with light pink flowers and purple seedpods.

# Shell Ginger
## *Alpinia zerumbet*

### When, Where, and How to Plant

Plant from nursery containers spring through summer, in moist well- amended soil in full sun (along the coast) or bright shade (hot inland and valley gardens). Follow planting directions in the Perennials introduction. Incorporate organic fertilizer into the planting hole. Soak the soil after planting and add a thick layer of mulch. To grow in containers, choose one large enough to hold several seasons growth. Use a rich, well-draining potting mix. Add slow release fertilizer, water, and top-dress with a layer of pebbles or gravel to hold in moisture.

### Growing Tips

Gingers like water and fertilizer. Keep soil moist (not wet) spring through early fall, and damp in late fall and winter. Feed with balanced organic fertilizer from spring to the end of summer (follow label directions). Mulch to retain soil moisture. If you have a pet rabbit, mulch with rabbit pellets (no need to compost them).

### Care

Cut old canes to the ground after bloom. Watch for ragged holes left by snails and slugs. (See "Tips and Techniques").

### Companion Planting and Design

Zone your garden to be water wise. Place thirstiest plants, such as shell ginger, nearest to the house, and the most drought tolerant plants place furthest away. Placing shell ginger near the house also allows you to best enjoy its beautiful leaves and flowers and to appreciate its heavenly fragrance. For a tropical garden vignette, plant ginger with king palm, angel's trumpet, reed orchid, and banana.

### Try These

Dwarf variegated shell ginger (*Alpinia zerumbet* 'Dwarf Variegated') is a 3-foot-tall slow grower good for containers. Dwarf cardamom (*Alpinia nutans*) is a ginger grown for leaves, not flowers. This knee-high ginger makes large patches of the bright green foliage that, when crushed smells of clove and citrus! Related to *Alpinia*, *Hedychium* ginger has fragrant butterfly-shaped flowers arranged in upright clusters or cones: Kahili ginger (*H. gardnerianum*) blooms yellow with long red stamens. Garland flower ginger (*H. coronarium*) flowers white.

*Nothing gives a garden a tropical look like summer blooming gingers. "Ginger" is a catchall term for several different, but related, plants. One of the gingers best suited for California gardens is shell ginger, an evergreen (in frost-free areas). Five- to eight-foot-tall stems of furled leaves emerge from underground rhizomes in spring. Leaves are bright green or variegated, two feet long × five inches wide. They resemble skinny banana leaves. In late summer, each ginger stalk produces an arching cascade of coral-tinged white flower buds that resemble the shells of sea snails. As buds open, they form tubular white flowers with fringy yellow lips and blood red throats. Flowers are long lasting and extremely fragrant.*

### Bloom Period and Seasonal Color

Summer buds are coral-tinged white, opening white with red and bright yellow throats.

### Mature Height × Spread

5 to 8 ft. × 3 ft. and multiplying

### Minimum Temperature

Root hardy to 15° F.

Hardy to 8B

Min. Temp. 15° F

# Spider Lily

## *Hymenocallis* spp.

*Ever wonder how plants get their common names? Look at the spider lily. These deciduous perennial bulbs produce long, strappy green leaves and 2-foot-tall flower stalks. Each stalk is topped with five or more fragrant white blooms that open a few at a time, creating the illusion of a long bloom. The flowers look like lilies gone bezerk. Each is at least 5 inches across with two sets of petal-like parts. Six petals form a central trumpet with green or yellowish striped throats. Behind the petals are six narrower petals that arch forward, enfolding the trumpet and six white with yellow tipped stamens. One might imagine a gardener referring to the points of the star or to the skinny stamens as resembling spider legs.*

**Other Common Name**
Peruvian Daffodil

**Bloom Period and Seasonal Color**
White, sometimes pale yellow summer flowers.

**Mature Height × Spread**
2 to 3 ft. × 2 to 3 ft.
and multiplying

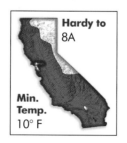

**Hardy to 8A**

**Min. Temp. 10° F**

### When, Where, and How to Plant

In fall or winter, plant dormant bulbs into well-amended and well-draining soil in full sun along the coast, part sun or bright shade everywhere else. Set spider lily bulbs just below the surface of the soil. Follow basic bulb planting directions in the chapter introduction. Space bulbs 12 inches apart. Water the soil until it is saturated, and top with thick mulch. In containers, plant bulbs the same distance apart but leave the neck of the bulb just above the soil. Place pot in part or bright shade and water until the soil is thoroughly saturated. Mulch with an inch or so of rounded gravel.

### Growing Tips

Spider lilies are thirstier bulbs that prefer moist (not wet) soil at all times. Place them nearest the house with other high water plants. Water deeply and regularly and mulch well. In early spring, top-dress with organic bulb fertilizer. Follow directions on the package label.

### Care

Once spring bloom is over, leave stems and foliage in place. They will stay green for a long time, then decline in late summer. Watch for ragged holes in leaves and buds that tell you snails and slugs are present. See "Tips and Techniques" for treatment.

### Companion Planting and Design

Plant spider lilies in a perennial bed where they won't be disturbed very often. Site beneath a tree that tolerates regular water and casts dappled spring and summer shade, such as Hong Kong orchid tree. Combine with lower growing plants so their greenery will hide or distract from fading spider lily foliage (such as dwarf Peruvian lily, low growing cuphea, hellebores, and celery scented or peppermint geranium).

### Try These

*Hymenocallis* × *festalis* is the white form of the spider lily. Trumpet petals have scalloped edges on variety 'Zwanenburg'. '*Hymenocallis* 'Sulfur Queen' is an heirloom variety with soft yellow flowers, green and yellow striped throats, and a light citrus fragrance.

# Walking Iris
## *Neomarica caerulea*

### When, Where, and How to Plant
Plant walking iris from 1- or 5-gallon containers fall through spring. Follow directions in the Perennials introduction. Plant into well-draining and well-amended soil. Plants tolerate full sun, but do better in bright shade. Water well and mulch. Where winter temperatures regularly dip into the 20s, grow in a large container. Move to a greenhouse, under the eaves, or to another protected location in winter.

### Growing Tips
In gardens where the soil is well mulched and winters are frost-free, walking iris are evergreen. If you mulch well, plants will bloom without much fertilizer. Smallish flowers or yellowing leaves suggest the need for organic fertilizer.

### Care
As walking iris finish flowering, "plantlets" replace flowers. The name "walking iris" comes from the way these easy rooting plantlets "walk" away from the mother plant and make new plants. To help them along, bend the flowering stalk to the ground so the base of the plantlet touches the soil. Weigh the stem down with a rock or other object. For container grown plants, bend the flower stalk and pin the base of the plantlet onto the surface of potting soil in a separate pot. After a few months, tug at the plantlet (remove the weight first) to test whether it is rooted. Once well rooted, simply sever the flower stalk from the mother plant. Pruning and pests are not an issue.

### Companion Planting and Design
Plant in the bright shade under the high canopy of jacaranda or under a floss silk tree. For a tropical look, plant with ground cover African daisy and flowering maples. Walking iris offer their tall sculptural shape to many kinds of container compositions. For best results, mix with long-lived perennials such as ornamental oregano and Jerusalem sage. Start with a container large enough to accommodate several years of growth. The larger the plants, the more flowers.

### Try This
Look for the walking iris *Neomarica caerulea* 'Regina,' whose flowers are bluer than the species.

At summer solstice, my garden produces a most mysterious looking flower with the odd name of "walking iris." This member of the iris family makes tall fans of sword-shaped green leaves that are perennial in warm climate gardens. Flattened flower stalks rise above walking iris foliage and produce clusters of buds that open a few at a time. Each flower has two types of petals. Three broad, flat petals ("falls" in iris lingo) are royal purple. Where the falls fuse at the base, they form a brown- and gold-striated cup. Between the falls are small, upright petals ("standards"), curved like the head of a cobra preparing to strike. The purple and white striped standards transition to gold and brown where they fuse with the falls.

### Bloom Period and Seasonal Color
Early summer blooms in purple and white on the outside, gold and brown patterns inside.

### Mature Height × Spread
4 to 6 ft. × 3 to 4 ft.

Hardy to 9B

Min. Temp. 25 to 30° F

# Fruits *for California*

Nothing tops the experience of strolling through the garden to pick fresh figs for breakfast, a juicy tangerine for snack, or a pomegranate to decorate the Thanksgiving table.

Fruits from all over the world grow in California gardens. At last count, my garden included more than fifty fruiting trees and shrubs. My little citrus grove produces lemons, limes, grapefruits, kumquats, and mandarins (the proper name for tangerines). A quintet of pineapple guava trees produce sweet tasting pink spring flowers and egg-shaped late fall fruits. Tropical guavas alongside my patio ripen in winter, which always strikes me as odd—the most heat loving fruits ripen in the coldest time of year.

While some fruiting plants such as avocado and pomegranate take a few years until they mature enough to fruit, many such as grape and fig fruit from the start. My trio of figs ripens in sequence over many months. We feast on 'Brown Turkey' figs in late summer, followed by green and yellow striped 'Panache' figs in fall. Apple-sized 'Big Yellow' figs ripen last in late fall and hang on the tree after frost (yes, we get frost in San Diego County).

I have a pair of low-chill apples bred in Australia that are excellent when fresh and make wonderful applesauce. They are best eaten warm out of the pot in winter. The stone fruits, however (apricots, nectarines, peaches, plums, pluots, cherries, etc.) are strictly summer fruits. I grow low chill blueberries too, in pots nestled in my herb garden.

## Consider the Chill

If you live in a mild winter area like I do, pay attention to chill ratings for deciduous fruit trees and shrubs. These plants, primarily stone fruits, apples, and berries, require a dormant period in order to fruit well in spring.

In the world of deciduous fruits, varieties are rated according to the number of chill hours they need to set fruit. Growers label them as low, medium, or high chill, calculated as an accumulation of nighttime hours below 45 degrees Fahrenheit, from November 1st to February 15th. Typically, low-chill

*Citrus unshiu* 'Owari Satsuma'

fruits require no more than 40 chill hours. Medium chill require 400 to 800 hours, and high chill require more than 800 hours. Ask about your community's chill rating at your local nursery or Master Gardeners' office.

Keep in mind that chill hours are not a hard and fast rule of nature. Rather, they are a human construct based on a mathematical model. Use chill hours as a guide for choosing varieties, but don't feel tied to them. California has so many microclimates that you might be successful with a fruit that is rated for more chill than you expect in your garden. If the difference isn't too great, give it a try. But if after several years you've had no fruit, don't hesitate to yank the tree or shrub and try a different variety (sometimes easier said than done).

Fruiting plants are also rated as early, mid season, or late season producers. These terms give you an idea of when a crop is expected to mature. Plant a combination of early, mid, and late season producers so you can harvest ripe fruits over many months.

Banana, citrus, and other fruits are self-fruitful, but some fruit (avocado and stone fruits being prime examples) need a second variety nearby for cross-pollination. Read the plant label or ask the nursery which fruits require cross-pollenizers and how to pick the best producing combination.

When it comes to pruning, most evergreen fruiting plants (citrus for example) don't require pruning though they can be pruned to shape. Deciduous fruits on the other hand produce more fruit when pruned. Before you prune, do your homework so you know which branch parts produce fruit: old wood, new wood, or the fruiting spurs that develop along the branches. That way, you'll know what to cut off and what to leave.

## What About Water?

Lest you think that fruiting plants require lots of water, think again. Several of the fruits in this chapter require little irrigation once established. In fact, a grape expert once told me that irrigating established grapevines for an entire year takes as much water as irrigating the same area of lawn for *one hour*.

As for the thirstier, more tropical fruits (banana, citrus, avocado, tropical guavas, etc.), this is a situation when it is worth investing the extra water. Your reward is a harvest of fresh, delicious fruits.

## Designing with Fruits

I intentionally grow fruits in all areas of my garden rather than relegate them to a dedicated orchard. These beautiful trees, shrubs, and vines fit right in with plants that are strictly ornamental. In addition, integrating them allows me to site each one where it gets the optimum amount of light and water.

Finally, don't forget that edibles are extremely attractive. Don't hesitate to grow these plants in pots to decorate your deck or patio.

www.digplantgrow.com

# Avocado
*Persea americana*

Take a rich buttery avocado, and add chopped onion, jalapeno, tomato, and a squeeze of lemon for the world's best guacamole. Avocado fruits grow on tall handsome evergreen trees that flower in spring. Each flower cluster has hundreds of tiny white blooms pollinated by bees. Flowers mature to fruits that soften only once picked. Because avocados are subtropical, fruits need summer warmth to mature. Guatemalan avocado trees produce large, leather-skinned fruits and produce best in mild winter gardens. Mexican avocado trees (P. drymifolia) produce small, thin skinned fruits and tolerate colder winters inland. Coastal and valley gardens from San Diego to Santa Cruz, the Central Valley's "banana belt," and the Bay Delta area are all backyard avocado country.

**Bloom Period and Harvest Season**
Tiny white flowers in spring. Harvest depends on variety.

**Mature Height × Spread**
Standard:
30 to 40 ft. × 40 to 50 ft.
Dwarf:
10 to 15 ft. × 10 to 15 ft.

**Minimum Temperature**
Depends on variety.

Hardy to 9A

Min. Temp. 20 to 30° F

## When, Where, and How to Plant
Plant in early spring, in full sun and in well-draining soil. Follow planting and staking directions in the Trees introduction, taking care not to minimize root disturbance (see "Tips and Techniques"). Do not amend the soil. In areas with clay soil, create a well-draining planting mound.

## Growing Tips
Water weekly (except in the rainy season). Water twice weekly when temperatures top 95 degrees F. Saturate soil 3 inches deep each time. Poke the soil with an unwound wire hanger or a moisture probe to test how deep the water penetrates. Allow fallen leaves to accumulate a thick soil-insulating layer of mulch. Apply organic citrus and avocado food according to label directions.

## Care and Harvest
Lowest branches shade tree trunks, but prune branch tips so they don't touch the ground. Protect from mealybug and scale (see "Tips and Techniques"). Avocado's biggest challenge is root rot, typically from overwatering. Purchase trees grafted onto 'Dusa' or another rot resistant rootstock. Ripening time depends on variety. Pick a test fruit and allow it to soften at room temperature. If it tastes bad or doesn't fully soften, try again after several weeks.

## Companion Planting and Design
Avocado is a very large tree with dense shade and shallow roots that resent disturbance like digging or weeding. Grow alone or in an orchard rather than in a garden bed.

## Try These
To ensure cross-pollination, plant an "A" variety with a "B" variety. Trees already in your neighborhood may be good pollenizers. Mexican avocados include green skinned 'Bacon' (B). Harvest fall/winter in warm climates and in late spring in cooler areas. Green skinned 'Zutano' (B) matures in fall/winter in warm climates and late spring in cooler gardens. Black skinned 'Mexicola' (A) matures late summer/fall. Guatemalan varieties include green skinned 'Gwen' (A), a 15 feet × 15 feet matures winter/fall. Black skinned 'Hass' (A) matures spring to fall; green skinned 'Holiday' (A) matures summer through winter 10 feet x 12 feet dwarf.

# Citrus

*Citrus* spp.

## When, Where, and How to Plant

Plant spring through fall into a 6- to10-inch tall mound of well-drained, well-amended soil in full sun and in the warmest part of the garden. Cover surface roots with *no more* than ¹/₂ inch of soil. Water to saturate soil several feet deep. Mulch the soil beyond the canopy, but not below it. In cold winter gardens, grow citrus in large containers and move to a protected location in fall.

## Growing Tips

Use organic citrus fertilizer. Follow label directions. Water young plants deeply, once or twice weekly to keep soil damp (*not wet*) through the first year (see avocado watering directions). Year two onward, deep water every week or two, from spring through early fall and when winter rains are sparse.

## Care and Harvest

Prune to remove dead or diseased wood, to keep branches off the ground or to shape. Discolored leaves suggest nutritional problems or poor drainage. Ant and aphid infestations make leaves pucker (see "Tips and Techniques"). Protect young trees from frost by covering with a floating row cover. Fruiting usually starts after year three. Fruits ripen on the tree. Color is one indicator, but trial and error will tell you when fruit is ready. Ripe fruits hang on the tree a long time, so there is no need to pick fruit all at once. They eventually drop, making fruits easy to collect.

## Companion Planting and Design

Citrus make beautiful garden landscape plants, even planted as hedges. Allow plenty of room and do not plant other plants beneath their branches. Grow potted dwarf citrus on patios, courtyards, and entryways.

## Try These

Different citrus varieties have different winter hardiness and needs for summer heat. 'Oroblanco' grapefruit (yellow skin, sweet yellow flesh) ripen in winter. Spring/fall ripening lemons include 'Eureka' (thick skin and tart flesh) and 'Improved Meyer' (thin golden skin and tart flesh). Mexican (thin skin and aromatic fruit) and 'Bearss' limes (thin skin, tart fruit) ripen in fall, even in cool summer gardens. Winter ripening 'Clementine' and 'Satsuma' mandarins (tangerines) are sweet and easy peeling.

*Citrus arrived in California with Spanish missionaries, but took off in a big way after 1873 when Riverside County farmers planted the first Washington navel orange trees. Soon bright green citrus trees with yellow and orange hanging fruits blanketed San Diego County north through Orange County (guess how it got its name), San Bernardino County, Riverside County, Los Angeles County (including the San Fernando Valley where I grew up), and Ventura County. In spring, sweet citrus flowers perfumed the region. While homes now grow in place of citrus, gardens from Redding to Yuma, from Santa Cruz to Chula Vista are still filled lemons, limes, oranges, grapefruit, mandarins, and kumquats in the ground or in pots that move indoors for the winter.*

### Bloom Period and Harvest Season

Small white flowers, most in spring. Harvest time depends on variety.

Hardy to 8A

Min. Temp. 10 to 28° F

### Mature Height × Spread

Standard: 20 to 30 ft. × 20 to 30 ft.
Semi-dwarf: 15 to 20 ft. × 15 to 20 ft.
Dwarf: 8 to 15 ft. × 8 to 15 ft.
All depending on variety and rootstock.

### Minimum Temperature

Depends on variety and rootstock.

# Edible Banana
## *Musa* spp.

*Bananas are great edible plants for warm climate gardens. Their huge leaves suggest tropical breezes and lazy afternoons (unless you are a banana picker). Bananas serve as tall vertical features whose silver- or burgundy-tinged stems and green leaves add garden drama. These fast growing plants have spreading underground rhizomes, while their stalks are made of layers of leaves that unfurl one by one. When growing conditions are just right, each stalk produces a huge showy flower cluster sheathed in deep wine or purple colored bracts. Tubular white flowers emerge from beneath each bract and soon develop into fruits. As flowers develop, their weight pulls the stalk towards earth. The result is a pendulous structure that makes an "upside down" flower, a sort of fruit chandelier.*

**Bloom Period and Seasonal Color**
Green, red, yellow, burgundy, and/or purple clusters flower sporadically through the year.

Hardy to 9B

Min. Temp. 28° F

**Mature Height × Spread**
8 to 15 ft. × 6 to 10 ft.

**Minimum Temperature**
Plants die to the ground, but roots usually survive at 28 degrees F.

### When, Where, and How to Plant
Plant bananas as soon as ground warms in spring. Amend soil heavily with compost and follow Tree planting directions. Choose a sunny warm spot in a coastal garden and a slightly shaded, cold-protected spot in hot inland gardens. Shield from wind. In cooler climates, grow in large plastic pots and move to a protected spot in winter.

### Growing Tips
Bananas are both thirsty and heavy feeders. Mulch with a 3-inch layer of composted manure. Apply balanced, organic fertilizer during the warm months of the year, according to label directions. Monitor soil to keep it evenly damp at all times from the surface to several feet deep.

### Care and Harvest
Control ants to prevent scale, aphids and sooty mold (see "Tips and Techniques"). Flowers appear at different times of the year. A banana shoot requires ten to fifteen frost-free months to flower and fruit. To encourage flowering, remove all but one or two stalks. Cut unwanted pups at the base, leaving roots attached. Pot pups to plant elsewhere or share. Once stalks flower, prop the branches with wood stakes. After fruits color-up (color depends on variety), cut the entire fruiting hand at once and let ripen at room temperature. Eat bananas as they ripen. Do not refrigerate. Since stalks die after fruiting, cut them away and let new stalks develop.

### Companion Planting and Design
In a tropical theme garden, plant banana with canna, sugar cane, Peruvian lily, king palm, butterfly weed, and Hong Kong orchid tree. Mass bananas as a background screen or use as the centerpiece of a planting bed. Use leaves and buds in flower arrangements.

### Try These
'Goldfinger' (14 feet) resists soil fungus and makes short straight fruits. 'Manzano' (14 feet) and reddish leaved 'Mysore' (15 to 18 feet) produce petite, "ladyfinger" fruits. Leaves of 'Ice Cream' are silver-blue on the undersides. Fruits can be eaten fresh or cooked, as can the square, yellow fruits of 15- to 18-foot 'Better Select' (also called 'Orinoco').

## When, Where, and How to Plant

Plant into full sun in fall through spring when soil can be worked. Along the coast, plant in the hottest part of the garden. Follow tree planting directions. Protect fig roots from hungry gophers by planting into a cage of hardware cloth. To grow in a pot, choose one at least 20 inches by 20 inches (see "Tips and Techniques").

## Growing Tips

Water to saturate soil 2 to 3 feet deep the first year to establish (see Avocado description). Year two and after, and in gardens with well draining soil, deep water once every week or two in summer, but no water in winter. Water slightly more often in desert gardens. Water less in heavy soils. No fertilizer for plants in the ground. Feed container-grown plants with a balanced, organic fertilizer.

## Care and Harvest

Pick fruits when they are very soft. Rodents and birds are the biggest fig pests, but resist the urge to harvest early to foil pests, as figs ripen only on the tree and unripe figs taste terrible. Many varieties produce a light crop in early spring and a heavier crop in fall. Fig mosaic discolors leaves and can cause stunting. There is no known control. Prune branches after the fall harvest to remove weak wood, create a strong structure, and encourage the next year's crop. Leave lower branches so fruit is easy to reach.

## Companion Planting and Design

Fig trees make spectacular shade trees. They set the tone in Mediterranean gardens, tropical gardens, and Asian style gardens. Espalier flat against a sunny wall. While fig trees can be incorporated into garden beds, do not plant beneath fig branches. Their roots don't like the disturbance or the competition.

## Try These

'Improved Brown Turkey' fruits are dark brown with amber flesh and are good for Southern California. 'Black Mission' has purple black fruit with pink flesh and is good throughout the state. 'King' ('Desert King') with yellow/green fruit and red flesh is best suited for cool, northern gardens.

*Cleopatra may have loved Marc Anthony, but she adored figs. No surprise, since at 55 percent sugar content, figs are the sweetest fruits and ones with a long history. Archeologists have found figs in 7000-year-old archaeological sites; they grew in the Hanging Gardens of Babylon; and Spanish conquistadors brought them to the New World in the 1500s. Franciscan friars planted California's first fig at Mission San Diego de Alcala 250 years later. The rest, as they say, is history. Fig trees are deciduous trees with fantastic gnarled branches, white bark, and big, shiny green lobed leaves (think Adam and Eve). Some varieties have two crops, one in spring and a heavier crop in late summer/fall. Easy to grow, low water, and delicious, figs are a garden must-have.*

**Bloom Period and Harvest Season**
Flowers inconspicuous. Light crop in spring, heavier crop in fall.

**Mature Height × Spread**
10 to 30 ft. × 10 to 30 ft.

**Minimum Temperature**
15 degrees F when dormant, 30 degrees F in leaf.

Hardy to 8B

Min. Temp. See below

# Grape
## *Vitis* spp. and hybrids

*Did you know that grapes are berries? Vines emerge from rough twisted trunks and sprout broad, shiny green leaves that turn fall colors and drop in winter. Their fruits develop in clusters on deciduous vines that grow long and fast. In the warmest parts of summer, a grapevine can grow 10 to 12 inches in a week! There are both edible and ornamental grapes, but from a gardener's standpoint, they all grow the same way. As is typical of plants that have been cultivated for millennia, there are a staggering number of grape varieties. Some have seeds, others are seedless; they are green, blue, black, yellow, or red. Some are best for eating, others for making juice, wine, and/or raisins. Young, tender grape leaves can be blanched and stuffed for dolmades.*

**Bloom Period and Harvest Season**
Flowers insignificant, grapes ripen in summer

**Mature Height × Spread**
An unpruned grape can grow 200 to 300 ft. long.

**Minimum Temperature**
Depends on variety.

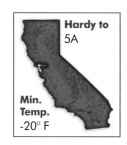

Hardy to 5A

Min. Temp. -20° F

### When, Where, and How to Plant
Purchase and plant grapes as dormant rooted "whips" in winter or as potted leafed-out vines in spring. Choose a spot in full sun and deep soil. If your soil drains poorly, prepare a planting mound. Follow shrub planting directions ("Tips and Techniques"). Mix in balanced organic fertilizer. Mulch with a 3-inch layer of compost. Grapes can be grown in large pots too.

### Growing Tips
Water deeply the first three summers to encourage deep roots (see Avocado watering directions). Established grapes are extremely drought tolerant and produce best on a low-water diet. Early California farmers grew grapes on rainfall alone. Fertilize minimally, if at all. Too much nitrogen makes for lush leaf growth at the expense of fruit.

### Care and Harvest
There are several methods for training grapevines, all of which are designed to prevent vines from tangling, keep fruit off the ground, and ensure both good ventilation and sunlight penetration. Prune in early spring, just before new growth starts. Since grapes fruit on year-old wood, learn to identify fruiting wood before you start cutting. Grape pests range from mildew to four-legged critters. Still, growing grapes is very easy and tremendously rewarding. Check with your local Master Gardeners for information on local grape pests and how to manage them.

### Companion Planting and Design
Grapevines are beautiful and functional as garden plants. Train them onto walls, over fences, or onto arbors for fast summer shade and warm sunshine in winter. Use cut grapevines to weave wreaths.

### Try These
There are grapes for nearly every microclimate of California. These varieties perform reliably throughout the state: 'Reliance', a seedless pink/red table grape that ripens midseason, 'Lakemont', a seedless green table grape, 'Alden', a reddish blue wine and table grape with seeds. 'Swenson' is an early season red grape (with seeds) suitable for table, juice, and wine.

# Olive

*Olea europaea*

## When, Where, and How to Plant

Plant in early fall or early spring into well-drained soil and full sun. Poor soils are fine. Keep away from sidewalks and other structures that could be damaged by surface roots. To grow several trees, space 20 feet apart. Water deeply and mulch after planting.

## Growing Tips

Water young trees deeply once a week through the first summer and less often in spring. Established trees are extremely drought resistant, but to produce olives, water deeply, monthly in summer. Avoid overwatering, which causes root rot. Apply all-purpose organic fertilizer before tiny spring flowers appear.

## Care and Harvest

In early spring remove dead or diseased wood. Prune fruiting olives to a vase shape for good light penetration, air circulation, and to keep fruit accessible. Prune ornamental olives to a single trunk or multi-trunk. Ants, black scale, and sooty mold are typical problems (see "Tips and Techniques"). Other pests and diseases affect olives in different regions (check with your local Master Gardeners). Fruiting starts after about four years in the ground. For lye curing, harvest olives when they turn from green to straw colored. For salt, sun, or oven drying, harvest olives black.

## Companion Planting and Design

Gnarled branches that reach gracefully towards the sky, smooth gray bark, and gray-green leaves make olive trees valuable landscape plants. Olive trees are adaptable to a wide range of situations and tolerant of extreme neglect. Full-sized specimens are defining features of Tuscany, Greek, French, Spanish, and Middle Eastern style gardens. Plant as a grove, screen, or espalier. Plant dwarf olives as hedges, borders, or container plants. **Note:** Some people have respiratory allergies to olive pollen.

## Try These

Ornamental olive trees make few or no fruits. Dwarf 'Little Ollie'™ is 4 to 6 feet tall and wide, 'Skylark Dwarf' is 16 feet × 16 feet, 'Swan Hill'™ is 35 feet tall and wide. For olive fruits, plant 'Manzanillo' or 'Mission' and to crosspollinate, plant 'Sevillano'. To make olive oil, try Tuscan 'Leccino' or 'Maurino' in cool winter areas.

*Years ago my husband and I visited friends in Italy whose family owned an abandoned olive orchard in the hills overlooking Florence. The couple spent many years rescuing ancient olive trees from a tangle of wild cherries, figs, and more. They lived in a romantic little flat over the old olive mill where they pressed their own oil. It was hard work, but one taste of their olive oil and we immediately understood their enthusiasm. Today, olive orchards and boutique olive oils are the rage for those with acreage in California. But you needn't have acres of space to enjoy olive trees in your own garden, whether to harvest or simply to enjoy for their graceful structure and soft green leaves.*

## Bloom Period and Harvest Season

Inconspicuous cream or yellow flowers in spring. Harvest fall/winter.

## Mature Height × Spread

20 to 30 ft. × 20 to 30 ft.

Hardy to 8B

Min. Temp. 15° F

# Persimmon
*Diospyros* spp.

*The cooler shorter days of autumn bring edible color to the garden. Pumpkins turn bright orange, pomegranates turn ruby red, and persimmons turn from bright green to red, orange, or gold. Persimmons are native to China and other parts of Asia. They grow on handsome trees, 25 feet tall and wide or wider. In mild winter gardens, persimmon's large, shiny green leaves turn fall colors before they drop around the time of Thanksgiving. In colder gardens, leaves drop with the first frost. Either way, the tennis-ball size fruits hang around a bit longer. Their round, oblong, flat, square, or acorn-shaped silhouettes dangle from bare branches like enormous Christmas ornaments against the blue, blue winter sky. Some are eaten hard and others must be soft as jelly to be palatable.*

### Bloom Period and Harvest Season
Spring flowers are inconspicuous. Fruit ripens red, orange, or gold in fall and winter.

### Mature Height × Spread
25 ft. × 25 ft. or wider

Hardy to 8A

Min. Temp. 10° F

## When, Where, and How to Plant
Plant young persimmon trees from fall through spring into deep, well-drained soil, in full sun along the coast and in sun or part shade inland. Trees tolerate poor soils. Follow Trees introduction planting directions. Plant into a gopher cage (see "Tips and Techniques"). Take care not to kink or coil the tree's long taproot. After planting, cut the main trunk to 3 feet high. New branches will sprout at that point and form a nice structure. Paint trunks with one part latex paint mixed with three parts water to prevent sunburn.

## Growing Tips
Water to wet the entire rootball when soil is dry—three inches down for the first two years. After that, water deeply but infrequently during spring and summer (a bit more often in desert gardens). Fertilize with citrus and avocado food, following the recommendations for avocados. If a fruiting persimmon tree develops too much non-fruiting wood, cut back on fertilizer.

## Care and Harvest
Persimmon trees fruit after a few years. Heavy and light crops often alternate years. Thin fruits to one per shoot. Prune when dormant. Prune away damaged wood and shape trees. Do not to cut back too far, as trees fruit on one-year-old branches. Ants, mealybugs, and scale can be a problem (see "Tips and Techniques"). The bigger problem is hungry birds, possums, gophers, and even coyotes. Plant enough to share, or pick fruit before completely ripe and ripen following directions below.

## Companion Planting and Design
Plant persimmon trees as specimens to show off their fantastic fall/winter display. Leave the ground beneath the branches bare rather than planted with perennials or other plants.

## Try These
"Astringent" persimmons are inedible until jelly is soft and translucent. Pick hard and let ripen in a paper bag or freeze overnight. Thaw to eat. 'Hachiya' has astringent, acorn shaped, deep orange fruit when ripe and is very sweet. It is self-pollinating. Non-astringent persimmons are sweet and edible—apple hard or tomato soft. 'Jiro' ('Fuyu') has non-astringent, flat, round fruit with orange skin. It is self-pollinating.

# Pineapple Guava
## *Feijoa sellowiana*

### When, Where, and How to Plant
Plant fall through spring in frost-free gardens, and in spring in gardens where the ground freezes. For maximum flowering and fruiting site guavas where they can reach full size rather than cram them into a too-small space and prune constantly. Fruiting is best in well-drained soils, but plants survive in nearly any soil, moist or dry. Provide full sun in coastal and valley gardens, afternoon shade in hotter inland and desert gardens. Follow planting directions in Trees introduction. Water deeply and mulch after planting.

### Growing Tips
Soak regularly through the first two summers to encourage deep roots so your guava will be drought tolerant for life. After the second summer, cut way back on water. Guava can survive solely on rainfall in coastal and northern gardens though fruiting might suffer. For best crop, irrigate deeply every week or two during flowering and fruiting seasons. Fertilize with balanced, all-purpose organic fertilizer in spring.

### Care and Harvest
Prune to shape in fall after the harvest is over. Selectively remove branches at their base rather than cut them short. Pests are not a problem. Fruiting starts after a few years in the ground. In early fall, guava fruits' rough skin smoothes out a bit and gains a yellow/green tone. Fruits plump then drop when fully ripe. Rather than picking guava fruits, simply collect them from the ground (shake branches periodically to help loose fruit drop). Eat them fresh. Cut fruits in quarters the long way and take a bite! Don't eat the rind.

### Companion Planting and Design
Pineapple guava are beautiful large shrubs, taller than wide. They fit perfectly into Mediterranean theme gardens. Plant several as an informal hedge, screen, or background. Prune for a formal hedge (but you'll sacrifice flowers and fruit). Prune up lower branches to form a small, multi-trunk tree.

### Try These
If you have a pineapple guava that doesn't fruit well, plant a second to improve pollination. Try 'Coolidge', a variety whose flowers are white, red, and purple and fruit is about 4 inches long.

*Pineapple guava is not a true guava, but rather an evergreen edible/ornamental with shiny, silvery green leaves and pink edible flowers with a bright red fringe of stamens. The petals are fleshy and sweet, the perfect surprise for a fruit salad or floating in a punch bowl. Don't pick too many flowers though, or you'll miss the guava fruits. These fall-ripening fruits are rounded or oval, 2 to 3 inches long with ridged, waxy, blue-green skins. As they ripen, fruits tend to plump, turning olive/yellow and eventually dropping just as they turn perfectly edible. Pick them up, and slice into quarters the long way to bite into the pale gold, sweet flesh for a flavor treat unlike any other. Pineapple guava is also known as Acca sellowiana.*

### Bloom Period and Harvest Season
Spring/summer flowers are red on top, curled to reveal pale pink undersides and a bright red fringe of stamens. Fruits ripen in fall.

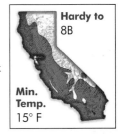

Hardy to 8B

Min. Temp. 15° F

### Mature Height × Spread
10 to15 ft. × 10 to 15 ft.

# Pluot
## *Prunus* hybrid

Bite into a pluot and you'll find the flavor to be ten times as intense as any plum you've ever tasted. Pluots are fairly recent arrivals to our summer fruit menu. These plum-like plum and apricot hybrids have smooth skin in shades of orange, red, green, and green mottled with red. Their flesh has the texture of a firm plum. Pluots, plums, and apricots are in the same family as peaches, nectarines, and cherries. All of these are stone fruits—fruits with hard stone-like pits. All are deciduous and are similarly easy to grow. To produce a good crop, you need two varieties of pluot trees, or a pluot and a 'Burgundy' plum as a cross-pollinator. Pick your favorite two and start planning for summer fruit!

### Bloom Period and Harvest Season
Flowers in spring; harvest late spring through summer

### Mature Height × Spread
Tree height depends on the rootstock.
 Standard: 20 to 30 ft. × 20 to 30 ft.
 Semi-dwarf: 15 to 20 ft. × 15 to 20 ft.
 Dwarf: 10 to 12 ft. × 10 to 12 ft.

### Minimum Temperature
Varies depending on variety.

### When, Where, and How to Plant
Plant trees bare root in winter and from nursery containers in spring. Site in full sun and in well-amended soil. Allow room for the tree's full size. Follow planting directions in the Trees introduction. Water deeply and mulch after planting.

### Growing Tips
Water regularly through growing season. When trees are dormant in winter, they require no supplemental irrigation except during long dry spells or dry Santa Ana winds. Use organic fruit tree fertilizer. Follow directions on the label.

### Care and Harvest
Prune after fruit harvest in summer or when trees are bare in winter. Prune young trees far back in order to focus energy on roots and not fruits. Peach leaf curl, aphids, scale, and other pests can be a problem. Control starts with resistant rootstock suited to your soil type and climate (check at the nursery or ask your local Master Gardeners). Discard rotten fruit, and spray trees in winter with dormant oil, following directions on the label. In early spring, thin fruits to one per cluster every few inches along a branch. Fruits are best if ripened on the tree but soften off the tree as well.

### Companion Planting and Design
To increase the varieties of stone fruit in your garden, plant several trees 18 inches apart. Prune in summer to no more than 8 feet tall. This approach, known as "backyard orchard culture," is gaining in popularity as backyards grow smaller.

### Try These
'Dapple Dandy' ('Dinosaur Egg') has red skin mottled green and red flesh late season harvest (400 to 500 chill hours). 'Flavor Supreme' has green-maroon mottled skin, sweet red flesh (500 chill hours). 'Flavorsa' is plum purple with sweet mild flavor, is earliest ripening (300 chill hours), is not suited for mountain gardens. 'Geo Pride' has smaller fruit with red skin and yellow flesh with fruiting mid to late season (500 chill hours). For earliest and heaviest fruiting, plant 'Emerald Drop' whose smaller emerald-green fruit and juicy yellow flesh ripens midsummer (400 chill hours). 'Splash' is apricot orange and ripens before 'Emerald Drop' (400 chill hours). 'Flavor Grenade' has late season harvest (300 chill hours).

# Pomegranate
*Punica granatum*

## When, Where, and How to Plant
Plant fall through spring in frost-free gardens and in spring in colder areas. Plant into full or part sun (the more sun, the more fruit). Well-draining soil is best but pomegranates adapt to very poor soils. Place plants away from walkways so thorny branches don't snag skin or sweaters. Water well after planting and mulch. To grow in a pot, choose one that is at least 3 feet × 2 feet. Place in full sun, saturate with water, and mulch thickly.

## Growing Tips
Water in-ground pomegranates deeply twice a month through the first spring/summer (more often in desert gardens). Established plants are extremely drought tolerant (even abandoned trees can fruit generously). If yours doesn't fruit after the fourth fall, water more frequently in spring/summer. Fertilize young plants once in early spring and mature plants not at all.

## Care and Harvest
If appearance doesn't matter, prune simply to remove dead wood, suckers, and water sprouts. If appearance does matter, prune young pomegranate to shape, either as a shrub, single, or multi-trunk tree. Mature shrubs can be reshaped but should be done gradually over several years. Fruits ripen on the tree in fall. Harvest once they color-up and are heavy, but before they split. No significant pests bother pomegranate.

## Companion Planting and Design
Plant where you can enjoy pomegranate's fall colors. Use as screens, foundation plants, hedges, and background shrubs. Combine with other Mediterranean climate plants including fig, Australian willow, grapes, flowering sages, yellow African bulbine, New Zealand flax, and emu bush.

## Try These
Edible pomegranates: 'Balgal' has sweet, 3-inch-diameter fruit, pale pink inside and out. Seeds of 'Eversweet' are lighter pink with little pith and do not stain. 'Utah Sweet' has sweet, dark pink fruit. 'Wonderful' has crimson fruit, tough skin, and hard tart seeds good for juicing. Ornamental pomegranates: double flowers of 'Legrellei' ('California Sunset') are striped coral/salmon pink. 'Nochi Shibari' has double, deep red-orange flowers.

*Who can resist the charms of the pomegranate? Its leathery skin peels back to reveal translucent gem-like seeds filled with sweet and often astringent juice. Take a bite, but just be sure your clothes are protected from the deep red pigments that give pomegranate seeds their rich hues. Pomegranates are some of California's oldest cultivated plants. They are native to a region from Iran to northern India, but arrived here with olives and figs brought by Spanish settlers in the late 1700s. These tall shrubs are adaptable to being pruned into single or multi-trunk trees with lovely arching branches. To produce well, pomegranates need full sun and a long, hot summer. They are easy to grow, and once established are extremely tolerant of both cold and drought.*

**Bloom Period and Harvest Season**
Brilliant scarlet or orange red flowers in spring; crimson fruit in fall.

**Mature Height × Spread**
8 to 10 ft. × 8 to 10 ft.

Hardy to 8A

Min. Temp. 12° F

# Southern Highbush Blueberry
## *Vaccinium* hybrids

*Visitors often inquire about the pretty shrubs in my herb garden. "They're blueberries," I say and watch their faces. "I thought blueberries don't grow here" they respond, eyes wide. They do, I explain, but not all blueberries. These are special hybrids called southern highbush blueberries. Native blueberries grow in forests and swampy areas throughout the U.S., but not in the southwest. We just don't have the wet acidic soils and long cold winters they require for good fruiting. Breeders have long worked to push those boundaries. Several years ago, they introduced hybrids that don't need acid soils and require only minimal winter chill. Whether you live in Mendocino or Murrieta, southern highbush blueberries are bred to produce a respectable crop of berries in your garden.*

**Bloom Period and Harvest Season**
Small white flowers in spring, fruit early summer through fall.

**Mature Height × Spread**
3 to 6 ft. × 3 to 6 ft.

Hardy to 6A

Min. Temp. -10° F

## When, Where, and How to Plant
Plant blueberries as bare-root plants (see "Tips and Techniques"). in winter or as potted plants in spring. In California gardens, blueberries do great in 20-inch plastic pots (not black, they get too hot in the sun), each filled with a handful of soil sulfur added to a mixture of 30 percent small pathway bark, 30 percent peat moss and 30 percent forest humus. Site in full sun (bright shade in hottest inland gardens) and mulch.

## Growing Tips
Use drip irrigation to keep shallow roots moist (not wet) and leaves dry. Fertilize in late spring before harvest and again in late winter before flowering. Use a formulation for acid loving plants (such as for azaleas and camellias), or mix your own using 50 percent cottonseed meal and 50 percent fishmeal. Water well after fertilizing, and then mulch thickly.

## Care and Harvest
Remove first year flowers so plants put their energy into roots, branches, and leaves. From the second year on, prune just after harvest, cutting the year's new growth by half. Don't cut any more since next year's fruit develops on this year's late summer and fall growth. Once leaves drop, remove branches that are three or more years old. Remove diseased or dead branches and prune to shape. Berries are very sweet, deep blue, and slightly soft when ripe. Touch them and they'll fall. Hungry birds are the biggest blueberry pests. Cover bushes with netting or plant extras so you have enough to eat *and* to share.

## Companion Planting and Design
Handsome blueberry bushes deserve to be a focus in any garden. Place potted blueberries on sunny decks, along walkways, or do as I do and nestle pots among other plants in garden beds. For maximum fruiting, combine two or more varieties (and plant two bushes per blueberry eater).

## Try These
For early summer fruit, try standard sized (5 to 6 feet tall) 'O'Neal', 'Reveille', 'Sharp Blue', or 'Southmoon'. Midsummer to fall fruits come from standard sized 'Georgia gem' and 'Jubilee', as well as from the 3-foot compact 'Sunshine Blue'.

## When, Where, and How to Plant

Plant in spring and early summer, into dappled shade in desert gardens and full sun elsewhere. Well-drained, well-amended soil is best, but guavas tolerate a wide range of soils. Follow Trees introduction for planting directions. Water deeply and mulch after planting. Grow guava in large containers, at least 20 inches by 20 inches. Place in a sunny spot and mulch to keep moist.

## Growing Tips

Water young trees deeply and weekly through the first spring and summer. Established trees are drought tolerant along the coast but produce more fruit with occasional deep watering. Still, the trees in my old garden fruited fine with no water. In hotter inland and desert gardens, water deeply every week or two, spring through fall. Fertilize with citrus and avocado food. Follow directions on the label.

## Care and Harvest

Prune only for aesthetic value. If whitefly, mealybugs, or thrips appear, treat as per directions in "Tips and Techniques." With extreme frost, trees may die back to the ground, but they will sprout again in spring. In some cultures, guava are eaten apple hard and dipped in salt and ground chili pepper. For sweet fruit, harvest just as they soften and let ripen in a paper bag or allow them to soften fully on the tree. Cut fruit in half. Spoon out the flesh and enjoy!

## Companion Planting and Design

Grow guava as a shrub or prune to maintain a tree-like shape. Plant trees 10 feet apart to create an informal hedge or screen. Prune for a formal hedge though fruit might be limited.

## Try These

The 8-ounce fruits of 'Beaumont', are delicious fresh or juiced. The large fruits of 'Bangkok Apple', and 'Red Indian' are popular in Mexican and Asian communities. If your garden is too cold for tropical guava but you can grow citrus, try strawberry guava (*Psidium cattleianum*) and lemon guava (*Psidium cattleianum lucidum*). They make smaller, rounded fruits that ripen red (strawberry) or yellow (lemon). Fruit is sweet, musky, and slightly spicy. (Hardy to 22 degrees F).

*I once lived in a house in Santa Barbara that had a relic guava orchard in the backyard. Six or seven beautiful trees (actually large shrubs) each stood about 15 feet tall. Their graceful branches were covered in shaggy, mottled brown/green bark. Their long leaves had rounded tips and a rough texture that looked almost corrugated. In a colder winter, the leaves dropped. But in warmer winters they hung on. The fragrant white spring flowers were more like tufts of white brushy stamens than proper flowers or petals. Round, green fruits appeared in early fall, turned matte yellow and softened in late fall or winter. The flesh was pale pink, creamy, and sweet with musky overtones. We never pruned or watered but we always had guava.*

**Bloom Period and Harvest Season**
White flowers in spring. Harvest depends on region and variety.

**Mature Height × Spread**
15 to 20 ft. × 15 to 20 ft.

Hardy to 9B

Min. Temp. 25° F

# Ground Covers *for California*

'Henfield Brilliant' sunrose shows bright orange flowers against silvery gray foliage

One of my nursery owner friends has a great response to people who come in looking for ground covers. "All plants," he says, "cover the ground." He is right of course. All plants do cover the ground. But plants generally referred to as ground covers tend to be short, fast growing, and spread horizontally, often by underground stems that knit the soil together and control erosion.

Perennials work as ground covers, as do many grasses and small shrubs. The ground covers in this chapter are all low water plants from Mediterranean climates, so you can plant them on dry slopes or place them beneath and around the trunks of low water trees and shrubs. Many are also compatible with succulents.

These evergreens create deep green, bright green, or gray-green fields with their foliage. If you are looking for a green carpet, substitute ground covers for thirsty, higher maintenance turfgrass. And if you need something tough, South African silver carpet handles considerable foot traffic in full sun and intense heat, with little water or fertilizer.

Ground covers are perfect to fill in the empty spots in the garden. They keep weeds down and insulate the soil beneath shrubs and trees. Planted atop a low wall or between large boulders, ground covers soon spill over the edges. Similarly, plant ground covers to cascade over the side of a hanging basket or brightly colored ceramic container, planted with tall ornamental grasses, flowering perennials, and variegated-leaved annuals.

Ground covers planted between stepping stones or pavers round out angular edges and bring softness to hard surfaces. Ornamental oregano is a particularly good choice. It spreads by underground rhizomes much like its close cousin mint. Mint, however, quickly grows out of control, whereas oregano is not nearly as aggressive. If you want to grow mint, do it ONLY in a container, not in the ground.

All of these ground covers flower, and one, honeybells, has the tiniest and most unexpectedly fragrant blooms. Other ground covers bloom in different seasons, but even when out of flower, all of these evergreens have foliage that beautifies the garden.

Peppermint geranium is one of my all-time favorite and atypical leafy ground covers. Peppermint geranium has big, wide, furry green leaves that release a strong peppermint smell when crushed. When my children were small, I planted peppermint geranium beneath a tire swing suspended from a branch of our mulberry tree. The geranium quickly grew into a wide, thick, velvety mat. As the children jumped (or fell) from the swing, the geranium softened their landing. They loved smelling like mint, and I liked the minty smell, too.

## Create a Tapestry

If you are planting a large area, avoid the urge to plant only one type of ground cover. Instead, create a tapestry of two or three ground covers, with multiple plants of each type clustered together and arranged in large, curving sweeps. Choose varieties that bloom in different seasons. Also pay attention to leaf color and shape. Wide, flat leaves contrast with narrow pointed leaves; bright green leaves contrast with blue-gray leaves. Don't plant alternate or checkerboard style. No matter how well intentioned, checkerboard planting matures to a tangled mess.

Plant ground covers as you would any other shrub or perennial. Some ground covers are sold in nursery flats; others are sold in 4-inch pots or 1-gallon nursery containers. For good coverage, set plants *slightly* closer than you would for other applications. Don't skimp on the number of plants you start out with. If a ground cover is supposed to top out at 12 inches in diameter, then set the plants 10 inches apart—but not closer than that. For a naturalistic appearance, arrange plants in a triangular pattern or an "X" rather than in a row or straight line.

Ground covers that spread by creeping stems respond well to yearly haircuts. Don't be afraid to cut back geraniums, African daisy, oregano, and germander sage (pot up the cuttings to plant elsewhere or share with a friend). Use a light hand when pruning woodier ground covers such as honeybells and sun-rose. If you cut back into the hardwood, you risk losing the whole plant. Mat-forming silver carpet needs no cutting back. If the mat grows too wide, simply dig up the offending plantlets and transplant them to a different area of the garden.

Plants in other chapters can also be used as ground covers, including vines such as bougainvillea, chocolate vine, coral vine, yellow orchid vine, and grapes. Check out other chapters for low growing Australian *Grevillea*, lavender, prostrate rosemary, California lilac, native manzanita, native flannel bush, and California currant.

Ornamental oregano

# African Daisy

*Arctotis* hybrids

At first glance, you might mistake African daisy for Gazania, the freeway daisy. Both are low water, evergreen ground covers with gray-green leaves and daisy-shaped flowers. From a gardener's perspective, the biggest difference between the two is aesthetic. Gazania flowers are subtle colored combinations of orange, pink, brown, black, cream, and yellow. African daisies bloom in clear, bright yellow, brick red, coppery orange, magenta pink, and tangerine, often with a contrasting dark ring of color at the center of each flower. Flowers open with morning and close at sunset. Broad silvery evergreen leaves have a felty texture from the fine hairs that cover the surface. They make handsome expanses of foliage, even in the hottest months of the year.

### Bloom Period and Seasonal Color

Brick red, lemony yellow, magenta pink, coppery orange, tangerine flowers from spring into through fall (not always in summer).

### Mature Height × Spread

6 to 15 in. × 1 to 3 ft.

### Minimum Temperature

Grown as an annual in colder areas.

Hardy to 9A

Min. Temp. 20° F

### When, Where, and How to Plant

Plant from gallon containers into well-draining garden soil in fall through late spring in frost-free gardens. In colder climates, plant in spring. Plants tolerate heavier soils but avoid areas that are constantly moist. Plant in full sun in coastal gardens and in sun or part sun in hotter inland gardens. Space plants 12 to 18 inches apart. Follow planting directions in the Perennials introduction. Water well and mulch after planting.

### Growing Tips

Deep water to keep the root zone moist through the first summer. After that, allow soil to dry several inches deep between waterings. Apply all-purpose organic fertilizer in spring and fall.

### Care

Remove spent flowers. Cut plants back to just a few inches in winter so they don't develop woody stems. Expect no pest problems. If African daisy begin to look ratty after a few years, simply replace them. Salvage old plants by cutting stems into sections, removing lower leaves, and setting the stems in damp sand or potting soil mixed with sand. Within a month or two, you will have new plants. Or look for a spot where a stem has rooted. Sever the stem from the mother plant and wait a few weeks. The newly independent plant can be left in place, transplanted, or shared with a friend.

### Companion Planting and Design

Bright colored and profuse flowering African daisy is perfect for "filling in the spaces," large or small. Have an empty spot that needs some color? Plant African daisy. Need a spaceholder until you decide what to plant? Stick in some African daisy. African daisy looks beautiful cascading from a container, hanging from a basket, or edging a flower bed. Plant several African daisy around a large specimen plant such as agave, pink-flowering Hong Kong orchid tree, or purple-leaved smoke tree. Plants soon knit together, forming a tapestry of texture.

### Try These

Some of the prettiest African daisies include the deep orange and very compact 'Pumpkin Pie', deep pink 'Big Magenta', lemon yellow 'Big Gold', pink with orange 'Pink Sugar', and bright orange 'Sun Spot'.

# Germander Sage
## *Salvia chamaedryoides*

## When, Where, and How to Plant
Plant from nursery containers during fall through spring in mild winter areas, and plant in spring in cold winter gardens. Choose a spot in full or part sun and with well-draining soil. Poor soils are fine. Follow planting directions for Perennials introduction. Water deeply after planting and mulch. Germander sage can be grown in a container as well.

## Growing Tips
Through the first summer, keep soil moist through the root zone. Once established, this sage is extremely adaptable to infrequent or frequent watering as long as the soil drains well. If you water weekly or water monthly, plants will respond about equally. No fertilizer is required.

## Care
Shear plants back to 3 or 4 inches tall in early spring or whenever they grow out of bounds or appear too ragged. No pests bother this plant.

## Companion Planting and Design
Plant beneath bronze-trunked manzanita or arbutus. In a succulent garden, plant to fill in the spaces between red yucca or century plant. Mix with deep-green rosemary for a study in contrasting blues and greens. Or grow with golden yellow perennial marigold. In a container, combine with burgundy-leaved New Zealand flax or bronze-leaved fountain grass. Try a combination of sages—germander sage with red flowered pineapple sage or purple flowered *Salvia guaranitica* 'Purple Majesty'.

## Try These
Other low growing ground cover sages include native hummingbird sage (*Salvia spathacea*) with bright green fragrant leaves and spires of rose-pink flowers much beloved by hummingbirds. *Salvia transsylvanica* makes 1-foot × 3-foot mounds with purple/blue summer flowers and tongue shaped dark-green leaves. Native creeping sage (*Salvia sonomensis*) grows ¹/₂ to 1 foot × 10 feet with lavender-blue flowers in spring and summer. Eyelash-leaved sage (*Salvia blepharophylla*) is a Mexican native that grows 1¹/₂ feet tall and spreads by rhizomes. It blooms scarlet on and off through the year with a peak in summer.

*Among the many garden-worthy ornamental sages there are several lower growing spreaders that work quite well as ground covers. Often these sages spread by underground runners, much like their cousins, the mints. One of the best and easiest growing ground cover sages is germander sage. Native to high elevations in eastern Mexico, germander sage has small rounded gray-green leaves. The bluest of blue flowers appear on and off through the year, peaking in late spring and early fall. Plants mature at about 2 feet tall (shorter with less water), making loose mounds that expand to colonize a slope in just a few growing seasons. Germander sage is extremely drought tolerant, surviving on just monthly summer irrigation in coastal gardens. To learn more about sages, see the Salvia entry in Perennials.*

### Bloom Period and Seasonal Color
Blue flowers on and off all year.

### Mature Height × Spread
2 ft. × 2 ft.

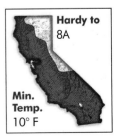

Hardy to 8A

Min. Temp. 10° F

# Honeybells
## *Hermannia verticillata*

Honeybells is a small plant that packs a big punch. Its tiny yellow flowers have a sweet honey perfume that fills the air for a surprising distance. This small stature South African native shrublet grows only 2 feet tall, but its mounding form spreads to 4 feet or wider. Honeybells has tiny evergreen leaves that cover mahogany-colored trailing branches. In mild coastal gardens, the branches are covered in blooming flowers nearly year-round. In inland and northern gardens, honeybells flowers primarily through winter and spring. They are wonderful cascading down a slope or planted beneath a knife-leafed acacia with its bright yellow flowers and gray-green, triangular leaves. In a pot or in the ground, honeybells is a bit of sunshine in the middle of winter.

**Bloom Period and Seasonal Color**
Tiny yellow flowers, year-round on the coast, winter through spring elsewhere.

**Mature Height × Spread**
2 ft. × 4 ft. or more

Hardy to 9A

Min. Temp. 20° F

### When, Where, and How to Plant
Plant from 4-inch or 1-gallon nursery cans from fall through spring in mild winter gardens, and in spring in cold winter gardens. Site in full sun, part sun, or light shade (especially in hotter inland gardens and gardens north of Santa Barbara). Pick a spot with well-draining soil. Follow perennial planting directions (see Perennials introduction). After planting, water well and mulch. Honeybells can also be grown in a container (see "Tips and Techniques").

### Growing Tips
Water to keep root zone moist through the first summer. Once established, honeybells is quite drought tolerant in coastal gardens. In warmer inland and desert gardens, more frequent watering is needed to keep it going. Experiment to see how often to water. No fertilizer is needed.

### Care
No pruning necessary, but it can be done if a plant grows too wide. Avoid cutting into the hardwood. Don't be surprised if you wake up one morning in the hottest part of summer and find a formerly thriving honeybells suddenly brown and dead. Simply replant and enjoy the next generation. Pests tend to ignore honeybells.

### Companion Planting and Design
Use to cover a slope or plant beneath a low water shrub such as grevillea. Combine with yellow flowering Jerusalem sage for a bright spot in the garden. Plant honeybells with blue flowering California lilac and the olive-and-coral colored leaves of New Zealand flax 'Maori Queen'. In a container or hanging basket, honeybells cascade over the side for that "dripping with flowers" look. Create a similar effect by planting along the edge of a low wall.

### Try These
Place fragrant plants near the house to enjoy their perfume. Spot fragrant plants here and there throughout the garden to create a scent trail. Try angel trumpet (*Brugmansia* spp.) along with any of the fragrant bulbs such as baboon flower (*Babiana*), bugle flower (*Watsonia*), Yellow marsh Afrikaner (*Gladiolus tristis*) and naked ladies (*Amaryllis belladonna*). California lilac (*Ceanothus* spp.) has a subtle but wonderful springtime perfume.

# Ornamental Oregano

## *Origanum* spp.

### When, Where, and How to Plant

Plant fall through spring in mild winter areas, spring in colder climates. Start with nursery flats, 4-inch pots or 1-gallon containers. See directions for planting in the Herbs introduction. Site in full or part sun and in well-draining soil. Water well after planting and mulch.

### Growing Tips

Keep soil moist down 4 to 6 inches deep (that is about as deep as the roots go) until plants are established. After that, water when soil is dry 2 to 3 inches below the surface in summer. Fertilizer makes more lush growth but is not necessary.

### Care

If you grow oregano as a lawn substitute and want it to look uniform, mow (or shear) it back once every two weeks in the summer. For a more naturalistic look, let it grow with no shearing. Protect from slugs and snails (see "Tips and Techniques").

### Companion Planting and Design

Plant mounding ground cover oregano between stepping stones or pavers—especially in a children's garden where their steps release the musty perfume of oregano into the air. Plant flowering oregano with purple, blue, or pink flowering ornamental sage, anise hyssop, lavender, and/or pink muhly grass—in pot or in the ground.

### Try These

Lawn substitute oreganos include (*O. marjorana*) 'Betty Rollins' (3 inches tall), a dense, tight, mat of dark green leaves and light pink flowers. Creeping golden marjoram (*Origanum vulgare* 'Aureum') has tight, 6-inch mounds of chartreuse leaves. Creeping oregano (*Origanum vulgare* 'Humile') makes 4- to 6-inch × 12-inch mounds of green leaves. For flowering oregano, plant 'Kent Beauty', (8 inches × 12 inches) whose narrow wiry stems are covered in soft green leaves and tiny lavender pink flowers in shell pink bracts. 'Santa Cruz' (1 to 2 feet × 1 to 2 feet) has green leaves on red stems with large rose-colored bracts and tiny lavender flowers. 'Dittany of Crete' has white-felted green leaves, rose colored bracts and pink flowers. 'Dingle Fairy' (6 to 12 inches × 6 to12 inches) has smooth bright-green leaves, rose tinged bracts, and tiny lavender pink flowers.

You might think of oreganos as culinary herbs, but there is another group of oreganos valued primarily as ornamentals rather than as edibles. Many ornamental oreganos have sprawling, relaxed stems, rounded green leaves, and cascades of large, pale green, pink, or purple flower bracts that surround tiny pink or lavender flowers. These oreganos are beautiful cascading over the side of a pot or window box or hanging over the side of a low wall. There are also creeping, low-growing ground cover oreganos whose tight mounds of leaves knit together to make a wonderful low water and low maintenance alternative to lawns. They may not be tough enough for dogs or for a good play area, but they do handle a surprising amount of foot traffic!

### Bloom Period and Seasonal Color

Summer and fall flowers in combinations of pink, lavender, pale green.

### Mature Height × Spread

3 to 24 in. × 24 to 36 in.

### Minimum Temperature

Varies depending on species.

# Peppermint Geranium
## *Pelargonium tomentosum*

There is more to geraniums than bright red or pink flowers that spill out from flower pots and window boxes. Geraniums are a wonderfully diverse group of plants, some flowery, some succulent, and some grown for their scented foliage. One of the easiest growing of the scented geraniums is peppermint geranium, which has long, lax stems that form a mounding mat, 6 feet or more across. The stems are obscured by floppy green leaves, 6 inches across and covered with fine hairs for a velvety texture. When crushed, the leaves release a strong fresh peppermint scent. Plant for a soft, aromatic landing pad beneath a tire swing on the branch of a shady tree. Your children will love the minty smell on their arms and legs!

**Bloom Period and Seasonal Color**
Spring blooms of white flowers.

**Mature Height × Spread**
1 to 2 ft. × 6 ft.

Hardy to 8B

Min. Temp. 15° F

### When, Where, and How to Plant
Plant fall through spring in frost-free areas and in spring in colder winter gardens. Provide full sun along the coast, part sun or part shade in valley and inland gardens. Plants prefer well-amended soil but tolerate most soils as long as they drain well. Follow planting directions in the introduction to Perennials. Water deeply and mulch after planting. Peppermint geranium is great for containers as well (see "Tips and Techniques").

### Growing Tips
Water to keep soil moist 6 inches deep through the first summer. After that, water when soil is dry several inches beneath the surface. In containers, keep potting soil moist year-round. No fertilizer is needed but do keep constant layer of mulch around the base of the plant.

### Care
No pruning. If a plant grows beyond its bounds, snip off the offending branches just above a leaf joint. To make more plants, cut the pruned-off stem into lengths with three or four sets of leaves each. Remove all but the top set of leaves. Bury the rest of the stem in damp potting mix, making sure to leave only the topmost leaves above soil. Place in a shaded location and keep moist until you see new growth, then transplant. Watch for snails, slugs, and whiteflies (see "Tips and Techniques").

### Companion Planting and Design
Plant beneath a large tree, to fill a planter bed, or to cover a slope. Peppermint geranium is the perfect plant to cascade over a low wall or fill a large brightly glazed pot.

### Try These
Other geraniums that can be planted as ground covers include *Pelargonium* 'Islington Peppermint', which is a bit smaller than the peppermint geranium. Its two-toned flowers have a pair of burgundy petals on top with three white petals below. Chocolate mint geranium (*Pelargonium* 'Chocolate Mint') is 1 foot × 6 feet with velvety leaves that are green splashed in deep chocolate brown. Pink 'Fairy Cascades' (*Pelargonium ionidiflorum*) grows 8 to 12 inches tall with lacy bright-green leaves. Mounds are covered in a riot of bright clear-pink flowers with ruby markings on the upper two petals.

# Silver Carpet
## *Dymondia margaretae*

### When, Where, and How to Plant
Plant from flats in all but the hottest months. Choose a spot in bright sun with well-drained soil. Plants in the flat may look to be all connected but they separate as you pull them out. Space 8 to 10 inches apart (closer for quicker fill). To plant between pavers, look for the largest joints. Dig a hole about 4 inches deep. Mix in a bit of organic fertilizer, then add the plant. Refill the hole with soil and soak well.

### Growing Tips
Water these shallow rooted plants to keep roots moist through the first summer. Once established, let soil dry out between waterings. Watch the plants to determine how often to water. Leaves on well-watered plants are nearly flat. Leaves on severely water stressed plants curl to the point of looking nearly white. Your goal is to be somewhere in between. No fertilizer is needed.

### Care
No pruning. No pests. Silver carpet is easy to divide and will spread to fill in empty spots. In spring or fall, simply snip the joints between stem sections (below the tufts of leaves). Rebury the lower part of the stem into the bare spot and water regularly until you see new growth. Alternatively, make several cuttings and bury the lower part of the stem into a pot or flat of well-draining potting soil (regular potting mix with a handful of construction sand thrown in). Once plants root, transplant them into the garden.

### Companion Planting and Design
Silver carpet makes a dense mat between pavers, spills over boulders, and finishes the edges of dry gardens and informal pathways. It can also make a beautiful thick variegated lawn. Use silver carpet as living mulch instead of leaving bare ground.

### Try This
For another very low growing, very low water ground cover, try woolly thyme (*Thymus pseudolanuginosus*). This dense creeping thyme has tiny green leaves covered in fine hairs that give the foliage a silvery sheen. Dense, 3-inch-tall mats occasionally sport pink flowers.

*Tough situations call for tough plants and silver carpet is one of the toughest. This low growing ground cover is an evergreen perennial member of the sunflower family and hails from South Africa. It grows flat against the ground in mats with 1- to 3-inch long leaves that look variegated. Get down on your hands and knees and you will see that the leaves are actually deep green on top with curled-up edges that reveal silvery white and slightly fuzzy undersides. In summer, silver carpet makes yellow dandelion-like flowers, but that is not the gardener's main focus. Instead, it is silver carpet's ability to make a dense, drought tolerant walkable ground cover that takes the heat. Silver carpet spreads quickly with regular water but does fine with very little water at all.*

**Bloom Period and Seasonal Color**
Yellow summer flowers.

**Mature Height × Spread**
1 to 3 in. × 18 to 24 in.

Hardy to
8B

Min.
Temp.
15° F

# Sundrops
*Calylophus hartwegii*

*Sundrops are woody perennials with yellow flowers and fine textured dark-green foliage that form mounds only a foot or so high and 3 feet wide. This mounding plant is native to the southwest U.S. and northern Mexico. Like its more aggressive relative, the evening primrose, sundrops have four crinkled petals that form a slightly cupped flower with an interesting lifecycle. Each flower opens lemon yellow. By afternoon, petals turn apricot pink. By evening, the flower is spent and fades away. Plants flower in spring and again in fall, often taking a break in the heat of the summer. This is a tough plant that takes the heat with little water. In some climates, foliage dies back in winter but sprouts again in spring.*

### Bloom Period and Seasonal Color
Yellow flowers spring and fall, sometimes summer.

### Mature Height × Spread
1 ft. × 3 ft.

Hardy to 7A

Min. Temp. 0° F

### When, Where, and How to Plant
Plant sundrops from fall through spring in mild winter gardens and in spring in colder areas. Site in full sun and very well-drained soil (poor soils are fine). Follow Perennials introduction planting directions. Water well after planting, and mulch. To grow this plant in a container, be sure to use a well-draining potting mix. Mulch the pot surface.

### Growing Tips
Water deeply to keep soil moist 6 inches deep through the first summer so plants become established. In subsequent years, sundrops do fine on a low water diet, though occasional deep irrigation promotes more flowers. Unless winter rains are sparse, Mother Nature will take care of these plants. Sundrops tolerate more frequent garden water only if soils drain well. Fertilizer is not necessary but can be applied to hasten growth in early spring. Use a balanced, organic formulation.

### Care
Sundrops spread by underground roots and need no pruning, but branches can be trimmed back in early spring if plants get too large, or too woody, or suffer frost damage. Pests and disease tend not to be a problem.

### Companion Planting and Design
This low profile, spreading plant makes a great ground cover for low water gardens. Plant it beneath Mediterranean climate shrubs such as rockrose and blue hibiscus and under trees such as granite bottlebrush. Lavender and penstemon make good partners as well. Add to a rock garden, planted to cascade over and between rocks. Plant sundrops in a container as a foil to colorful and sculptural succulents such as flapjack plant, shrubby candelabra aloe, or tall tree aloe. For a colorful, low water combination, plant yellow flowered sundrops beneath red-flowering red yucca and blue flowering, gray-leaved germander sage.

### Try These
If you prefer gray-green foliage to deep green, plant lavender leaf primrose (*Calylophus lavandulifolius*). Texas primrose (*Calylophus drummondianus*) is another *Calylophus* offered by California nurseries. This native Texan lies flat to the ground and spreads 2 feet across. Leaves are narrower than sundrops' and bright green.

# Sunrose
## *Helianthemum nummularium*

### When, Where, and How to Plant
Plant fall through summer in mild climate gardens and plant in spring in colder winter areas. Site in well-draining soil in a spot in full sun or bright shade. Space sunrose 2 feet apart. Follow Perennials introduction planting directions. Water deeply after planting and mulch. To grow in containers, use a well-draining planting mix and mulch with gravel.

### Growing Tips
Water to keep the root zone moist through the first summer so plants can become established. After that, cut back so soil dries several inches down between waterings. It will take some experimentation to find the right watering frequency. Take care not to overwater, or plants will rot. Fertilizer is not necessary if plants are well mulched. If you want to fertilize, use an all-purpose organic fertilizer in early spring.

### Care
Deadhead as flowers fade. After spring bloom, shear lightly to encourage a repeat bloom. Insects don't bother this plant, but it does rot in poor draining soils.

### Companion Planting and Design
Grow sunrose next to their cousin, blue chalk sticks, Jerusalem sage, ornamental grasses like blue fescue, and kangaroo paw. Combine with taller plants including shoestring acacia (it casts only light shade), and grevillea. Tiny rockrose flowers are best viewed at eye level, cascading over the edge of a pot or rock wall or on a slope.

### Try These
Sunrose flowers come in an amazing color range: 'Brunette' flowers are burnt orange, 'Mesa Wine' blooms burgundy red with a yellow center, 'Wisely Primrose' blooms yellow with gray-green leaves. 'Henfield Brilliant' has gray-green leaves and bright orange flowers with yellow centers. 'Belgravia Rose' has pink flowers and blue-green leaves. 'Dazzler' has dark green leaves and deep pink blooms. 'Shot Silk' has gray-green leaves and coral pink flowers. 'The Bride' has silver leaves and, as you would expect, white flowers. 'Stoplight' has bright red flowers and gray-green leaves.

*Sunrose is the perfect low profile flowering ground cover. It is a tiny evergreen shrub related to rockrose but growing no more than 8 inches high. These Mediterranean natives make round patches, 2 to 3 feet across, with small gray, green, or gray-green leaves. In the spring and sometimes again in fall, dozens of tiny rose-shaped flowers float just inches above the foliage. Some flowers are singles with bright yellow stamens, and some are doubles with stamens buried amid the petals. Blooms come in shades of red to burgundy, apricot to copper, pink to rose, to yellow and even white. Each flower lasts just a day or so but there are so many and they open over such a long time that the bloom lasts three months or longer.*

### Bloom Period and Seasonal Color
Late spring flowers are red to burgundy, apricot to copper, pink to rose, yellow, and white. Bloom sometimes repeats in fall.

### Mature Height × Spread
6 to 8 in. × 24 to 36 in.

Hardy to 7A

Min. Temp. 0° F

# Herbs *for California*

A few years back, I invited a good friend for a pasta dinner. By the time she arrived, the oregano and basil were picked and cleaned, but I had forgotten the bay. As the onions and garlic sizzled in hot olive oil, I asked her to pick some bay leaves. "It's the big tree to the left of the door," I told her, "you'll recognize the leaves." She came back in with a handful of the dark green, leathery foliage and a quizzical look on her face as she handed them to me. "So," she said, "don't you need to dry the leaves before you cook with them? I stifled the urge to laugh and suggested she crush the leaves and smell them. As she inhaled their spicy fragrance, I explained how much more potent fresh herbs are than dried.

She called a few days later, excited to tell me that she had just planted a little bay tree into a pot by her kitchen door. Smelling the fresh leaves made her realize how much she was missing by cooking with dried herbs. My friend and I agreed that once you cook with fresh herbs, the dried stuff tastes much like old lawn clippings.

## Growing Your Herbs

Many of the more common culinary herbs—bay, rosemary, oregano, thyme, and sage—are Mediterranean natives that are extremely easy to grow in our gardens. Nurseries offer these perennial herbs in 4-inch or 1-gallon pots. They are easy to propagate. For oregano or thyme, simply dig up a section of underground stem with some roots attached and put into a pot or plant directly into the ground. Anchor a branch of sage or rosemary to the ground with a rock or other heavy object, and after a few months it will root. Sever the rooted piece from the mother plant and you have a new independent plant. Bay trees are propagated by cuttings, which take a bit more skill.

Cilantro, dill, fennel, and parsley are common annual herbs, all of which are best planted from seed every few weeks through the growing season to ensure a constant supply. In the warmer days of summer, these spring- and fall-growers bolt—meaning that they bloom. Flowering signals the beginning of the end, but if you let the flowers turn to seed, you can harvest the seed or leave them to reseed and sprout the next crop.

Purple basil stands out in a crowd

The best location for an herb garden is in the full sun, in well-draining soil, with good air circulation and *near the kitchen door.* (Though you can always make mounds of imported, well-draining soil as described in "Tips and Techniques.") This last point is one that new gardeners often overlook, but is most important. The closer your herbs are to the kitchen, the more likely you are to cook with them.

## Design with Herbs

Gardeners typically group herbs together in formal or informal arrangements. These "segregators" keep culinary herbs segregated from garden ornamentals. In formal herb gardens, geometrically shaped beds—squares, rectangles, exploded circles—are laid out in regular patterns. Each bed is dedicated to a single type of herb, so there may be an oregano bed, a fennel bed, a garlic bed, and so on. Beds are often edged in brick set flush with the level of the soil. Brick serves both as a solid walkable surface and as an edging that keeps the herbs contained. Informal herb gardeners don't worry about keeping herbs separated. Instead they combine herbs in an aesthetic arrangement that appeals to the eye and works for the plants.

Finally, there are the people who make no distinction between herb beds and ornamental beds. They simply tuck herbs in wherever there is room or opportunity.

Personally, formal arrangements are too unnatural to me. In the herb bed outside my kitchen door bay grows with oregano, rosemary, lemon grass, pineapple scented sage, and chives. Over the years, I've mixed other things in with the herbs. Harlequin flowers (an early spring bulb from South Africa) have naturalized into my herb bed, as have lilies and other plants. Pots of blueberries sit nestled into the mat-forming oregano.

In other gardening, I've seen basil interplanted with coleus and ornamental gingers in a tropical theme. The solid green basil balances out the wild green, maroon, and chartreuse variegation of the coleus leaves. I've also seen bay used as a massive hedge, controlled with an electric hedge pruner to a height of about 8 feet tall rather than its natural 15- or 25-foot height. Grow bay in a pot and it will stay small enough for an apartment balcony.

Rosemary is also an incredibly versatile herb. In addition to their culinary use, upright rosemaries make nice flowering evergreen hedges that are shorter and more finely textured than bay. Prostrate (spreading) rosemary looks fantastic cascading over a wall or adorning a staircase or used simply as a deep green ground cover in place of lawn.

The oregano ground cover in my herb garden is a tapestry of green-leaved Greek oregano and variegated yellow and green oregano. Thyme, oregano's smaller cousin, grows in the cracks of the pavers adjacent to the herb garden.

Remember, children are drawn to herbs in a garden. At the school garden I helped create, the herb garden is the most popular spot of all. Early on, I showed the children how to crush and smell the leaves. I soon noticed a chain reaction as children crushed leaves for their friends and parents to smell as well. Herbs are also a great way to introduce children to the flavors of different cuisines, an entry point for discussing diversity and tolerance. Just another of the many lessons gardening has to teach us!

# Basil
## *Ocimum basilicum*

*Sing the praises of basil—it is beautiful, aromatic, delicious, and easy to grow. Basils have been cultivated for thousands of years; selected, crossed, and selected again, resulting in countless varieties. Some have large leaves, others tiny leaves; some grow tall, while others are minute enough to grow in a teacup. Green-leaved basils have white flowers; purple basils have pink tinged flowers. The aromatic oils that give basils their flavors vary with variety. There are Italian basils, Thai basil, licorice basil, cinnamon basil, lemon basil, and more. Some botanists regard lemon basil, purple-leaved basil, and holy basil as varieties of green basil, while others regard them as closely related but distinct plants. Basils are perennials in tropical climates, but we grow them as summer annuals.*

**Bloom Period and Seasonal Color**
Purple flowers.

**Mature Height × Spread**
8 to 24 in. × 8 to 24 in.

Hardy to 9A

Min. Temp. 20° F

### When, Where, and How to Plant
Plant once air and soil warms in spring. Site in full sun (bright shade in hot inland valleys). Incorporate a generous amount of compost into the soil, along with organic vegetable fertilizer (follow label directions). Start basil from seed (directions are in the Introduction to Annuals), sowing every month for a continuous crop or purchase seedlings at the nursery. For a 2-foot-tall basil, set seedlings 1 1/2 feet apart. A typical basil plant can fill a 12-inch pot.

### Growing Tips
Keep the soil constantly moist (not wet) through the growing season for seeds, seedlings, and mature plants. Fertilize regularly with organic vegetable fertilizer.

### Care and Harvest
Pinch out branch tips of young plants to promote bushy growth. Once plants have several branches covered in leaves, start to harvest. Cut branches just above a branching point (don't leave a stub). Never cut more than a third of the plant at once. Pinch out flower stalks as they develop to keep plant from declining. Sprinkle flowers into salad. Whiteflies sometimes attack basil. They appear as small white specks that fly off when you shake the plant; wash them off with a sharp stream of water (see "Tips and Techniques").

### Companion Planting and Design
Basils are beautiful garden plants that should not be limited to the herb garden. Use them to edge a flower bed, or mix basil with colorful variegated coleus for a stunning display of color in a tropical garden. Grow basil singly in a pot or use as a leafy accent in a color bowl.

### Try These
Italian large-leaf basil (24 inches tall and wide) has a full, spicy basil flavor. Thai basil (16 to 20 inches tall and wide) has clove-scented leaves, are purple, and turn green with age. Italian 'Windowbox Mini Basil' (8 to 10 inches tall and wide) has tiny leaves. 'Purple Ruffles' (12 inches tall and wide) has deep purple-cabernet colored leaves with undulating edges. African blue basil (to 24 inches × 24 inches), a shrubby perennial basil has purple tinged leaves and lavender flowers.

# Bay Laurel
## *Laurus nobilis*

### When, Where, and How to Plant

Plant from 1-, 5-, or 15-gallon containers. In colder winter gardens, plant in spring. In coastal gardens, plant fall through spring and site in full sun. In hot inland gardens, provide some afternoon shade. Bay laurel tolerates dry shade and poor soils that drain well. If your soil drains poorly, build a raised mound of well-draining soil (see "Tips and Techniques"). Follow tree planting directions in the Trees introduction. For directions for container planting, see "Tips and Techniques." Water all bay trees thoroughly after planting, then mulch.

### Growing Tips

Saturate the soil several feet deep to keep the root zone moist (not wet) from the first spring into early fall. Once this establishment period is over, bay is extremely drought tolerant, requiring water only once every few weeks in summer (more often in hotter inland gardens). Let Mother Nature water your bay the rest of the year—unless rains are sparse. Keep container-grown bay moist, but not wet. For faster growth, apply all-purpose organic fertilizer once in spring.

### Care and Harvest

Once branches are a few feet long, harvest leaves as you need them. Pluck from the underside to avoid bare spots. Prune to control size if needed. If leaves become covered with a black sooty mold, chances are scale and/or whiteflies are present (see "Tips and Techniques"). Wash leaves before using.

### Companion Planting and Design

Bays are beautiful, vertical garden elements at their full size. Plant them in rows and prune for wall-high hedges as they do in Europe. I once visited a Pasadena garden where two rows of bays were planted in opposing semi-circles to create an intimate outdoor dining room within a larger garden. Those bays were kept in scale by regular pruning. Bay is also quite happy in a medium sized pot on a condo patio.

### Try This

'Saratoga' is a cross between European and native California bays. It is lush and fast growing, to 10 to 25 feet tall. Crushed leaves are slightly sweeter than bay laurel. Hardy to 20 degrees F.

*Bay laurel is more than a dried out leaf that sits in a can on your pantry shelf. It is a wonderful aromatic evergreen shrub or tree that is extremely versatile in the garden—and convenient for making marinara sauce or chicken Marbella. Bay tree has a rounded or columnar shape with branches covered in leathery deep-green leaves 4 to 5 inches long. Bay laurel is native to the Mediterranean, where long ago ancient Greeks wove its branches into wreaths to crown their heroes. Like most herbs, bay is far stronger used fresh, than used dry. To harvest, choose a leaf from the interior of the plant (so its absence won't be noticed). Simply pick the leaf, rinse off any dust, and get cooking!*

**Other Common Name**
Sweet Bay

**Bloom Period and Seasonal Color**
Green leaves year-round. Flowers not notable.

**Mature Height × Spread**
15 to 25 ft. × 10 to 20 ft.

Hardy to 8B

Min. Temp. 15° F

# Cilantro
*Coriandrum sativum*

*No salsa fresca is complete without some chopped cilantro. Neither is stir-fry. This leafy fragrant herb is popular in dishes across Latin America, Asia, Europe, and Africa. Cilantro seeds, also known as coriander, are round and aromatic and typically ground and added to curries. Cilantro is an annual in the same family as dill, carrot, fennel, and parsley. These plants all produce flowers clusters shaped something like umbrellas. They all grow best in full sun and well-drained soil. Unless you grow these plants for their seed, look for "slow bolting" cilantros, those bred to maximize leaf production by delaying the onset of flowers in warm weather. Flowering leads to seed production and the final stage in the life of this annual.*

**Bloom Period and Seasonal Color**
White flowers in summer

**Mature Height × Spread**
3 ft. × 1 to 2 ft.

**Minimum Temperature**
An annual plant.

### When, Where, and How to Plant
For a continuous crop, plant cilantro seed every few weeks from September to October in hot desert areas. In coastal and interior valley gardens, plant in sequence from December to May. Site in full sun, in well-drained, well-amended soil. In hottest months of the year, provide part shade. Set seeds about 1/2-inch deep, in rows 1 to 2 feet apart. Start with 10 to 15 seeds per foot of row. Once plants sprout, thin to about 8 inches apart. (See the introduction to Annuals for more details about planting from seed.)

### Growing Tips
Water to keep soil evenly moist at all times through the growing season. That may mean once a week or once every few days depending on weather and soil. Fertilize young plants once with an organic vegetable fertilizer. Too much fertilizer makes plants taste bland.

### Care and Harvest
Once plants are at least 8 inches tall and have lots of leaves, you can start to harvest. Cut leaves as you need them, severing them at the base. Never take more than a third of the plant at time. Eventually even slow bolt cilantro will flower. Flowers can be harvested and added to salads. If you leave the flowers, seeds will ripen. Either harvest them once they dry or leave them to reseed. Watch for whiteflies (see "Tips and Techniques").

### Companion Planting and Design
While cilantro is prized as an edible, its flowers also attract bees and butterflies to the garden. Plant with butterfly bush, passion vine, and butterfly weed to attract those flying beauties.

### Try These
Cilantro 'Santo' has broad leaves, while 'Delfino' has long ferny leaves. Both are slow-bolt varieties. You might also plant dill (*Anethum graveolens*), which grows just like cilantro. 'Bouquet' is a standard dill with large flower heads. 'Dukat' has a slightly sweet flavor and plentiful blue-green leaves. Dwarf (18 inches tall) 'Fernleaf' dill produces over a long season. 'Long Island Mammoth' dill (3 to 5 feet) is grown commercially and by home gardeners.

# Edible Oregano
## *Origanum vulgare*

### When, Where, and How to Plant
In mild winter gardens, plant fall through spring. In colder areas, plant in spring. Oregano prefers full sun and well draining soil. Start with a 4-inch or 1-gallon plant, or transplant a stem of oregano with roots attached. Follow directions in the Perennials introduction. Plant cuttings so the roots are buried. Water well after planting and mulch. Or plant oregano into a wide, shallow pot. Place the pot in full sun near your kitchen door so you can cut a stem whenever you need it.

### Growing Tips
Water to keep the soil moist down to the bottom of the roots for the first spring through early fall. After that, water deeply once the top 3 inches of soil is dry. No fertilizer is needed.

### Care and Harvest
There is no need to prune oregano, but if stems grow beyond the garden bed, snip them off and cook with the leaves, or root to make more plants. If oregano gets too leggy cut all stems back to the ground in winter or early spring. Water and wait for stems to resprout. Protect from slugs and snails (see "Tips and Techniques").

### Companion Planting and Design
If you don't have the room (or the inclination) to plant a dedicated herb garden, simply plant oregano as a ground cover in any ornamental flower bed. From an ornamental standpoint, edible oregano makes a lovely, low, green carpet. Or plant a mixed herb garden in a large container with tall chives or dill and bushy basil or sage and let oregano cascade over the side.

### Try These
*Origanum vulgare* ssp. *hirtum*, true Greek oregano, (8 inches × 12 to 18 inches) is the primary culinary oregano. Its broad green leaves are covered in fine down. Look also for varieties that are compact, have variegated leaves, or white flowers. Do not confuse Greek oregano with Mexican oregano, (*Lippia graveolens*) a 6-foot-tall and wide woody shrub whose leaves have a similar flavor. Mexican oregano is popular in Mexican and Tex-Mex cooking. Hardy to 25 degrees F.

We know oregano as the herb that lends its zip to salad dressings, pasta sauces, marinades, and other dishes. Ancient Greeks, however, believed that the goddess Aphrodite created oregano's spicy scent as a symbol of happiness, so they crowned bridal couples with oregano wreaths. Romance aside, all gardeners and cooks should grow their own oregano. Not only is oregano easy to grow, it thrives in California gardens. Oregano forms horizontal stems covered in deep green, almost crinkled leaves. Those creeping stems root wherever they touch the ground, so a single plant soon makes a good-sized patch. To harvest, simply snip a branch, rinse off any dirt clinging to the leaves, then strip the leaves off the stem. Be aware that fresh oregano is much *more flavorful than dried.*

### Bloom Period and Seasonal Color
White or pink flower clusters in summer and early fall.

### Mature Height × Spread
8 in. × 24 to 36 in.

Hardy to 5B

Min. Temp. -15° F.

# Garden Thyme
## *Thymus vulgaris*

*No herb garden is complete without a patch of thyme, an herb popular in many cuisines. It is a major component, for example, of French fine herbs, along with chervil, parsley, bay, French tarragon, and a handful of others. Culinary thyme has a surprisingly pungent aroma for its tiny leaf. There are also scented thymes that are good to cook with: lemon thyme, lime thyme, orange balsam thyme, and caraway thyme. Some are stronger flavored and some milder, but they add a twist to omelets, pastas, and sauces. Thyme is a short, creeping plant, less than a foot tall. The tiny pointed green (sometimes variegated) leaves line creeping stems. Its diminutive size may be why European folklore has long associated thyme with fairies.*

**Other Common Name**
English Thyme

**Bloom Period and Seasonal Color**
Spring and early summer blooms in tiny rosy lavender, dark pink, or white.

**Mature Height × Spread**
2 to 12 in. × 5 to 12 in.

Hardy to 7A

Min. Temp. 0 to 15° F

### When, Where, and How to Plant
Plant thyme from fall through spring in mild winter gardens and in spring in cold winter areas. Site in well-drained, well-amended soil. Thyme tolerates part sun but performs best in full sun. Thymes are typically sold in 4-inch pots but eventually grow to a foot across. Measure the planting area and calculate the number of plants you need, allowing them to overlap a few inches. See both Perennials and Ground Covers introductions for more planting information. Water well after planting, and mulch to keep thyme's shallow roots moist.

### Growing Tips
Culinary thyme prefers weekly water from spring through fall. If winter rains are normal, let Mother Nature cover winter irrigation. Otherwise, water to completely saturate the root zone every few weeks in winter. No fertilizer is needed.

### Care and Harvest
Every time you snip a piece, you have, in effect, pruned your thyme. Cut culinary thyme back by a third of its height after bloom unless you use it often. Lower growing ground cover thymes need no pruning. Pests aren't a problem.

### Companion Planting and Design
Thyme can be upright or low and spreading. Traditional culinary thyme is an upright type that can be planted as an edging in the garden, particularly in an herb garden. Creeping thymes, on the other hand, are good for low profile, low water ground covers planted between pavers (they handle light foot traffic), around the base of other plants with similar cultural needs, or to cover a temporary bare spot while other woodier plants fill in. Both upright and creeping thyme can be grown in a pot.

### Try These
Silver thyme and 'Hi Ho Silver' thyme (both *Thymus argenteus*) have green and white variegated leaves and wonderful flavor. Italian oregano thyme has a flavor reminiscent of oregano. For low growing (not necessarily culinary) thyme to grow as a low water ground cover, try diminutive elfin thyme (1 to 2 inches × 5 inches). Mint thyme fills the spaces between pavers and releases its scent when stepped on, as does lavender thyme, which has more needle-like leaves than its other thyme brethren.

# Lavender

## *Lavandula* spp.

### When, Where, and How to Plant

Plant lavender from 4-inch or 1-gallon containers, early fall through spring in areas where winter temperatures don't fall much below freezing. In colder areas, wait until spring. Site in full sun. Lavender performs best in well-amended, well-drained soil but tolerates poor soils. Follow planting directions in the Perennials introduction. Water well after planting, and mulch.

### Growing Tips

French lavender, Spanish lavender and other North African lavenders are more drought resistant than the English lavenders and their hybrids. Water all lavenders at least weekly to thoroughly moisten the root zone, through their first growing season so they become established. After that, water English/ hybrid lavenders when the top 3 inches of soil is dry. Allow Spanish and other African lavenders to go dry between watering. Fertilize in early spring with a balanced organic fertilizer.

### Care and Harvest

Prune to control lavender size and increase longevity. Harvest flower wands as they reach their brightest and fullest color, severing them where they emerge from the foliage. Next, prune branches back by a third to promote bushiness and refresh foliage. Unpruned lavender grows heavy and woody after a few years, often splitting in the middle. Lavender is pest-free but overwatering can cause fatal root rot.

### Companion Planting and Design

Plant lavender in herb gardens, cottage gardens, Mediterranean style gardens, even knot gardens. Use them as a low, fragrant hedge or to edge a flower border. Grow them in containers as well.

### Try These

'Munstead' lavender is an English lavender with sweet fragrance, gray leaves, and bright purple flowers. The rich fragrance of 'Provence' lavender is used for perfumes. Spanish lavender has gray leaves and pineapple-shaped flower clusters topped in colorful bracts that are referred to as "bunny ears" because they look like perky, colorful bunny ears. 'Madrid Pink' is a Spanish lavender with rose colored flowers and pale pink bracts. 'Madrid Purple' has purple flowers and pale purple bracts. 'Lemon Leigh' has chartreuse flowers and blue-gray foliage.

*The first time I was offered a lavender cookie, I expected it to be purple. Then it dawned on me that the cookie was made with lavender. I was surprised by the taste—slightly sweet, slightly spicy, slightly resinous, and very aromatic. As I think about it now, I suspect it was made with either an English variety (Lavandula angustifolia) that has a sweet fragrance, or the hybrid lavender 'Provence' (Lavandula × intermedia), which is a bit milder. Both are used in cooking. Not all lavenders are edible and not all are grown for their fragrance. Some lavenders, like Spanish lavenders (L. stoechas), are grown for their large colorful flowers, the newest of which are pink, white, or chartreuse yellow.*

### Bloom Period and Seasonal Color

Blue, purple, pink, white, or yellow flowers in spring or summer.

### Mature Height × Spread

1 to 3 ft. × 5 to 6 ft. (depending on species)

### Minimum Temperature

English and hybrid lavenders hardy to −10 degrees F; Spanish and all others hardy to 15 degrees F.

# Lemon Grass
## *Cymbopogon citratus*

*Nothing can beat a cool refreshing glass of iced lemon grass tea on a hot summer day. Add some mint leaves and touch of honey. Delicious! Lemon grass is an ever-green bunching perennial grass native to India and Ceylon. In cool winter climates, plants are often grown as annuals. This tall grass has long arching leaves 4 to 6 feet long and an inch wide. Lemon grass is not too different from the grass in your lawn, just larger and better smelling thanks to fresh, lemony scented citral oil. Thai and Vietnamese cooks cut ivory-colored lemon grass stalks at their base. They chop it finely to use in soups, salads, and curries. Lemon grass oil is used in soaps, creams, and deodorants.*

### Bloom Period and Seasonal Color
Bright green grass takes on a light purple tinge in winter.

### Mature Height × Spread
4 to 6 ft. × 4 ft., mounding

### Minimum Temperature
25 degrees F planted in the ground.

**Hardy to 9B**

**Min. Temp. 25° F**

### When, Where, and How to Plant
Lemon grass is most often available in a 4-inch or 1-gallon pots. Plant lemon grass in full sun or bright shade from spring through midsummer. Follow planting directions in the Ornamental Grasses introduction. Plants are not particular about soil but do best in soil that drains well. Allow room to accommodate the plant's ultimate height and width. If space is limited or your climate too cool for lemongrass to overwinter in the ground, grow it in a container that you can move to a greenhouse or under the eaves for winter protection from cold. Wherever you grow it, be sure to give lemon grass enough space, both vertical and horizontal.

### Growing Tips
Water deeply in the warm months to keep root zone moist. To avoid overly vigorous growth, use little, if any, fertilizer. If you do fertilize, use a balanced organic fertilizer.

### Care and Harvest
To harvest, cut stalks at the base. In warm areas where plants overwinter in the ground, remove brown leaves once spring arrives. When plants grow too large, cut them back (see the Ornamental Grasses introduction), then divide (see "Tips and Techniques"). Save damaged plant parts for cooking. In cooler areas, plants may die back to the root or die altogether in winter. Pests and diseases are rare.

### Companion Planting and Design
Lemon grass is also an attractive landscape plant whose green foliage is as much at home in a tropical style landscape as in a traditional perennial border. Combine with canna, purple sugar cane, tall palms, and flowering gingers. In a traditional border, site a pair of lemon grass plants on either side of a walkway to create an elegant transition between garden spaces. Grow as a container plant, either alone or combined with variegated coleus, flowering zinnias, and canna. Don't hesitate to cut stalks for cooking. The plant will replace lost stalks soon enough.

### Try This
If you prefer an even milder scent, try East Indian lemon grass, *Cymbopogon flexuosus*.

# Rosemary
## *Rosmarinus officinalis*

### When, Where, and How to Plant

Plant rosemary from fall through spring in mild winter gardens and in spring in colder winter areas. Choose a spot in full sun. Rosemary tolerates almost any garden soil but does best in well draining soils. Space plants to accommodate their full size—both the height and width. Follow planting directions in the Perennials introduction. Water well after planting and mulch. Grow rosemary in a container with good quality potting mix. Mulch with gravel or small pebbles.

### Growing Tips

Water deeply through the first spring and summer to saturate soil down through the rootball. After that, allow soil to dry out several inches from the surface before watering again. When you do water, water deeply. Apply an all-purpose, organic fertilizer in early spring if you wish to speed growth. In a container, keep soil moist (not wet). Replace the potting mix every few years.

### Care and Harvest

Rosemary care is simple. Every time you snip a sprig, you've pruned it. Prune more if you want to shape it. Not only do pests ignore rosemary, rosemary plants and oils are used as insect deterrents!

### Companion Planting and Design

Rosemary is equally at home in an ornamental garden and in an herb garden. Grow as a single specimen or line up plants as an evergreen screen. Trim for a more formal hedge. Plant prostrate rosemary into a pot, over a wall, or among rocks where it can cascade.

### Try These

A popular prostrate rosemary is 'Lockwood de Forest' (also called Santa Barbara rosemary), named for the famed Santa Barbara artist and designer. It grows 1 to 2 feet tall and up to 8 feet wide with light blue flowers. 'Tuscan Blue', is an upright variety valued for it size (4 to 6 feet × 4 to 5 feet) and large bright blue flowers. Some more unusual upright varieties available include 'Golden Rain' that has blue flowers and golden yellow leaves, and 'Majorca Pink' (3 to 5 feet × 3 to 5 feet) with lavender pink flowers.

The aroma of crushed rosemary leaves is unmistakable, pungent, slightly resinous, and hinting at far away lands. Though we mostly cook with rosemary, its aromatic oils have been used since ancient times when it was respected for strengthening the memory. It therefore became the emblem of fidelity for lovers, making it a popular decoration at weddings, funerals, as incense in religious ceremonies, and in magical spells. Rosemary casts its magic in our gardens as well. There are two basic forms. There is the traditional upright shrub and a prostrate spreading form. The upright form is the one used primarily for cooking and cosmetics. Rosemary is a Mediterranean native with dark green, needle-like leaves and flowers traditionally in shades of blue. Rosemary thrives in California gardens.

### Bloom Period and Seasonal Color

Late winter through spring flowers in pale to deep blue, lavender, pink, or white.

### Mature Height × Spread

1 to 6 ft. × 8 ft. depending on variety

Hardy to 7A

Min. Temp. 15 to 20° F

# Ornamental Grasses & Grass-like Plants *for California*

Ornamental grasses and grass-like plants are essential elements of well-designed gardens. Every garden needs wispy foliage spires that bend and sway and rustle in the breeze. Even more interesting are grand masses of mixed ornamental grasses that create a symphony of texture in a vast space or soften an angular structure.

Here are some grass facts: The grass family has more than 9000 species. Grasses are found on every continent except Antarctica. Grasses have a long horticultural history. Bamboo (a giant grass) has been used in gardens for eons. Other ornamental grasses like silver grass have been grown in Japanese gardens for more than 100 years.

The most fundamental feature of any grass is the shape and color if its leaves. Grasses in this chapter range from 40-foot-tall bamboos to 6-inch-tall sedges and fescues. There are grasses whose leaves are bright green, blue-green, or silver; some that have yellow and green horizontal stripes or cream and green vertical stripes. Grasses with orange and wine-red leaves are included as well. Some have blades that stand upright while others arch out like the spray of a fountain. Bamboo and sugar cane (both true grasses) have distinct jointed stems, while the others are virtually stemless.

Beautiful bamboo

Ornamental grass adds texture to a mixed planting

Grasses flower, but unlike other plant flowers, grass flowers don't have showy petals. Instead, their flowers range from tiny, barely noticeable flowers to tall, wheat-like stalks, columnar, flattened, or shaped like a tassel. Some grass flowers are festooned with what look like fine hairs that enhance their ethereal appearance. Grass flowers are colored too: ochre, pink, coral, burgundy, green, blue-green, brown, and black.

Once grasses flower, those flowers turn to seeds. It is not unusual for grass seeds to sprout, especially if grown in an irrigated part of the garden. While some reseed freely (gardener's euphemism for almost out-of-control), the grasses in this chapter are not that prolific. In my own garden, I regard grass seedlings as free plants. I dig them up and move them or share them with other gardeners. In fact, having grasses to spare has freed me to try them in unconventional growing conditions and in unusual plant combinations.

Notice that this chapter is titled "Grasses and Grass-like Plants" There are ten entries that describe fifty-six species and cultivars in this chapter. Roughly half are true ornamental grasses. The other half have grass-like forms with narrow blade-shaped leaves that form tufts or mats. For the sake of simplicity, they are presented as a single chapter.

## Good for Drier Gardens

While turf grasses (lawn grasses) require ongoing watering, fertilizing, mowing, and weeding, these ornamental grasses require nearly the opposite. The majority do well in drier garden conditions, though one, Japanese sweet flag, is a bog plant that thrives along the edges of ponds and streams.

High nitrogen fertilizer gets grasses off to a good start at planting time. Wait at least a year, though, before you consider fertilizing again. If your grasses have good color and seem to be growing well, wait. If they grow slowly or their color is poor, apply a small amount of high nitrogen fertilizer (preferably organic). Lawn fertilizer at half or quarter the recommended amount should suffice.

Generous water and fertilizer makes for fast, lush growth. With less water and little or no fertilizer, grasses grow just fine, but not quite as quickly nor as full—a plus in many situations. Mowing is virtually a non-issue except for those fescues and sedges that can be mowed for a more formal, lawn-like presentation. Other than that, kiss your lawnmower goodbye.

East Coast gardeners cut ornamental grasses back every year, but here on the West Coast, we treat grasses differently. All of the grasses in this chapter are perennial, and many are evergreen. Except for seasonal grooming and clean up, evergreen grasses do not require cutting back.

Silver grass and several other perennial grasses do go dormant in winter, but don't let that keep you from growing them. As the leaves die, blades and flowers turn wonderful shades of blonde and gold, creating strong silhouettes for winter garden interest. Cut them back in February or just as you see new green blades sprouting at the base. Cutting back doesn't affect the health of the plant. New blades sprout no matter what, but cutting back does keep the overall size of each clump under control—if that is important to you.

A tapestry of variegated grass with aloes and flowering ground covers

Porcupine Grass (*Miscanthus sinensis* 'Strictus')

Here's an easy way to cut back tall grasses: Gather leaves together by wrapping strong twine around the perimeter of the clump, 6 to 8 inches above ground. Pull tight to gather the leaves into a tight sheaf, then knot the twine. Once the blades are gathered tight, it is easy to cut across the sheaf (below the twine). Leave a stubble no more than 5 inches tall. If you have an informal or naturalistic garden, leave the trimmings in place as mulch. Not only will they add to the organic matter, improve the soil texture, hold in water, and suppress weeds, but also the leaf mulch recycles the nutrients right back into the grasses.

Grasses make fantastic container plants. Larger grasses can fill an entire container on their own. Or underplant a shrub or tall perennial with orange sedge or teal-leaved blue fescue. Add trailing African daisy to spill over the side of the pot, and your composition is complete.

# Bamboo
## *Bambusa* spp.

*Bamboo is one of the world's most useful and fastest growing plants. On a weight basis, bamboo is stronger than steel. Its young shoots are edible. In parts of the world, everything from spatulas to scaffolding to flutes are made from bamboo culms (stems). In the garden, evergreen bamboos fit into the serene green of an Asian garden, or into a loud and colorful tropical garden. Some people are scared by bamboo's reputation for growing out of control. That is true of uncontained running bamboos planted without sturdy root barriers to keep them in check. Clumping bamboos, on the other hand, mind their manners and stay pretty much where you plant them. Before you buy bamboo, ask whether it is a clumper or a runner.*

**Bloom Period and Seasonal Color**
Green, gold, or variegated stems, year-round.

**Mature Height × Spread**
3 to 40 ft. depending on species

**Minimum Temperature**
-30 to -20 F depending on species.

Hardy to 5A

Min. Temp. See below

## When, Where, and How to Plant
Install a root barrier before planting (see "Tips and Techniques"). Plant fall through spring into full sun. Some species prefer part sun in hot inland gardens. Bamboos prefer well-drained soils heavily amended with organic matter. In containers, use a rich potting mix. Water deeply after planting and mulch well.

## Growing Tips
A grove of bamboo takes as much water as the same area of lawn. Water well through the first summer. Cut back on water the second year but not so much that leaves start to curl—the signal that it is past time to water. Fertilize from April to September with high nitrogen fertilizer, at the same rate as grass. *Avoid fertilizers that contain grass killer.* Allow a 6-inch layer of fallen bamboo leaves to cover the base of the culms to hold in moisture and recycle silica into new growth.

## Care
Prune in early spring. Remove the oldest culms of running bamboo by the time they reach four to six years old. Remove rhizomes of both running and clumping bamboos that climb over the edge of the root barrier. Control ants to control scale and mealybugs.

## Companion Planting and Design
Bamboo fits into tropical, Asian, and woodland style gardens. Smaller varieties are gorgeous container plants, while tall growing bamboos can screen out a two-story townhouse or form the walls of an outdoor room.

## Try These
Clumping bamboos: 'Alphonse Karr' (*Bambusa multiplex*) grows to 26 feet tall with golden culms striped dark green. Hardy to 18 degrees F. fernleaf bamboo (*Bambusa multiplex* 'Fernleaf') is a 15-foot-tall clumper with double rows of small ferny leaflets. Hardy to 18 degrees F. The slender weeping culms of Mexican weeping bamboo (*Otatea acuminata aztecorum*) reach 15 feet tall. Hardy to 22 degrees F. Whorls of tiny leaves line 17-foot-tall culms of crown bamboo (*Chusquea coronalis*). Hardy to 30 degrees F. Skewer-thin, blue-blush culms of dwarf blue bamboo (*Himalayacalamus hookerianus* 'Baby Blue') are 6 to 8 feet tall with long dark-green leaves.

## When, Where, and How to Plant

Plant from fall to spring into well-draining soil. No soggy soils. Plant in full sun along the coast, and in part sun or part shade inland. Plant odd numbers of plants (3, 5, 7, etc.) in clusters for a natural look, or mass plant for a meadow (see Sedges entry for meadow planting). Spacing depends on variety. Water deeply and mulch well.

## Growing Tips

In the northern part of the state, water deeply and weekly through the first two springs and summers. After that, deep water non-natives in the north and all fescues in the south several times in summer. Follow fertilizing instructions in the Grasses introduction.

## Care

These evergreen grasses do not need pruning or cutting back. Mass plantings can be mowed for a groomed look. Otherwise remove dead foliage carefully with a metal rake in fall. Better yet, comb the dead leaves out with your hands and leave them around the base as mulch. Pests are no problem.

## Companion Planting and Design

Fescue's blue tones add a zing to the garden. Plant it into garden borders or mass on hillsides to control erosion. Plant between pavers. California fescue is drought and shade tolerant enough to grow beneath oaks if planted at least 4 feet away from the trunk (to protect the tree). Mulch well, and water by hand or by drip irrigation for the first two summers until grasses are established.

## Try These

'Siskiyou Blue' (2 feet × 3 feet) prefers part shade in cooler gardens. 'Elijah Blue' (8 to12 inches) is a silvery blue mound. Amethyst fescue (*Festuca amethystina*) 'Aprilgrun' (10 to 12 inches) has fine emerald foliage and prefers sun or shade. Native Idaho fescue (*Festuca idahoensis*) produces 6-inch mounds of silvery green and tolerates desert conditions. 'Tomales Bay' is blue, sturdy, and compact. It prefers cooler gardens. California fescue (*Festuca californica*) a 2-foot mound, silvery to greenish blue with blue flowers, is especially good for northern California. Atlas fescue (*F. mairei*) produces 2½-foot gray-green mounds and is well suited to southern California.

I once visited a Japanese style garden where a meticulously pruned pine tree floated in a sea of startling teal blue grasses. Their short vertical tufts contrasted with the black trunk and the deep green needles that covered the horizontal branches. The grass wasn't labeled, but appeared to be a blue fescue. Fescue is a perennial bunching grass that forms rounded tufts of narrow blades. In summer, the tufts are topped with wands of wheat-like flowers that blow in the breeze. Some members of these evergreen, cool-season grasses (they grow actively when the weather is cool and slow in warm weather) have handsome deep-green blades, but the blue fescues are the ones that always catch my eye. Blue fescue is also sold as Festuca glauca.

**Bloom Period and Seasonal Color**
Year-round colorful foliage. Summer flowers blue to pinkish.

**Mature Height × Spread**
6 to 24 in. × 12 in.

Hardy to 7A

Min. Temp. 0° F

# Cape Rush
## *Chondropetalum tectorum*

*Cape rush looks like a giant wiry grass, but it is not a grass at all. Instead, cape rush is a member of the Restio family, a group of tufted, evergreen plants that grows in seeps and marshes in the fynbos of Southern Africa. "Fynbos" is Afrikaans for "fine bush" and refers to the fact that fynbos plants have tough, narrow, needle-like foliage, a common adaptation to harsh dry climates. In the case of cape rush, stems are cylindrical and jointed, with sepia colored sheaths. They are so tough that they are used to make thatched roofs. Cape rush shares the fynbos with other restios and at least 6000 other species of plants native to nowhere else in the world, including Protea and geranium!*

**Other Common Name**
Cape Thatching Reed

**Bloom Period and Seasonal Color**
Small brown flowers in summer/fall followed by long-lasting black seedheads.

**Mature Height × Spread**
2 to 6 ft. × 3 to 8 ft.

Hardy to 9A

Min. Temp. 20° F

### When, Where, and How to Plant
Plant fall through spring in full sun and well-draining soil where there is good air movement. Cape rush will grow in the shallow water at the edge of a pond, in soils that stay moist most of the year, or in standard garden beds. Alternatively, plant cape rush in a large container filled with very well-draining soil.

### Growing Tips
Water cape rush regularly so the soil around its roots stays moist through the first summer. After that, plants will be well enough established to allow the soil to dry out somewhat between waterings. If planted into a spot that is naturally wet, it may not need to be irrigated at all. Because soils in the fynbos are poorer than soils in California, there is no need to feed cape rush. If you want to fertilize, feed once with all-purpose organic fertilizer early in spring. Apply at half the recommended rate or less.

### Care
Remove dead stems and older stems at their bases when new stems emerge in spring. Do not prune or cut back stems from the tips, or cut stems will die back and the clump will decline. No pests bother cape rush.

### Companion Planting and Design
Cape rush's narrow, arching stems give it a dramatic and sculptural form that works beautifully as a specimen in the middle-to-back of a garden bed or in a large container. It can be used as a visual anchor in a pond or stream. If sited in a breezy area, cape rush's arching stems wave in the breeze. Plant cape rush instead of the beautiful but aggressive horsetail (*Equisetum hyemale*) or the stunning but horribly invasive pampass grass (*Cortaderia selloana*), a pest throughout California.

### Try This
*Chondropetalum elephantinum*, usually labeled "large cape rush" grows 6 feet tall and wide. Other than that, the two are identical in the garden.

## When, Where, and How to Plant

Plant spring through fall and in full sun or part sun. Rich, well-drained soil is best but fountain grasses tolerate a wide range of soils. Be sure to site fountain grasses where they can reach their full width without smothering nearby plants or requiring constant pruning. Water well and mulch thickly.

## Growing Tips

Most fountain grasses are quite drought tolerant once established. Water deeply through the first spring/ summer season. After that, water deeply but only occasionally in summer, most often where summers are hot, and less often in clay soils as those soils hold water for a long time. See the introduction for fertilizer instructions.

## Care

Once foliage goes dormant, cut it back or leave it until the first new growth appears in spring. After a few years, overly large clumps can be divided when dormant (see introduction for instructions). Some fountain grasses reseed in irrigated areas of the garden. If you find one growing where you don't want it, simply dig it out, move it, or give away. Pests aren't a problem.

## Companion Planting and Design

Dwarf fountain grasses are small enough for containers or to be used as edging plants. Larger varieties are suitable for planting as single specimens or massed as foundation plants. They contrast well with shrubs in a mixed border. In a mixed planting, group plants in odd numbers (3s, 5s, etc.).

## Try These

The true fountain grass, *Pennisetum setaceum*, can invade native habitats throughout the state. Instead, plant these better-behaved cultivars: 'Eaton Canyon' (also called 'Red Riding Hood') grows 1 to 3 feet × 1 to 2 feet with bronzy foliage and reddish brown flowers. 'Fairy Tails' (4 feet × 4 feet) has blue-green foliage. Green leaved *Pennisetum alopecuroides* cultivars work especially well in northern California. Look for 'Hameln' ($2^{1}/_{2}$ feet × $2^{1}/_{2}$ feet), 'Little Bunny' (10 to 12 inches × 10 to 12 inches), and 'Moudry' (2 to 3 feet × 2 to 3 feet) with unusual, almost-black flowers. In southern California, grow the purple majesty millet (*Pennisetum glaucum* 'Purple Majesty').

*Planted against a deep colored stucco wall in a modernistic garden or a beneath pines in a cozy bungalow garden, fountain grasses simply cannot be beat. Fountain grasses are some of our most versatile ornamental grasses. These mid-sized grasses make 2- to 4-foot-tall fountainy mounds of narrow green and/or burgundy leaves. From sometime in summer until fall, the mounds are graced with tall arching stems, atop which are fuzzy plume-like flowers tinged pink, burgundy, near black, or pale green. As the flowers turn a straw-buff color, their contrast against leaves becomes even more outstanding. In late fall, leaves begin to turn the color of straw, as fountain grass sinks into winter dormancy. Leave the handsome mounds to add seasonality to your garden.*

**Bloom Period and Seasonal Color**
Pinkish, pale green, burgundy, near black, or buff colored flowers in late summer into fall.

**Mature Height × Spread**
1 to 5 ft. × 1 to 5 ft. depending on species

**Minimum Temperature**
Depends on species

Hardy to 9A

Min. Temp. See below

# Japanese Sweet Flag
## *Acorus gramineus*

There are tall grasses, short grasses, and non-grass grasses. One of my favorite non-grass grasses is a perennial with long sleek leaves that are flat and pointed, a bit like diminutive iris leaves. The leaves of Japanese sweet flag make fans, about a foot tall and wide. Some varieties have deep green leaves while others are striped green and cream, or yellow and green with stripes running the length of the foliage. Since Japanese sweet flag spreads by underground stems, it eventually forms a mat up to 5 feet across. Japanese sweet flag can be planted along the edge of a pond or stream since it is one of the most water-tolerant of the grass-like plants. It also makes a great no-mow ground cover or bed edging.

### Bloom Period and Seasonal Color
Green, green and yellow, or green and cream striped leaves.

### Mature Height × Spread
6 to 14 in. × 10 in., spreading to 5 ft.

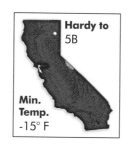

**Hardy to 5B**

**Min. Temp. -15° F**

### When, Where, and How to Plant
Japanese sweet flag is a bog plant, so while it does fine in regularly watered garden beds, it also thrives at the edge of a water garden and even a few inches underwater. Plant in full sun (along the coast) to full shade (everywhere else) in fall through spring. If planting along the edge of a water garden, you are essentially planting into mud. Just make sure that the soil around the roots is stable so it won't wash away.

### Growing Tips
Water regularly to keep soil moist unless sweet flag is planted in a pond or bog, in which case watering is not needed. Burned leaf tips indicate that the plant is too dry. Fertilize in-ground plants once in early spring with all-purpose organic fertilizer.

### Care
No pruning. If a wide clump dies out in the middle simply divide it and replant (see "Tips and Techniques").

### Companion Planting and Design
Use in an Asian theme garden with camellias, iris, and purple-leaved Japanese maples. Mass as a ground cover, use to edge a bed, plant between stepping stones in a shade garden, or surround the base of a bamboo hedge. Submerge pots of Japanese sweet flag into a pond or water garden for bright color. Use in a container arrangement as the bright colored vertical element along with Peruvian lily and bronze leaved coleus.

### Try These
My favorite is variegated sweet flag (*Acorus calamus* 'Variegatus'), the 4-foot-tall "big brother" to *Acorus gramineus*. Leaves are wide and green with cream colored edges, much like variegated iris. Dwarf sweet flag (*Acorus gramineus* 'Pusillus') grows 4 to 5 inches × 4 to 5inches with green leaves that tolerate some foot traffic; Grassy leaved sweet flag (*Acorus gramineus* 'Variegatus') grows 6 to 12 inches × 6 to12 inches with dark-green leaves striped cream. Golden variegated sweet flag (*Acorus gramineus* 'Ogon') is 6 to 12 inches × 6 to 12 inches and green with yellow striped edges. Dwarf gold sweet flag (*Acorus gramineus* 'Minimus Aureus') is 3 inches × 12 inches with green and pale yellow striped leaves.

# New Zealand Flax
## *Phormium* spp.

### When, Where, and How to Plant
Plant fall through early summer into well-draining soil and full sun (light shade in inland or desert gardens). In a mass planting, be sure to allow enough space for plant's natural widths. Water well and mulch.

### Growing Tips
New Zealand flax tolerates long dry periods but looks better with occasional deep water in summer. No fertilizer is needed.

### Care
As New Zealand flax spread, some varieties tend to revert to the green or bronze color of their hybrid parent. Simply cut the offending sprout (or leaf) off at the base. Divide plants if they grow too large for their spot or if clumps die out in the center (see "Tips and Techniques"). Watch for mealybugs. Check for and destroy snails hiding amidst leaves (see "Tips and Techniques").

### Companion Planting and Design
Flax's strong profile fits all garden styles. Plant largest varieties as a background with trees and shrubs. Edge flower borders or assemble flower bowls with tiny 'Jack Sprat', medium-sized 'Shiraz', and chartreuse-leaved 'Golden Spirit' smoke tree. Or combine yellow-leaved 'Yellow Wave' and red-leaved redbud *Cercis* 'Forest Pansy'.'

### Try These
There are dozens of cultivars and hybrids to choose from, so be sure to match size to space. Avoid planting large flax into too small a space or you will end up with a monster. *Phormium tenax* 'Atropurpureum' is 6 to 8 feet tall with red/purple foliage. Phormium hybrid 'Maori Queen' is 4 to 6 feet tall with upright olive green leaves edged in coral red. 'Sea Jade' leaves are 3 to 5 feet tall with upright green leaves and a bronze center stripe. Dwarfs include: 'Yellow Wave' (3 to 4 feet) with arching yellow and green stripes; 'Platt's Black' (2 to 3 feet) with arching leaves in deep maroon, nearly chocolate; 'Shiraz' (or 'Shirazz') with wine colored leaves; 'Tom Thumb' (2 to 3 feet) has green leaves with bronze margins. 'Wings of Gold' (2 to 3 feet) has upright olive-green leaves with yellow margins. Miniature 'Jack Sprat' stands only 18 inches tall with curled, deep bronze/chocolate leaves.

*Every garden needs strong foliage plants, and New Zealand flax fits that bill perfectly. Its fans of strappy and sometimes arching evergreen leaves come in countless shades of olive green to red, yellow, bronze, nearly purple, chocolate, and bright green—often in combination. Though summer brings tall spikes of dark colored flowers shaped a bit like tiny bird of paradise blooms, it is the New Zealand flax's low maintenance and colorful leaves that make it such a great garden plant. There are dozens of varieties, from 18-inch dwarfs to 8-foot giants, all a bit taller than wide. These tough plants are tolerant of fairly harsh conditions as long as they get lots of sun. Good in the ground and in containers, they are water thrifty as well.*

### Bloom Period and Seasonal Color
Evergreen leaves are green, deep bronze, gold, yellow, coral, olive, red, nearly purple, and combinations thereof.

### Mature Height × Spread
1 1/2 to 8 ft. × 1 1/2 to 18 ft., depending on variety

Hardy to 8B

Min. Temp. 15° F

# Pink Muhly Grass
## *Muhlenbergia capillaris*

One of my favorite ornamental grasses is a North American native whose broad mounds of rounded and pointed green leaves sit demurely along a dry streambed in my front garden. Sometime in October, those modest mounds put on the show of shows. It happens quite suddenly; narrow flower spikes rise above the foliage, doubling the mound height. The last 8 or so inches of each stalk splits to reveal a full, feathery plume of rose-purple flowers that look a bit like tiny seeds. The bloom covers the mound in a purple haze that undulates gently with the slightest breeze and lasts for a month or longer. The grass is pink muhly grass, one of the many members of the late-season blooming genus Muhlenbergia.

**Hardy to 6A**

**Min. Temp. -10° F**

**Other Common Name**
Purple Muhly

**Bloom Period and Seasonal Color**
Rose-purple blooms in early fall.

**Mature Height × Spread**
2 ft. × 2 ft. and slightly wider

### When, Where, and How to Plant
Pink muhly grass is tolerant of most soils and watering regimes, but not of overwatering. From fall through spring, set plants in full or part sun (especially in hot desert gardens). Plant in clusters, spacing plants 2 1/2 feet or more apart. A bit of extra room makes it easier to appreciate each plant's silhouette and flowers. Muhly is suitable for high elevation gardens. Water deeply after planting and surround in a 2- to 3-inch layer of organic mulch.

### Growing Tips
Keep soil moist through the first two summers. Once established, pink muhly grass prefers moist soils in hot gardens and tolerates drier conditions along the coast. More water means more flowers and a longer growing season, but do not overwater. Apply no fertilizer in the first year after planting. Then fertilize once a year *only* if plants grow slowly or if their color is off. Use lawn fertilizer at half or quarter strength.

### Care
This evergreen grass does not require pruning. Old leaves turn straw colored and fall out. You can also remove them with a gentle tug and leave them around the base as mulch. If you choose to shear pink muhly grass, wait until after the flowers fade. Leave 2 or 3 inches of leaf length. Pink muhly reseeds in irrigated gardens, but unwanted seedlings are easy to move or remove. No pests.

### Companion Planting and Design
Plant clusters of pink muhly grass as accents in garden beds. To show off the flowers, site plants where they will be backlit in fall. Plant en mass for a meadow or as a grassland beneath sycamores. Combine with redbud 'Forest Pansy' to highlight both plants' rose-purple color tones.

### Try These
Mexican muhly grass (*Muhlenbergia pubescens*) has gray-green or blue-green blades in 2-foot mounds with purplish blue flowers. Bamboo muhly (*Muhlenbergia dumosa*), a southwest desert native, forms 3- to 6-foot-tall jointed stems that look like petite bamboo. Feathery foliage waves in the breeze. Native deergrass (*Muhlenbergia rigens*) grows 4 to 5 feet × 6 feet with silvery gray foliage and yellow flowers.

# Purple Leaf Sugar Cane
### *Saccharum officinarum violaceum*

### When, Where, and How to Plant
Plant spring through early fall in mild winter areas, and in spring in colder areas. Choose a spot with full sun and well-drained soils. Though sugar cane likes lots of water, it doesn't want to sit in wet soil. Water deeply and mulch with a generous layer after planting.

### Growing Tips
Sugar cane takes regular water, especially through the summer. Fertilizer is not necessary if plants are kept well mulched.

### Care
In warmest winter areas, purple sugar cane is ever-green, though each cane eventually dies and is replaced. In cooler winter areas, all canes die back in winter. Either way, groom regularly and cut dead canes back to the base. Pests are not a problem.

### Companion Planting and Design
Sugar cane is a plant to site in the highest watering zone nearest the house. For a tropical composition, combine with canna and banana. Plant along a fence for a medium size privacy screen in place of bamboo. Purple sugar cane's architectural shape and amazing color make it perfectly suited for a modernistic planting with gray-leaved succulents, pink flowering sages, and apricot flowering anise hyssop. Since these other plants take less water than the sugar cane, rather than overwater everything, grow sugar cane in a large terracotta pot set in the garden bed. The combination gives the bed architecture, enhances the color contrast, and adds height since the pot adds 2 feet to the stature of the sugar cane.

### Try These
To propagate sugar cane, simply cut a stem into sections, each long enough to include at least one "joint." Strip the leaves off and set the piece horizontally into the soil, a few inches deep. Keep the soil damp, and soon you will see new roots growing into the soil and a new bud sprouting vertically from the section of stem. Once the piece is firmly rooted, transplant into a container or in the ground.

*Believe it or not, sugar cane is a perennial grass. This tropical/subtropical native comes from Southeast Asia. Green sugar cane is the standard variety, but for ornamental use, I far prefer purple sugar cane. It has 10- to 15-foot-tall chocolate-wine colored shoots with stems an inch or two across. Long arching leaves emerge and mature to wine and olive green. Strip the leaves away and you'll see that the stems are jointed much like bamboo. The overall tall profile and coarse foliage make a striking vertical accent in the garden. If you live in an area where it is warm enough, purple sugar cane makes pink tassel flowers that turn silvery. Sugar cane juice (actually sap) has been extracted to make crystallized sugar for at least 2500 years.*

**Bloom Period and Seasonal Color**
Olive green to wine colored stems and foliage year-round

**Mature Height × Spread**
4 to 12 ft. × 5 to 10 ft.

**Minimum Temperature**
25 degrees; root hardy to 10 degrees F

**Hardy to 8A**

**Min. Temp.** See below

# Sedge
## *Carex* spp.

*Sedges look like grasses and grow like grasses, but they are not grasses. Instead they are related to papyrus and edible water chestnut. These evergreen perennials are easy to grow, low maintenance, and add a wonderful character to the garden. Want a lawn that you don't have to mow? There are creeping sedges to fit that bill. Want color in your garden beds without relying on the seasonal come-and-go nature of flowers? There are clumping sedges for that purpose. Some sedges have long billowy leaves that resemble long-haired "Cousin It" from the 1960s television series* The Addams Family. *Others have shorter blades that hearken back to the spiky punk hairstyles of the 1980s. Either way, once you grow sedge in your garden, you'll be hooked.*

### Bloom Period and Seasonal Color
Evergreen foliage is green, blue-green, bronze, or orange.

### Mature Height × Spread
6 in. to 24 in. × 16 in. to 24 in.

### Minimum Temperature
Depends on species

Hardy to 8B

Min. Temp. 15° F

### When, Where, and How to Plant
Plant fall through spring, in part to full sun near the coast and in some shade in valleys and deserts. Sedges are tolerant of many kinds of soil. Plant from pots or plugs (small plants). Water deeply and mulch well.

### Growing Tips
Along the coast, water occasionally in summer. In inland valleys, water when the soil is dry 3 inches down. No fertilizer needed unless plants fail to thrive. Then apply a single feeding of lawn fertilizer at half to quarter strength.

### Care
Dead blades turn wheat colored and loosen from the center. To remove them, gently comb the plants with your fingers or a wide-tooth comb. Plant en mass and leave unmowed for a naturalistic meadow. Cut back once in fall or mow monthly for a more traditional lawn. Transplant or share unwanted seedlings. Pests aren't a problem.

### Companion Planting and Design
Plant colorful clumping sedges to spill over walls, to grow between stepping stones, to mix in containers, or to edge garden beds. Mix orange sedge with blue fescue and surround both with creeping wooly thyme, which blooms palest pink in spring. Plant creeping sedges to stabilize slopes, as a ground cover, a formal lawn, or meadow. For lawns or meadows, cover the area in organic mulch, 2- to 3-inches thick. Use a bulb planter to bore holes through the mulch for plugs. Set plugs so crowns are at the same level as in the nursery container. Water deeply.

### Try These
Colorful clumping orange sedge (*Carex testaceae*) has 1- to 2-foot-long arching blades that emerge bright olive and mature carrot-orange, especially in full sun. For meadows and lawns, try 6-inch creeping blue sedge (*Carex glauca*), which handles some traffic and tolerates heavy, poorly draining soils. Try natives Pacific dune sedge (*Carex pansa*) and clustered field sedge (*Carex praegracilis*) spaced 6 to 8 inches apart in well-draining soils. Plant Berkeley sedge (*Carex tumicola* AKA *Carex divulsa*), a green 2-foot-tall clumper into gardens as a ground cover (but not near a wetland, as it can be invasive).

# Silver Grass
## *Miscanthus sinensis*

### When, Where, and How to Plant
Plant fall through spring, in full sun or part sun (especially in hot desert gardens) and in well-draining soil. Water deeply after planting and mulch thickly.

### Growing Tips
Silver grass tolerates both wet and dry conditions, but growth slows and plants flower a bit less when grown on the dryer side. Water regularly and deeply (wet the soil about 6 inches deep) through the first two summers until plants send roots deep. After that, water when top 3 inches of soil are dry.

### Care
Blades dry to a straw color by late November. Cut them back or enjoy until new blades sprout in spring. The new blades will eventually hide the old. To cut back, loop twine around the circumference of the blades, about 8 inches above ground. Tighten the loop, then tie it off. Cut the sheaf, leaving 2 to 3 inches of stubble. Silver grass can reseed in areas of the garden that stay constantly moist. Avoid planting near a wetland as this grass can be invasive. Pests aren't a problem.

### Companion Planting and Design
Plant silver grass as an accent, as a screen, or as a background plant. Grow it as a tall element in a meadow of sedges or place it in a large pot and underplant with trailing nasturtium, cape fuchsia, or germander sage. Harvest flowers for dried arrangements.

### Try These
*Miscanthus sinensis* 'Morning Light' (5 feet × 5 feet) has pinkish flowers and white-edged green blades that turn russet in fall. Blades of 'Variegatus' (4 to 8 feet × 4 to 6 feet) and 'Cosmopolitan' (8 feet × 5 feet) have green and cream stripes along the length of the blade. 'Strictus' (4 to 8 feet × 4 to 6 feet), 'Zebrinus', and 'Kirk Alexander' (3 feet × 3 feet) have horizontal bands of green and yellow. The blades of 'Graziella' (7 feet × 4 feet) are silver. 'Purpurascens' (4 feet × 4 feet) has gray-green blades and pinkish flowers. Unlike other species, *Miscanthus transmorissonensis* (4 feet × 3 feet) is both evergreen and everblooming.

While ornamental grasses have become trendy relatively recently, silver grass has a long horticultural history. For more than 100 years, this tall stately grass has graced Japanese gardens, lending its graceful and textural blades to sophisticated compositions. In California gardens, silver grass works in both formal and informal gardens. Different varieties have different colored blades, from silver to striped (vertical or horizontal), to deep green; some are broad, and some are narrow. This clumping grass has large feathery flowers that rise above the blades in late summer or fall. As is typical with warm season grasses, silver grass goes dormant in winter, at which point flowers and blades turn the color of wheat, sometimes with reddish overtones. Even dormant, silver grass is beautiful in the garden.

**Other Common Name**
Eulalia Grass

**Bloom Period and Seasonal Color**
Summer through fall flowers are silver, cream, reddish, bronze, or copper.

**Mature Height × Spread**
2 to 8 ft. × 1 to 6 ft.

**Minimum Temperature**
Depends on variety.

Hardy to 5A

Min. Temp. -20 to 5° F

# Perennials *for California*

Mexican tulip poppy in border

Flowering perennials are the most beloved of garden plants. These soft-stemmed herbs grace the garden with a kaleidoscope of leafy texture and flowers for years on end.

What is a perennial? Whereas annuals live a single year and biennials for two years, perennials live three years or more. Some can live for decades while others are rather short-lived, making way for new perennials or filling space on a temporary basis while you wait for innately slower growing shrubs to fill out. Because perennials grow faster than shrubs or trees, their presence tends to dominate young gardens but balance more mature gardens.

This chapter includes plants and varieties that perform extremely well in our typically dry Mediterranean garden conditions, as well as in California's rainier areas.

These perennials represent tremendous diversity. Some grow only 6 inches tall and others grow 8 feet tall! Some burst with flowers, while others present a sophisticated combination of both blooms and foliage. While many are sun lovers, a few prefer shade, and some go either way. In fact, perennials that thrive in full sun in coastal gardens often need shade from the intense sun and heat in hot inland valley and desert gardens.

## Shopping for the Best Plants

Though most of the perennials in this chapter can be started from seed, cutting, or division, most gardeners purchase them in the nursery as 4-inch or 1-gallon plants. Some are also available in 5-gallon containers, but perennials are much like children—smaller ones adapt more quickly to being transplanted. So while a 5-gallon plant is larger initially, a 1-gallon size will match it and outgrow it in a year or two.

In fact, the best buys are not always the bushiest plants, those with the tallest branches, or those with the most flowers. The best buys are those with the largest, healthiest roots that can nourish the plant from the time of planting until it reaches the end of its natural life.

As you shop in the nursery, don't be shy about turning a plant out of its pot to check what's inside. Look for a network of fine pale white roots. If you see no roots, chances are that the plant was recently moved from a smaller pot and the roots have yet to fill the potting soil. There is nothing wrong with this plant, but if there is a plant with a more developed and extensive root network then choose that one first. Avoid plants with dead, brown, or black roots, with a bad odor, and (with few exceptions) those with roots that wrap round and round in an impenetrable mass—these are by definition rootbound plants. After you inspect the roots, set each plant and its label carefully back into the pot.

Once you get a plant home, make sure to keep it well watered until it goes into the ground. Nursery plants are accustomed to daily (or every other day) watering. I have many times made the mistake of bringing home a carload of plants and losing several before they made it into the ground—simply because I didn't keep up with watering.

## Planting Your Perennials

To plant a perennial, dig a hole just as deep as the rootball and $1\frac{1}{2}$ to 2 times as wide as the nursery container. I like to saturate both the plant in the container and the planting hole before planting so everything is nice and moist. Plan enough time for the hole to drain completely before you plant. Sandy soils tend to drain in a few hours and clay soils take longer.

Spurge with chartreuse blooms shines against a background of purple *Felicia echinata*

If your soil takes more than a few hours to drain, you have what we call "heavy" soil. Consider building a large planting mound of well-amended and well-draining soil. I am not talking about a series of little mole hills a foot or so across, but rather bed-sized mounds a foot or two tall with curves and peaks that create nooks and gullies for new planting opportunities. A good friend taught me years ago that garden beds with this kind of contour and topography are much more interesting than flat beds. Beyond the aesthetic advantage, creating raised planting mounds allows us gardeners to import well-draining soils to support the kinds of plants we want to grow.

Blanket flower

When it comes to planting, the majority of perennials in this chapter require minimal soil amendment (none if you are planting into raised mounds). Research and experience suggest that plants adapt better if planted in unamended or only lightly amended soils. Some gardeners like to mix fertilizer into the planting hole, but I don't do that. I add a small amount of worm castings instead. Worm castings (a genteel term for worm poop) are rich in nutrients and at a concentration and in a form that don't burn plant roots. As an added bonus, worm castings also improve soil structure. For example, natives such as monkey flower and Matilija poppy get a great start from a handful or two of worm castings added directly into the bottom of their planting holes. For non-natives, you might want to add 2 handfuls of organic compost along with a handful of worm castings into the backfill for a 1-gallon sized planting hole (less for smaller plants, more for larger ones).

Set the plant into the hole at the level it was in the pot (no deeper) and tamp soil down around the rootball as you refill the hole. Once the hole is filled, set your hose to drip water slowly around the moat so the soil saturates all the way past the bottom of the rootball. Deep watering is a crucial step at planting time and afterwards. It settles the soil around the rootball, eliminating any air pockets that might dry roots out. In addition, deep water ensures that moisture stays available at the roots rather than wicking into the surrounding soil.

Spread a 2 or 3-inch thick layer of composted mulch over the soil surface, keeping the mulch well away from stems and branches. Water regularly for the first year or two. After that check the watering directions for each plant.

As branches start to put on length, pinch out the tips to encourage side branches. More side growth makes for fuller plants and since perennials tend to flower at branch tips, more branches mean more flowers too. Just remember to stop pinching once flower buds appear!

Evergreen perennials such as Jerusalem sage are in full leaf year-round. Others loose leaves or branches or go completely dormant in the heat of summer (bear's breech, native monkey flower, and artichoke) or in response to the shorter, colder days of winter (Matilija poppy, purple coneflower, spurge, and tall verbena).

Evergreens need an occasional cleanup to remove dead leaves. Evergreen doesn't mean each leaf lives forever, but rather that the plant always has leaves. Throughout the year, individual leaves die and are replaced. These evergreens don't need pruning except to control their size. Better yet, site the plant in enough space to accommodate its full size, and prune only to encourage bushiness and flowers.

Perennials that go through dormancy require a different approach. For those that die back completely, simply remove the spent leaves and stems. Unless they are diseased, add them to your compost pile. For spurges and other plants that send up new stems from the base, wait until new growth appears in spring and then cut the old stems to the ground.

Perennials like sage and anise hyssop may lose leaves in winter, but their branches remain if temperatures don't get too cold. In my garden, the outer branches often die in winter freeze. I leave them in place to protect the interior branches and roots from future freezes. In spring, I watch for new leaves to develop along lower stems. Once the last chance of frost is past (ask your local UC extension agent or Master Gardener for your community's last frost date), I prune the old stems to just above the lowest set of leaves. These plants don't require pruning and they would grow just fine if I left them alone, but they would be leggy and awkward looking.

Perennials are tremendously rewarding. The ones I've described in these pages are just a starting point for the nearly infinite palette of perennials in the marketplace. Try these, and if they don't work, then try others. In my garden, I play by the "three strikes and you're out" rule. If a plant dies, I am willing to give it another try and another, all in different locations and under different conditions. If it dies a third time, it wasn't meant to grow in my garden. It may disappoint me, but I never get too upset. It simply means that I have a spot to try something else!

# Anise Hyssop
## *Agastache* spp.

*The mint family is large and varied with some members grown for both their fragrant leaves and for their tall spires of colorful flowers. One of these flowery mint relatives is anise hyssop, a mid-sized perennial that is as at home in an English cottage garden as it is in a low-water Mediterranean garden. Anise hyssop has green crinkled foliage on 2- to 3-foot-tall stems that flowers from spring through fall. The flowers, which are sometimes fragrant, bloom in sunset colors: rose pink, raspberry, apricot, salmon pink, gold, lavender, and violet blue. Like all mints, anise hyssop has tubular two-lipped flowers arranged in whorls at the tops of flower spikes. They are easy to grow and much beloved by bees, butterflies, and hummingbirds.*

**Other Common Name**
Giant Hyssop

**Bloom Period and Seasonal Color**
Flowers spring through fall in sunset colors: lavender, violet blue, rose pink, raspberry, apricot, salmon pink, and gold.

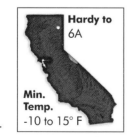

**Hardy to 6A**

**Min. Temp. -10 to 15° F**

**Mature Height × Spread**
2 to 3 ft. × 1 to 3 ft.

**Minimum Temperature**
Depends on species and variety.

## When, Where, and How to Plant
Plant fall through spring in mild winter gardens and in spring in colder winter gardens. Well-amended and well-drained soils are best, but poor soils are fine too. Plant in a spot in full or part sun. See the Perennials introduction for planting instructions. Water well after planting, and mulch.

## Growing Tips
Water needs depend on variety. Some anise hyssop needs only occasional deep summer watering, and others prefer more water. Apply organic fertilizer in spring before new growth starts, or mulch with compost.

## Care
Remove spent flowering stems to keep the plant neat and prolong bloom. To harvest for bouquets, snip flowering stems at their bases just as buds open. Anise hyssop has no serious pest problems and is often planted to draw beneficial insects into the garden.

## Companion Planting and Design
Anise hyssop is the perfect plant for any sunny perennial border in nearly any style garden. Stems sometimes fall over, so surround anise hyssop with hebe and other plants that have strong branches to support them. Anise hyssop belongs in every butterfly and herb garden. It also does well in large mixed containers.

## Try These
'Blue Fortune' (3 feet × 2 feet) has lavender blue flowers with maroon edges and dark green leaves (hardy to -10 degrees F). 'Summer Breeze' (3 feet × 3 feet) has orchid pink flowers and aromatic gray green leaves (hardy to -10 degrees F). *Agastache aurantiaca* 'Apricot Sunrise' (3 feet × 3 feet) has apricot and gold flowers in burgundy calyces and is drought tolerant (hardy to 15 degrees F). *Agastache* 'Tutti Frutti' (2 to 3 feet × 1 to 2 feet) has large fragrant whorls of lavender/raspberry flowers and leaves smell like lemon-mint (hardy to at least 0 degrees F). *Agastache cana* 'Bubble Gum Mint' (2 feet × 2 feet) has fragrant rose pink flowers and is drought tolerant (hardy to 20 degrees F). *Agastache foeniculum* 'Golden Jubilee' (20 inches × 20 inches) has purple flowers and golden yellow/green mint scented leaves (hardy to -10 degrees F).

# Artichoke
### *Cynara scolymus*

## When, Where, and How to Plant

Plant bare-root artichokes when available in the nursery in late winter. Set roots 6 inches deep and 5 to 6 feet apart. To grow from seed, start in August. Transplant seedlings at 4 to 5 inches tall. Artichokes started from seed often produce two crops their first year. Plant from 1-gallon pots anytime the ground is workable, set 5 to 6 feet apart, following planting instructions in the Perennials introduction. Artichoke prefers well-amended, well-draining soils and full sun. In poor soils, build planting mounds or raised beds (see "Tips and Techniques"). Container growing is another option. For seed starting and container growing information, see "Tips and Techniques."

## Growing Tips

Water regularly to keep soil moist (not wet) during the growing season. After flowering withhold water to force summer dormancy. Resume watering when leaves resprout at the base. Feed lightly with a balanced organic fertilizer each month through artichoke's growing season.

## Care

Groom to remove spent leaves. To harvest buds, cut the bud stalk in the crotch above the uppermost set of leaves. To harvest for cut flowers, wait until buds are nearly open and then cut the stalk to the desired length. After flowering, plants decline and go dormant. Cut all remaining stems back to 3- to 4-inch stubs. Slugs, snails, aphids, and ants are persistent problems (see "Tips and Techniques" for controls). Before cooking buds, submerge them in a bowl of water with a few drops of dish soap and vinegar. Agitate to remove hitchhiking aphids and then rinse.

## Companion Planting and Design

Artichoke's gray arching leaves serve as a sculptural accent in the garden. Plant in your permanent garden beds with other Mediterranean climate plants such as rockrose, lavender, and rosemary.

## Try These

'Emerald' (5 feet × 5 feet) has large, globe-shaped, and glossy-green buds that are thornless. It is frost and heat tolerant. 'Improved Green Globe' (3 to 5 feet × 3 to 5 feet) has purple-tinged buds and ferny foliage, and is cold tolerant. 'Violetto' from Northern Italy has violet-colored buds.

*Artichoke is a tri-purpose plant. It is a delicious vegetable eaten for its lovely hearts and meaty leaf-like bracts. It is a perennial with long, jagged-edged gray-green leaves that emerge like fountainy sprays from the base, and it is also a beautiful cut flower. Its flowering stalks emerge from the plant's center and form numerous buds at the tips. Those unopened buds are the delicacies we eat. Harvest them large, or small as baby "chokes." As you cut the buds, plants produce side shoots that produce buds as well. The more you harvest, the more you get. If left on the plant, buds open up to reveal beautiful thistle-like flowers in shades of rose to purple to blue. Just don't try to eat the flowers!*

### Other Common Name
Globe Artichoke

### Bloom Period and Seasonal Color
Buds develop in early spring and by summer open fringes of rose-purple or lavender blue stamens.

### Mature Height × Spread
3 to 5 ft. × 3 to 5 ft.

### Minimum Temperature
10 degrees F (Zone 8A) as perennial, grown as annuals in cooler climates.

# Bat-faced Cuphea
## *Cuphea llavea*

*One plant in my garden has flowers that make me smile. Bat-faced cuphea is a shrubby perennial with pointed evergreen leaves and branches tipped in amazing and amusing flowers. Their color is amazing—scarlet red with deep purple. Their shape is amusing—they truly look like little bat faces. Each flower has two large red petals shaped like mouse ears atop a purple "snout" with white "eyes" and a proboscis-like "mouth." This Mexican native tolerates hot, hot climates and blooms much of the year. In my own garden, Bat-faced cuphea inspired the color scheme for a garden bed to which I added scarlet amaryllis, red Peruvian lilies, and purple flowering 'Black Knight' butterfly bush. Between the butterfly bush and the cuphea, my garden is filled with butterflies.*

**Bloom Period and Seasonal Color**
Red and purple flowers on and off all year, peaking in spring through fall.

**Mature Height × Spread**
1 to 2 ft. × 2 to 3 ft.

Hardy to 9B

Min. Temp. 25° F

## When, Where, and How to Plant
Plant into moderately amended soil and in full or part sun (especially in desert gardens). Well-drained soils are important for avoiding root rot. As long as they are watered, cuphea tolerate inland valley and desert heat, while also performing well along the coast. Follow planting directions in the Perennials introduction and then water deeply and mulch well. This cuphea is ideal for growing in a container (see "Tips and Techniques").

## Growing Tips
Though these plants can handle extreme heat, they don't always handle drought. Keep soil damp (not wet) during the flowering season. Mulch heavily to conserve soil moisture. When the air cools in winter, cut back on water. Fertilize with all-purpose organic food in early spring.

## Care
Pruning is not necessary but can be done to shape the plant. Pinch branch tips to keep it bushy. Prune with a light hand, cutting only the green parts and not the woody parts of branches. Watch for aphids and whiteflies (see "Tips and Techniques").

## Companion Planting and Design
Children love the funny little bat faces of cuphea flowers. Include them in school gardens and other gardens where children play. Incorporate bat-faced cuphea into perennial borders and butterfly and hummingbird gardens. Plant at the base of tall shrubs as a transition to lower growing perennials. The relaxed branches also hang gracefully over the sides of hanging baskets and window boxes.

## Try These
Some cuphea are more shrub-like with tiny flowers but I prefer larger and bold colored flowers of varieties such as 'Georgia Scarlet' ('Tiny Mice') (1 to 2 feet × 2 to 3 feet) with tube flowers that are more petite and narrower than traditional bat-faced cuphea. Purple throats and white-fringed stamens enhance the look of the tiny mouse faces. 'Flamenco™ Rumba' (16 inches × 16 inches) is more compact with lots of larger flowers. 'Flamenco™ Tango' is like 'Rumba' but with pink and purple flowers. *Cuphea × purpurea* 'Firefly' (8 to 14 inches × 8 to 14 inches) has magenta red flowers with a white crown in the center.

# Bear's Breech
## *Acanthus mollis*

### When, Where, and How to Plant
Plant bear's breech from fall through spring in mild winter climates and in spring in colder winter gardens. Start with a 1- or 5-gallon plant. Follow planting directions in the Perennials introduction. Bear's breech prefers moist well-amended soil that drains well but will adapt to most soils and watering regimens. Plant in full sun to part shade, especially in hot inland gardens. Allow enough space for the plant's ultimate expanse. Water well and mulch after planting. Bear's breech can be container grown as well. A large pot will accommodate its size.

### Growing Tips
If grown on a low-water diet, bear's breech leaves die back in the heat of summer and then return when the weather cools. For year-round greenery, irrigate through summer, but be aware that in a well-irrigated garden, beer's breech multiplies. Dig up extra plants and pass them on to friends. Keep a thick layer of organic compost around the base of the plants. Use a balanced organic fertilizer monthly through the growing season.

### Care
Groom to remove spent flower stalks and leaves. Protect from snails and slugs (see "Tips and Techniques").

### Companion Planting and Design
Use bear's breech as a specimen plant or mass plant them in a wide border. For a rich green look, combine with bay laurel, iris, hellebore, shrub fuchsia, and camellia. Plant bear's breech at the base of a tall crape myrtle or grow masses of them beneath an oak grove. Bear's breech makes a bold statement when planted in a white garden. It also holds its own in a tropical planting with ginger, guava, banana shrub, and tree ferns.

### Try These
'Tasmanian Angel' (3 feet × 3 feet) variegated bear's breech has deep green leaves mottled with white and with white margins. Pink and cream flowers line a 3-foot stalk. 'Oak Leaf' (4 feet × 4 feet) has large oak leaf-shaped leaves. *Acanthus spinosissimus*, (sometimes sold as *Acanthus spinosus*) (2 feet × 2 feet) is smaller scale and more refined looking than *Acanthus mollis*.

*Bear's Breech is a classic Mediterranean perennial with deep green arching leaves 2 to 3 feet long and 1 foot or more wide arranged in a rosette. The leaves are deeply sculpted and tipped in soft spines. In spring, bear's breech sends up column-like flower stems 5 to 6 feet tall and lined with blooms. Each flower has olive/gold stamens sandwiched between a canopy-like dusty purple bract above and a white petal below. Irrigated plants stay evergreen through summer. Un-irrigated, they go dormant briefly. Bear's breech leaf is a classic design motif used since ancient times. Greek artisans carved ornate bear's breech leaves into fluted Corinthian columns. Renaissance weavers incorporated bear's breech designs into textiles. Victorians adorned furniture, decorative prints, and borders (printed, not planted) with bear's breech leaves.*

### Bloom Period and Seasonal Color
Early spring into summer, white/dusty purple with olive/gold stamens.

### Mature Height × Spread
4 to 5 ft. × 4 to 5 ft., flower stalks to 6 feet

Hardy to 7A

Min. Temp. 0° F

# Blanket Flower
## *Gaillardia aristata*

*Blanket flowers are bright colored, flowering evergreens that thrive in heat and drought. These North American natives form rosettes of sculpted green or gray-green leaves from which emerge tall, wiry flower stalks topped with 3-inch daisy-like flowers in Indian blanket colors: scarlet, wine, or orange and tipped in yellow. The bloom often lasts from spring through fall. As flowers fade, they release their large seeds. A patch of blanket flower sprouted in a decomposed granite walkway in my garden. It blooms most of the year in full sun and with no irrigation. I cut the flowers for arrangements with green and yellow variegated canna leaves, orange or pale yellow Peruvian lily flowers. A long, deep purple flower wand of anise-scented sage adds a zip to the combination.*

**Bloom Period and Seasonal Color**

Earliest spring through fall blooms in hot scarlet, wine, or orange, most often with yellow tips.

**Mature Height × Spread**

8 to12 in. × 8 to18 in. with flower stalks to 2 ft.

**Hardy to 4B**

**Min. Temp. -30° F**

### When, Where, and How to Plant

Plant fall through spring in frost-free gardens and in spring in cold winter gardens. Blanket flower likes full sun (some afternoon shade in deserts) and well-draining soil. Rich and poor soils are both fine. Follow directions for planting in the Perennials introduction and then water deeply and mulch well. Blanket flower is almost as easy to start from seed as it is to transplant from nursery six-packs or pots. Follow seed planting directions in "Tips and Techniques." Blanket flower also does well in pots, preferably unglazed ceramic pots. Container planting directions are also in "Tips and Techniques."

### Growing Tips

Water deeply and regularly the first growing season so plants develop deep roots. Blanket flower is very drought tolerant once established but more water encourages more flowers and more lush foliage. No fertilizer is needed.

### Care

Deadhead spent flowers through the season for ongoing bloom. Don't worry if flowering stops in the heat of summer; another round of blooms will start in the cool of fall. When fall bloom ends, rejuvenate by cutting stems back to just a few inches tall. New leaves will soon sprout. Protect from slugs. Sunlight and good air circulation help prevent powdery mildew in coastal gardens (see "Tips and Techniques" for more on managing pests and disease).

### Companion Planting and Design

Blanket flower's bright red, orange, and yellow blooms liven flower borders, perennial gardens, cutting gardens, and low water gardens. Mass plant for a ground cover or meadow. Plant dwarf varieties between stepping stones.

### Try These

'Arizona Sun' (18 inches × 18 inches) has very large full flower heads with deep red petals edged in yellow. 'Burgundy' ('Burgunder') has raspberry flowers with yellow centers (24 inches × 24 inches). 'Fanfare' (12 inches × 18 inches) petals are red edged with yellow and flare like trumpets. 'Oranges and Lemons' (18 to 24 inches × 18 to 24 inches) has blooms of citrus orange petals tipped in yellow and fringed. 'Summer's Kiss' (12 inches × 18 inches) flowers in pale coral, yellow, or apricot.

# Butterfly Weed
## *Asclepias curassavica*

### When, Where, and How to Plant
Spread seeds in summer (see "Tips and Techniques") either onto the ground or into pots. Plant the seedlings or set out plants from the nursery in 4-inch or 1-gallon pots in spring through fall, according to planting instructions in the Perennials introduction. Choose a spot in full sun or light shade and with occasional irrigation. Butterfly weed is adaptable to about any kind of soil. Water seedlings well after planting and mulch.

### Growing Tips
Water deeply and frequently through the first summer. Once established, plants survive with little water but prefer regular irrigation in summer. Fertilizer is not necessary, though a single application of organic fertilizer in early spring can promote growth. If you get lush growth but few flowers, cut back on fertilizer. **Note:** This plant is poisonous. The milky sap irritates eyes.

### Care
To control the spread of this plant in the garden, remove seedpods before they open. In fall, cut plants back to the base. Aphids like butterfly weed, but even a heavy infestation is seldom problematic. If leaves appear to be eaten, congratulations, you have monarch butterfly caterpillars! Do not remove the black, white, and yellow striped caterpillars, they are the best reason to grow this plant.

### Companion Planting and Design
When my children were small, I planted butterfly weed in a bed outside the windowseat in our living room. We spent hours sitting in the window and watching the butterflies in action. My children learned to inspect the plants for yellow and white striped monarch butterfly caterpillars and the hanging jade green chrysalises that form as caterpillars start their transition to butterflies. Today butterfly weed sprouts from many of my garden beds and from cracks between walkway pavers. Every day the sun is out, from spring into fall, my garden is alive with the antics of flittering of orange and black butterflies.

### Try These
'Silky Gold' is like the species but its flowers are completely golden yellow; 'Silky Deep Red' flowers are golden yellow and deep red rather than fiery orange.

*Every butterfly garden requires two kinds of plants: those with nectar-rich flowers for adult butterflies to sip and those with leaves for hungry caterpillars to chomp. Butterfly weed has both and is a special favorite of monarch butterflies. This South American perennial forms tall, green stalks lined in narrow leaves. From spring through fall, stems are topped with 4-inch clusters of fiery red-orange buds that open to reveal star-shaped, golden yellow, flower-like parts. Each bloom is replaced by a 3-inch-long sickle-shaped seedpod that opens to reveal large brown seeds attached to pieces of white fluff that float away in the breeze. Seeds germinate wherever they land. Find an unwanted butterfly weed volunteer? Simply pull it out.*

**Other Common Name**
Bloodflower

**Bloom Period and Seasonal Color**
Spring through fall blooms, fiery red-orange with golden yellow.

**Mature Height × Spread**
3 to 4 ft. × 2 ft.

Hardy to 8A

Min. Temp. 10° F

# California Fuchsia

*Epilobium canum ssp. canum*

*California fuchsia could easily be called California hummingbird plant. This low-spreading native perennial has narrow evergreen leaves in gray-green, silver green, or yellow-green. When many California natives go dormant in the heat of late summer, that is when California fuchsia blooms kick in. Long, trumpet-shaped flowers explode in shades of brilliant salmon or coral-orange (sometimes soft pink). These flowers bloom for a long time, attracting hummingbirds by the score. The little birds zip and dive as they maneuver for a turn to poke their narrow beaks deep into a bloom for sweet nectar. Smaller forms of California fuchsia make nice tight mounds, while larger varieties are somewhat gangly and look best in informal gardens where they can sprawl.*

**Other Common Name**
Hummingbird Trumpet

**Bloom Period and Seasonal Color**
Late summer to fall flowers, brilliant salmon orange, coral, or pale pink.

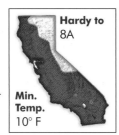

Hardy to 8A

Min. Temp. 10° F

**Mature Height × Spread**
6 to 12 in. × 36 in.

### When, Where, and How to Plant
California fuchsia is suitable for all gardens including those in high elevations and desert areas. Plant fall through spring in mild winter areas and in spring where winters are freezing. Provide full sun and soil with excellent drainage, though plants are adaptable to heavier soils. Water deeply after planting and mulch. See the Perennials introduction for planting instructions.

### Growing Tips
In cool summer and coastal gardens, California fuchsia is drought tolerant. Water deeply the first spring through fall, then only periodically in the hot summer. In hotter valley and desert gardens, water established plants more frequently. No fertilizer.

### Care
Prune scraggly branches or cut back mounds after the bloom ends and before new growth begins. Some varieties tend to wander via underground roots and fertile seeds. To prevent seeding, simply cut off flowers as they end their bloom. To contain underground runners, use a root barrier (see "Tips and Techniques"), plant in a pot sunk into the ground, or simply keep an eye on the runners and remove them as they appear. No pests.

### Companion Planting and Design
Plant California fuchsia into any dry garden that needs a color boost in late summer or early fall. Mix with natives and other Mediterranean climate plants that have similar cultural needs. Plant beneath California lilac or manzanita, on a slope or hillside to help stem erosion.

### Try These
*Epilobium canum* ssp. *canum* is also sold as *Epilobium californica* and as *Zauschneria californica*. Varieties include 'Bowman's' with orange flowers on upright branches. 'Cloverdale' has bright green leaves topped in orange-scarlet flowers. 'Solidarity Pink' has yellow-green leaves and soft pink flowers. 'Catalina' (3 to 4 feet tall) has silvery white leaves with red-orange flowers in summer and tolerates part shade. Humboldt County fuchsia (*Epilobium septentrionale*) is native to north coastal ranges and is especially good for northern gardens. Low mat varieties (6 to 12 inches × 12 to 18 inches) include 'Select Mattole' with silvery foliage and bright scarlet flowers.

# Cape Fuchsia
*Phygelius capensis*

## When, Where, and How to Plant

Cape fuchsia does best in full sun. These plants tolerate light shade (especially in the hottest gardens) but too much shade makes them flower sparsely. Provide well-drained and moderately amended soil. In a multiple planting, space 3 to 4 feet apart. Follow planting instructions in the Perennials introduction. Water deeply and mulch. Cape fuchsia is a very good choice for containers (see container planting information in "Tips and Techniques").

## Growing Tips

Water deeply and frequently through the first summer and fall. Once established, cape fuchsia is quite drought tolerant. Fertilize with general-purpose organic fertilizer in spring before new growth begins.

## Care

Deadhead through the flowering season to keep plants blooming. Between the time when bloom is completely done for the season and new growth starts in spring, you can (but don't have to) cut branches back by a half or two-thirds. Remove stray branches and pull out wayward running stems any time of year. Pests are no problem.

## Companion Planting and Design

This relaxed plant looks best in a relaxed environment. Plant into a perennial bed or between shrubs to fill empty spaces with color. Cape fuchsia can be used to cascade over a low wall, in a glazed pot of a contrasting color, or trailing over the edge of a hanging basket. For a tremendous flower display, plant with sundrops, daylily, canna, naked ladies, red-hot poker, and angel trumpet. Draw hummingbirds to your garden by planting cape fuchsia with bright flowering sages, California fuchsia, California buckeye, penstemon, fuchsia, and daylily.

## Try These

'African Queen' has orange-red tubular flowers. 'Trewidden Pink' flowers are dusky pink. 'Moonraker' flowers are pale yellow. 'New Sensation' ('Blaphy') has raspberry-purple colored flowers. *Phygelius × rectus* 'African Queen' has coral red flowers. 'Yellow Trumpet' has soft yellow flowers (to 5 feet tall).

*Some plants are sheer color and joy. Such is the case with cape fuchsia, a shrubby evergreen perennial from South Africa. Narrow deep green leaves with tiny serrated edges lines the stems, while big loose tiers of bright orange, pink, red, or yellow flowers hang from cape fuchsia's tall spire-like flower stalks. Each flower is an elongated trumpet that ends in a star-shaped flare, often with a gold or yellow throat. The flowers are shaped a bit like fuchsia flowers, but cape fuchsia is not a fuchsia at all. Instead it is related to penstemon. Lax, trailing branches spread by underground runners that are relatively contained in a low water garden but make large patches in well-watered gardens.*

**Other Common Name**
Cape Figwort

**Bloom Period and easonal Color**
Bright orange, red, pink, coral, or pale yellow summer blooms.

**Mature Height × Spread**
3 to 4 ft. × 3 to 4 ft. or wider

**Minimum Temperature**
Evergreen to 25 degrees F; root hardy to 10 degrees F.

# Curry Plant

## Helichrysum italicum

*Rub the pale green leaves of curry plant and you'll immediately know how it got its common name. The leaves contain aromatic oils with a familiar, sweet, rich curry fragrance. Surprisingly they are not really edible. Though the leaves of curry plant are distilled for essential oils, they are not used to make curry. True curry is a mixture of ground herbs and spices altogether different from this plant. Still this beautiful petite evergreen is a valuable garden plant. At 2 feet tall and wide, curry plant is covered in narrow needle-like leaves that are silvery gray, almost white. In summer tiny yellow flowers cover the branch tips. This Turkish native comes from dry, rocky, and sandy areas. Curry plant is also sold as* Helichrysum angustifolium.

### Bloom Period and Seasonal Color
Yellow summer to fall flowers.

### Mature Height × Spread
2 ft. × 2 ft.

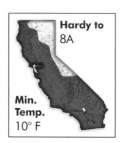

**Hardy to 8A**

**Min. Temp. 10° F**

### When, Where, and How to Plant
Plant fall through spring in mild winter climates and in spring in colder climates. Plant in full sun with well-draining soil (see directions in the Perennials introduction). Water well and mulch after planting. Curry is a good container plant too (see "Tips and Techniques" for container planting).

### Growing Tips
Water deeply to keep the rootball moist (not wet) through the first summer. After that, water only occasionally from spring until winter rains. These are drought tolerant plants that prefer to be kept on the dry side. No fertilizer is needed.

### Care
To shape, prune back soft part of branches in spring. Do not cut into hardwood. Pests do not bother curry plant.

### Companion Planting and Design
Site curry plant where passersby can brush up against the foliage to release its rich curry fragrance. In a garden for children, create a tapestry of texture and fragrance by planting soft, spicy curry plant with fuzzy, fragrant peppermint geranium and the velvety leaves of lamb's ear. Though not edible per se, curry plant is still a terrific choice for an herb garden, especially when mixed with low-growing oreganos and creeping thyme. Mass it as a low hedge in front of the deep green leaves of bay tree. Plant curry in a low water perennial bed mixed with, for example, purple and blue flowering plants such as anise-scented sages, Mexican sage, and blue hibiscus. Add a golden flowered perennial marigold for contrast. In a Mediterranean planting scheme, mix curry plant with bear's breech, bougainvillea, and yucca.

### Try These
Strawflower (*Helichrysum bracteatum*) is a 2- to 3-feet × 1-foot annual closely related to curry plant, but grown for its 2$\frac{1}{2}$-inch flowers. Strawflower leaves are greener, wider, and longer than the curry plant but lack fragrance. Summer flowers are shades of gold, red, orange, white, and pink. Flowers can be cut, dried, and used in flower arrangements. Strawflower is best started from seed and planted out in full sun with little to moderate water once established. See seed starting directions in "Tips and Techniques."

# Foothill Penstemon
### *Penstemon heterophyllus*

### When, Where, and How to Plant
Plant in fall as rains begin. Site in full sun (light shade in hot valleys) and in well-drained soil. Poor soils or rocky soils are fine. Penstemon tolerates clay if not overwatered. Follow planting directions in the Perennials introduction. Water deeply after planting and mulch.

### Growing Tips
If winter rains are sparse, water through the first winter. If rains are plentiful, wait until spring to start watering, then water deeply and regularly until rains arrive in late fall. After the first year in the ground, foothill penstemon needs only occasional water in areas that receive 12 inches or more rainfall per year. In drier areas, water occasionally through summer. Trial and error will help you determine the best watering frequency for your garden conditions. No fertilizer is needed.

### Care
Cut off spent flower spikes to encourage longer bloom cycle. Prune to shape and to remove last flower spikes once seeds have been released (so you have more plants the next year). Powdery mildew often results from overwatering. Cut back on water and see if plants recover. If not, replace them.

### Companion Planting and Design
Foothill penstemon is at home in the front of a flower border. Plant with other natives such as orange flowered California poppy, burgundy monkey flower 'Ruby Silver', and other native penstemon (see below). In a more cosmopolitan Mediterranean scheme, plant with red- and purple-flowering bat-faced cuphea, yellow-flowered sundrops, and an evergreen hebe. Foothill penstemon is adaptable to containers as well.

### Try These
'Margarita BOP' (1 foot × 3 feet) is larger and more floriferous than the species and more disease resistant and tolerant of garden conditions. 'Lodoga Strain' (2 feet tall) has bright blue flowers. 'Blue Springs' (18 inches tall) flowers are bluest blue. Scarlet bugler (*Penstemon centranthifolius*) (2 to 4 feet × 2 feet) makes tall spikes of red flowers in spring and summer. Showy penstemon (*Penstemon spectabilis*) has bright lavender-purple flowers in spring and summer on 3- to 5-foot spikes.

*Penstemons are spreading perennials that send up tall spires of colorful, long lasting flowers. One of my favorite is foothill penstemon, a smaller penstemon with narrow two-lipped, trumpet-shaped flowers in translucent violet with a blue blush, or bright blue with lavender or pink throats. The foliage makes loose mats of 1-foot-tall branches, densely clothed in narrow and pointed blue-green leaves. In spring and summer, pale yellow buds form and open to the purple/blue/pink flowers. This relatively short-lived evergreen is native to dry areas of California's low- and mid-elevation grasslands, chaparral, and open areas along the coastal mountains and Sierra Nevadas. These are areas with poor soils, little rainfall, and lots of sun. If you can emulate those conditions, these plants will thrive.*

### Other Common Name
Foothill Beardtongue

### Bloom Period and Seasonal Color
Spring to fall flowers in combinations of violet, blue, and pink.

### Mature Height × Spread
1 to 3 ft. × 1 to 3 ft., or slightly wider

Hardy to 7B

Min. Temp. 5° F

# Heartleaf Bergenia
## *Bergenia cordifolia*

Heartleaf bergenia is a low growing evergreen perennial with large heart-shaped green leaves that form a rosette. The leaves sit at various angles, creating a low plane of texture. This shade loving and moisture tolerant perennial has been a favorite of plant breeders for many years. As a result, we have a selection of varieties with leaves in many colors: variegated golden yellow/green, burgundy, bronze, or green turning burgundy/bronze as the weather cools. Heartleaf bergenia's springtime flower clusters range from almost magenta to palest pink. During my Los Angeles childhood, I remember seeing heartleaf bergenia planted beneath broad-leaf bear's breech, tropical bird of paradise, and raspberry flowering bougainvillea. This combination was a Los Angeles invention though, as Bergenia is native to the woodlands of Mongolia and Siberia.

**Bloom Period and Seasonal Color**
Deep pink spring flowers.

**Mature Height × Spread**
1 to 2 ft. × 1 to 2 ft.

Hardy to 5A

Min. Temp. -20° F

## When, Where, and How to Plant
Plant in spring into a location in full sun along the coast, part sun to part shade elsewhere, according to directions in the Perennials introduction. These plants are adaptable to many kinds of soils but prefer those that are well amended with organic matter. Space plants 1 foot apart. For a naturalistic appearance, plant in odd numbers and stagger plants rather than planting them in a straight line. Water well after planting and mulch with organic matter.

## Growing Tips
Water well the first year to establish plants. In subsequent years water when the soil is dry 3 to 4 inches down. Fertilize early in spring with an all-purpose organic fertilizer. Fertilize again if leaves start to look pale. A thick layer of organic compost greatly reduces the need to fertilize and water.

## Care
Divide clumps every few years if they get too wide. Groom to remove spent leaves and flowers. Protect from slugs and snails (see "Tips and Techniques" for more on care and pest controls).

## Companion Planting and Design
Plant this shade lover beneath almost any tree except an oak. Use it to surround the base of tall shrubs, or mass it as a ground cover. Create a woodland look by planting with Japanese maple, bear's breech, daylily, and hellebore.

## Try These
'Tubby Andrews'™ (10 to 14 inches × 10 to 14 inches) has golden yellow and green splashed leaves. 'Winterglut' (12 inches × 24 inches) has deep rosy-red flowers in spring. 'Evening Glow' (12 inches × 24 inches) has pink springtime flowers and leaves that are dark olive and burgundy. 'Bressingham Ruby' (12 inches × 14 inches) has ruby red spring flowers and green leaves that age to ruby in fall and winter. Winter blooming bergenia (*Bergenia crassifolia*) is the same size as and looks much like heartleaf bergenia but blooms in winter and has taller flower stalks. Frilly bergenia (*Bergenia cilliata*) is deciduous with round leaves covered in fine hairs and pale pink flowers in spring and summer.

# Hellebore
## *Helleborus* spp.

### When, Where, and How to Plant
In frost-free gardens, plant fall through spring, following the directions in the Perennials introduction. In cold winter gardens, plant in spring. Hellebores prefer well-amended and well-draining soil. They tolerate full sun only along the coast so provide some shade everywhere else. Water deeply after planting, and mulch.

### Growing Tips
Water deeply and regularly through the first summer into fall. Once established, water sun-grown hellebore from spring through fall and water shade-grown hellebore only in the hottest months. Keep mulched. Apply balanced organic fertilizer, according to label directions. Feed container-grown hellebore regularly with diluted liquid fertilizer.

### Care
Groom to remove spent flowers and leaves once they turn brown. Watch for snails, slugs, whitefly, and sooty mold (see "Tips and Techniques" for managing these pests).

### Companion Planting and Design
Hybrid and Mediterranean native hellebore are best suited for California gardens. Their round foliage complements woodland gardens, Asian gardens, and traditional perennial gardens. In more northern gardens where rainfall and humidity are higher than in the south, plant them beneath oak trees and water sparingly until plants are established. Let Mother Nature water after that.

### Try These
Corsican hellebore (*Helleborus argutifolius* or *Helleborus corsicus*) is 2 to 3 feet × 2 to 3 feet with chartreuse flowers. Leaves are blue-green above and blush pink below and along stems. Stinking hellebore (*Helleborus foetidus*) is 18 to 30 inches × 24 to 36 inches and doesn't really smell. Its mounds of feathery, swirling, curved leaves are deep green or gray-green. Pale green flowers are edged in burgundy. Livid hellebore (*Helleborus lividus*) makes an 18 inch × 18 inch mound of green leaves with silver or purplish veins and undersides. Pale green flowers are blushed purple. *Helleborus* × *nigersmitthii* 'Ivory Prince' (12 to 18 inches × 12 to18 inches) flowers blush pink to plum on the backside, palest green to ivory on the inside.

*Dry shade gardens can be quite a challenge. Nurseries offer foliage plants for those conditions, but finding plants with beautiful flowers is far harder. Hellebore is one of the few exceptions. This mounding perennial has great leaves and great flowers. Hellebores are divided into 3 to 9 inch-long pointed leaflets, with some having serrated edges. Leaflets can be wide or narrow and feathery in dark green, blue-green, or variegated. Some leaves have silvery veins, and others have burgundy or purple stems and leaf undersides. Clusters of cup-shaped flowers form on short stems. Their petal-like sepals are the subtle calm colors of winter—combinations of pale green, ivory, dusky purple, velvety plum, creamy peach, and soft chartreuse. Note: This plant is poisonous if eaten.*

**Other Common Names**
Lenten Rose, Christmas Rose

**Bloom Period and Seasonal Color**
Late fall/early spring bloom in combinations of pale jade, near ivory, dusky purple, velvety plum, creamy peach, soft chartreuse.

Hardy to 8A

Min. Temp. See below

**Mature Height × Spread**
18 in. × 24 to 36 in.

**Minimum Temperature**
Depends on species.

# Jerusalem Sage

## Phlomis fruticosa

*Starting in spring, my perennial beds are filled with the tall tiers of golden yellow flowers belonging to Jerusalem sage. This tough, low water perennial comes not from Israel but from dry rocky cliffs in hot inland areas around the Mediterranean. Jerusalem sage is a shrubby evergreen with leaves 2 to 3 inches long. Leaves are soft felty gray-green on top, fuzzy white underneath and line upright branches that form mounds 3 to 4 feet tall and wide. Jerusalem sage flowers are shaped a bit like snapdragon flowers and arranged in golf-ball sized whorls. Plants reseed under ideal conditions but produce only a seedling or two each year—making them easy to dig up and move or share with a friend.*

**Bloom Period and Seasonal Color**
Spring/summer blooms, golden yellow.

**Mature Height × Spread**
4 ft. × 4 ft.

Hardy to 9A

Min. Temp. 20° F

### When, Where, and How to Plant
In warm winter gardens, plant spring through fall in full sun, following the directions in the Perennials introduction. In cold winter gardens, plant in fall. In hotter inland or desert areas, choose a site with part shade. Jerusalem sage tolerates most soils, poor or rich, but prefer soils with adequate drainage. Water well after planting and mulch thickly.

### Growing Tips
This low water plant likes regular water through the first summer and early fall to become established. After that, occasionally summer irrigation is all that is necessary, though plants will tolerate more frequent watering in well-draining soils. In hot desert or inland areas, water regularly through summer and minimally the rest of the year. No fertilizer is necessary, especially if you mulch well with composted organic matter. If you prefer to fertilize, do so lightly in early spring using a balanced organic fertilizer.

### Care
Groom to remove spent flowers and to promote ongoing bloom. After major bloom is over, cut plants back by a third to maintain their shape and promote flowering. Pests are no problem.

### Companion Planting and Design
Create a yellow, low water garden by combining Jerusalem sages with yellow and green striped variegated century plant (*Agave americana variegata*), the succulent leaves of yellow and green variegated *Aloe*, yellow blooming stonecrop, and the sunny yellow flowers of ground cover African Daisy 'Big Gold'. For color contrast, mix Jerusalem sage with a 'Rosenka' bougainvillea (pale pink and soft orange bracts) and burgundy leaved 'Shirazz' or 'Platt's Black' New Zealand flax.

### Try These
Purple phlomis (*Phlomis purpurea*) stands 4 to 6 inches × 4 to 6 inches and has pale purple flowers topping large, silvery, gray-green leaves with white undersides. Stems are lanky so plant in the middle of the garden bed and support with rockrose, lavender, and rosemary. Jerusalem Sage (*Phlomis lanata*) forms a 3-foot × 4-foot mound with small rounded leaves that are felty, olive green on golden stems.

# Kangaroo Paw
## *Anigozanthos* spp.

### When, Where, and How to Plant
Plants prefer full sun and well-drained soil. Fall through spring are the best times to plant. Follow directions in the Perennials introduction. In cooler areas, plant in a south-facing garden (for heat) or under the eaves (for protection). Space plants to accommodate their eventual width and to provide good air circulation. Water deeply after planting and mulch well.

### Growing Tips
Water deeply with drip irrigation once a week or so in spring and summer (more often in hot valley and desert gardens) and occasionally in dry winter. Plants do fine with no fertilizer but grow lush with a light application of balanced organic fertilizer in early spring.

### Care
At the end of the bloom season, cut spent flower stalks at the base. The fuzzy outer parts of the flowers irritate skin, so wear long sleeves and gloves. Remove dead leaves. Divide clumps every few years as flowers fade or tiny new fans appear in spring. Protect from snails and slugs (see "Tips and Techniques"). Watch for leaf blackening at the tips, which suggests black spot fungal disease caused by plants being too close together, without good air circulation, in too much shade, or damaged by pests. Treat with fungicide (ask at the nursery) or choose disease resistant varieties.

### Companion Planting and Design
Plant en masse for a really impressive show (purchase all at once and in bloom so you can be sure of their color). In addition to their wonderful flowers, kangaroo paw leaf fans make an excellent background for shorter plants in low water gardens. Combine with California natives or other Australian plants such as emu bush, grevillea, and cone bush. Cut flowers last long in arrangements.

### Try These
'Harmony' is 6 feet tall with iridescent yellow flowers on bright red stems; 'Pink Joey' is a 2- to 3-foot dwarf with pink flowers (some taller, pink flowering kangaroo paw are also sold as 'Pink Joey'); 'Gold Fever' has saffron orange flowers on 3- to 4-foot stems. The 'Bush Gem' series of kangaroo paw are particularly disease resistant.

These evergreen perennials form fans of long strappy green leaves. In spring, slender stems arise from the center of the fans, each topped with a cluster of fuzzy tubular flowers that resemble miniature kangaroo paws. Kangaroo paw hails from western Australia. Their brilliant flowers so inspired hybridizers that kangaroo paws are available in colors ranging from red to burgundy, saffron, pink, iridescent yellow, soft yellow, bright green, and almost fluorescent green. Often stems are one color and flowers are a contrasting color. Plants also come in different heights, from dwarfs (2 feet tall in bloom) to standard (6 feet tall in bloom). Kangaroo paw multiplies by a thick fleshy rhizome that creates new sets of fans.

### Bloom Period and Seasonal Color
Flower in shades of orange, red, burgundy, pink, soft yellow, gold, day-glo yellow, and fluorescent green. Usually kangaroo paw bloom starts in spring and ends in fall.

Hardy to 7A

Min. Temp. 2° F

### Mature Height × Spread
3 to 6 ft. × 2 ft. and multiplying
Dwarfs: 1 to 2 ft. × 1 to 2 ft.

# Matilija Poppy
## *Romneya coulteri*

*Matilija poppies are the giants of the poppy family. Each plant sends up multiple stalks, 8 feet tall and thicker than a finger, clothed in fringy blue-green leaves. Come late spring, the tip of every stalk develops marble to walnut-sized buds that erupt into crepe paper flowers as large as salad plates. The combination of white petals and the bright yellow center earns this plant the nickname "fried egg plant." Flowers start to open around the end of May and keep going into the summer—depending on your location and the weather. Once considered for state flower (and beat out by the California poppy), Matilija poppy is native to chaparral and coastal sage scrub habitats, primarily from Santa Barbara County south into Baja.*

**Other Common Name**
Fried Egg Plant

**Bloom Period and Seasonal Color**
Huge white flowers with yellow centers, late spring into summer.

**Mature Height × Spread**
8 ft. × 6 ft. or more

Hardy to 8B

Min. Temp. 15° F

### When, Where, and How to Plant
Plant in fall and winter and into full sun and well-draining soil. Plants tolerate—and spread slower in—clay soils. If surrounded with a root barrier, place it at least 6 feet out from the rootball so the plant can spread wide enough for a good show of flowers. The key to successful transplant is not disturbing the rootball during planting. For instructions on root barriers and planting with minimal root disturbance, see "Tips and Techniques."

### Growing Tips
Water deeply every week or so through the first summer to establish. Then turn off the tap to limit growth. No fertilizer is needed.

### Care
In warmer winters, stalks either remain green through winter dormancy or, as in colder climates, turn brown. Tops may be dead, but roots are fine. Either way cut stalks down to 3 to 4 inch stubs in fall. This is a big job and I'll admit to leaving mine uncut for a year or two with no noticeable loss of stems or flowers. Wear long sleeves and gloves to protect your skin from irritating plant hairs. This plant can be invasive. If you are an energetic gardener (and didn't install a root barrier at planting) cut the roots around the base of each plant yearly. Watch for sprouts a surprising distance from the mother plant. No significant pests.

### Companion Planting and Design
These beautiful plants spread by orange colored rhizomes that expand seemingly forever in well-draining soil, especially when well watered. This is not a plant for small spaces, but don't let its exuberant growth scare you away. Matilija poppies make a beautiful background for gold flowered perennial marigolds, coral flowering desert mallow, and the tiny blue blooms of ground cover germander sage. Add a succulent agave for leaf contrast.

### Try These
'White Cloud' has slightly smaller leaves and even more flowers than the species. Also look for Coast Matilija poppy (*Romneya trichocalyx*) that has a fuzzy calyx beneath the petals and slightly smaller leaves. It also may be a bit less aggressive.

# Mexican Bush Marigold
## *Tagetes lemmonii*

### When, Where, and How to Plant
Plant fall through spring in mild winter gardens and in spring in cold winter gardens. Site in full sun (part sun in hottest valley and desert gardens) and well-draining soil. Plants tolerate heavy and poor soils too. Follow planting directions in the Perennials introduction. Water deeply after planting and mulch.

### Growing Tips
Water well through the first summer or two so plants establish deep roots. Water deeply, but only occasionally (once every few weeks), in subsequent summers along the coast. In hotter gardens, you may need to water more regularly in summer.

### Care
To prevent marigold branches from becoming leggy, pinch tips back early in the growing season before flower buds develop. Remove spent flowers to extend bloom. After flowering, cut branches back by a third. Pests aren't a problem.

### Companion Planting and Design
Use Mexican bush marigold where you need a spot of color. Plant in a Mediterranean border along with rosemary, desert mallow, Matilija poppy, bay, and coral tree. Mix Mexican bush marigold with red-flowering pineapple sage, lemon grass, and edible oregano. Plant several as a low informal hedge or screen. The colorful flowers really stand out against a deep colored wall or evergreen background.

### Try These
'Low Huntington Form' (5 feet × 4 to 5 feet) is a compact selection. Mexican Tarragon (*Tagetes lucida*) forms mounds 2½ to 3 feet with late summer/early fall flowers that are more yellow than gold and are pretty, though less showy than Mexican bush marigold flowers. Try sprinkling them into salads. The tarragon/anise scented leaves are ferny and deep green. They can be used as a substitute for French tarragon or as a brew to make tea. Citrus Scented Marigold (*Tagetes nelsonii*) grows tall and narrow (8 feet × 3 feet). In fall, clusters of golden yellow marigold flowers top narrow and lanky branches lasting until frost. The finely cut leaves have a strong citrus fragrance when crushed or bruised. Lower branches root where they touch the ground.

If "marigold" makes you think of orange and yellow pompom flowers, then it is time to broaden your perspective. Annual marigolds are great in summer flower gardens, but for a long lasting and dynamic show, try perennial marigold Mexican bush marigold. Mexican bush marigold grows 3 to 6 feet tall with clusters of small (half-inch across) golden yellow flowers at branch tips. Flowering peaks in spring and fall. In milder gardens it continues on and off year-round, especially when faded flowers are removed promptly. Mexican bush marigold branches sprout from the base and are covered with wispy or feathery green leaves. Leaves release a strong citrus/mint fragrance when bruised or crushed. These natives of Arizona and Mexico are evergreen in warmer climates and deciduous in cooler climates.

### Other Common Name
Copper Canyon Daisy

### Bloom Period and Seasonal Color
Golden yellow flowers peak in fall, bloom on and off through the year in milder gardens

### Mature Height × Spread
3 to 6 ft. × 6 to 8 ft.

### Minimum Temperature
Perennial to 20 degrees F. Grown as an annual in cooler climates.

Hardy to 9A

Min. Temp. See below

# Mexican Tulip Poppy
*Hunnemannia fumariifolia*

There is a distinct familial resemblance between yellow flowered Mexican tulip poppy and the bright orange California poppy. Both have feathery blue-green foliage and both have cup-shaped flowers of four petals. Mexican tulip poppy, however, is the taller and larger of the two. It has broad flattened leaves that grow on plants reaching 2 to 3 feet tall and spreading out several feet. Yellow petals serve as a bright backdrop for a fringe of golden orange stamens in the center of each flower. In cold winter areas, this Mexican desert native is grown as an annual, much like California poppy. In warmer gardens, these low water poppies live from year to year, reseeding gently through the garden and filling empty spaces with bright spots of color.

## Bloom Period and Seasonal Color
Yellow flowers almost year round in mild coastal gardens, from spring into early fall in colder climates.

## Mature Height × Spread
2 to 3 ft. × 2 to 3 ft.

## Minimum Temperature
Perennial down to 15 degrees F; grown as an annual in colder climates.

**Hardy to 8B**

**Min. Temp.** See below

## When, Where, and How to Plant
Plant from seed in fall and in full sun (directions in "Tips and Techniques") or plant from 6-packs or 1-gallon pots (see directions in the Perennials introduction). Take care not to disturb the poppies' deep taproots. Often, transplanted poppies die at the end of their first season, but because they reseed freely, you will have a new crop the following spring.

## Growing Tips
Tulip poppies are drought tolerant and will survive on rainfall alone in most areas. In hot desert gardens, offer some supplemental water every few weeks in summer. No fertilizer is needed.

## Care
Groom to remove faded flowers and leaves. If plants get woody, cut back to a few inches aboveground after the seeds are all released in the fall. If seedlings pop up in areas where you don't want them (if such a location exists), gently dig them up when very young to move or share with another gardener. No significant pests bother this plant.

## Companion Planting and Design
Mexican tulip poppies are the perfect filler plants for low water gardens. Their spreading habit makes them best suited for informal gardens. For a yellow theme garden, plant Mexican tulip poppy beneath yellow-flowering palo verde or knife-leaf acacia. Add perennials Jerusalem sage, chartreuse flowering spurge (*Euphorbia rigida*), and succulent bulbine. For a twist, add the orange tones of bulbine 'Tiny Tangerine'. For more color contrast, plant Mexican tulip poppy next to grevillea, cone bush, Texas ranger, low water sages (especially blue and purple flowering species), burgundy-leaved New Zealand flax or smoke tree, succulent aloes, California lilac, and desert spoon.

## Try These
Horned poppies (*Glaucium flavum*) have deeply sculpted lacy blue-gray leaves in a rosette. In late spring or summer of their second year, horned poppies produce tall branching wands of golden yellow or apricot (my favorite) flowers. Blooms are replaced by curved horn-shaped seedpods that split to release their seeds and spread their beauty. These Mediterranean seashore natives prefer full sun, dry conditions, and well-draining soils.

# Purple Coneflower
## *Echinacea purpurea*

### When, Where, and How to Plant

Plant purple coneflower when the soil warms in spring. These plants can be started from seed (see "Tips and Techniques") but are easier and more reliable in our climate if transplanted from a nursery container (see the Perennials introduction for directions). Choose a spot in full sun with well-amended soil that drains well. Water deeply after planting, and mulch.

### Growing Tips

In California's spare rainfall climates, coneflowers do best if watered regularly from the time that leaves emerge in spring until they finish blooming in fall. In wetter northern parts of the state, they can get by with far less irrigation. Be patient. It may take a few years for plants to grow large enough for a significant show of flowers. Use all-purpose organic fertilizer in early spring.

### Care

Deadhead spent flowers early in the season to keep bloom going. Leave the last of the season's flowers so birds can eat the seeds. When leaves turn completely brown, cut plants back to the ground. Clumps slowly increase in size and can be divided if they get too large. Plants sometimes are infected with powdery mildew. For information on dividing plants and treating mildew, see "Tips and Techniques."

### Companion Planting and Design

Purple coneflower is a traditional choice for a cutting garden, perennial garden, or old-fashioned cottage garden. Mix with cape fuchsia, geraniums, breadseed poppies, and iris. Add Peruvian lily in different shades of pink or white. Plant against a background of bay, butterfly bush, or Arabian lilac.

### Try These

'Double Decker' has 5-inch rose pink flowers with a second set of petals atop the cone that make the flowers look like swirling dancers. 'Magnus' petals curve downward, away from the center. 'White Swan' is white flowered. New hybrids come in hot colors such as 'Sunrise', a yellow coneflower hybrid with 4- to 5-inch fragrant flowers, the orange/coral/pink blush tones of 'Katie Saul' ('Summer Sky'™), and shocking magenta pink (also fragrant) flowers of foot-tall 'Emily Saul' ('After Midnight'™).

*Purple coneflower is a traditional perennial with large rosy purple flowers from summer through fall. These winter-deciduous plants form thick roots. Deep green, textured leaves shaped like long tongues emerge from the roots, as do tall flower stalks topped in multiple daisy-like flowers typical of the sunflower family. Petals tend to curve back away from deep brown or coppery orange "cones" in the center. The cones are the reason for this plant's tongue twister of a botanical name, Echinacea. It comes from the Greek root echinos that means hedgehog. According to legend, the spiny round seedhead of purple coneflower reminded a long ago botanist of a spiny hedgehog. Purple coneflower is native to woods, prairies, and bushy thickets in central and eastern U.S.*

**Bloom Period and Seasonal Color**
Summer to fall blooms in shades of purple and rose-purple.

**Mature Height × Spread**
2 to 4 ft × 1 to 2 ft.

**Hardy to** 4A

**Min. Temp.** -30° F

# Red-hot Poker

## *Kniphofia* spp.

*From South Africa comes a group of evergreen drought tolerant lily relatives known as red-hot poker. These perennials have long relaxed green strappy leaves. Dwarf cultivars stand only 1 foot × 1 foot while standard varieties grow as big as 7 feet × 6 feet. The plants are named for the shape and color of their flowers. Their tall slender flower spikes rise above the foliage. At the tips are conical clusters of narrow tubular flowers, much like aloe flowers. Buds are typically soft red, bright orange, or coral, opening to pale yellow. They open in sequence from bottom to top forming a poker point. The effect is of a glowing red-hot fireplace poker, though it should be noted that some varieties of red-hot poker plants have all-yellow buds and flowers.*

### Other Common Name
Torch Flower

### Bloom Period and Seasonal Color
"Heads" are combinations of soft red, coral, bright to pale yellow, and salmon orange to bright orange. Blooms from summer through fall and some year-round in mild climates.

Hardy to 8A

Min. Temp. 10° F

### Mature Height × Spread
1 to 7 ft. × 1 to 6 ft. depending on species and hybrid

### When, Where, and How to Plant
Plant fall through spring in mild winter gardens and in spring in colder gardens. Site in well-draining soil and in full or part sun or even dry bright shade. Follow planting directions in the Perennials introduction. Water well after planting and mulch.

### Growing Tips
This plant is very drought tolerant once established, but summer water promotes flowers. Most red-hot pokers tolerate more frequent water in soil that drains well, but resent too much water in heavy soils. Little or no fertilizer is required.

### Care
Groom to remove dead leaves and flower stalks throughout the year. As plants multiply, they may outgrow their spot. Divide them in spring, following directions for plants with rhizomes in "Tips and Techniques." Protect from ants carrying aphids, as well as from snails and slugs (see "Tips and Techniques" for controls).

### Companion Planting and Design
The green grass-like foliage of red-hot poker fits into any style garden, while the colorful flowers lend themselves to tropical, Mediterranean, succulent, and desert gardens. For an especially interesting color presentation, surround red-hot pokers with paddle plant. This low-growing succulent has dense clusters of large round leaves in the same coral, orange, red, and yellow tones of red-hot poker flowers.

### Try These
'Shining Sceptre' (2 to 3 feet × 1 foot) has blue-green foliage and early to midsummer pale orange buds opening to yellow flowers. 'Christmas Cheer' (5 feet × 6 feet) has deep orange buds opening to yellow flowers from fall through spring or until frost. 'Little Maid' (1 foot × 1 foot) has greenish yellow buds opening to yellow flowers. *Kniphofia caulescens* (3 feet × 3 feet) has blue-green foliage and coral-orange buds opening yellow from late summer through fall. *Kniphofia citrina* (3 feet × 3 feet) has pale yellow flowers. *Kniphofia galpinii* 'Orange Flame' (1 to 2 feet × 1 to 2 feet) has bright orange spring/summer buds opening to yellow-orange. Giant poker (*Kniphofia northiae*) (2 to 4 feet × 2 to 4 feet) has reddish spring flower buds opening pale yellow.

# Sage
## *Salvia* spp.

### When, Where, and How to Plant
Plant fall through spring in frost-free gardens and in spring in colder winter areas. Provide full sun and well-drained soils, though some species tolerate heavy soils. Follow planting directions in the Perennials introduction. Allow enough room for plants to reach their full size. Water deeply and mulch heavily after planting. Sages are excellent container plants.

### Growing Tips
Native and South African sages are typically drought tolerant. Sages from more temperate or tropical climates need occasional to frequent deep watering. Those that prefer more water also like an occasional dose of organic fertilizer in spring. Follow label directions for fertilizing perennials.

### Care
Prune according to growth form. For sages that form upright branches from a single point, prune once new growth appears near the branch base after blooms fade. Cut back to 12 or 18 inches, leaving the new growth intact. Sages that spread by underground runners such as the Mexican bush sage can be cut to the ground after flowers fade. Groom rosette-forming sages by removing spent leaves and flowers. Sages are delightfully pest free.

### Companion Planting and Design
Plant in all style gardens. Drought tolerant sages are perfect for Mediterranean and desert gardens. More water-loving sages fit right into traditional perennial beds, cutting gardens, and even herb gardens.

### Try These
'Waverly' (3 feet × 3 feet) has wands of rose-blush white flowers from summer into fall and prefers sun to part shade (hardy to 20 degrees F). Anise-scented sage (*Salvia guaranitica*) 'Black and Blue' (5 feet × 5 feet) has blue-violet flowers much of the year with chartreuse foliage (hardy to 20 degrees F). Water weekly. Mexican bush sage (*Salvia leucantha*) (4 feet × 4 feet or wider) combines velvety white petals with bright purple calyces in spring/fall. Green leaves are flocked white beneath. It is drought tolerant. 'Midnight' has purple petals in a purple calyx. 'Santa Barbara' is only 2 feet × 3 feet (hardy to 15 degrees F). Pineapple sage (*Salvia elegans*) blooms scarlet-red in late summer/fall and crushed leaves smell like pineapple.

To some folks, sage is an herb for turkey stuffing. But to gardeners, sage is a huge group of plants in the genus *Salvia*. Perennial sages come from deserts, coastlines, mountains, and valleys around the world, including California. They can be tiny or tall with leaves that are bright green, dark green, silver, or blue-gray. Some sage leaves are smooth, others corrugated or fuzzy from 1/4 inch to 6 inches across, on plants with upright, spreading, and low growing branches, and even a few rosette forms. Flowers come in every color of the rainbow, and some are multicolored. All sages are square-stemmed in cross-section and tipped in whorls of tubular two-lipped flowers that look like mini-snapdragons. Plant sages for year-round bloom and for year-round hummingbirds.

### Bloom Period and Seasonal Color
Flowers in every color of the rainbow and some multicolored blooming in different seasons, depending on the species.

### Mature Height × Spread
1 to 8 ft. × 1 to 8 ft., depending on species

### Minimum Temperature
Varies depending on species.

139

# South African Geranium
## *Pelargonium sidoides* 'Burgundy'

*South African geranium is a low growing, perennial ever-green with small velvet-burgundy flowers. These delicate looking blooms appear in clusters of six or more on stalks held several inches above mounds of heart-shaped blue-green leaves. Leaves are velvety and crenulated with edges that curl slightly to reveal silvery undersides. The color and texture of the leaves contrast with the flowers for an absolutely beautiful plant suitable for borders or contain-ers. As an added bonus, this geranium requires very little water, making it the perfect plant for our Mediterranean climate. In its native grassland, South African geranium dies back and goes dormant to survive the hot months of summer. Here it stays evergreen. This plant is often sold simply as* Pelargonium sidoides.

**Other Common Name**
Kalwerbossie Geranium

**Bloom Period and
Seasonal Color**
Velvet burgundy flowers much of
the year.

**Mature Height × Spread**
12 in. × 12 in.

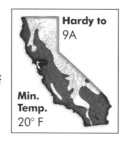

Hardy to
9A

Min.
Temp.
20° F

### When, Where, and How to Plant
Plant fall through spring in full sun and well-drain-ing soil. Follow planting directions in the Peren-nials introduction. Water well and mulch after planting. In cooler winter gardens, grow as a con-tainer plant and move to a protected spot for winter.

### Growing Tips
Provide occasional deep watering from spring to fall and if there is a long dry spell in winter. Keep plants mulched. Only potted South African geranium needs fertilizer. Use a balanced organic fertilizer.

### Care
Over time these geraniums can become leggy. In November or December, cut stems back to within a few inches of the ground. Winter rains will bring a new growth cycle. Set cuttings into a moist potting mix and you'll soon have more lovely geraniums (for more details, see directions for propagating perennials in "Tips and Techniques"). No pests bother this plant.

### Companion Planting and Design
Mass South African geraniums for a long border edging or grow as a single tuft of leaves and flowers in any sunny flower bed. Alternatively, plant along the edge of a large pot and let the geranium cascade over the side. In a low water perennial bed, com-bine with Mexican bush sage so purple wands wave above burgundy flowers. Add tall grasses such as the blue-green leaved 'Fairy Tales' fountain grass.

### Try These
The species *Pelargonium sidoides* is not as floriferous as 'Burgundy', but its flowers are nearly as black and are fragrant in the early evening. Heartleaf geranium (*Pelargonium cordifolium*) is shrubby, (4 feet × 3 feet) with soft green, heart-shaped leaves. Spring through fall flowers are large and pink. It is drought tolerant (hardy to 25 degrees F). Kidney-leaf geranium (*Pelargonium reniforme*) (10 inches × 12 inches) has bright magenta-pink petals that have ruby markings. Angel face pelargoniums are 15- to 24-inch mounding hybrids with large rounded flowers in spring through fall. Their two-color petals can be twisted or ruffled. They prefer part sun or part shade in hotter inland and desert gar-dens (hardy to 30 degrees F). 'The Tamar' has lilac pink petals with upper petals splashed with maroon.

# Spurge
## *Euphorbia* spp.

### When, Where, and How to Plant
Plant fall through spring in frost-free gardens and in spring in colder winter gardens. Choose a spot in full sun and in well-drained soil. Follow planting directions in the Perennials introduction. Water well and mulch after planting.

### Growing Tips
Water these very drought tolerant plants regularly the first summer and only occasionally in summer after that. In coastal gardens, spurges often reseed into dry areas of the garden and do just fine. In hotter gardens, some deep water in the growing season produces more flowers. No fertilizer is needed.

### Care
After flowers fade, seedpods shoot their seeds into the air with a loud "pop!" If you start with just a few plants, you'll soon have a patch. Pull up unwanted seedlings to share. Remove spent flowers and stems before winter. New stems will sprout from the base. Some types of spurges face significant pest problems, but the ones listed below are generally pest free.

### Companion Planting and Design
Spurge fits succulent gardens of aloes, agave, dragon tree, Mexican grass tree, blue chalk sticks, and red yucca. In a perennial bed, plant with purple flowering sages, tall verbena, African geranium, and pink or orange flowered African daisy. Use spurges to edge the beds, mix them into beds, or use them to fill empty spaces throughout the beds. Use these same plants with other spurges in large container plantings.

### Try These
'Tasmanian Tiger' (3 feet × 3 feet) has green and cream variegated leaves and flowers. *Euphorbia characias* ssp. *wulfenii* (3 to 4 feet × 3 to 4 feet) has blue-green foliage and chartreuse flower clusters. *Euphorbia griffithii* 'Fireglow' (3 feet × 2 feet) has deep blue-green leaves with burnished orange stems and bright orange bracts. *Euphorbia myrsinites* (6 inches. × 24 inches) flowers chartreuse with red and yellow centers, and its geometric leaves are silvery blue-green. *Euphorbia pithyusa* 'Faded Jeans' (6 to 14 inches × 6 to 14 inches) has finely textured ice-green leaves and minute silver/olive flowers. Gopher plant (*Euphorbia rigida*) has chartreuse flowers. It does NOT repel gophers.

*Spurge is a terrific plant with a dreadful name. There are more than 2,000 kinds of spurges. Many are clumping perennials grown as ground covers and small shrubs. In mild climate gardens, spurges serve as a flower bridge linking winter gardens to spring gardens. Flowers open in late winter, typically in bright chartreuse. By the time spring arrives, spurges are winding down, though some last into early summer. Look closely at spurge flower to see that outer bracts, not petals, are the showy parts. Spurge has upright or trailing succulent stems clothed in deep green, burgundy, or blue-green foliage that adds texture and contrast to the garden. Protect your skin and eyes from irritating and toxic milky sap.*

**Other Common Name**
Gopher Plant

**Bloom Period and Seasonal Color**
Showy chartreuse bracts that sometimes have a bright orange caste and/or tiny red, green, or burgundy flowers in the center. Blooms late winter to summer.

Hardy to 8A

Min. Temp. 10 to 15° F

**Mature Height × Spread**
1/2 to 4 ft. × 1 to 5 ft., depending on species and variety.

**Minimum Temperature**
Depends on variety.

# Sticky Monkey Flower
## *Mimulus aurantiacus*

*Monkey flower is one of our best and easiest to grow flowering natives. Of the several species and numerous varieties of monkey flower, the most widespread is sticky monkey flower. Sticky monkey flower grows throughout the state on sunny hillsides, canyons, slopes, in the chaparral, and in forests. This 2- to 3-foot-tall and wide perennial is a fast grower with sticky narrow green leaves and in undisturbed areas, it has large creamy yellow-orange, five-petal flowers pollinated by insects. Interestingly, in areas where humans have significant impact on the environment, the same monkey flowers produce smaller red flowers pollinated by hummingbirds. Though monkey flower plants are not long lived, their variety, their beauty, and their profuse flowering with almost no water or care make them ideal garden plants.*

**Other Common Name**
Bush Monkey Flower

**Bloom Period and Seasonal Color**
Spring through summer, sometimes fall

**Mature Height × Spread**
1 to 3 ft. × 2 to 4 ft.

Hardy to 8B

Min. Temp. 15° F

### When, Where, and How to Plant
Monkey flower is a good choice for coast, inland valley, foothills, and low elevation mountain gardens. Plant fall through spring in frost-free gardens and in spring in colder areas. Monkey flowers take sun, part sun, or part shade, and tolerate many soils as long as water is limited. Follow planting directions in the Perennials introduction. Water deeply and mulch after planting.

### Growing Tips
Deep water occasionally through the first spring/summer to establish. Stop watering when branches turn brown in summer. Once established, monkey flower survives on rainfall alone, especially in mild coastal and cool northern gardens. In hotter climates, provide an occasional deep drink in summer. Individual monkey flower plants last only a few years.

### Care
Pinch branch tips to keep plants bushy. In the hottest summer months, plants may turn brown and go dormant. Cut back the soft wood but not the harder wood of the branches. They will resprout in fall. To make new monkey flowers, weigh a few branches down with rocks. They will root where nodes touch the ground. Once they are well rooted, sever the connecting branches from the mother plant. Good air circulation prevents fungal diseases. Watch for aphids (see "Tips and Techniques" for treatments).

### Companion Planting and Design
Combine monkey flower with California poppy, native sages, native fescue, and flannel bush. Add monkey flower to a dry Mediterranean garden with grevillea, winter cassia, sunrose, and rockrose. To stem erosion on a slope, plant monkey flower with California fuchsia, California lilac, and manzanita.

### Try These
'Apricot' (3 to 4 feet tall) has soft apricot color flowers. *Mimulus* 'Ruby Silver' (2 feet × 2 feet) has many deep ruby flowers. 'Trish' (1 to 2 feet × 1 to 2 feet) has soft pink blooms with yellow throats. 'Jack' (1 to 2 feet × 1 to 2 feet) has deep burgundy flowers. Orangey azalea-like flowers of monkey flower (*Mimulus bifidus*) are the largest monkey flowers.

## When, Where, and How to Plant

Plant fall through spring in mild climate gardens and in spring in colder winter gardens. Tall verbena tolerates well-amended to poor soils. It does best where soils drain well but tolerates heavier soils if not overwatered. Space plants 18 to 24 inches apart. Follow planting directions in the Perennials introduction. Water well and mulch.

## Growing Tips

Irrigate occasionally through the first spring through fall to establish. In my garden, tall verbena reseeds freely. With winter rains, seeds sprout in unirrigated decomposed granite walkways and in sandy spots in cracks between pavers. These dry-grown plants are slightly shorter but grow as quickly and flower as well as those in irrigated flower beds. Fertilize with all-purpose organic fertilizer in early spring or mulch with compost.

## Care

Flower stems die back by the end of summer in hot gardens. After dried seedheads release their seeds, cut stems back to the base and they will resprout. Leave plenty of room for air to circulate between plants to prevent powdery mildew.

## Companion Planting and Design

The narrow upright wands of tall verbena make an open, wispy, vertical element that enhances any garden bed. Create a purple butterfly garden bed by planting tall verbena with lavender, bat-faced cuphea, 'New Sensation' cape fuchsia, butterfly vine, butterfly bush, and Arabian lilac. Add silver-leaved curry plant for contrast. Near patios and walkways, plant tall verbena a few feet into the flowerbed since dried seedheads and leaves are scratchy.

## Try These

Lilac verbena (*Verbena lilacina*) is a 2- to 3-feet × 3- to 6-feet loosely mounding verbena with lacy bright green leaves covered in fragrant pale lilac flower heads from spring through fall. Like tall verbena, this one tolerates sun or part sun and regular to little irrigation. Where summers get very hot, this verbena goes dormant to avoid the heat but pops back up in fall. Butterflies love it. Selection 'De la Mina' from Cedros Island off the coast of Baja has deep lilac flowers (hardy to 20 degrees F).

Take a walk through the bedding plant section of your local nursery and you'll see many low-growing verbenas in brilliant red, purple, bright white, and deep burgundy. Those plants are great fillers, but for my money, I prefer a different verbena, one that looks like a verbena on stilts. Tall verbena is exactly that, a perennial verbena with 3- to 6-foot upright and open flowering stems. Stems are very angular (examine them in cross section and you'll see that they are square). Small deep green leaves with serrated edges run the length of the stems. Topping each one is a 2- to 3-inch-round cluster of tiny lilac verbena flowers. Together the flowers and stems look like tall wands in the garden. Also sold as Verbena patagonica.

**Other Common Name**
Purple Top Verbena

**Bloom Period and Seasonal Color**
Lilac colored flowers, spring to fall.

**Mature Height × Spread**
3 to 6 ft. × 2 ft.

**Minimum Temperature**
Annual in colder areas.

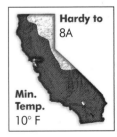

Hardy to 8A

Min. Temp. 10° F

# Shrubs *for California*

Indian mallow

Shrubs contribute width and substance to the garden. Shade tolerant shrubs planted beneath tall trees make the "walls" of the garden. Sun-loving shrubs serve as the taller elements in flower borders. They can stand alone as specimens or work in combination with other shrubs in the foreground or background of any garden.

This chapter covers nearly 180 species and varieties of shrubs suited for California gardens. They range from 2 to 30 feet tall, most are evergreen, and all flower, though some are grown more for foliage than for flowers. Additional shrubs are scattered through other chapters of this book. Some are included in the Herbs chapter (such as rosemary), the Ground Covers chapter (such as sunrose), and Fruits chapter (such as blueberry).

If you find that confusing, keep in mind that humans, not nature, divide plants into familiar categories of perennials, shrubs, trees, and herbs. These terms create a common vocabulary for describing the world around us. When we encounter plants that don't fit nicely into a category or fit into several categories, it can be hard to know what to do with them.

The prototypical shrub stands 4 to 8 feet tall with a woody upright trunk that supports woody side branches. While technically perennials (meaning they live for several years), it is the woody stems that distinguish shrubs from soft-stemmed herbaceous perennials. Still there are perennials that develop wood to some degree and shrubs with trunks and branches that are fairly soft. The dividing line is not so clear.

The distinction between shrubs and trees is fuzzy as well. We would all agree that a woody plant 50 feet tall with a single trunk is a tree, but what about one that grows 18 feet tall with branches lining the entire length of the trunk? Is it a shrub? If you prune off the lower branches, is it a tree? What about woody-stemmed plants that grow a foot tall and spread many feet horizontally—are they shrubs or are they ground covers? They can be both.

## Mediterranean Climate Shrubs

Terminology aside, the focus of this chapter is Mediterranean climate shrubs, including many of the most garden-worthy plants from California's chaparral, scrub, woodland, mountain, and riparian habitats. Several other entries hail from the southwest deserts and adapt very well to garden conditions. All of these shrubs are low water, low maintenance, and very beautiful.

Each plant description includes design ideas and/or plant combinations for your garden. While California gardeners use shrubs to divide spaces, we seldom plant formal shrubbery hedges so typical in East Coast and European gardens. Perhaps it is our informal lifestyle, or maybe it has to do with the fact that few gardens are large enough to accommodate such massive hedges. Either way, we are more likely to mix evergreen shrubs to create naturalistic green screens that hide unsightly views, create intimate spaces, and even muffle street noise.

While tall shrub screens create privacy, shorter ones suggest divisions without blocking the view. Plants with open "see-through" foliage suggest separate spaces—but don't draw a hard line. In fact, designed strategically, this kind of screen enhances a view rather than blocking it.

Massed shrub plantings make a wonderful green backdrop for a bounty of brightly flowering perennials, annuals, and roses. Roses are the focal point when they are in bloom, but out of bloom they

Bush anemone

www.digplantgrow.com

Angel's trumpet decorates a wall

are most unattractive. Planted against a background of evergreen shrubs and surrounded with flowering perennials and ornamental grasses, they become part of a bed that looks great year-round.

The best informal evergreen hedges include shrubs of different heights that bloom in different seasons. Don't line them up like soldiers; create staggered layers instead. Shorter shrubs go towards the front and taller ones to the rear. Space them so that the branches touch but don't overlap; that will greatly reduce the need to prune them. Be sure to choose shrubs that like the same amounts of water and sun.

## Varied Choices and Uses

Consider leaf texture as you consider combinations. Try broad-leaved evergreens, such as camellias, behind or beside sculpted-leaved flowering maples. Pay attention to flower color as well. In my early spring garden, a deep blue flowering California lilac blooms simultaneously with a golden orange flowering flannel bush. The two have grown too intertwined to distinguish between them, but that is no problem. When they bloom, they are a gorgeous combination.

I am especially enamored of the many Australian shrubs that have come into the marketplace in the last several years. Not only are they from climates and soils similar to ours, they have the most interesting foliage and flowers. Grevilleas in particular range from ground cover to tree size with foliage that can be feathery and needle-like to broad and finely cut. Leaves are gray, green, or silver.

The foliage, together with sizeable clusters of tiny, curled, and colorful flowers (much fought over by humming-birds), are fantastic in cut-flower arrangements.

California flannel bush

The flower bed is another place for shrubs. Plant hebe and other small-profile shrubs to support more lax-branched plants such as Peruvian lily, Canary Island sage, cape fuchsia, and bush anemone. Spotted emu bush flowers nearly as profusely as any of the perennials in the garden and mixes well with them too. Surround honey bush with burgundy-flowered South African geranium and a pink flowering kangaroo paw.

When it comes to growing shrubs in containers, smaller and slower growing shrubs are your best choice, though most, if not all, of these shrubs grow fine in containers for at least several years.

Plant shrubs as you do trees (see Trees introduction) though there is no need to stake them. For more information on planting shrubs, see "Tips and Techniques."

# Angel's Trumpet
## *Brugmansia* spp.

Angel's trumpet is a plant of heavenly beauty and fragrance. These tall tender shrubs produce long green leaves and trumpet-shaped flowers that hang elegantly from branches summer through fall. The trumpets are huge, 6 to 10 inches long and flaring 6 inches across at the mouth; blooms come in shades of white to fiery orange with yellow veins. At sunset they release their sweet musky perfume. These Andean natives are thirsty, vigorous growers with soft stems up to 15 feet tall and wide, but easily pruned to single or multi-trunked "trees." Because of their mountain origins, they appreciate the cool nights that typify much of California, especially in our coastal gardens. Leaves drop briefly at temperatures below freezing. It is excellent for growing as a potted plant.

**Bloom Period and Seasonal Color**
Summer into fall blooms in white to apricot, yellow, soft pink, coral or fiery orange, some deepen in color as they age.

Hardy to 9B

Min. Temp. 25° F

**Mature Height × Spread**
8 ft. to 15 ft. × 8 ft. to 15 ft.

**Minimum Temperature**
Loses leaves below 32 degrees F.

### When, Where, and How to Plant
Plant when soil is warm from spring and into late summer. Provide full sun along the coast and bright shade in hot valley and low desert gardens. Well-draining and heavily amended soils promote best growth. Follow shrub-planting directions in "Tips and Techniques." Water deeply after planting and mulch. To grow in a container, choose a pot that is at least 18 inches × 18 inches.

### Growing Tips
These are thirsty plants best grown in the garden bed that gets the most frequent water. While more drought tolerant plants require moist or damp soil only through the first year or two, angel's trumpet requires moist soil throughout its life. Pay special attention to potted angel's trumpet. Droopy leaves are a cry for a drink. Fertilize regularly with higher nitrogen organic fertilizer, rabbit manure (fresh), or composted chicken manure. **Note:** All parts are poisonous if ingested.

### Care
Remove dead and weak growth after flowering each year. Reduce stems to one or three for a tree or umbrella shape and then prune off lower branches to force top growth. Keep sprouts from regrowing along lower branches. Watch for aphids, mealybug, scale, and whitefly (see "Tips and Technique" for treatments).

### Companion Planting and Design
Plant angel's trumpet outside a window and allow it to perfume your home. For a tropical effect, combine with palms, sugar cane, flowering maple, pineapple lily, and banana—all plants on the high water side.

### Try These
'Betty Marshall' has single white flowers. 'Charles Grimaldi' has single flowers in pastel yellow or gold. 'Frosty Pink' has extra-wide flowers in salmon pink that darkens with age. 'Miner's Claim' has variegated cream and green leaves with cream flowers that age to pink. *Brugmansia* × *candida* 'Double White' has a white, double ruffled trumpet. *Brugmansia sanguinea* 'Inca Queen' has long, narrow-fluted flowers in bright orange-red with yellow veins and throat. It is the most cold hardy (down to 20 degrees F) and prefers full sun along the coast and light shade elsewhere.

# Anisodontea

## *Anisodontea × hypomandarum*

### When, Where, and How to Plant

Anisodontea thrive from coast to desert. Plant fall to spring in mild winter gardens and in spring and summer in cold winter gardens. Provide full sun along the coast, some shade in hot inland gardens, and well-drained soil. Allow enough room to accommodate the shrub's full size. Follow planting directions in "Tips and Techniques." Water well after planting and mulch. Or grow in a container. Mulch and water until water runs out the bottom of the container.

### Growing Tips

Anisodontea is drought tolerant enough to survive once it is established with just a few deep waterings through summer. Water more often in the desert. In all gardens, more frequent irrigation encourages lusher growth. Fertilize with organic formulation early in spring if desired. Mulched plants need no fertilizer.

### Care

Pruning is not necessary but can be done to shape shrubs. To keep plants full and compact, cut back by a third each fall. Aphids and whiteflies can be a problem (see "Tips and Techniques").

### Companion Planting and Design

Anisodontea are some of the brighter flowering, dry growing shrubs. Use smaller varieties to edge borders or as low hedges. Grow in perennial beds with lavenders, rosemary, and yellow-flowering perennial marigold. Use larger varieties as screens, hedges, and background plants. Interplant anisodontea with pineapple guava for an attractive, informal evergreen hedge.

### Try These

'Blushing Lady' has pale pink flowers with a deep pink flare at the base of each petal (2 feet × 2 feet). 'Elegant Lady' has magenta pink flowers (5 to 6 feet × 4 to 5 feet). Bushy 'Tara's Pink' (8 feet × 6 feet) has beautiful pink flowers and is drought tolerant. 'Tara's Wonder' (5 feet tall) has darker, softer green leaves and pink flowers with a deep rose center. Both 'Tara' varieties tolerate temperatures into the high teens. *Anisodontea julii* (6 feet × 6 feet) has deep pink flowers and large velvety leaves. False mallow (*Anisodontea scabrosa*) is an upright 4-foot shrub with sticky stems, dark green leaves, and pale pink flowers.

*My first anisodontea grew quickly to 6 feet tall and wide, obscuring an ugly wooden fence in a dry area of my garden. Petite pink hibiscus-type flowers, 2 inches across, covered the branches every day of the year. When the bush died, it left behind seedlings that quickly filled its spot. Some grew taller than the mother plant and some shorter, but all were equally flowery and colorful. Today there are several varieties of these low water evergreens available to home gardeners. Their deep green, three-lobed leaves are edged in rounded teeth. Flowers come in different shades of pink with deep colored lines that run the length of each petal. In their native South Africa, those pink lines act like arrows, pointing insect pollinators to the flowers' sweet nectar.*

**Other Common Name**
Cape Mallow

**Bloom Period and Seasonal Color**
Pink flowers year-round in mild winter areas, spring to fall elsewhere.

**Mature Height × Spread**
2 ft. to 6 ft. × 2 ft. to 6 ft.

**Minimum Temperature**
Depends on variety.

Hardy to 8B

Min. Temp. 15 to 28° F

# Arabian Lilac
*Vitex trifolia* 'Purpurea'

*Arabian lilac is one of my top ten favorite shrubs. It has graceful open branches and wonderfully colorful foliage. This smaller cousin to the chaste tree has 3- to 4-inch oblong leaves that are olive-green on top and a most unexpected dusky lilac-purple beneath. Some of the fragrant leaves are divided into three leaflets; all are gently creased along the midrib, as if to show off the colorful undersides. In late summer or early fall, branch tips develop 8-inch spikes of tubular purple flowers. While the flowers are beautiful, it is the leaves that put on the bigger show. In warmer gardens, these shrubs are evergreen. In colder winter areas, Arabian lilacs loose their leaves briefly during the coldest months.*

**Other Common Name**
Purple Lilac

**Bloom Period and Seasonal Color**
Purple leaves year-round and purple flower clusters in summer and fall.

**Mature Height × Spread**
6 to 8 ft. × 6 to 8 ft.

Hardy to 9A

Min. Temp. 20° F

### When, Where, and How to Plant
Plant from fall through spring in warm winter climates. In areas where overnight winter temperatures often dip below freezing, wait until spring. Arabian lilac is adaptable to low water gardens in most California gardening climates, including dry valley and desert gardens. Plant in full or part sun and in well-draining soil. Follow planting directions in "Tips and Techniques." Water well after planting, and mulch. If growing in a container, use one large enough to accommodate the ultimate size.

### Growing Tips
In year one, water regularly and deeply from the time soil dries in spring to the arrival of winter rains. Starting in year two, water only occasionally, but deeply, in summer. Fertilize with a balanced organic fertilizer before new growth starts in early spring.

### Care
Arabian lilac's natural shape is open and rounded. Enjoy the shape or prune off lower branches to reveal graceful stems. If you choose to prune, do so after fall bloom or in early spring. No significant pests bother this plant.

### Companion Planting and Design
Arabian lilac adds important year-round color to the backbone of the garden, especially during seasonal transitions when no flowers are in bloom. If you can, place Arabian lilac in a spot where its leaves are in clear view. The best-placed specimen I have ever seen was planted alongside a garden stairway at the Kimberly-Clark House and Garden in Redlands, California. A single specimen was sited part way up the slope, so everyone ascending the stairs would view the undersides of the foliage. Planted en mass, these shrubs make an excellent hedge. They are also great foliage plants for containers. Create a Mediterranean patio garden with potted Arabian lilac, lemon, rosemary, and tall pittosporum.

### Try This
Arabian lilac 'Variegata' (10 feet × 8 to 12 feet) has blue flowers and gray-green leaves with creamy white edges and soft gray fuzz on the undersides. Grow it as a large shrub or small tree.

# Baja Fairy Duster
## *Calliandra californica*

### When, Where, and How to Plant
Plant fall through spring in frost-free gardens and in spring in colder gardens. Plant into well-draining soil and in full sun (part sun in hot inland or desert gardens). Baja fairy duster tolerates clay as long as you water sparingly. Follow shrub-planting directions in "Tips and Techniques." Water deeply after planting and mulch.

### Growing Tips
To establish deep roots, water deeply (but infrequently) through the first two years, from the time soil dries in spring until winter rains arrive. After that, water only in summer months, monthly in milder climates, and twice monthly in hot desert or inland areas. If plants look stressed, increase water frequency. No fertilizer is needed.

### Care
Deadhead fading flowers to promote longer bloom. Prune to trim off weak or damaged wood in fall. Prune lightly to shape if desired. Pests are not a problem.

### Companion Planting and Design
This beautiful and colorful plant is perfect as an entryway specimen, foundation, or patio plant. Mass plant fairy duster to create an informal screen or hedge. Combine with red yucca, aloe, and ornamental grasses for a spectacular dry border. A Baja fairy duster next to a giant variegated century plant is the perfect complement for Tuscan, Mission Revival, and Spanish Colonial architecture. Fairy duster's bright red flowers and bright green foliage also fit in a dry tropical landscape when planted with dry growing palms such as triangle palm or Guadalupe palm.

### Try These
'Maricopa Red' is a variety of Baja fairy duster with especially bright red flowers. Fairy duster (*Calliandra eriophylla*) is a California native with gray-green leaves and pink flowers almost year-round. Its overall structure is a bit daintier than its red cousin's and flowers are wispier. (1 to 3 feet × 3 to 4 feet). The leaves drop briefly (hardy to 5 degrees F). *Calliandra* 'Sierra Star'™ is a cross between fairy duster and Baja fairy duster. Its overall structure is a bit denser than its parents'. Flowers are the color of maraschino cherries (4 to 5 feet × 4 to 5 feet).

*Baja fairy duster is a large, stunning evergreen shrub covered in bright, crimson-red, ping-pong-ball sized powder puff flowers. The flowers develop at the tips of branches and appear to float over lacy, bright green, fern-like leaves that fold closed each evening. The red flowers (actually colorful stamens rather than petals) are magnets for hummingbirds that fight over them. Baja fairy duster is native to sandy washes and hillsides in Baja but grows well in drier gardens as well. Flowering starts in early spring and, with some supplemental water, lasts through summer and into fall. As is typical of plants in the legume family, fairy duster fruits are shaped like pea pods (don't eat them). Plants sometimes reseed but are not a problem.*

**Other Common Name**
Red Fairy Duster

**Bloom Period and Seasonal Color**
Bright red (sometimes purple or plum) flowers year-round, peaking in spring.

**Mature Height × Spread**
3 to 6 ft. × 4 to 8 ft.

Hardy to 9A

Min. Temp. 20 to 25° F

# Blue Hibiscus
*Alyogyne huegelii*

*Imagine a hibiscus with a lilac-colored flower. Now add deeply lobed, olive-green leaves that resemble scented geranium leaves. You've pictured the drought tolerant blue hibiscus of Australia. In the garden, blue hibiscus is an upright, evergreen shrub that quickly reaches 9 to10 feet tall and about half as wide. Much of the year the shrub is covered in large five-petal flowers with a crepe papery texture typical of the mallow family. Some are lilac and others deep purple. Occasionally one finds pink or deep magenta flowering individuals, and there is even a white variety. Like thirsty tropical hibiscus, blue hibiscus flowers have yellow centers. These shrubs are extremely versatile and easy to grow. Each plant is relatively short-lived, but the great flowers make them worth replacing again and again.*

**Bloom Period and Seasonal Color**
Lilac to deep purple flowers (occasionally pink, magenta, or white) most of the year.

**Mature Height × Spread**
8 to 10 ft. × 4 ft. to 5 ft.

Hardy to 9B

Min. Temp. 25° F

## When, Where, and How to Plant
Plant fall through spring in warm winter gardens and in spring in gardens that frequently dip below freezing in winter. Choose a spot in full or part sun and in well-drained soil or heavy soils. Follow planting directions in "Tips and Techniques." Water deeply after planting, and mulch.

## Growing Tips
Deep water weekly for the first two or three weeks and then monthly until winter rains. In subsequent years, start watering when soil dries in late spring and then water deeply each month. More water brings more flowers and lusher growth—to a point. Always let the soil dry between waterings. Since most Australian plants come from areas where soils have even less nutrients than ours, they don't need fertilizer.

## Care
Prune often to shape and to promote bushiness and more prolific flowers. Left unpruned for a long time, branches tend to lose some of their lower leaves and get lanky. Avoid overwatering to prevent root rot and deadly soil fungi. Watch for scale and aphids (see "Tips and Techniques").

## Companion Planting and Design
In cooler gardens, site blue hibiscus against a south- or west-facing wall. These evergreens can fill a spot where you need a narrower upright shrub, a flowering evergreen screen, a foundation plant, or a specimen plant. Mix blue hibiscus with yellow flowering plants such as Mexican marigold and any of the ground covers such as sundrops, honey bells, or raspberry flowered sunroses. Pink or white flowering shrubby rockroses are a good complement as well. Add a granite bottlebrush tree, a few white flowering succulent stonecrop and your full sun, low water flower bed is complete.

## Try These
'Monterey Bay' has violet-blue flowers. 'Mood Indigo' has the deepest violet-blue flowers. 'Santa Cruz' has light purple flowers. 'Swan River' has medium purple-blue flowers. 'White Swan' has white flowers with a lilac tinge. Somewhat rarer, red-centered hibiscus (*Alyogyne hakeifolia*) has red centered flowers, narrow needle-like leaves, and a more graceful appearance. Flowers are in shades of yellow or purple 6 to 8 feet tall and almost as wide.

# Bush Anemone
## *Carpenteria californica*

### When, Where, and How to Plant

Plants tolerate most soils, but prefer well-draining soils. These shrubs do fine in both low-water gardens and those watered regularly, as long as the soil drains well. In coastal or mild summer gardens, plant in full sun and provide more shade in hot inland gardens. See "Tips and Techniques" regarding planting natives. Water deeply and mulch.

### Growing Tips

For the first two years, water bush anemone deeply and regularly from the time soil dries in spring until winter rains. After that plants should be established enough to survive with only occasional summer water—a bit more in hot inland areas. Feed lightly with organic fertilizer if desired.

### Care

Groom occasionally to remove dead leaves. Once the annual bloom is over, you can cut the bush back by 1/3 to 1/2 its size to stimulate new growth and a strong shape. Watch for aphids, ants, and scale (see "Tips and Techniques").

### Companion Planting and Design

Bush anemone is the perfect specimen plant for any garden, native or exotic. Plant several as a hedge, use as a foundation plant, or plant on a steep hillside to help stem erosion. Plant bush anemone in a dry woodland garden with salmon-pink flowering forest lily, native iris, mariposa lily, bear's breech, tall currants, native grape, or blue-eyed grass. Near the coast, bush anemone thrives in full sun with other low-water plants such as the bright blue germander sage, Mexican tulip poppy, red hesperaloe, and shrubby aloe.

### Try This

Bush anemone 'Elizabeth' is a bit more compact than the species. It makes even more flowers, up to twenty per flower cluster! According to the State of California and the California Native Plant Society, bush anemone is under threat because its native habitat is being lost to development. So if you would like to grow bush anemone in your garden, purchase it from a reputable nursery. Do not dig it up and do not collect seed in the wild.

*Bush anemone's shiny, dark green leaves suggest a lush exotic habitat in far-away China. In fact, bush anemone comes from the California foothills, northeast of Fresno. There it grows along seasonal creeks, in the chaparral and oak woodlands, often in the company of native grapevines and California bay. To complement the beauty of the evergreen foliage, three- to four-year-old and older bush anemone put on show-stopping bloom from spring to early summer. Copious clusters of slightly fragrant flowers in pure white are 3 to 4 inches across with fringy yellow stamens in the center. They look like a cross between a Japanese anemone and an old-fashioned white rose. When flowers fade, petals fall, leaving behind flower-like star-shaped bracts of pale yellow-green.*

### Other Common Name
Tree Anemone

### Bloom Period and Seasonal Color
Pure white flowers with fringe of yellow stamens at the center from spring to early summer.

### Mature Height × Spread
8 to 12 ft. × 6 to 8 ft.

Hardy to 8A

Min. Temp. 10° F

# Butterfly Bush
## *Buddleja* spp.

*Every garden needs plants with tasty leaves for caterpillars and with sweet nectar for adult butterflies. Butterfly bush falls into the latter category. These large vigorous shrubs produce 10-inch-long fragrant flower clusters that are butterfly magnets. The most commonly planted butterfly bushes are varieties of Buddleja (also spelled Buddleia) davidii, a deciduous shrub that grows to 10 feet × 15 feet but can be kept smaller by pruning. Long pointed leaves are shiny green or blue-green on top (some variegated) and silvery white below. Flowers range from deep to light purple and from rose-pink to white. Other species of Buddleja have yellow or orange flowers. They all look beautiful when covered in yellow swallowtail or black and orange monarch butterflies. The flowers are lovely in a vase as well.*

### Bloom Period and Seasonal Color
Summertime blooms in deep purple, lavender, white, rose-pink, yellow, orange-gold, often with an orange eye.

### Mature Height × Spread
Standard: 8 to 10 ft. × 15 ft.
Dwarf: to 6 ft. × 5 ft.

**Hardy to 8A**

**Min. Temp. 10° F**

### When, Where, and How to Plant
Site in full sun or part shade along the coast and in part shade in hot inland and desert gardens. Plant fall through spring in mild winter areas and in spring in cold winter gardens. Provide moderately amended, well-draining soil. Allow plenty of room for branches to spread. See "Tips and Techniques" for details regarding planting. Water well after planting, and mulch.

### Growing Tips
Irrigate regularly from the time soil dries in spring until winter rains. Starting in year three, butterfly bushes in coastal gardens need only occasional deep summer water. In hotter areas, water regularly and deeply during the growing season. Apply balanced organic fertilizer in early spring.

### Care
Deadhead to prolong bloom. To control size and shape, cut upright stems back to knee high in fall or winter. Or reveal the plant's vertical arching form by selectively removing all but one, three, or five stems. Then remove lower branches and all new sprouts as they develop along the stems. No notable pests or diseases bother this plant.

### Companion Planting and Design
Butterfly bush makes an excellent screen either pruned or unpruned. Plant several (spaced 10 feet or farther apart) or integrate with other shrubs. If you prefer not to prune on a regular basis, place butterfly bush in the background where its large size can perfume the air without dominating the garden. Alternatively, train butterfly bush to arch over a walkway.

### Try These
'Black Knight' (8 to 10 feet × 8 to 10 feet) has very fragrant, deep purple flowers. 'Harlequin' (4 to 6 feet × 3 to 5 feet) has variegated leaves, olive-green with cream margins, and violet-blue flowers. 'Monite' (Petit Snow™) has white flowers (6 feet × 5 feet). For something completely different, try woolly butterfly bush (*Buddleja marrubifolia*), an extremely drought tolerant desert native with crenulated, fuzzy, gray-green leaves, only 3/4-inch long. Branch tips produce ball-shaped flower clusters, 1 1/2 inches across with tiny bright gold and golden orange flowers. This 5-foot × 5-foot shrub is open branching. It is hardy to 15 degrees F.

# California Flannel Bush

*Fremontodendron* spp.

## When, Where, and How to Plant

Plant in fall and winter in full sun and in well-draining soil (or build raised beds as described in "Tips and Techniques"). Protect from wind that can blow over these shallow rooted shrubs. Allow enough room for this plant's ultimate size. Keep away from paths and walkways, as the fuzzy flocking on the leaf undersides is irritating to the skin. See "Tips and Techniques" on planting natives. Water well and mulch.

## Growing Tips

Deep water occasionally through the first fall and in winter too if rains are sparse. Let soil dry several inches down between waterings. Avoid all summer water. Flannel bush often succumbs to deadly fungi that proliferate in wet warm soil. In my native garden (average 11 inches of rainfall per year), I plant flannel bush when the weather cools in early fall. I water at planting and then *never again*. No fertilizer is needed.

## Care

Flannel bush can be pruned but does not require it. If you prune to shape the plant, do so after flowering and wear long sleeves to protect your skin from the irritating fuzz.

## Companion Planting and Design

In my own garden, I adore the combination of flannel bush and California lilac. Over the years, the branches have interwoven so that in spring they bloom together with the flannel bush's golden yellow-orange flowers next to cobalt blue lilac flowers and all against deep green leaves. Flannel bush can be planted en mass as an evergreen screen in an informal garden. In a more formal garden, it can be trained as espalier.

## Try These

'Ken Taylor' is a spreading form, 6 to 8 feet × 12 feet with 3- to 4-inch flowers. 'Pacific Sunset' grows 12 to 20 feet × 12 to 20 feet with 4-inch orange-yellow flowers. 'San Gabriel' grows upright and spreads 10 to 18 feet × 8 to 12 feet, with bright yellow flowers. 'California Glory' is one of the largest at 20 feet × 20 feet. It has yellow flowers and is suitable for mountain gardens.

Fast growing evergreen California flannel bushes (F. californicum) are some of our most beautiful native shrubs. Flannel bushes have cupped golden yellow flowers shaped like a star, 3 to 4 inches across, that take on a coppery tint as they age. The bright colored flowers make a strong contrast against olive-green and deeply lobed leathery leaves that are flocked on the underside with coppery fuzz. Flannel bush cultivars have different forms and sizes. Some are low growing, mounding ground covers, some are large shrubs, and some almost tree-sized at 20- feet tall and twice as wide. The most important thing to know about flannel bush is that they are extremely vulnerable to fungi that thrive in wet soil during warm summer months. Success comes from withholding water though the summer.

**Other Common Name**
Fremontia

**Bloom Period and Seasonal Color**
Early spring blooms yellow to golden yellow or orange yellow.

Hardy to 8B

Min. Temp. 15° F

**Mature Height × Spread**
4 to 20 ft. × 6 to 40 ft. depending on cultivar

# California Lilac
## *Ceanothus* spp.

*Once winter rains end, I start watching for the brilliant blue blooms of California lilac. I grow several California lilacs, ranging from a 3-foot tall mounding ground cover 'Louis Edmunds' to 18-foot-tall 'Ray Hartman'. 'Dark Star' (6 feet tall) joins the show with unbelievably deep blue flowers. Against equally deep green leaves of 'Dark Star', the bright chartreuse and green variegated leaves of Ceanothus thyrsiflorus 'El Dorado' shine like a beacon. These fast growing evergreen natives (and their hybrids) vary not only in their sizes and growth forms but also in their flower color. Leaves and flowers are both fragrant. Busy bees visit their flowers (and pollinate nearby fruit trees), while the hungry caterpillars of native butterflies relish California lilac leaves.*

### Bloom Period and Seasonal Color
Late winter to spring flowers in violet-indigo to the palest blue and even white. Some repeat in fall.

### Mature Height × Spread
1 to 30 ft. × 8 to 15 ft., depending on species.

Hardy to 8A

Min. Temp. 10 to 15° F

### When, Where, and How to Plant
California lilac is extremely drought tolerant once established. Plant fall through spring in mild winter gardens and in spring in coldest winter gardens. Provide full or part sun and well-draining soil. See "Tips and Techniques" for details on planting natives. Water well after planting, and mulch.

### Growing Tips
Provide occasional deep water from the time that soil dries in spring until winter rains begin. Let soil dry several inches down between waterings. Keep water off leaves. After the second summer many garden cultivars survive on rainfall alone. In my coastal garden, I water established California lilac monthly in summer and not at all the rest of the year. No fertilizer is needed.

### Care
Prune if desired, just after bloom to remove dead wood and shape plants. Avoid cutting into the hardwood. Watch for aphids, mealybugs, scale, and whiteflies (see "Tips and Techniques").

### Companion Planting and Design
Low-mounding varieties help stabilize slopes or form a "green carpet" in place of lawn. Mass plant larger varieties for blooming evergreen screens or hedges. Ceanothus are especially effective lining a long driveway. Large specimens can be shaped as small trees. Combine with other natives and Mediterranean climate plants. My all-time favorite combination is California lilac with California flannel bush. Their intertwining branches bloom simultaneously, putting on a knockout show of blue and gold.

### Try These
'Concha' (6 to 9 feet × 6 to 9 feet) has narrow green leaves with serrated edges and magenta buds that open dark blue. It's easy to grow especially in mountain gardens, beach gardens, and in heavy soils. 'Dark Star' (6 feet × 8 to 12 feet) has small, dark green leaves with burgundy buds that open to cobalt blue flowers. It's good for coastal gardens with well-drained soils. 'Ray Hartman' (18 feet × 20 feet) is a large shrub or small tree with bright-blue flowers. It tolerates heavy soils and heat along the coast or inland. *Ceanothus gloriosus* 'Heart's Desire' is a mounding ground cover (1 foot × 4 to 6 feet) with pale blue flowers. It's good for coastal gardens.

# Caribbean Copper Plant

*Euphorbia cotinifolia*

### When, Where, and How to Plant
In mild climate gardens, plant Caribbean copper plant in the warm months of the year when its branches are covered in leaves. Choose a spot in full sun with well-draining soil. Follow shrub planting directions in "Tips and Techniques." Water well after planting, and mulch. Where winter temperatures regularly dip below freezing, grow in a pot and move to a protected spot in winter. Place in full sun and monitor the soil so it doesn't dry out too much. Or grow it as an annual.

### Growing Tips
These subtropical plants prefer moist (not wet) soil, though they will survive in drier soils. Drooping or dropping leaves in summer mean it is past time to water. Mulch with compost and feed with all-purpose organic fertilizer in early spring as growth resumes. **Note:** This plant is poisonous. It's milky sap irritates eyes and skin.

### Care
To grow Caribbean copper plant as a tree, simply reduce the number of upright stems at the base to one or three. Watch for new sprouts along stems and remove them as they develop. As with all spurges, the plants' milky sap is a skin and eye irritant. Wear gloves, long pants, long sleeves, and eye protection when you prune. This plant is pest free.

### Companion Planting and Design
Plant Caribbean copper plant in a spot where its leaves will be backlit and appear to glow. In a tropical landscape, mix with king palm and fragrant angel's trumpet. Pink-flowering naked ladies bring out the red tones in copper plant leaves. Group potted copper plant with pots of plants that bloom in bright-saturated colors: exotic reed orchid, orchid cactus, and Peruvian lilies. Or plant Caribbean copper plant with the variegated New Zealand flax, yellow-flowering Jerusalem sage, green needle-like rosemary, yellow or green flowered kangaroo paw, orange-flowered beach sage, or silver-leaved germander sage.

### Try These
'Atropurpurea' makes clouds of tiny white flowers and wine-red leaves (10 feet × 4 feet). 'Burgundy Wine' has tiny yellow flowers and dusky red leaves (2 to 4 feet × 2 to 4 feet).

*Plants in the spurge family come in all shapes and sizes. Caribbean copper plant is a Euphorbia that grows as a tall, narrow shrub or small tree. While Caribbean copper plant flowers, the blooms are insignificant compared to the beautiful, large, round, coppery-wine colored leaves that cover its branches in the warm months of the year. Its many upright stems are covered in soft, corky, gray bark. In summer's heat, stems grow quickly to 10 feet or taller. With a light frost, leaves drop. With more frost, stems die back to the base or die altogether. Grow this heat-lover in the ground along the coast. In cooler areas, grow in a pot and move to a sheltered location in winter.*

**Other Common Name**
Mexican Shrubby Spurge

**Bloom Period and Seasonal Color**
Coppery-wine colored leaves

**Mature Height × Spread**
10 to 16 ft. × 6 to 8 ft.

Hardy to 9B

Min. Temp.
25 to 30° F

# Conebush
## *Leucadendron* spp.

*From South Africa come the conebushes, evergreen shrubs (and some small trees) in the same family as the beautiful and odd-looking Protea. Most conebushes are 6- to 8-foot-tall shrubs with narrow upright branches, which in some species are covered in needle-like leaves. Most conebush leaves, however, are flat and green, covering the branches like overlapping fish scales. From winter through spring, branch tips end in what we call flowers. Look closely, however, and you'll see that they are bright colored leaf-like bracts in shades of red, yellow, gold, scarlet, pink, and/or orange. In the center are small colorful cones (male and female cones form on separate plants). The foliage and blooms of these low water and low care evergreens spice up any garden or cut flower arrangement.*

### Bloom Period and Seasonal Color
Colorful foliage in green, yellow, gold, scarlet, pomegranate pink, and/or orange.

### Mature Height × Spread
6 to 8 ft. × 6 to 8 ft.

### Minimum Temperature
Depends on hybrid or species.

**Hardy to 9A**

**Min. Temp. 20 to 25° F**

### When, Where, and How to Plant
Plant fall through spring in frost-free gardens and in spring in cold gardens. Full sun brings out the best leaf color. Build a planting mound of well-draining soil, then follow shrub planting directions (see "Tips and Techniques"). For potted conebush, add coarse bark or pumice to the potting mix to improve drainage. Water well and mulch.

### Growing Tips
Water deeply every week for the first two to three weeks and then monthly until winter rains. Starting in year two, deep water monthly from late spring until winter rains, more often in hot valley gardens. Drip irrigation is ideal for these shrubs, but do spray leaves periodically to rinse away dust. No fertilizer is needed for mulched plants in the ground. Feed potted plants with slow-release fertilizer *low in phosphate.*

### Care
Prune back hard after flowering to keep plant vigorous. Avoid overwatering to prevent root rot and deadly soil fungi. If leaves pale, sprinkle soil with iron sulfate or powdered sulfur and iron chelate (follow label directions). Water well. Leaves will color up over several weeks. No significant pests.

### Companion Planting and Design
Conebush adds color and texture to any low-water garden. Mix into a border with palo verde, honeybells, and African daisy. A line of conebushes makes a good hedge, screen, or windbreak. Cut branches for flower arrangements (fresh or dried).

### Try These
'Cloudbank Ginny' ('Cloudbank Jenny') (6 feet × 6 feet) has dense grey-green leaves tipped red with bright red or orange cones surrounded by pale yellow and green bracts. 'Safari Sunset' (8 to 10 feet × 6 to 8 feet) has dark green leaves with wine blush on burgundy stems. Deep red flower bracts surround small pale yellow centers. 'Red Gem' (4 feet × 4 feet) has red bracts surrounding yellow female cones. 'Jester' ('Safari Sunshine') (5 feet × 5 feet) has colorful striped leaves, pink-blush yellow with a green center stripe and red edge. Flower bracts are pale yellow with pink blush. *Leucadendron discolor* 'Pom Pom' (7 feet × 5 feet) has pale yellow bracts surrounding bright orange or red cones and blue-gray leaves.

# Desert Mallow
## *Sphaeralcea ambigua*

### When, Where, and How to Plant
Purchase plants in bloom to be certain of their flower color. Plant fall through spring in mild winter gardens and in spring in coldest winter gardens (see shrub planting directions in "Tips and Techniques"). Site in full sun and in well-draining soil. Soils with little organic matter are fine. Water well after planting and mulch.

### Growing Tips
In the first year or two, apply occasional deep water from the time soil dries in spring until winter rains. After that, water deeply and only occasionally during spring and fall and a bit more in summer, especially in hot inland and desert gardens. Let soil dry several inches down between waterings. Water the soil and not the leaves. No fertilizer is needed.

### Care
Prune back branches by a third or so after flowering and if plants become too leggy. Avoid cutting into harder wood. Prune out the occasional dead branches. Wear long sleeves and long plants, as some people have an allergic reaction to the hairs on the leaves. No insect pests are a problem.

### Companion Planting and Design
For a spectacular spring display in a dry garden, plant desert mallow with purple-flowered foothill penstemon, white flowered Matilija poppy, and golden orange California poppies. The gray-green leaves complement deep green foliage plants such as Mexican grass tree and native bush anemone. Because desert mallow is fairly open and lanky, you get a better show from three or five plants grouped together. In a Mediterranean garden, plant desert mallow beneath sculptural dragon tree or next to a succulent shrub aloe. Try desert mallow in a terracotta pot with a well-draining potting mix.

### Try These
'Louis Hamilton'™ has watermelon colored flowers and gray-green leaves. 'Papago Pink'™ blooms light pink. Fendler's globemallow (*Sphaeralcea fendleri*) is a mounding shrub with gray-green leaves with pale orange to bright orange and even purple flowers (3 feet × 3 feet). Munro's globemallow (*Sphaeralcea munroana*) has apricot flowers, silver foliage, and upright branches (2 to 4 feet × 2 to 4 feet). It tolerates clay soil if you water sparingly.

*On springtime trips through the desert, I often pull the car over to photograph desert mallow blooming orange or red along the roadside. In my own garden, I grow desert mallow in a dry sunny spot in a corner and next to a large granite boulder. The petite shrubs erupt in wands of miniature hibiscus flowers that bloom in shades of raspberry, watermelon, pink, orange, and coral, on and off throughout the year and peaking in spring and summer. They are so eye-catching that neighbors often knock on the door to ask about them. Evergreen desert mallow grows quickly to 2 feet × 3 feet. Their small silvery green leaves are covered with fine hairs—typical adaptations for plants native to hot, dry, sunny environments.*

**Other Common Name**
Globe Mallow

**Bloom Period and Seasonal Color**
Spring into late summer in raspberry, watermelon, pink, orange, and coral.

**Mature Height × Spread**
2 ft. × 3 ft.

Hardy to
7A

Min.
Temp.
0° F

# Dune Sage
## *Salvia africana-lutea*

Most sages are herbaceous perennials, but many are shrubby with woody stems. Some are native, and some come from other Mediterranean climate regions. Dune sage falls into the latter category. This very drought tolerant and unusual looking sage is from the Cape of Good Hope in South Africa where it grows on coastal sand dunes and dry rocky banks. It has small, rounded, olive-gray leaves that sit at a slight angle to the stem, perhaps a way of minimize exposure to hot sun. Dune sage grows 5 feet tall and at least as wide. The calyx is rusty orange and olive-green. The flower color is most unusual, emerging butter yellow and aging to a rusty apricot.

**Other Common Name**
Beach Salvia

**Bloom Period and Seasonal Color**
Flowers rust colored, butter yellow, and rusty apricot that peak in spring and sporadically through the year.

**Mature Height × Spread**
5 ft. × 5 ft.

**Hardy to**
9A

**Min. Temp.**
20° F

### When, Where, and How to Plant
Plant in all but the hottest months of the year in mild winter gardens, or spring in cold gardens. Site in full sun with well-draining soil. Poor soils are fine. See shrub planting techniques in "Tips and Techniques." Water well after planting, and mulch.

### Growing Tips
In the first year or two, water deeply and regularly from spring until winter rains. Once established, cut back to occasional water in spring and fall, a bit more in summer, especially in hot inland and desert gardens. Let soil dry several inches down between waterings. Water the soil, not the leaves. No fertilizer is needed.

### Care
Allow sages to find their own shape or prune them to shape after flowering. If branches get too straggly, cut back by a third, but don't cut into hardwood. Over time, underground stems eventually make a small colony. If they become too massive, merely dig out unwanted stems. Replant elsewhere or share with a friend. No significant pests bother dune sage.

### Companion Planting and Design
The unusual bronzy undertones of dune sage flowers are brought out by copper, bright pink, yellow, orange, and gold, including red hot poker, gold-flowered Jerusalem sage, wine-colored smoke tree foliage, and lavender-pink flowers of round leaf tea tree. Add yellow and green variegated New Zealand flax such as 'Yellow Wave', or the burgundy leaved 'Shirazz'. Dune sage also makes a good mid-sized informal screen or hedge.

### Try These
All of these shrubby sages are drought tolerant and hardy to 20 degrees F: 'Kirstenbosch' is a dwarf dune sage (2 to 3 feet × 2 to 3 feet). Cleveland sage (*Salvia clevelandii*) is an aromatic California native (3 feet × 4 feet) with violet-blue flowers. It has gray-green leaves. Rocky mountain sage (*Salvia lanceolata*) is a seemingly misnamed salvia from South Africa. It grows 2¹/₂ feet × 8 feet and wider with highly aromatic, silver, blue-gray leaves. See Ground Covers and Perennials for more sages.

# Feathery Senna
## *Senna artemisioides*

### When, Where, and How to Plant
Feathery senna thrives in coastal gardens as well as hot inland and desert gardens. Plant in fall through late spring, into a spot with full sun and with well-draining soil. In freezing winter areas, plant in spring. Poor soils are fine. See "Tips and Techniques" for shrub planting directions and for building planting mounds to deal with heavy clay soils. Water deeply and mulch.

### Growing Tips
Water deeply weekly for the first two or three weeks and then monthly until winter rains arrive. In year two, start watering monthly from when soil dries in late spring until winter rains. After that, the roots are likely to be deep enough to require just a few deep waterings in summer. Since most Australian plants come from areas where soils have even fewer nutrients than ours, they don't need fertilizer.

### Care
Don't prune senna. Pests aren't a problem. Avoid overwatering to prevent root rot and deadly soil fungi.

### Companion Planting and Design
Feathery senna's fantastic foliage is striking against a dark wall or when combined with bronze colored plants such as giant dracaena 'Dark Star'. Add deep green leaved and bright blue flowered California lilac. For a winter show, plant yellow flowering cassia with coral flowering aloes. Flowers complement each other, while the wispy silver leaves of senna contrast with the thick succulent aloe leaves. Feathery senna is also suited for massing as an informal evergreen screen or planted around a pool.

### Try These
The family resemblance between feathery senna and silvery senna (*Senna phyllodinea* or *Cassia phyllodinea*) is unmistakable. The two are about the same size with the same color flowers. Silvery cassia flowers peak in winter and fall. Leaves are shaped like small sickles. Technically they are not leaves but flattened stems that have taken on the functions of leaves. Silvery senna is extremely drought tolerant and requires very little water in summer, though it appreciates a bit of shade in hottest desert and inland gardens. This one is hardy to 20 degrees F.

*Feathery senna is a fast growing mounding shrub that reaches 6 feet × 6 feet. Despite its delicate look, this is one tough drought tolerant plant. Branches are clothed in narrow needle-like leaves arranged like geometric feathers. Each leaf is covered in short white hairs that give the foliage a pale, ghostly appearance. From winter into spring, these evergreens are smothered in small pea-like iridescent yellow flowers that form on short spikes. Lesser summer and fall blooms are common in milder climate gardens as well. Flat, bright, green pea-type seedpods follow the flowers and eventually turn mahogany, an added bonus of contrast against those nearly white leaves. Feathery senna is a classic Mediterranean climate plant that is native to Australia. This plant is sometimes sold as Cassia artemisioides.*

**Other Common Name**
Silver Cassia

**Bloom Period and Seasonal Color**
Iridescent yellow pea-shaped flowers on and off through the year, peaking in winter and spring.

Hardy to 8B

Min. Temp. 15° F

**Mature Height × Spread**
3 to 6 ft. × 3 to 6 ft.

# Flowering Maple
## *Abutilon* spp.

*Subtlety can be a virtue in the garden. More reserved and subtler plants balance those with huge flowers or brightly colored foliage that scream "Look at me!" Some of the most subtle plants are hybrid Abutilon, the flowering maples. Not really maples, they are delicate evergreen shrubs with open branches and deep green (sometimes variegated) leaves shaped like miniature maple leaves. Flowering maple produces pendant (downward hanging) bell-shaped flowers. Thanks to breeders and nursery folks, we have cultivars with springtime flowers blooming in shades of ivory, yellow, pink, orange, raspberry, and deep red. Some are yellow with orange or reddish veins, while others have light colored petals with deep toned sepals.*

### Bloom Period and Seasonal Color
Peak bloom in spring, but some bloom nearly year-round in shades of ivory, yellow, orange, pink, raspberry, and deep red.

### Mature Height × Spread
2 to 12 ft. × 2 to 12 ft., depending on cultivar

### Minimum Temperature
Evergreen to 20 degrees F. Deciduous to about 10 degrees F. Grown as an annual in colder areas.

### When, Where, and How to Plant
Provide full or part sun in milder coastal gardens and provide part shade or shade in warmer inland gardens. Provide well-draining and well-amended soil. Plant fall through spring in warm climates and in spring in colder climates. Follow shrub planting directions in "Tips and Techniques." The more lax-branched flowering maples benefit from staking at planting time or planting among sturdier shrubs for branches to rest on. Well suited for containers. Water deeply after planting and mulch.

### Growing Tips
Water deeply and regularly, especially in hot inland gardens. Along the coast, plants require less frequent water. Water once the top 3 inches of soil are dry. A thick layer of mulch insulates the soil from water loss and reduces the need to water. Feed with all-purpose organic fertilizer before new growth starts in early spring.

### Care
Pinch branch tips or prune after flowering to promote compact bushy growth. Remove weak or spindly branches and those that point inward. Control scale and whitefly (see "Tips and Techniques").

### Companion Planting and Design
Sprawling forms can be planted in hanging baskets. Use more upright forms for espalier or airy visual screens. Integrate flowering maple into shady woodland or Asian theme gardens with forest lily, bush anemone, daylily, Japanese maple, and bear's breech. For an interesting effect, combine flowering maples of similar flower color but different shades, i.e. one with garnet red flowers and one with soft pink flowers. In cold areas, grow in containers and move to a protected location in winter.

### Try These
'Nabob' (6 to 8 feet × 4 to 5 feet) has deep garnet red flowers. 'Apricot' (2 to 3 feet × 2 to 3 feet) has profuse pale apricot blooms with red sepals. 'Alba' (8 to 12 feet × 8 to 12 feet) has pale white blooms with prominent yellow stamens. 'Luteus' (8 to 12 feet × 8 to 12 feet) makes bright yellow flowers mostly spring through summer. 'Lavender Pink' (4 feet × 4 feet) has small, silver-pink flowers.

# Giant Dracaena
## *Cordyline australis*

### When, Where, and How to Plant
Plant into well-draining soil and full sun or dry shade. Plant in fall through spring in frost-free gardens, and in spring in colder winter garden. Poor or well-amended soil will be fine. Follow shrub planting directions in "Tips and Techniques." Water well and mulch. Giant dracaena grows well in a container.

### Growing Tips
Water deeply weekly for the first two or three weeks and then monthly until winter rains arrive. In subsequent years, start watering when soil dries in late spring. A deep monthly watering should do, but these plants tolerate more frequent watering too. Spray periodically to rinse dust off leaves. Mulch with well composted organic matter. Apply all-purpose organic fertilizer in early spring.

### Care
Groom to remove spent leaves. It is okay to cut the top of a too-tall stalk. Stalks will resprout leaves and severed tops can be potted to root and become new plants (wait a few days for the cut end to dry). Avoid overwatering to prevent root rot and deadly soil fungi. Watch for mealybugs and scale (see "Tips and Techniques" for controls).

### Companion Planting and Design
Plant as a vertical element in nearly any garden. In a Mediterranean garden, underplant with white or pink flowering rockrose and yellow flowering ground cover honeybells. For more subtlety, plant plum colored 'Red Sensation' with silvery Rocky Mountain sage. Combine with palms, gingers, and canna around a swimming pool. Giant dracaena looks right at home in a mixed succulent garden where colorful foliage and texture are the main focus.

### Try These
'Chocolate' (3 to 4 feet tall) has red-chocolate colored leaves. 'Krakatoa' (20 to 30 feet × 10 to 15 feet) has brown leaves striped pink. 'Pink Stripe' (12 to 20 feet × 8 to 10 feet) has gray-green leaves with a pink center stripe. 'Red Sensation' (15 to 25 feet × 8 to 10 feet) has plum colored leaves on stems that branch with age. 'Red Star' (8 to 10 feet × 5 feet) has burgundy red leaves. 'Sundance' (20 to 30 feet × 8 to 10 feet) has green leaves with narrow pink center stripe.

*At first glance, you might confuse this tall, drought tolerant evergreen with yucca. Giant dracaena leaves, like yucca leaves, form in rosettes at the tops of corky stems. But where yucca leaves are stiff, succulent, and sharp-spined, the long and sword-like leaves of giant dracaena are soft and flexible. Its flowers are quite different too, but neither plant is grown for its flowers. Instead this New Zealand native is grown for its tall narrow profile and long arching foliage that spirals around the stem. For years, nurseries offered green leaved giant dracaena. Recently the nurseries have expanded their offerings with plants whose leaves are shades of bronze, burgundy, raspberry, and combinations thereof. Giant dracaena stems branch after they flower. Giant dracaena is also called Dracaena australis.*

### Other Common Name
Cabbage Tree

### Bloom Period and Seasonal Color
Focus on evergreen foliage: green, chartreuse, bronze, burgundy, raspberry-colored, some multicolored.

**Hardy to 9A**

**Min. Temp. 20° F**

### Mature Height × Spread
8 to 30 ft. × 10 to 15 ft., depending on cultivar.

# Grevillea
## *Grevillea* spp.

*Grevillea is a huge family of handsome woody shrubs, trees, and mounding ground covers from Australia. These Protea cousins have large showy flower clusters, each made of tiny tubular flowers, only an inch or two long and curled. Protruding from the center of each is what looks like a curved colored antenna. The "antenna" is actually a long pistil. With some grevillea, the petals and pistil are the same color. In others, they differ. Either way, grevillea has soft needle-like leaves (some have flattened leaves) that are the perfect backdrop for their most unusual and beautiful flowers. Grevillea bloom in fall, winter, and spring, and some bloom year-round. Birds, especially hummingbirds, love these plants. Grevillea can be picky about their location but once you find the right spot, they thrive.*

### Bloom Period and Seasonal Color
Bright red, maroon, raspberry coral, cream, buttery yellow, apricot, and bright gold flowers peak fall through spring. Some flower year-round.

Hardy to
9A

Min.
Temp.
20° F

### Mature Height × Spread
2 to 10 ft. × 5 to 15 ft., depending on cultivar

### Minimum Temperature
Depends on cultivar.

### When, Where, and How to Plant
Grevillea are suited to all California garden climates except those with hard frosts. Plant in fall through spring in frost-free gardens and in spring in colder winter gardens. Grevillea prefer full sun but will tolerate light shade (though flowering may diminish). Well-draining soils are best, poor soils are fine. See "Tips and Techniques" for more details on planting. Water well and mulch.

### Growing Tips
Water deeply each week for the first two or three weeks, then monthly until winter rains arrive. In year two, start watering when soil dries in late spring. Water deeply each month until winter rains. After that roots are likely to be deep enough to require just a few deep waterings in summer. Since most Australian plants come from areas where soils have even less nutrients than ours, they don't need fertilizer. If leaves yellow, sprinkle the soil beneath the branches with iron sulfate or powdered sulfur and iron chelate (follow directions on the label). Water deeply and wait. Leaves green up over several months.

### Care
Pruning promotes new branches. Flowers form at branch tips, so pruning ultimately promotes flowering. Remove no more than a third of a plant in one season. No significant pests. Avoid overwatering to prevent root rot and deadly soil fungi.

### Companion Planting and Design
Use grevillea as a single specimen, background shrub, screen, ground cover, informal hedge, or clipped for a formal hedge, and to attract birds. Branches are dramatic in cut flower arrangements.

### Try These
'Long John' (10 feet × 15 feet) has wispy bright green foliage, copper colored new stems, and large clusters of coral and red flowers. 'Moonlight' (15 feet × 6 feet) has gray fern-like leaves and large soft yellow flowers, and tolerates part shade. 'Robyn Gordon' (4 to 6 feet × 4 to 6 feet) has fern-like foliage and red flowers. It tolerates part shade. *Grevillea lanigera* (2 feet × 5 feet) has short gray-green, needlelike leaves. Flowers are salmon and cream. It tolerates desert and beach conditions.

## When, Where, and How to Plant

Plant hebe in full sun in coastal gardens and in part sun in hot inland gardens. Well-draining soils are best since soggy soils can lead to root rot. Nutrient poor soils are fine. Follow planting directions in "Tips and Techniques." Water well and mulch.

## Growing Tips

Water deeply each week for several weeks after planting, then monthly until winter rains arrive. In year two, water deeply and monthly (somewhat more often in hot inland gardens) from spring until winter rains begin. After that, plants are likely to require only a few deep summer waterings. In cool coastal gardens, water sparingly, and in hot inland gardens, be careful to water enough. Apply all-purpose organic fertilizer in early spring.

## Care

After flowering, cut branches back up to half to stimulate growth. Shrubs can be shorn if they get ratty after winter. To avoid leaf spot, avoid using overhead sprinklers.

## Companion Planting and Design

Plant taller hebe beneath high windows (they won't grow tall enough to interfere with views) or as low hedges. Display shorter varieties in pots next to potted citrus and other evergreens in earth-tone ceramic pots on a patio. Use hebe instead of dwarf boxwood to outline a formal planting bed. Hebe take a bit of shearing, while their stiff upright structures can help support Peruvian lilies, bush anemone, and other plants with stems that need some extra support.

## Try These

'Autumn Glory' (2 feet × 2 feet) has diminutive green leaves edged in red with violet flowers summer to fall. 'Great Orme' (4 feet × 4 feet) is round with bright pink fading to white flowers (summer to frost) and shiny bright green leaves. 'Carl Teschner' (2 feet × 3 to 4 feet) has glossy green leaves and deep violet flowers that fade to white in summer. 'Amy' (4 feet × 4 feet) has elongated glossy green leaves tinged purple when young and purple flowers summer to fall. 'Red Edge' is a 2-foot mound with small gray-green leaves edged in red with pale violet-blue flowers midsummer to fall.

*Today's smaller gardens often require smaller-scale evergreens for foundation plants, edging garden beds, forming low hedges, and serving as backgrounds for colorful flowers. That is a tall order to fill, but one that is well filled by a group of short shrubs called hebe. Hebe are drought tolerant plants native to Australia, New Zealand, and South America. These compact evergreens are extremely versatile, thanks primarily to the dense foliage that lines their short stems. The smooth leaves can be deep green, shiny green with a purple or red blush, silver green, or even variegated green and cream. Hebe foliage looks good year-round, but summer brings out their flowers. Tiny flowers form dense clusters on short plumes in shades of white, purple, or pale blue.*

**Bloom Period and Seasonal Color**
Summer flowers in purple, violet blue, rosy pink, often deep tones fading to white.

**Mature Height × Spread**
1 to 4 ft. × 1 to 4 ft., depending on species

**Minimum Temperature**
Depends on species.

Hardy to 7A

Min. Temp. 0 to 20° F

# Honey Bush
## *Melianthus major*

*Honey bush has a place of honor on my list of top ten garden plants. The leaves of this South African native are big jagged fronds of smooth, icy blue-green with serrated edges. They form at the ends of thick corky stalks that grow both upright and spreading, often reaching 10 feet in my garden. In spring each stalk forms a huge handsome deep maroon bud that slowly unfurls into a 1- to 2-foot-tall column of similarly colored tubular flowers. The flowers look a bit like red versions of bear's breech flowers. There must be honey in those flowers as hummingbirds fight mightily for a spot sipping the nectar. The contrast of deep red and pale green with the sculptural leaves draws human admirers as well.*

**Other Common Name**
Honey Flower

**Bloom Period and
Seasonal Color**
Winter/spring flowers in
deep maroon.

**Mature Height × Spread**
8 to12 ft. × 8 to 12 ft.

**Minimum Temperature**
Root hardy to at least 15 degrees F.

Hardy to
9A

Min.
Temp.
20° F

### When, Where, and How to Plant
In frost-free gardens, plant fall through spring. In colder winter areas, wait until spring. Site in full or part sun. Well-draining and well-amended soil is optimal, but honey bush also tolerates poorer soils and heavier soils. Follow shrub planting directions in "Tips and Techniques." Water deeply and mulch. For container culture, start with a large container. This fast growing and vigorous plant will fill it quickly.

### Growing Tips
Honey bush is adaptable to both frequent and infrequent irrigation. In the first year, water regularly and deeply from spring until winter rains. In subsequent years, water regularly but less often. Apply all-purpose organic fertilizer in early spring or maintain a constant layer of composted organic mulch. Mulch reduces the need to water. This plant is poisonous if ingested.

### Care
This plant is naturally multi-stemmed and sprawling. Limit it to three or five stalks if you want it to grow tall instead of wide. Spent flowers can be removed or left in place. If you let them develop seeds, you may find two or three new seedlings nearby to dig and share with friends. After flowering, new stalks sprout at the base. At that point, cut old stalks to the ground and allow the plant to rejuvenate. Black sooty mold often appears, probably from sticky nectar that leaks from flowers onto leaves. Either ignore it, wash the leaves with water, or prune off infected leaves.

### Companion Planting and Design
Use honey bush as a specimen in a dry garden, mixed with aloes, grevillea, geraniums, kangaroo paw, and other classic Mediterranean climate plants. The leaves have a slightly waxy surface that rubs off if you touch them. They also emit a musty smell, so site the plant a few feet away from where anyone would brush up against the leaves.

### Try These
*Melianthus minor* (4 to 6 feet × 4 to 6 feet) is a smaller cousin to honey bush. The plant is bushier with narrow stems and deep green leaves that reach only about 8 inches across. Bright red flower clusters are arranged more like tassels.

# Indian Mallow

## Abutilon palmeri

### When, Where, and How to Plant

Plant Indian mallow from fall through spring in frost-free gardens and in spring in colder winter gardens. Choose a spot in full or part sun and in a warmer area of your garden. While these shrubs prefer well-draining soils, they are adaptable to heavier soils as well. Follow directions for planting natives in "Tips and Techniques." Water well and mulch.

### Growing Tips

In the first year, water deeply when soil is dry 3 inches down, starting when soil dries in spring, ending with winter rains. After that, these drought tolerant plans may do fine on rainfall-only diets, but tend to grow larger with occasional deep water. Water the soil, not the leaves. Drip irrigation is ideal for native plants like Indian mallow. No fertilizer is needed.

### Care

Indian mallow reseeds occasionally. The seedlings are easy to transplant or pot up and share with a friend. Prune out twiggy and damaged growth in early spring. Then, prune the entire shrub back by $1/3$ or $1/2$ to stimulate bloom.

### Companion Planting and Design

Indian mallow is appropriate for planting along walkways, driveways, and amongst boulders. Site Indian mallow against a deep purple or terracotta colored wall for maximum visual impact. Combine with other California natives such as Cleveland sage, woolly blue curls, penstemon, and California lilac. Or combine with low water plants from other Mediterranean climates including tall succulent tree aloes, shrubby grevillea 'Long John', orange sedge, and tall fountain grasses such as 'Red Bunny Tails'. In children's gardens, plant an Indian mallow near a pathway so the children can touch it as they walk past.

### Try These

Chaparral mallow (*Malacothamnus fasciculatus*) is another fuzzy, gray leaved, native mallow. This drought-tolerant evergreen shrub is the taller cousin to Indian mallow. It has a tall narrow profile of upright branches that can reach 12 feet × 4 to 6 feet. Chaparral mallow has pink to lilac-pink flowers in summer and fall. 'Casitas' is a variety with lavender flowers.

*How many plants can you think of that have fuzzy leaves? Meet Indian mallow, a beautiful small shrub with mahogany-brown stems, golden yellow flowers, and velvety gray-green leaves. The leaves are so soft and inviting that you can't help but reach out and pet them. Indian mallow is native to deserts of California and Arizona where it grows on dry rocky slopes. In our gardens, this mounding shrub grows dense and compact in full sun and more sprawling in part sun. While the hybrid flowering maples (Indian mallow's cousins) have bell-shaped pendant flowers that hang downward, Indian mallow has more cup-shaped flowers pointing up. Each shines like a golden gem against the background of soft green leaves that delight children as much as they do adults.*

**Bloom Period and Seasonal Color**
Golden yellow flowers from spring into fall.

**Mature Height × Spread**
3 to 6 ft. × 3 to 4 ft.

Hardy to 9A

Min. Temp. 20° F

# Island Bush Poppy
## *Dendromecon harfordii*

*Have you ever seen poppy flowers covering a bush? If not, get acquainted with island bush poppy. This tall evergreen shrub has upright woody stems densely covered in oval pale green or blue-green leaves with a waxy blush. In spring and summer (and throughout the year in mild winter gardens), branches are covered in bright yellow poppy flowers, 3 inches across, each with a row of fringed stamens at the center. As flowers fade, petals drop, leaving behind long narrow seedpods that look just like the seedpods of its cousins, the orange California poppy and bright yellow Mexican tulip poppy. Island bush poppy is native to chaparral habitats of the Channel Islands, just off the coast of Santa Barbara. It is an excellent choice for a wild garden.*

### Bloom Period and Seasonal Color
Bright yellow flowers peak in spring and summer.

### Mature Height × Spread
3 to 10 ft. × 3 to 10 ft.

**Hardy to**
8A

**Min. Temp.**
10° F

### When, Where, and How to Plant
In mild winter gardens, plant in fall through early spring. These shrubs prefer full to part sun and well-drained soil. They tolerate part shade as long as it is dry shade. Follow shrub planting directions, taking care to minimize root disturbance while planting (see "Tips and Techniques"). Water well and mulch after planting.

### Growing Tips
Once plants are established (after the second summer), they should survive on rainfall alone. Watering deeply in summer will extend the blooming season, but be careful not to overwater. No fertilizer is needed.

### Care
Bush poppy does not *require* pruning, but regular pruning keeps it looking its best. New shoots are produced each year, so older branches can be cut back safely by a third as soon as flowering is over. Alternatively, wait for new branches to sprout in late winter and selectively prune out some older ones. Remove dried leaves that linger. Pests do not bother bush poppy.

### Companion Planting and Design
Island bush poppy can be used as a background shrub or even as an informal screen. Its light colored leaves contrast beautifully with native shrubs that have dark green leaves such as toyon, manzanita (especially those with darkest mahogany bark), and California lilac (look for one with deep blue flowers such as 'Dark Star'). Add native perennials including any of the penstemon, woolly blue curls, Cleveland sage, and pink flowered hummingbird sage. Blue fescue and other ornamental grasses complement shrub poppy as well.

### Try These
Chaparral bush poppy (*Dendromecon rigida*) is island bush poppy's mainland relative. It is native to chaparral from coastal mountains to the Sierra Nevada foothills. Chaparral bush poppy leaves are the same color, but longer and narrower. Branches are more upright with yellow flowers that are slightly smaller, but during their spring peak there are so many that it doesn't matter. Overall chaparral bush poppy is slightly more cold hardy and more tolerant of clay soils, as long as you leave the irrigation to Mother Nature.

# Kohuhu

## *Pittosporum tenuifolium*

### When, Where, and How to Plant

Plant fall through spring in frost-free gardens and in spring in colder winter gardens. Kohuhu prefers full sun, part sun, or even part shade and well-draining soils. Nutrient poor soils are fine. Follow shrub planting directions in "Tips and Techniques." Stake taller specimens. Water well and mulch. To grow in a container, start a small plant in a small container and move it to a larger pot as the plant grows.

### Growing Tips

Water deeply each week for the first two or three weeks and then monthly until winter rains arrive. In year two, start watering when soil dries in late spring. Water deeply each month until winter rains. After that, roots are likely to be deep enough to require just a few deep waterings in summer, though kohuhu tolerates moist soils that drain well. Spray lightly every so often to rinse dust off leaves. Feed with an all-purpose organic fertilizer in spring. **Note:** This plant is poisonous if ingested.

### Care

Prune only if you want to shape the shrub. Shear for a formal presentation or leave natural for a less formal look. Watch for aphids (see "Tips and Techniques" for controls).

### Companion Planting and Design

Kohuhu is an excellent choice to mass as a privacy screen or "room divider" in a large garden. Foliage plants like kohuhu can be used as a serene green background for an otherwise exuberant or chaotic show of colorful flowering plants. These shrubs are lovely in containers on a patio, in front of an upright column, or along a walkway.

### Try These

'Silver Sheen' (12 to 15 feet × 6 to 8 feet) is narrow and upright with slender black stems and small green leaves that shine silver in bright sunlight. 'Marjorie Channon' (8 to 12 feet × 6 to 8 feet) has variegated leaves, deep green with creamy white margins. 'Golf Ball' (20 to 24 inches × 20 to 24 inches) is dense and round, perfect for a low-border edging or container. Willow Pittosporum (*Pittosporum phillyreoides*) forms a slender small tree with long, narrow, weeping leaves (15 to 20 feet × 10 to 15 feet).

*Kohuhu is a large group of shrubs and trees grown for their foliage and for the structure they bring to the garden. Kohuhu is from New Zealand (hence the unusual common name) and has small deep green leaves. The leaves are a sharp contrast to the upright dark brown or black stems. These evergreens produce sweetly fragrant purplish or reddish flowers that are so minute, you'd have a hard time finding them. Kohuhu has been extensively hybridized and selected so nurseries offer many cultivars, each a different form, width, height, leaf shape, and leaf color. All are fast growing and require little water. Pittosporum tenuifolium is sometimes sold as Pittosporum nigricans.*

**Other Common Name**
Tawhiwhi

**Bloom Period and Seasonal Color**
Grown for green or variegated foliage.

**Mature Height × Spread**
15 to 25 ft. × 10 to 15 ft.

Hardy to 8B

Min. Temp. 15° F

# Lilac
## *Syringa vulgaris*

*I love to visit California's gold country, especially in early spring. Auburn, Ione, Placerville, and other historic mining towns along Highway 49 (named for the 1849 gold rush) have old main streets and historic homes, many of which have lovely gardens with plenty of winter chill for spectacular springtime displays of lilacs. Lilacs are large deciduous shrubs with heart-shaped green leaves. They are most beloved for their large colorful and heavily perfumed flower clusters in shades of white, pink, rose, maroon, purple, and lilac. If you live in an area with little or no winter chill (along the coast or in the southern part of the state), don't despair, hybridizers have developed low-chill lilacs for your gardens as well.*

**Bloom Period and Seasonal Color**
Spring blooms are white, purple, lilac, rose, pink, maroon, and multicolored combinations.

**Mature Height × Spread**
8 to 12 ft. × 6 to 12 ft., depending on cultivar

**Minimum Temperature**
Traditional lilac: -40 degrees F.
Low chill hybrids: 10 degrees F.

## When, Where, and How to Plant
Plant in early spring, in full or part sun, when lilacs are offered bare root or in nursery containers, along the coast. Provide afternoon shade or day-long filtered light in hot inland gardens to protect flower color. Plant in well-amended and well-draining soil. See shrub planting directions in "Tips and Techniques." Set potted lilac an inch or two higher than it was in the nursery container, taking care not to disturb the rootball. Mulch the exposed part of the rootball and surrounding soil to bring the level up to what it was in the nursery can. Don't let mulch touch the trunk. Water well.

## Growing Tips
For the first three years, keep the soil and rootball moist so roots become well established. After that, water deeply and weekly during the growing season. Cut back water towards the end of summer to push lilac into the dormancy it needs for a good bloom. In February or March, feed with blood-meal and bonemeal. In year four, add a May or June feeding of organic low-nitrogen fertilizer.

## Care
Prune after blooming to stimulate new wood that will flower the following year. Remove spent flower clusters, cutting stems just above a pair of leaves (don't leave a stub). In year four, prune out suckers, weak wood, and crossing branches so the center of the lilac is open to light and air. Avoid overhead water to keep leaves dry and avoid leafspot and mildew. Watch for scale (see "Tips and Techniques").

## Companion Planting and Design
Place lilac where you can enjoy its spectacular bloom and heavenly fragrance. Grow lilacs as specimen plants, foundation plants, large hedges, or screens.

## Try These
'Michael Buckner' (also spelled 'Buchner') (10 to 15 feet tall) has rose-lilac colored flowers. 'Charles Joly' (10 feet × 6 feet) has dusky red flowers. In low chill climates, try 'Lavender Lady' (12 feet × 6 feet) with lavender flowers. 'California Rose' (15 to 20 feet × 12 to 15 feet) has pink flowers, or 'Angel White' (10 feet × 6 to 8 feet) has white flowers.

# Manzanita
## *Arctostaphylos* spp.

## When, Where, and How to Plant

Manzanita grows in nearly every California garden except in deserts and in highest elevation mountains. Plant in fall in full or part sun along the coast, and plant in part sun to part shade inland. Provide unamended but well-draining soil. See native planting directions in "Tips and Techniques." In humid coastal gardens, space out plants out to prevent leaf spot and keep water off leaves. Water deeply and mulch.

## Growing Tips

Provide deep periodic water through the first year to establish. After that, manzanita will survive on rainfall alone or with occasional deep summer water. Let soil dry several inches down between waterings. No fertilizer is needed.

## Care

Prune to shape just after bloom or fruiting. Occasional dead branches result from fungal "manzanita branch dieback." Prune the dead branches off in summer. Cut a few inches into healthy-looking live wood. Sterilize pruning shears between cuts and after you finish to avoid spreading the spread fungus (see "Tips and Techniques").

## Companion Planting and Design

Use low growing manzanita to create a drought tolerant "green carpet" instead of lawn or to help stabilize a slope. Shrub-sized manzanita makes great screens, hedges, and foundation plants. Tree-sized manzanita make fabulous specimens, especially when pruned to reveal their gorgeous branching structure and beautiful bark.

## Try These

'Emerald Carpet' (1 to 2 feet × 3 to 6 feet) has small leaves and pale pink flowers. *Arctostaphylos hookeri* 'Sunset' (5 feet × 5 feet) has pink flowers. Coppery leaves mature bright green. *Arctostaphylos densiflora* 'Howard McMinn' (4 to 6 feet × 4 to 6 feet) is adaptable to heavy soils. It has pale pink flowers. Parry manzanita (*Arctostaphylos manzanita*) performs best in central and northern California. Pale pink to white flowers complement green, blue-green, or olive-green leaves (10 to 12 feet × 10 to 12 feet). Bigberry manzanita (*Arctostaphylos stauca*) has blue-green leaves with white flowers. Good in Southern California.

*Between native species and cultivars, there are several hundred wonderful evergreen manzanitas, all with leathery, deep green leaves. Some leaves are the size of peas, others the size of silver dollars, and some covered in silvery hairs. In summer, manzanita produce clusters of sweetly fragrant, upside-down, pitcher-shaped flowers, white to pale pink, turning to reddish berries that draw birds. Upright manzanita have gnarled and twisted branches the color of mahogany, some so smooth that they look like sculpture. Once a year, the bark sheds, revealing patches of cinnamon-colored wood beneath. Low-growing manzanita make terrific ground covers, while the tallest are almost small trees. There are so many manzanita to choose from and so little space to plant them! If only all gardening dilemmas were so enjoyable.*

### Other Common Name
Bearberry

### Bloom Period and Seasonal Color
Pale pink to white flowers in fall through early spring, followed by reddish berries.

### Mature Height × Spread
As shrub: 3 to 10 ft. × 3 to 10 ft.

Hardy to 8B

Min. Temp. 15° F

# Pink-flowering Currant
## *Ribes sanguineum* var. *glutinosum*

*They grow under oak trees and in other dry shady places. Their slightly toothed, fuzzy, mini-maple-shaped leaves line upright branches. Hanging tassels of pale pink or rose-colored flowers (occasionally white) are often visited by hummingbirds. Flowers turn to bluish black fruits much beloved by jays, finches, robins, and other birds. These are pink-flowering currants, one of many shade-loving evergreen and deciduous currants native to scrub, chaparral, and woodland areas from Baja to Oregon and from mountains to the coast. This tall, narrow garden shrub grows in all but desert and high mountain gardens. Pink flowering currant is a summer deciduous currant. Its show runs in the "off" season from winter through early spring, making it especially valuable for extending garden interest through the year.*

### Bloom Period and Seasonal Color
Winter through early spring flowers pale pink, deep pink, occasionally white.

### Mature Height × Spread
5 to 12 ft. × 3 to 6 ft.

**Hardy to 5A**

**Min. Temp.** -20° F

### When, Where, and How to Plant
These currants are best suited for coastal, valley, and foothill gardens. Plant any time of year except summer. Currants handle full sun right along the coast and shade everywhere else. Well-draining soils are best, but pink flowering currant also tolerates heavy soils.

### Growing Tips
Water deeply and regularly through the first year to establish. Currants in the wild survive on rainfall; however, once a plant is established, a bit of supplemental garden water through the growing season makes for a lusher plant currant. In milder gardens, currants need little to no water when dormant in summer. In hot inland gardens, water occasionally in summer. Mulch with composted organic matter. No fertilizer is needed.

### Care
Prune if desired after flowering (or after berries are gone) to shape and encourage additional bloom the following year. Pruning for good air circulation prevents rust, as does keeping water off leaves and not watering too much in summer. Watch for thrips and spider mites (see "Tips and Techniques" for controls).

### Companion Planting and Design
Plant at the same time as new oaks or sycamores. Combine with redbud, toyon, and hummingbird sage. Currant's tall and narrow profile fits into narrow planting strips as well.

### Try These
'Inverness White' and 'White Icicle' (both 8 feet × 6 feet) have white flowers. 'Claremont' (8 feet tall), with pale pink to rose-pink flowers, and 'Tranquillon Ridge' (10 feet), with deep pink flowers both tolerate the more arid conditions of the southern part of the state. Chaparral currant (*Ribes malvaceum*) is an easy-to-grow currant with many upright stems covered in bright green leaves. It has hanging 2- to 6-inch pale pink to red flower clusters followed by almost-black berries, and gnarled stems with shreddy bark. 'Dancing tassels' (6 to 8 feet × 6 to 8 feet) has full 8- to 12-inch-long tassels of pale pink flowers starting in fall. Beautiful! Catalina perfume (*Ribes viburnifolium*) is evergreen ground cover with tiny deep-green fragrant leaves. Small burgundy flowers appear in winter to early spring.

# Rockrose
## *Cistus* spp.

### When, Where, and How to Plant

Plant fall through spring in warm winter climates and in spring through early summer in cold winter climates. Choose a spot in full sun with well-draining soil. Rockrose is native to areas with poor soils that drain well. If your soil drains poorly, build a raised garden bed or mound of well-draining soil. Be gentle with the roots to minimize damage at planting (see "Tips and Techniques" for more on building mounds and planting).

### Growing Tips

Water deeply and regularly through the first year to establish. In subsequent years, water only occasionally but deeply from the time the ground dries in spring until winter rains. Rockrose is very drought tolerant but a bit of supplemental water through the growing season encourages lusher growth. Mulch with composted organic matter. Fertilize with all-purpose organic fertilizer in early spring if desired.

### Care

Rockrose does not *require* pruning, but if you can, remove dead or damaged branches before growth starts in spring. Do not cut into the woody part of the plant. Few if any pests dare bother the sticky stems of rockrose.

### Companion Planting and Design

Rockrose is at home in flower borders, massed as informal hedges or evergreen screens, used to control erosion on a steep bank, or dressing up a seaside garden. What more could one ask from a garden plant?

### Try These

'Blanche' (5 feet × 5 feet) has pure white flowers on branches clothed in deep green leaves. 'Sunset' (4 feet × 8 feet) has magenta flowers. Both leaves and flowers are a bit smaller and more delicate looking than other *Cistus* hybrids. 'Victor Reiter' (4 feet × 3 feet) has hot pink flowers with pale pink centers and gray-green leaves. *Cistus* × *skanbergii* (4 feet × 6 feet) blooms profusely with small pale pink flowers. Leaves are small and gray-green. *Cistus* × *purpureus* (4 feet × 4 feet) has a deep magenta-purple flower with a red spot at the base of each petal that contrasts dramatically with bright yellow stamens in the center of the flower.

*These aromatic-leaved evergreen shrubs grow in scrubby dry habitats much like California's sage scrub and chaparral. Their spring through early summer flowers look like crepe-papery old-fashioned roses (hence the common name). Each flower has five petals in white, pink, rose, or even deep purple, all with yellow centers. In some varieties, the base of each petal is decorated with a burgundy spot. Rockrose thrives in the toughest conditions—in the heat and intense sun of the desert or the harsh salt spray next to the sea. An impressive display of wild rockrose grows on the hillsides overlooking Cinque Terre, the five seaside towns on the coast of the Mediterranean in northern Italy.*

### Bloom Period and Seasonal Color

Spring to early summer flowers are pale to deep pink, crimson, purple, or white, with a yellow center and often with a deep maroon spot at the base of the petals.

Hardy to 7A

Min. Temp.
0 to 15° F

### Mature Height × Spread
2 to 4 ft. × 6 to 8 ft.

### Minimum Temperature
Depends on cultivar.

# Round-leaf Tea Tree

## *Leptospermum rotundifolium*

Round-leaf tea tree is an 8- to 10-foot-tall and wide evergreen shrub, native to New South Wales, Australia. Its small round ("rotundus") leaves ("folium") distinguish it from other types of tea trees, including the more commonly grown New Zealand tea tree (Leptospermum scoparium), which has narrow, more needlelike leaves and an upright and jagged branching structure that is attractive only when pruned. Round-leaf tea tree, on the other hand, is more open with an airy, naturally graceful structure of curved branches. Large lavender or rose-pink flowers cover the branches in spring. The round, five-petal structure and soft colors contrast the glossy green or blue-green leaves. As shrubs mature, their multiple branches become more gnarled, adding to their character.

### Bloom Period and Seasonal Color
Rose or lavender pink flowers in spring and summer.

### Mature Height × Spread
8 to 10 ft. × 8 to 10 ft.

**Hardy to 9A**

**Min. Temp. 20° F**

### When, Where, and How to Plant
Plant fall through spring in frost-free gardens and in spring in colder winter gardens. Round-leaf tea tree prefers well-draining soils but tolerates heavy soils and nutrient poor soils. Plant in full or part sun. Follow shrub planting directions in "Tips and Techniques." Water well and mulch. To grow as a potted plant, start small plants in small containers. Move plants to larger containers as they gain height and width.

### Growing Tips
Deep water weekly for the first two or three weeks, then monthly until winter rains arrive. Starting in year two, water deeply each month from the time soil dries in spring until winter rains. Rinse dust off leaves periodically with a light spray. Since their native soils have even less nutrients than ours, these plants don't need fertilizer.

### Care
Pests have little interest in round-leaf tea tree. Discourage root rot and deadly soil fungi by limiting water. Pruning is not necessary but can be done for shape and bushiness. Perform any pruning right after flowering. See pruning directions in "Tips and Techniques."

### Companion Planting and Design
Grow round-leaf tea tree as an accent in a dry garden along with California natives or other Mediterranean climate plants. Set against a background of dense-leaved shrubs, this tea tree's open branching structure lightens the presentation, especially when flowers are present. It's adaptable to growing in a container. It's excellent as a cut flower.

### Try These
'Manning's Choice' (6 feet × 9 feet) has blue-green leaves and green-eyed lavender-pink flowers that peak in spring. Shining tea tree (*Leptospermum turbinatum* 'Flat Rock' or *Leptospermum nitidum*) is a spreading shrub 6 to 12 feet × 6 to 12 feet. Small half-inch white flowers contrast against small gray-green leaves that have a touch of bronze when they first emerge. It's hardy to 20 degrees F. *Leptospermum laevigatum* 'Reevesii' (or 'Reevesii Compacta') is a 3- to 5-foot × 3- to 5-foot evergreen with white spring flowers and oval blue-gray leaves. It is hardy to 25 degrees F.

## When, Where, and How to Plant

Plant in early spring or early fall into well-drained and slightly acidic soil and full or part sun. These camellias manage in that tough spot that gets full shade in winter and full sun in summer. Follow basic shrub planting directions (see "Tips and Techniques") but amend the soil so you refill the planting hole with 50 percent organic matter and 50 percent native soil. If your soil is basic, sprinkle in soil sulfur to help acidify it. Loosen camellia roots and plant a few inches high in the hole. Build a water basin around the trunk. Water deeply and mulch to keep roots cool and shaded.

## Growing Tips

Protect sun-grown camellias with shadecloth for their first three summers. Water deeply to keep the rootball moist through the first four years, then cut back. Once established, sasanquas are relatively drought tolerant. Apply balanced organic fertilizer every six weeks when plants are *not* blooming from February through August.

## Care

Prune to shape after flowering ends and before new growth begins. Watch for scale, aphids, mealybugs, and whiteflies (see "Tips and Techniques"). Many diseases threaten camellias. Ask your local Master Gardeners about diseases in your region and how to treat them.

## Companion Planting and Design

Use sasanquas as background shrubs or specimen plants, screens, espaliers, or hedges. Grow in containers or bonsai.

## Try These

'Showa No Sake' (5 feet × 6 feet) has soft pink semi-double flowers. 'Shishi Gashira' (5 feet × 5 feet) has shocking pink or rosy red double flowers. 'White Doves' ('Mine-No-Yuki') (6 feet × 6 feet) has large white, semi-double flowers. 'Kanjiro' (10 to 12 feet × 10 to 12 feet) has single to semi-double hot pink or rose-red flowers. 'Setsugekka' (10 to 12 feet × 10 to 12 feet) has large semi-double white flowers with ruffled petals. 'Hana Jiman' (12 to 15 feet × 12 to 15 feet) has semi-double white flowers with pink edges. 'Narumigata' (15 feet × 15 feet) tree has large cup-shaped flowers tinged pink.

*Few plants are as consistent and reliable as the camellia, and few plants have lovelier flowers. Camellias are large evergreen shrubs with shiny dark-green leaves and large flowers (some fragrant) that bloom white to pink, deep red, and combinations thereof. There are even yellow flowered camellias. Most gardeners are familiar with* Camellia japonica, *an Asian native that blooms early in the year, but for my garden I prefer sasanqua camellias. While japonicas prefer a shady spot with moist soil, sasanquas tolerate sun and drier soils, important characteristics in our arid Mediterranean climate. Sasanqua camellias start blooming as early as the end of August along the coast and in September inland. Bloom continues until February when* Camellia japonica *takes center stage. Plant both for a long season of bloom.*

### Bloom Period and Seasonal Color

Late summer through late winter in white to pink, deep red, and combinations thereof.

### Mature Height × Spread

5 to 15 ft. × 5 to 15 ft., depending on variety.

**Hardy to 7A**

**Min. Temp. 0° F**

# Sky Flower
## *Duranta erecta*

*Beautiful and easy to grow, sky flower shrubs have gained in popularity over the last decade. These attractive thorny evergreens grow quickly to about 12 feet tall. Their small, serrated leaves are bright green, gold, or variegated green with cream or yellow. From spring to summer, sky flowers are decorated in long sprays of fragrant flowers arranged in tapering clusters. Flowers are white, light blue, intense blue, or lilac blue. Some varieties have deep purple flowers edged in white. Flowers turn into clusters of golden berries, though not all at once. It is common to see these graceful shrubs with both purple flowers and golden berries at the same time—a winning combination! Sky flower is also sold as Duranta repens. Note: Sky flower is poisonous if ingested.*

### Other Common Name
Golden Dewdrop

### Bloom Period and Seasonal Color
Spring to summer flower clusters are white, light blue, intense blue, lilac blue, and deep purple edged in white. Golden berries appear throughout the year.

Hardy to
9B

Min.
Temp.
25° F

### Mature Height × Spread
2 to 15 ft. × 2 to 12 ft., depending on cultivar.

## When, Where, and How to Plant
Plant into full or part sun, especially in the hottest inland gardens. Sky flowers prefer well-drained soil but tolerate even heavy clay. These shrubs thrive in spots that are in full sun part of the year and shade the rest. Plant any time of year except hottest summer months. Follow basic shrub planting directions in "Tips and Techniques." Water deeply and mulch.

## Growing Tips
Sky flower requires deep weekly water from spring to late fall in the first two years. After the second year, cut back water frequency. If the leaves droop, increase the frequency (not duration) of watering. Apply all-purpose organic fertilizer in early spring.

## Care
Prune to remove dead, diseased, or damaged wood, or to shape. Sky flowers are naturally multi-trunked shrubs but can be pruned to more of a tree-like shape or to espalier against a wall. Sky flower has no major pests.

## Companion Planting and Design
Plant sky flower en masse as an informal hedge. Prune it to a single plane to grow as an espalier or to one or three trunks to grow as a small tree. Sky flower is a great container plant. Look for a very large ceramic pot glazed teal, purple, or terracotta.

## Try These
'Alba' (15 feet × 8 to 12 feet) has white flowers and gold berries. 'Gold Tip' (6 feet × 6 feet) is a slow growing, compact sky flower with bright yellow-gold foliage turning purplish in cold weather. 'Variegata' (15 feet × 8 feet) has green and cream variegated leaves with lilac-blue flowers and golden berries. Plant in part shade in hot inland gardens to protect foliage. 'Gold Edge' (10 feet × 10 feet) has lilac flowers and golden-yellow leaves that look best in part sun. 'Sapphire Showers' (25 feet × 25 feet) has spreading and arching branches adaptable to growing as an upright tree. Flowers are intense blue with a white edge. 'Sweet Memory' (6 to 8 feet × 6 to 8 feet) has deep purple flowers edged in white.

# Spotted Emu Bush
## *Eremophila maculata*

### When, Where, and How to Plant
Emu bushes are excellent small shrubs for all gardens except high deserts and mountains. Well-draining soils are best, but plants tolerate heavy soils if kept on the dry side. Plant fall through spring in frost-free gardens and in spring in colder winter gardens. Follow shrub planting directions in "Tips and Techniques." Water well and mulch.

### Growing Tips
Water deeply each week for the first several weeks and then monthly until rains arrive. In year two, water deeply each month from spring until winter rains. After that, deep water only occasionally in summer. More frequent watering encourages faster growth. Since Australian soils have fewer nutrients than ours, there is no need to fertilize. If leaves pale, sprinkle soil around the base with iron sulfate or powdered sulfur and iron chelate (follow directions on the label). Water deeply and wait. Leaves color up over several months.

### Care
Prune branch tips after flowers fade to encourage new flowering stems. If plants split or decline, rejuvenate by cutting branches back by a third. No significant pests bother this plant. Limit water to discourage root rot and deadly soil fungi.

### Companion Planting and Design
Incorporate mounding emu bushes into low water perennial borders, plant on slopes to control erosion and in succulent gardens to add color and fine texture. Feature them in collections of potted plants.

### Try These
'Aurea' has yellow flowers (3 to 5 feet × 3 to 5 feet) and is hardy to 20 degrees F. Red flowers of 'Valentine™' bloom winter to early spring, peaking in February (4 feet × 4 feet). It is hardy to 15 degrees F. Yellow Emu Bush (*Eremophila glabra*) has soft gray-green leaves and warm golden orange blooms that peak in winter/early spring (4 to 5 feet × 6 to 8 feet) and is hardy to 20 degrees F. 'Kalgoorlie' (2 to 3 feet × 2 to 3 feet) has grey-green leaves and bright orange flowers. 'Ouyen' (2 to 3 feet × 2 to 3 feet) has grey foliage and green flowers. *Eremophila laanii* has arching branches and pink springtime flowers (5 to 8 feet × 5 to 8 feet).

*The genus of Emu bush is Eremophila, which loosely translated from Latin means "desert lover." The name is well suited for these low mounding evergreens that hail from arid regions of Australia. There are 214 species of emu bushes, a handful of which are available in California nurseries. Spotted emu is one of the more commonly available species. It has narrow green leaves and tubular snapdragon-like flowers. The flowers are spotted red or magenta pink. They bloom year-round in milder winter gardens, and their show peaks in summer. Other species have gray or gray-green leaves with scarlet, pumpkin, lavender, or golden yellow flowers. These beautiful low-water shrubs are moderate to fast growers, easy to care for, and perfectly suited to our arid Mediterranean climate gardens.*

### Bloom Period and Seasonal Color
Spotted red or magenta pink flowers year-round, peak in summer.

### Mature Height × Spread
3 ft. × 3 ft.

Hardy to 7A

Min. Temp. 0° F

# Sweet-pea Bush
## *Polygala × dalmaisiana*

*If you could create your dream shrub, it would probably be easy to grow, always in flower, tolerate lots or little water, have no pests, and be easy to prune. That list is more than fulfilled by sweet-pea bush. This evergreen shrub has dense branches that are covered in oval green leaves and topped in vibrant violet sweet pea-like flowers. These flowers' most prominent features are a pair of wing shaped petals and a beard of white fringes. The flowers bloom nearly twelve months of the year, even in gardens where temperatures dip down into the 20s several nights each winter. These shrubs make beautiful evergreen screens or hedges, clipped formally (though you loose some bloom) or left to their natural rounded shape.*

### Other Common Name
Sweet-pea shrub

### Bloom Period and Seasonal Color
Violet and white flowers, year-round.

### Mature Height × Spread
4 ft. × 4 ft.

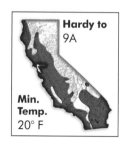

**Hardy to**
9A

**Min. Temp.**
20° F

### When, Where, and How to Plant
Plant fall through spring in frost-free gardens and in spring in colder gardens. The most prolific bloom is in full sun, a bit less in part sun. These shrubs tolerate the heat of low desert gardens. They prefer well-drained soils. Follow shrub planting directions in "Tips and Techniques." Water well and mulch.

### Growing Tips
Sweet-pea bush growing along the coast is quite drought tolerant. In my garden, one seeded itself into the unwatered cracks of a dry-stacked concrete stair. It is not as large or lush as its irrigated neighbors, but it puts on a good show of flowers. In all areas, water deeply and regularly through the first summer to help plants become established. In subsequent years, water deeply but infrequently along the coast in summer and more regularly in valleys and low deserts. Apply all-purpose organic fertilizer before new growth in spring.

### Care
Plants require no pruning but can be clipped and shaped as desired or to rejuvenate a poor performing plant. Prune the softwood and avoid cutting into the hardwood branches. No significant pests.

### Companion Planting and Design
Polygala makes an excellent specimen, hedge, border (space 5 feet apart), or low screen. Try a border of sweet-pea bush mixed with butterfly bush, sages, and ornamental grasses.

### Try These
*Polygala fruticosa* (4 to 6 feet × 4 to 6 feet) features red to violet flowers spring through summer. Heart-shaped blue-green leaves have a purple tint. 'Petite Butterfly' ('Petite Butterflies') is a dwarf (2 feet × 3 feet) with a rounded form and is excellent in containers or narrow borders. It is hardy to 15 to 20 degrees F. Purple broom (*Polygala apopetala*) has the form of a small tree (4 to 8 feet × 3 feet). Its single green "trunk" splits into multiple branches with a sprinkling of narrow green leaves. Branches are topped with sprays of vibrant purple flowers with purple fringes from winter through early summer. It is root hardy to 10 degrees F. Boxleaf sweet-pea bush (*Polygala myrtifolia*) is larger (8 feet × 8 feet) and has darker green leaves and larger flowers than the sweet-pea bush.

# Texas Ranger
## *Leucophyllum* spp.

### When, Where, and How to Plant

Plant in frost-free gardens in fall, or in spring in colder areas. Utilize full sun and very well-draining soil. If you have heavy soil, build a planting mound (see "Tips and Techniques"). Texas ranger grows in most California garden climates, even in the extremes of high desert gardens. Nutrient poor soils are fine. Follow shrub-planting directions in "Tips and Techniques." Water deeply and mulch after planting.

### Growing Tips

Water deeply and frequently through the first two summers to help plants become established. After that, provide only periodic summer water. No winter watering is needed once plants are established. There is no need to fertilize either.

### Care

Prune to shape (especially if shrubs grow lanky), in early spring before new flower buds develop. Alternatively, allow your Texas ranger to find its own natural shape. Avoid overwatering to prevent root rot. Texas ranger has no pest problems.

### Companion Planting and Design

Texas ranger performs well as both a specimen plant and a background shrub. Use in streetscapes, in parking lot planters, and in curbside strips. Plant en mass as evergreen screens and informal hedges. In a mixed garden bed, balance with rosette-forming plants such as Mexican grass plant, yucca, and agave. Combine with Mediterranean climate plants such as maleleuca, bougainvillea, and burgundy flowered South African geranium. In a native garden, plant with dark-green leaved California lilac and arbutus.

### Try These

*Leucophyllum frutescens* 'Compacta' (5 feet × 5 feet) has silver foliage and dark pink flowers. It tolerates heavier soils and more water. 'Green Cloud'™ (6 to 8 feet × 6 to 8 feet) has deep green leaves and rose-purple flowers and is deciduous in cold winter gardens. 'White Cloud'™ (6 to 8 feet × 6 to 8 feet) has grey foliage and white flowers. *Leucophyllum laevigatum* (5 feet × 5 feet) has flat green leaves and blue flowers. *Leucophyllum langmaniae* 'Lynn's Legacy' (5 feet × 5 feet) has green leaves and lavender colored flowers.

*"White leaf" is the translation of Texas ranger's scientific name* Leucophyllum. *Aptly named, many varieties of this fast growing evergreen shrub are densely clothed in tiny leaves, each covered in a fine down that gives them a silvery sheen. These are tiny leaves, a half-inch or so long and slightly cupped—all common adaptations for plants native to hot, sunny, and dry habitats. These are good-sized shrubs, some with leaves that are greener and others with leaves that are grayer. Flower color too differs, depending on variety. Texas ranger has 1-inch summertime flowers ranging from a deep purple to pale purple to white and sometimes pink. The contrast between leaf color and flower color is one of Texas ranger's most attractive traits.*

**Other Common Name**
Texas Sage

**Bloom Period and Seasonal Color**
Summer blooms in deep purple to pale purple, white or pink.

**Mature Height × Spread**
3 to 8 ft. × 3 to 8 ft.

Hardy to 8A

Min. Temp. 10° F

# Thyme-leafed Fuchsia
## *Fuchsia thymifolia*

*I remember our fuchsia days. We lived at the beach where the air was humid and patios were filled with hanging baskets overflowing with fuchsias. When we moved a few miles inland, the air was drier and our fuchsias struggled to maintain their looks. I soon satisfied my fuchsia love with in-ground species, including shrubby, thyme-leafed fuchsia. This fine-textured fuchsia doesn't have large fancy multi-colored flowers of the hybrids. Instead a profusion of tiny trumpet-shaped magenta or rose-pink flowers appear at branch ends in the warmer months of the year. Small glossy green leaves with finely toothed edges cover the somewhat arching, semi-woody branches that typically reach 4 or 5 feet long but under the best circumstances, can grow to 10 feet. What a show!*

**Bloom Period and Seasonal Color**
Magenta or rose-pink flowers late spring through fall.

**Mature Height × Spread**
4 to 10 ft. × 4 to 10 ft.

**Hardy to 9A**

**Min. Temp. 20° F**

## When, Where, and How to Plant
Plant thyme-leaved fuchsia in spring or early summer into well-amended and well-draining soil. This fuchsia can handle full sun, but only right along the coast. Otherwise provide part sun to dappled shade. When planted in full shade, flowers diminish. In hot gardens, protect it from wind and sun. Follow shrub planting directions in "Tips and Techniques." Water deeply after planting, and mulch. Thyme-leaved fuchsia does well in a glazed or plastic container as well. Use a rich organic potting mix. Top-dress with pebbles or gravel to conserve moisture.

## Growing Tips
Fuchsias both in pots and in the ground require constantly damp (not wet) soil. Those in the ground benefit from a thick layer of composted organic matter year-round to seal in moisture. Add organic matter as the mulch breaks down. Whether in a pot or in the ground, feed them regularly with organic fertilizer in the growing season. Follow directions on the label.

## Care
To encourage new blooms and bushier plants, pinch back branch tips or clip branches back in early spring before new growth starts. This plant is resistant to the fuchsia mite. Watch for aphids (see "Tips and Techniques").

## Companion Planting and Design
Thyme-leaved fuchsia is extremely versatile. Create a shade garden with bear's breach, Japanese maple, hellebore, bergenia, Japanese sweet shade, and a shade loving bamboo. Thyme-leaved fuchsia can also be grown in a container placed at the entry to a courtyard, patio, or any location out of the direct sun.

## Try These
'Variegata' doesn't grow as fast as the species but has deep green leaves with creamy white edges. Another of my favorite shrub fuchsias is lilac fuchsia (*Fuchsia arborescens*). This fuchsia's scale is the diametric opposite of thyme-leaf fuchsia. Shrub fuchsia has long leaves (8 inches) on a large shrub (8 to 10 feet × 8 feet) with abundant clusters of petite tubular rose-colored flower buds that open to dusky pink stars. Flowers are often visited by hummingbirds.

# Toyon
## *Heteromeles arbutifolia*

### When, Where, and How to Plant
Toyon grows well in full sun or in the bright shade of a tall oak (planted at the same time) or other tree. They are suitable for all gardens except those in the deserts and highest mountains. In a beach garden, keep them out of the spray zone. While toyon prefers well-draining soils, they also tolerate clay. Plant in fall or winter, according to shrub-planting directions in "Tips and Techniques." Water deeply and mulch after planting.

### Growing Tips
Water regularly and deeply through the first year or two to help roots go deep. Once established, toyon can survive on rainfall in most gardens, but grows faster and looks lusher with deep monthly summer water. Too frequent water, however, can lead to root rot. Maintain a thick layer of organic mulch beneath all toyons. No fertilizer is needed.

### Care
Young toyon grow slowly, then speed up as plants mature, ultimately forming a large shrub that can be pruned to be a small multi-trunk tree (very old plants can reach 20 feet tall). These shrubs flower (and make berries) on the previous year's growth. If your toyon needs pruning but you want berries, selectively remove branches rather than pruning it back. Cut all branches at the base. Toyon is susceptible to aphids, mealybugs, thrips. Fire blight results in dead branches that look burnt. Prune off infected branches and trash immediately (don't compost), sterilizing pruning shears between cuts and after you finish. Pruning directions, tool sterilization, and pest control information can be found in "Tips and Techniques."

### Companion Planting and Design
One of my favorite fall displays is a toyon in full red berry alongside blue fall-blooming California lilac and the bright gold fall flowers of perennial marigold. Add yellow blooming daylilies, tufts of teal blue fescue, and a purple leaf New Zealand flax for contrast.

### Try This
Toyon 'Davis Gold' grows just like the species but with narrower leaves and gorgeous golden yellow berries in fall.

*We think of Hollywood as the birthplace of the movie industry, but long before that it was known for toyons. When easterners first arrived, Hollywood's hillsides were covered in thickets of evergreen shrubs with leathery, deep green, toothed leaves and bright-red fall berries. Not surprisingly, they referred to the shrubs as hollies and eventually named the area for the shrubs. Toyon (the native American name) is common in chaparral and oak woodlands throughout California. Garden-grown toyons are big beautiful shrubs that fill open spaces in short time. They are a fantastic background for flowering plants and quickly stabilize slopes, screen out neighbors, and hide unsightly fences. Birds love the berries, but they are not for human consumption. Toyon is easy to grow and drought tolerant.*

**Other Common Name**
California Holly

**Bloom Period and Seasonal Color**
White summer flowers become bright red berries in late fall through winter.

**Mature Height × Spread**
6 to 15 ft. × 6 to 10 ft.

Hardy to 8A
Min. Temp. 10° F

# Winter Cassia
## *Cassia bicapsularis*

*Have you ever heard gardeners talking about California's "second spring"? Our second spring arrives when the temperatures cool in fall. It is both a planting time and a blooming time. One of the showiest "second spring" bloomers in my garden is winter cassia. This shrub has bright green, feathery foliage and a broad rounded form. Covering the branches are large, round petaled, golden yellow flowers that look like pieces of buttered popcorn. These South American and Caribbean natives are extremely vigorous and very easy garden plants. Naturally multi-stemmed, winter cassia can be pruned to just a few stems or to one stem and grown as a shrub or pruned up to a small tree. Winter cassia is also sold as Senna bicapsularis.*

**Other Common Name**
Christmasbush

**Bloom Period and Seasonal Color**
Bright yellow flowers from late summer to early winter followed by brown seedpods.

**Mature Height × Spread**
5 to 12 ft. × 5 to 12 ft.

Hardy to 9A

Min. Temp. 20 to 25° F

### When, Where, and How to Plant
Plant fall through spring in frost-free gardens and in spring in colder winter gardens, in full or part sun. Provide well-drained soils that are sandy or loamy. If you have heavy soil, build a planting mound. Directions for building planting mounds and for general shrub planting directions are in "Tips and Techniques." Water well after planting, and mulch.

### Growing Tips
Winter cassia is fairly drought tolerant, especially in milder coastal gardens. Deep watering for the first year helps winter cassia establish deep roots. Water regularly through summer, especially in drier inland gardens. Apply a balanced organic fertilizer in early spring.

### Care
Pinch branch tips to encourage bushiness. Stake or prune young plants to create a strong network of main branches. Weak wood and heavy canopies can cause slender branches to bend and break. Don't be afraid to prune winter cassia. They recover from even the most extreme (even botched) pruning. Frost may kill off branches, but they sprout back, even if frozen to the ground. Pests are not a problem, though caterpillars sometimes eat the leaves. Tolerate the chewed leaves and you will be rewarded with butterflies.

### Companion Planting and Design
My favorite fall to winter color combinations are yellow flowering winter cassia planted with purple flowering Mexican bush sage or blue-flowering Mexican sage. Add a ground cover of orange flowered sunrose 'Henfield Brilliant' or burgundy 'Mesa Wine'. Pineapple lily beneath the branches, gets just the right amount of summer shade while livening up the composition before the winter cassia bloom. Winter cassia attracts yellow winged-sulfur butterflies.

### Try These
'Butter Creme' ('Worley's Butter Crème') has soft yellow flowers. Golden Medallion Tree (*Cassia leptophylla*) is a tree-like cassia with a broad canopy and rounded pom-poms of bright yellow flowers in summer. Lacy foliage is deep green and evergreen. Like winter cassia, leaves may drop during prolonged cold periods (20 to 25 feet × 30 feet). It is very drought tolerant and hardy to 25 degrees F.

## When, Where, and How to Plant

Plant in all but the hottest summer months or during freezing temperatures. Yellow bells is adaptable to a wide range of soils, from rocky, soils to well-amended and well-draining soils. Pick a spot in full sun where the plant has room to spread. Follow shrub planting directions in "Tips and Techniques." Water well after planting, and mulch.

## Growing Tips

Water deeply and regularly for the first year to help establish deep roots. In subsequent years, maximize flower production by watering plants deeply every other week (more or less depending on soil and climate) during bloom. Reduce water frequency in winter, especially when plants are dormant. Fertilizer is not necessary.

## Care

Cut back spent flower stems after bloom. Prune off frost damaged branches in early spring after danger of additional frosts is past. Prune to shape anytime the plant is not in bloom and has no flower buds. Monitor young plants for tomato horn worm (caterpillars). Pick caterpillars off by hand or treat with the bacterial spore *Bacillus thuringiensis* (Bt).

## Companion Planting and Design

Plant yellow bells singly as a specimen, or cluster plants for an informal hedge or screen. In a tropical landscape, combine yellow bells with dry climate palms, pink orchid vine, and bougainvillea. Don't site this plant too close to a swimming pool, however, as it generates quite a bit of leaf and flower litter. For an unusual combination, plant rock purslane at the base of yellow bells. The contrast of bright magenta purple flowers and golden yellow or orange flowers is particularly striking.

## Try These

'Orange Jubilee' (12 feet × 8 feet) has tangerine orange flowers. *Tecoma* × Sunrise (8 feet × 8 feet) is my favorite. Its trumpet-shaped flowers are golden yellow inside with apricot colored veins. On the outside, they are shaded deep apricot to pale apricot from the base to the mouth. I grow *Tecoma* × Sunrise against a terracotta colored wall. When it blooms, friends and strangers stop me to ask what it is and where to find one for their own.

*Not all low water plants are succulent, gray leaved, or tiny flowered. One of the showier dry climate plants is the very tropical looking yellow bells. This tall shrub (or small tree) has large clusters of trumpet-shaped golden flowers, sometimes blushed with apricot and orange. Its flowers are the most striking features, but part of the attraction is the contrast between the bright color flowers and the shiny deep green leaves. Such lush foliage allows low water yellow bells to look right at home in tropical landscapes. In drier landscapes the green leaves provide a welcome relief from the grays and blue-greens. In the warmest regions, yellow bells is evergreen. Where winter temperatures dip much below 30 degrees F, plants loose their leaves in winter.*

**Other Common Name**
Yellow Trumpet Flower

**Bloom Period and Seasonal Color**
Bright gold flowers with tangerine or yellow, orange, and apricot. Blooms from spring through fall.

Hardy to 7A

Min. Temp. 0 to 20° F

**Mature Height × Spread**
6 to 12 ft. × 6 to 8 ft., depending on variety.

# Succulents *for California*

The San Diego County Fair is one of my favorite places to see garden displays. Some years I have the honor of judging displays, some years I enjoy them simply as a visitor, and one year I was invited to design and install one. That year, as we slaved to finish our display in time for opening, I noticed a crowd gathering around another display. I wandered over to take a look. What I saw floored me. It was a perfect underwater scene. There were anemones, coral, starfish, and more—done completely in succulents!

The garden's creator, Jeff Moore of Solana Succulents in Solana Beach, California, told me that people wandering through his nursery often comment on how one succulent or another looks like it should be growing underwater. The comments inspired Jeff to try his hand at creating an underwater garden scene. The display was so clever and convincing that it garnered a lion's share of awards. Jeff was then invited to recreate the display at the Philadelphia Flower Show. A similar composition is on permanent display at Quail Botanical Gardens in Encinitas, California, just north of Jeff's nursery.

Foxtail agave behind green and black aeoniums

Californian gardeners' love affair with succulents goes back to the Victorian era, if not earlier. At the turn of the century garden designer Rudolph Ulrich created lavish formal landscapes for the likes of railroad barons Leland Stanford and Charles Crocker in Palo Alto and Monterey. They were extensive and expensive plant collections that included Ulrich's renowned "ribbon beds" and "carpet beds" that were vast, ornate, tapestry-like designs created with succulents carefully chosen for their texture and color.

Today, as in Ulrich's day, gardeners are attracted to succulents for their sculptural and architectural value. Moreover, we love their weird appearances, their incredibly diverse shapes, their colors, and their easy care.

Succulents add interest even in small spaces

## What Are Succulents?

Succulents are not a separate group of related plants but rather an adaptation that occurs across the plant kingdom. In some families like the agave family, all members are succulent. But there are also succulent geraniums, succulent leaved oreganos, succulent amaryllis, succulent begonias, succulent orchids, succulent members of the cucumber family, and many more. Succulence describes a plant's ability to store water in its leaves, stems, or roots. Water storing tissues become thick and fleshy ensuring a plentiful supply in environments where water is extremely limited. Plants evolve as succulents not just in deserts, but in other dry environments such as dry tropics, dry mountains, and along coastlines. To plants, beaches bear a striking resemblance to deserts: freshwater is limited, soils are porous and dry, the sun is intense, and plants are subject to constant drying wind.

One interesting, but seemingly contradictory, habitat for succulents is humid tropical jungles. Plants such as orchid cactus and reed orchid hail from these habitats. These plants are epiphytes—they live in the branches of trees rather than in the ground. As such, they get moisture from the atmosphere, not from roots sunk into the ground. This situation evidently prompted their development of fleshy succulent stems and roots.

Succulents have additional ways of adapting to challenging conditions. Some are covered in fine silvery hairs that look like fuzz and give the leaves a grayish cast. Those hairs shade the plant by reflecting sunlight away from the surface. They also create a vapor barrier that limits critical water evaporation, as does a whitish waxy covering that covers some leaves instead of hairs.

Many succulents have a special kind of metabolism that further limits water loss. Plant leaves have pores that open to exchange oxygen for carbon dioxide. Open pores allow water to evaporate as well. The process typically happens during the day while the sun is up and the plant is actively photosynthesizing. With these special succulents, however, the pores open only at night when the air is cool and evaporative stress is far lower than during the heat of the day.

Stunning aloe in a tall urn

## A Prickly Topic

All cacti are succulent, but not all succulents are cacti. Spines are the most obvious features that distinguish cacti from other succulents. Through evolution, cacti lost their leaves. Or more accurately, their leaves morphed into spines, typically arranged in clusters. Spines serve several purposes, among them, protecting plants from hungry predators (two- and four-legged), forming a protective layer similar to the fine hairs of succulents, and even collecting dew on their tips. The dew drops to the ground and serves as a source of moisture for the roots. Imagine a situation so dry that even a few droplets of dew count towards a plant's survival!

Also, some succulents have thorns instead of spines. Botanists tell us that where spines are modified leaves, thorns are modified stems and branches. Technical but interesting . . .

By the way, if you get those fine spines in your hand (ouch!), paint over them with rubber cement. Once it dries, rub it off and the spines will pull right out. Rubber cement can be hazardous, so some people prefer using duct tape instead.

This chapter covers more than fifty species and varieties of succulents. In addition to sharing succulent roots, stems, and/or leaves, all are shallow rooted plants that prefer extremely well-draining soil, whether

Flapjack plant with cobweb houseleek

A rosette of aeonium foliage against tall grasses and New Zealand flax

planted into a pot or into the ground. If you want to plant succulents in the ground but have heavy or poor draining soil, build a raised bed or planting mound of well draining soil (see Perennials introduction). The shallow roots make them easy to dig and move, too.

Succulents prefer full sun and have very little need for water with a few exceptions. Christmas cactus can burn in bright sun. Along with reed orchid, Christmas cactus needs regular water. Other succulents, however, do fine on a low-water diet. Water timing is most important during the growing season, which for some succulents is summer and for others is fall or winter. Watch for information on when *not* to water succulents. Aeonium, for example, can rot if overwatered in the winter.

Overall, succulents are extremely low maintenance plants. They grow slowly (another reason they make good container plants). Pruning is essentially a non-issue. Fertilization is minimal (except for tropical epiphytes), and they are extremely easy to propagate. Break a piece off and share it with a friend.

Pests can be pesky, especially sucking pests like aphids or mealybugs and, of course, the snails and slugs that are ubiquitous in our gardens.

Interestingly there are succulents with bright colored foliage—one of their most desirable characteristics—that develop only with tough love. The red pigments that create those fantastic colors develop in response to extreme cold, extreme heat, nutrient deficiency, or water stress. Brightly colored aloes and flapjack plant are examples. That is not to say that your goal should be to never water them or allow them to freeze. With some experimentation, the plants will show you the conditions that most encourage color. By the way, if you withhold water and your succulent starts to shrink, you have gone too far. Soak that plant right away!

# Aeonium
## *Aeonium* spp.

Gardeners are often challenged to keep their gardens interesting between bloom seasons. One solution is to include evergreens that have interesting leaf color and/or texture. Aeoniums are just those plants. Aeoniums form rosettes of spoon-shaped leaves that, at first glance, look like big succulent flowers. Some aeonium have bright green leaves, some are deep burgundy almost black. Then there are aeoniums with leaves of all shades and variations in between. One of the most beautiful aeoniums, 'Sunburst', has pale yellow leaves striped in green and edged in pink. In summer aeoniums form stalks of tiny yellow flowers that are nice, but less impressive than their leafy rosettes. Most aeoniums multiply making side shoots (pups), many forming broad colonies that make great low-water ground covers.

**Bloom Period and Seasonal Color**
Stalks of tiny yellow flowers in summer.

**Mature Height × Spread**
1¹/₂ to 4 ft. × 1 to 3 ft.

Hardy to 9B

Min. Temp. 25° F

### When, Where, and How to Plant
Aeonium is grown in well-draining soil in full sun along the coast. If your soil drains poorly, build a planting mound of well-draining soil (see "Tips and Techniques"). Aeonium tolerates dry shade, especially in hot inland gardens.

### Growing Tips
Aeoniums stop growing in summer, so be sparing with summer water or your plants will rot. Rains arrive during their winter growing season and should take care of their water needs, but do water occasionally if we have a dry winter. No fertilizer is needed.

### Care
Groom plants to remove dead leaves and spent flower stalks. There is no need to prune, but you can remove branches to shape. To root cuttings, allow them to dry for a few days. As you pot the cutting, set most of the bare stem below the surface in a well-draining soil mix. Place in indirect light. Keep soil moist but not wet until cuttings root. Few pests bother aeonium.

### Companion Planting and Design
Aeonium are the mainstay of many succulent gardens. You can also use them in combination with non-succulent, water-wise plants. Use *Aeonium* 'Sunburst' to light up deep green cape rush. Play burgundy 'Zwartkopf' off of bright green leaved Jerusalem sage, red-hot poker, and drought tolerant sages. Insert stems of aeonium into cracks in masonry walls or plant them in containers. They look especially good in aged terracotta.

### Try These
*Aeonium arboreum* 'Zwartkopf' grows 3 to 4 feet tall with nearly black rosettes. *Aeonium* 'Sunburst' is shorter with variegated green and pale yellow leaves edged in pink. *Aeonium* 'Blushing Beauty' leaves are green with red blush on the backsides, upper edges, and inner margins. *Aeonium* 'Cyclops' is a 4- to 5-foot-tall stem topped with a single rosette of deep burgundy and green leaves. *Aeonium undulatum* forms a low colony of 8-inch bright green rosettes. Dinner plate aeonium (*Aeonium tabuliforme*) forms rosettes only 2 inches tall that spread up to 18 inches in diameter, hence the name "dinner plate." This most striking aeonium is best grown in a container.

# Aloe
## *Aloe* spp.

### When, Where, and How to Plant
Plant aloes in any season, except winter in areas with winter freezes. Provide very well-draining soil in full sun and site in the hottest part of the garden. Water after planting, thoroughly soak the rootball, and mulch with gravel or other inorganic material. Aloes are excellent container plants. Use a cactus and succulent potting mix and mulch with gravel. Site in full sun.

### Growing Tips
Water summer growing (winter blooming) aloes once or twice a week in the hottest months of summer. Rainfall will water them the rest of the year. Keep summer water off winter growing (summer blooming) aloes. Allow soil to dry several inches deep between waterings. Withhold water from red-leaved aloes to encourage deep pigments. If in-ground plants don't flower, top-dress in spring with bonemeal or composted chicken manure. Feed container-grown aloes once, early in the growing season with a balanced organic fertilizer.

### Care
Remove spent leaves and flower stalks. Rotting center leaves or misshapen rosettes mean that ants and aphids are present. See "Tips and Techniques" for treatment suggestions.

### Companion Planting and Design
Use dwarf aloes in succulent dish gardens and rock gardens. Grow horizontal, colonizing aloes as bedding plants or low-water ground covers. Grow shrub aloes as single specimens in a succulent garden or mix with Mediterranean climate plants such as cassias, spurge, and bulbine. Use tall tree aloes as vertical elements that set a mood with their strong architectural structures.

### Try These
Shrub-type aloes such as *Aloe arborescens* often have multiple branches and multiple flower spikes, while some the leaves of single rosette aloes, such as *Aloe suprafoliata*, form in spirals. The buds of *Aloe speciosa* open in sequence, creating a gradation from pink buds at the top to yellow flowers with long, fringed, rust-colored stamens at the bottom. For a tall narrow plant, try tree-type aloes such as smooth leaved *Aloe barberae* (*Aloe bainesii*) or spiky *Aloe ferox* or *Aloe marlothii*. Leaves of *Aloe cameronii* turn carmine red when water-stressed.

*Aloes were a standard of California's Spanish Colonial Revival and Mission styles that were the rage in the early 1900s. Designers combined aloes with yucca, agave, and other succulents to complement white stucco walls, red tile roofs, turrets and arches. They used aloe's fleshy leaves and architectural shapes to create fascinating garden textures. They loved the candelabra of poker-shaped aloe blooms in fiery red, soft orange, pale yellow, salmon, coral, and pink. There are more than 400 species of aloe, all of which store water in their thick juicy leaves—an adaptation to dry climates of Africa, Saudi Arabia, and Madagascar. In those parts of the world, insects, birds, monkeys, and even children drink the sweet nectar of aloe flowers.*

### Bloom Period and Seasonal Color
Mostly winter and spring blooms in fiery red, soft orange, pale yellow, salmon, coral, and pink. Buds can be one color and open to a contrasting color.

### Mature Height × Spread
From 3 in. single rosettes to 40 ft. × 10 ft. trees, depending on the species

Hardy to 9B

Min. Temp. 25° F

# Blue Chalk Sticks

*Senecio mandraliscae*

*Have you ever seen a powder blue plant? While green, blue-green, and gray-green are common, powder blue is something special, especially when it is the thick, succulent, powder blue leaves of blue chalk sticks. Blue chalk sticks is a perennial succulent from South Africa. It has long trailing stems lined in smooth cylindrical leaves; each 3 to 4 inches long and arranged in 360 degrees around a tubular stem. Rub the stem or leaves and you'll see that they are actually bluish-green covered in a white waxy coating. Wax coatings are a typical water conserving strategy used by plants like this one that evolved to withstand hot, sunny, and dry environments.*

**Other Common Name**
Blue Finger

**Bloom Period and
Seasonal Color**
Powder blue foliage year round.
Flowers are not notable.

**Mature Height × Spread**
1 to 2 ft. × 2 to 3 ft.

**Hardy to
8B**

**Min.
Temp.
15° F**

## When, Where, and How to Plant

Plant spring through fall in frost-free gardens and in spring in colder winter areas. Select a spot in full sun (some shade in the desert). Well-draining soil is best, but plants will tolerate heavier soils if watered sparingly. Blue chalk sticks are fast growing, so don't hesitate to start with just a 4-inch pot. See the Perennials introduction for planting directions. Water well and mulch after planting. For container culture, use a cactus and succulent potting mix or combine standard potting mix with $1/3$ coarse construction sand. Top with 1 inch of rounded gravel or pebbles to conserve moisture.

## Growing Tips

Blue chalk sticks is extremely drought tolerant once established. Water twice monthly spring through fall in desert gardens, half as often elsewhere, and none in winters with regular rainfall. With more frequent water plants grow quickly—a blessing or a curse depending on the garden. No fertilizer is needed. **Note:** This plant is poisonous if ingested.

## Care

Snip off stray branches of blue chalk sticks. To pot these cuttings, strip off all but the top two sets of leaves and bury the bare stem in a pot of well-draining potting mix. Once they've rooted, replant into the garden or share with a friend. Dingy white flowers appear in spring. Remove them if you wish. Pests won't be a problem.

## Companion Planting and Design

Blue chalk sticks makes an excellent ground cover or bed edging. Surround the stout trunk of tall desert spoon with blue chalk sticks, the bright green, upright, succulent leaves of yellow African bulbine, and pink flowering African daisy. Set blue chalk sticks along the base of a wall or use to soften the edges in borders with succulent spurge. Use to cascade over the side of a pot of pink, lavender, and teal-leaved hen and chicks.

## Try This

Blue chalk fingers (*Senecio vitalis*) looks much like blue chalk sticks, but its leaves are slightly greener, more slender, and more graceful. The stems are more upright, giving this senecio a somewhat refined appearance.

# Desert Spoon
## *Dasylirion wheeleri*

### When, Where, and How to Plant
Plant into a very well-drained soil in full sun (some shade in the desert) in all but the hottest months of the year. Wear gloves, long sleeves, and long pants to protect your skin from the sharp teeth on leaf edges. Follow planting directions in the Perennials introduction. Water well after planting and mulch. For container culture, start with a plant small enough to handle easily. Use a large pot filled with cactus and succulent potting mix. Set the pot in full sun, drench until water comes out the holes in the bottom, and mulch with small pebbles or gravel.

### Growing Tips
This very low-water desert plant will survive solely on rainfall once established, though it will grow a bit faster with occasional summer irrigation. Be careful not to overwater. It requires no fertilizer.

### Care
Groom to remove old leaves and spent flower stalks. No pruning is needed and there are no significant pests.

### Companion Planting and Design
The magnificent architecture of desert spoon makes it an excellent choice for a garden focal point, especially for an area that gets little foot traffic. Desert spoon is striking in a large rustic ceramic pot. For a dry garden composition, plant with golden barrel cactus, Baja fairy duster, blue chalk fingers, flapjack plant, aloe, and century plant. Desert spoon makes a bold statement when planted en mass.

### Try This
Desert spoon's cousin is Mexican grass tree, *Dasylirion longissimum* (also known as *Dasylirion quadrangulatum*). Similar in profile to the desert spoon, Mexican grass tree has narrow, deep green leaves that form a rosette resembling a large tuft of grass atop a stout trunk. Over time it can reach 16 feet tall. Mexican grass tree flowers much like desert spoon. Because of its leaf color and structure, Mexican grass tree has more of a tropical look. Add it to a garden of palms, gingers, naked ladies, and Hong Kong orchid, taking care to make sure that the soil is well draining.

*Desert spoon is a large evergreen perennial in the lily family. This refined cousin of the yucca has a crown of strappy gray-green leaves with yellow sawtooth edges. Leaves are more than 3 feet long and radiate from a stout trunk that grows slowly to 5 feet tall. In late spring, desert spoon develops a yucca-like flower stalk that is 10 to 20 feet tall and covered in thousands of tiny greenish-white bell-shaped flowers. Desert spoon is native to the southwestern U.S. and northern Mexico where it grows in high elevation grasslands and open woodlands. Its distinctive and almost furry appearance is a wonderful addition to dry gardens throughout the state. Though native to desert climates, desert spoon grows well in more humid climate gardens across the U.S. and abroad.*

### Other Common Name
Sotol

### Bloom Period and Seasonal Color
Greenish-white flowers on a tall flower stalk in late spring and early summer; fruits in late summer.

**Hardy to 7A**

**Min. Temp. 0° F**

### Mature Height × Spread
5 ft. × 5 ft.; flower stalk to 20 ft.

# Flapjack Plant
## *Kalanchoe luciae* ssp. *luciae*

When it comes to fascinating leaf shape, texture, and color few plants beat those in the genus Kalanchoe. Despite its unglamorous name, flapjack plant is one of the most popular and beautiful kalanchoe of all. It looks like a series of flat rounded discs—flapjacks—set upright around a central stem. Lest that sounds unattractive, the discs are translucent green, fading to yellow-green, orange, and then to rosy or rusty red. Somewhere in that sunset color combination is a band of pink too. The colors give these plants a pizazz and make them incredibly valuable in the landscape both in the ground and as a container plant. Kalanchoe luciae ssp. luciae and the similar, though somewhat greener, Kalanchoe thyrsiflora are both called "flapjack plant." Both are great garden plants.

**Other Common Name**
Paddle Plant

**Bloom Period and Seasonal Color**
Green, orange, rose and rust colored leaves year-round. Yellow spring flowers.

**Mature Height × Spread**
1 to 2 ft × 2 to 3 ft.

**Hardy to 9B**

**Min. Temp. 26° F**

### When, Where, and How to Plant
Plant from spring through fall in full sun. Flapjack plants tolerate bright shade, but reddish colors develop best in full sun. In the ground, grow in amended and well-draining soil, following planting directions in the Perennials introduction. In a pot, use cactus and succulent potting mix. Water well after planting, and mulch.

### Growing Tips
These summer growers appreciate moist, but not wet, soil in summer. Cut back on winter water; flapjack plants don't mind dry cold, but they do mind wet cold. Fertilizer is not necessary, but if you like, apply organic cactus and succulent fertilizer in spring.

### Care
Prune off flower stalks to encourage production of side shoots (commonly called "pups"). If you remove pups root them in a potting mix to make new plants. If leaves lose their red color, move them to a sunnier spot and cut back on water. Stress stimulates the production of colorful pigments. Watch for snails, slugs, sooty mold, aphids, and mealybugs (see "Tips and Techniques" for controls).

### Companion Planting and Design
Flapjack plant is a wonderful colorful accent in any low-water garden. Use flapjack plants to surround the base of larger succulents such as aloes, agave, or giant false agave. They make a nice texture contrast for the upright succulent leaves of yellow African bulbine and pick up the pink tones in pink flowering African daisy (not succulent but drought tolerant). Tuck some flapjack plant in between buff-colored boulders to accentuate the rock's shapes and tones.

### Try This
Felt plant (*Kalanchoe beharensis*) is related to flapjack plant but looks very different and very prehistoric. This 5-foot-plus succulent has 5- to 12-inch-long triangular leaves with crenulated edges. The leaves are ice-green and covered with fine hairs that give them the texture of velour. Hairs on the top of leaves are rusty chocolate brown. On the underside, hairs are silver. Where old leaves fall off, a triangular scar remains giving the trunk and branches a twisted geometric pattern. Felt plant needs full sun to part sun.

## When, Where, and How to Plant

Plant anytime into well-draining soil. Heavy soils are okay, but water sparingly. Set plants an inch or so higher in the ground than they were in the pot. They will eventually settle to soil level. Backfill with a bit of compost mixed into the native soil. If planting into containers, use a cactus and succulent potting mix. Set plants a bit high in containers as well. When planting in the ground or in containers, water thoroughly after planting, and mulch with a layer of small pebbles or gravel.

## Growing Tips

Once established, foxtail agave is extremely drought tolerant. In desert gardens, water twice monthly in summer and every three weeks in spring and fall. Water coastal- and valley-grown plants less frequently. Provide deep slow water to saturate the roots. If leaves turn yellow or translucent in summer, water more. In-ground plants need no fertilizer. Fertilize container-grown plants occasionally with an organic cactus and succulent mix.

## Care

Remove spent leaves. Leaf tips and edges might frost when temperatures dip below freezing. Let them grow out on their own. As plants pup, allow them to form a colony or cut off and let root in moist sand to make new plants. Remove dead rosettes after flowering. No significant pests.

## Companion Planting and Design

Use as a specimen plant, or mass them in narrow planting strips or raised planters. Plant poolside or in a patio garden. Add to succulent borders, tuck in among boulders, or use as accents at the base of low water trees. Foxtail agave makes a beautiful container plant, especially in a deep burgundy, purple, or blue glazed pot.

## Try These

There are so many wonderful and garden worthy agaves that it is hard to choose! Try the huge spectacular century plant (*Agave americana*) with its arching blue-gray leaves, toothed edges, and sharp pointy spines. *Agave americana.* 'Marginata' is the same plant with green leaves and custard yellow stripes along the edges. Green spider agave (*Agave bracteosa*) is only 1 to 2 feet tall with smooth flexible leaves.

*Foxtail agave is one of our most popular garden succulents and for good reason. This Mexican native forms large graceful rosettes of pointed leaves that are slightly cupped along their length. Leaves spiral around a stout, grayish trunk that reaches 3 feet tall and is often encircled by pups. Leaves are smooth-edged without the sharp teeth and spines common in other agaves. In winter, a mature rosette produces a curved flower stalk 6 to 12 feet tall and covered in pale creamy green flowers. As with most agaves, once a rosette flowers, it dies and leaves its pups behind. All agave are well adapted to our Mediterranean climate. While Foxtail agave performs best in warmer coastal and hot inland gardens, others such as Queen Victoria agave are better suited for cooler gardens.*

**Other Common Name**
Dragon-tree agave

**Bloom Period and Seasonal Color**
Creamy greenish flowers in winter.

**Mature Height × Spread**
1 1/2 to 5 ft. × 2 to 4 ft. with blooms to 12 ft.

**Minimum Temperature**
Leaves damaged below 32 degrees F; plants die below 25 degrees F.

Hardy to 10A

Min. Temp. See below

# Giant False Agave
## *Furcraea foetida*

*Giant false agave is a tropical evergreen member of the agave family. It looks like a giant yucca but with soft leaves and no sharp spines. Each plant makes a tall, trunkless rosette of sword-shaped leaves, each up to 10 inches wide and 7 feet long. After a few years in the ground, a 25-foot flower stalk rises from the center of the plant. The stalk is lined with small, cream, ivory, or pale green flowers that hang like little bells. Each fragrant flower is soon replaced by a tiny green plantlet, which develops for a while and then drops off the stalk to root in the ground alongside the mother plant. The mother plant dies about a year later, leaving a colony of offspring behind.*

**Other Common Name**
Mauritius Hemp

**Bloom Period and Seasonal Color**
Cream, ivory, or pale green flowers in spring.

**Mature Height × Spread**
5 ft. × 8 ft. with blooms to 25 ft.

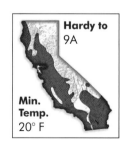

Hardy to 9A

Min. Temp. 20° F

### When, Where, and How to Plant
Plant fall through spring. Provide very well-draining soil and full sun along the coast, and filtered light elsewhere. Follow Perennials planting directions, but set plants in ground an inch or so higher than they were in the nursery container. They will eventually settle to soil level. Mulch with rock or stone to conserve moisture. In climates where winter temperatures regularly dip below freezing, grow in a ceramic pot and move to a protected area under the eaves or in a greenhouse. Plant into cactus and succulent potting mix. Water well and mulch with gravel or pebbles.

### Growing Tips
Keep watered through the first summer so plants become established. After that, in hottest desert gardens water weekly in summer and monthly in fall and spring. In other areas, water every three weeks to once a month in summer and half as often in fall and spring. No winter water is needed. In-ground plants do not need fertilizer. Feed container-grown plants with organic cactus and succulent fertilizer. Follow directions on the package.

### Care
Prune if you want to remove the flower stalk once plantlets drop. You can remove the entire mother plant at that time or wait until its leaves turn yellow from obvious decline. Pests are seldom a problem.

### Companion Planting and Design
Giant false agave is a big plant, so give it plenty of room. It can be used as the centerpiece of a dry garden along with silvery leaved feathery senna, colorful flapjack plant, succulent yellow African bulbine, tall, wispy shoestring acacia trees, and succulent echeveria. Giant false agave makes a wonderful container plant as well. Use it in a grouping of potted succulents chosen for their sizes, leaf colors, and textures.

### Try This
*Furcraea gigantea* is another name for giant false agave. *Furcraea gigantea striata* (*Furcraea foetida* 'Mediopicta') is a variegated form of giant false agave. Its sword-shaped leaves are striped green with yellow or green with white. This variegated giant false agave makes a very striking specimen plant.

# Golden Barrel Cactus

*Echinocactus grusonii*

## When, Where, and How to Plant

To plant in the ground, choose a spot in hot sun with well-draining soil. Poor soil is fine if it drains well. Planting a large golden barrel cactus can be painful. Wrap a wide strip of scrap carpet around the center of the plant. Face the backing towards the outside and use it to hold on to. Wear gloves. Roll the cactus gently into the planting hole. Refill the hole, water well, and mulch with stone or rock before you remove the carpet. In a container, use cactus and succulent mix. Mulch with small pebbles. Water well. Place the pot in a warm spot in full sun.

## Growing Tips

Water containers when the top few inches of soil is dry. Water in-ground cactus sparingly through the first summer to get it established. After that, stop watering in coastal and valley gardens. In desert gardens, water deeply once a month in summer only. For faster growth, fertilize in early spring with an organic fertilizer.

## Care

Groom to remove spent flowers. No pruning is needed. Watch for mealybugs on young plants. Treat as described in "Tips and Techniques."

## Companion Planting and Design

Golden barrel cactus' spectacular architectural shape can transform a garden bed from blah to fabulous. Larger specimens of these slow growing cacti can be costly. Buy the largest one you can afford and plant a cluster in a highly visible spot, but well away from walkways and areas where people or pets might brush against them. On the other hand, their spiny surfaces make a great deterrent to pets and pedestrians. Plant golden barrel cactus into a mixed succulent bed (cacti are a type of succulent). They look especially impressive next to a large boulder, a tall tree aloe, or a dragon tree to balance the composition. Smaller plants fit well into smaller spaces and especially into containers. Plant a small golden barrel cactus in a mixed succulent container. As they grow, remove other succulents until the top of the pot is completely filled with the golden barrel.

## Try This

While golden barrel cactus has several relatives, none quite match its beauty in the garden.

*The southwest native flora includes some very impressive plants, one of the most impressive being the golden barrel cactus. Golden barrel cactus has grown in California gardens for generations. It looks like a round, yellow and green hassock, but not one you'd like to put your feet on. If you tried, your feet would be pierced by thick curved spines that line deep vertical pleats in the cactus' green flesh. Golden barrel cactus grows very slowly, but ultimately becomes an elongated globe, 4 feet in diameter, with smaller globes sprouting around the base to eventually form large colonies. Come spring, rust colored flower buds encircle the top of larger golden barrels. Buds open to 2-inch bright lemon yellow flowers with the texture of tissue paper.*

**Bloom Period and Seasonal Color**
Spring flowers, bright lemon yellow.

**Mature Height × Spread**
3 to 4 ft. × 3 to 4 ft.

**Hardy to** 8B

**Min. Temp.** 15° F

# Hen and Chicks

## *Echeveria* spp.

Hen and chicks are easy-to-grow succulents that require little care but offer big rewards in the garden. Hen and chicks come in a huge variety of leaf shape, color, and size, but all have low-growing rosettes of leaves arranged geometrically around a central point. Some rosettes are only 3 or 4 inches across, while others can be a foot or more in diameter. Most form pups—the "chicks" part of hen and chicks—eventually creating colonies that carpet broad areas of the garden. Tall stalks of small orange or yellow flowers appear in spring or summer, but they take a back seat to hen and chicks succulent leaves that can be tiny and tight or large and relaxed, green, blue-green, gray, and even aqua and rose.

### Bloom Period and Seasonal Color
Colorful leaves are blue-gray, green with red highlights, aqua, blue-gray, teal, pink, and lavender.

### Mature Height × Spread
Rosettes range from 3 to 24 inches in diameter, often forming colonies several feet across.

**Hardy to 9A**

**Min. Temp. 20° F**

### When, Where, and How to Plant
Plant in full sun along the coast and in bright shade in valleys and deserts in all but freezing weather. Provide very well-draining soil. Water well after planting, and mulch with stones or pebbles. If soil is heavy, build a mound of well-draining soil or grow hen and chicks in a pot of cactus and succulent mix. Water well and mulch with small gravel.

### Growing Tips
Water frequently from spring through summer. Little to no water is needed in fall and winter. Feed with an organic cactus and succulent fertilizer once in spring, summer, and fall.

### Care
Remove spent flowers and dried leaves. If colonies grow too large, separate extra rosettes and pot them into containers to share or transplant. Simply separate the chicks by snipping the base of the stem where it attaches to the hen. Bury the stem into well-draining potting mix or soil, water in, and wait while they root. If mature plants start to decline, water a little more often (if you tend to spare water) or a little less often (if you tend to be generous). Also check for slugs, snails, aphids, or mealybugs (see "Tips and Techniques" for treatments).

### Companion Planting and Design
Use hen and chicks as a low-water ground cover, cluster larger hybrids as specimen plants, tuck single rosettes into cracks in walls, or plant between rocks or boulders. Grow in pots set on a sunny deck or patio.

### Try These
The most colorful varieties of hen and chicks include 'Zorro', 'Mauna Loa', 'Scarlet Curls', and 'Blue Wave'. They all form 1-foot rosettes shaped like large open heads of lettuce. Leaves are shades of aqua, blue-gray, teal, lavender, pink, and coral. Some leaves are wavy with crenulated edges (referred to as "petticoats"). Woolly rose (*Echeveria* 'Doris Taylor') has 8-inch rosettes comprised of pointed, bright green leaves, covered in fine silvery fuzz and tipped red. *Echeveria elegans* forms broad colonies of 4-inch rosettes of tight, pale green leaves. Plant it in a blue or deep red glazed pot.

# Mexican Lily
## *Beschorneria yuccoides*

## When, Where, and How to Plant

Plant Mexican lily any time except in the cold of winter. Choose a site in full sun (bright shade in hottest inland or desert gardens) with well-amended and well-draining soil. Be sure to allow plants enough room to spread. Water well after planting, and mulch with stones. Or plant into a container of cactus and succulent potting mix. Set in a sunny spot, water well, and mulch with pebbles or gravel.

## Growing Tips

Water in-ground plants deeply twice a month or so through the first summer. Established plants will tolerate periods of drought but perform better with occasional deep water in summer. Water container grown plants when top 5 inches of soil are dry. No fertilizer is needed.

## Care

Mexican lily is very low maintenance. While many agaves bloom once and die, Mexican lilies keep on growing. After blooming, mature plants form new pups around the base. Leave the pups in place, or when the weather warms in summer, sever pups from the mother plant, move them elsewhere, or set them onto a pot of fast draining cactus and succulent mix to root. Remove flower stalk after it fades. No significant pests bother is plant.

## Companion Planting and Design

Include Mexican lily in a traditional old-world Mediterranean planting scheme, in a succulent garden, or in a large informal dry garden. Mix with contrasting leaf forms and sizes such as the large, fuzzy green leaves of peppermint geranium, small triangular leaves of knife-leaf acacia, or the tiny needle-like foliage of *Grevillea lavandulaceae*. Site where the amazing flower stalks can be seen and appreciated near a walkway, driveway, or midpoint in a flower bed. Mexican lily looks fantastic as a single specimen in a large old terracotta pot. Because the leaves are soft, potted Mexican lilies pose no problem when sited on a patio or along a wide stairway.

## Try These

'Queretaro' is a smaller variety of Mexican yucca. Rosettes are 2 feet across, and flower stalks reach 5 feet tall.

*Lest you think that all succulents with long sword-shaped leaves that end in points are lethal yuccas or agaves, think again. Though related to yucca, the leaves of evergreen Mexican lily are soft and pliable. And its oversized shocking coral pink flower stalk is simply a showstopper. Mexican lily forms a rosette of leaves in soft blue-green with smooth edges. In early spring, mature plants form what appear to be giant pinkish spears of asparagus. Those spears are actually emerging flower stalks that eventually stretch to 7 feet or taller. As the large pink buds open, they reveal hanging clusters of tubular green flowers surrounded in coral pink bracts. In bloom, these plants have a comic-prehistoric look to them.*

**Bloom Period and Seasonal Color**
Bright coral pink flower stalks, buds, and bracts; bright green flowers in early spring.

**Mature Height × Spread**
4 to 6 ft. × 4 to 6 ft. Flower stalks 7 ft. or taller.

Hardy to 8B

Min. Temp. 15° F

# Orchid Cactus
## *Epiphyllum* spp.

If you are drawn to big exotic flowers and easy-to-grow potted plants, then orchid cactus is for you. Despite the name, orchid cactus flowers look nothing like demure and elegant orchid blossoms. Instead each enormous 3- to 8-inch bloom has rows of colored sepals and petals in translucent shades of white, yellow, orange, hot red, rose, pink, lemon, or gold. At the center is a fringe of white or yellow stamens and a starburst–shaped pistil. Many flowers are multicolored. These succulent epiphytes have 6- to 8-foot arching succulent green stems, some flat and some triangular. They are most often grown in hanging pots so stems have plenty of room and flowers are at eye level. In winter they need protection from the cold.

### Bloom Period and Seasonal Color
Spring blooms in shades of white, creamy yellow, sherbet orange, hot red, rich rose, pale and hot pink, lemon, gold, and multicolors.

### Mature Height × Spread
12 to 18 in. × 48 in.

### Minimum Temperature
40 degrees F is ideal, will survive to 32 degrees F.

Hardy to 10A

Min. Temp.
See below

### When, Where, and How to Plant
In spring, set orchid cactus cuttings into a pot—a hanging pot is best—filled with coarse, fast draining mix. Combine 1 part potting mix with 1 part perlite and enough small bark to make it "chunky." Add 14-14-14 slow-release granular fertilizer according to directions. Mist branches weekly after planting. In a month, start watering regularly. Hang pots in bright shade. Midday sun bleaches and burns stems.

### Growing Tips
Water each plant until water runs out the holes in the bottom of the pot. Keep potting mix damp but not wet. Apply slow-release granular fertilizer in spring. In winter, move pots to a protected location such as a greenhouse, indoors in a sunny window, or outdoors under the eaves.

### Care
Prune stems at joints if plants grow too lopsided, or to start a new plant (or share with a friend). Allow these cut ends to dry for a week, and then set several cuttings (cut end down) in a plastic hanging pot filled with damp potting mix. Insert cuttings 2 inches below the surface. Repot existing plants into new potting mix every other year and be sure to loosen the rootball when you replant. Since these are most often grown as hanging plants, they seldom have pest problems, but do keep pots weeded.

### Companion Planting and Design
Hang pots of orchid cactus so flowers are at eye-level. Suspend from an overhang covered in shadecloth or lath or from the branch of a leafy tree. Assemble a collection of varieties that bloom at different times through the spring for a season-long show.

### Try These
Buy orchid cactus in bloom so you can see the flowers. There are hundreds of hybrids. For yellow flowers, try 'Meadowlark'. 'Cassis' is a heavy bloomer with 4-inch-diameter flowers in lavender-pink that may rebloom late in the season. 'Zotz' makes 8-inch flowers with pink and white stripes. 'Wayfarer' forms 8-inch flowers that are solid red with a cerise throat. 'Mr. P' makes 8-inch-diameter flowers that are orange with a raspberry throat.

# Red Yucca

*Hesperaloe parviflora*

## When, Where, and How to Plant

Plant from fall through spring. Site red yucca in full sun (bright shade in hottest deserts) in well-draining soil. Water well after planting, and mulch with stone or rock. To grow in containers, use cactus and succulent potting mix. Set plants an inch or so higher in the pot than they were in the nursery can. Water deeply. Mulch with gravel.

## Growing Tips

In coastal and valley gardens, water in-ground plants once a month, and in desert gardens water twice a month during summer (more often in the first year while plants are becoming established). Water deeply (down to the roots) and slowly. Established plants can survive on rainfall alone except in hottest desert gardens. No fertilizer is required for in-ground planting. Water containers regularly and do fertilize occasionally and lightly with an organic fertilizer formulated for cactus and succulents.

## Care

Groom to remove spent flower clusters and dried leaves. Surround young plants with a cylinder of hardware cloth to deter hungry rabbits.

## Companion Planting and Design

Planted en mass, red yucca's striking profile complements plants such as barrel cactus, aloe, and agave in desert theme gardens. Alternatively, red yucca can be grown in a field of wildflowers or combined with Mediterranean climate plants such as red-flowered grevillea, blue flowered and gray leaved germander sage, and yellow sundrops.

## Try These

There are four other plants in the genus *Hesperaloe*. Yellow yucca (*Hesperaloe parvifolia* 'Yellow') is a custard-yellow flowered version of red yucca. Night blooming hesperaloe (*Hesperaloe nocturna*) is a bit larger plant. Its 12-foot-tall flower stalks have greenish-white blooms that open at night. Giant hesperaloe (*Hesperaloe funifera*) has 4- to 6-foot-long leaves that stand straight. Its 12-foot-tall flower stalks have greenish-white (sometimes purple tinged) flowers that open at nights. Bell flower hesperaloe (*Hesperaloe campanulata*) is much like the giant hesperaloe but reaches only 3 feet tall and wide. It has pink and white bell-shaped flowers on a 10-foot flower stalk.

*Succulent rosettes of yucca and agave have large coarse leaves with spiny tips. The rosettes of red hesperaloe have a similar profile but with slender leaves that are more refined and delicate looking. Its stiff dark green leaves arch from the base, each curling inward almost to the point of forming a long tube. As leaves mature, they typically extend to 2 feet long with a bit of white thread that curls off the edges. Starting in late spring, plants develop 5- to 9-foot arching flower stalks with coral red tubular flowers whose petals are yellow inside. Hummingbirds love them. These southwest natives can survive on rainfall in most parts of the state but grow faster with some deep summer water. This grass-shaped succulent perennial is tough—really tough.*

**Other Common Name**
Red Hesperaloe

**Bloom Period and Seasonal Color**
Coral colored flowers in spring through early fall.

**Mature Height × Spread**
3 to 4 ft. × 3 to 4 ft.

Hardy to 5A

Min. Temp. -20° F

# Reed Orchid
## *Epidendrum* spp.

*There are two types of gardeners: those who can grow orchids successfully and those who can't. If you are in the latter category, take heart. Reed orchids are so easy, so tough, and so forgiving, that anyone can grow them. Reed orchids have tiny orchid flowers in shades of lavender, papaya, butter yellow, orange, magenta, and red. The flowers develop in generous clusters at the tips of slender reedy stems. Their graceful vertical stems are lined with pairs of succulent green leaves that project left and right at 90-degree angles. Reed orchids form small plantlets called "keikis" (Hawaiian for "babies") along their stems. Simply break some off with roots intact and pot them up to make an entirely new reed orchid.*

**Other Common Name**
Poor Man's Orchid

**Bloom Period and Seasonal Color**
Lavender, papaya, butter yellow, orange, magenta, and red blooms continuously in warm weather.

**Mature Height × Spread**
1 to 3 ft. × 1 to 3 ft.

Hardy to 9B

Min. Temp. 25° F

### When, Where, and How to Plant
Grow reed orchids in the ground in the very mildest coastal gardens. Grow them in full sun. For good drainage, make a raised planting bed with 50 percent orchid bark (or other small redwood bark) and 50 percent planting mix. Set roots so that they are barely covered with planting mix. Water well. In all other garden climates, grow reed orchid in containers filled with a 1:1 mixture of orchid mix or small redwood bark and potting mix. Set roots so that they are secure in the pot but barely covered with potting mix. Water well and set in bright shade of full sun.

### Growing Tips
Reed orchids can survive on surprisingly little water but bloom best when watered several times a week through the growing season. Add diluted liquid all-purpose fertilizer every few weeks from spring through fall. Replace bark (for in-ground plants) or potting mix every few years as the bark decomposes.

### Care
Remove spent flowers and leaves. Divide plants when they climb out of their pots. Protect from hungry snails and slugs (see "Tips and Techniques" for controls).

### Companion Planting and Design
Plant a large container with a single color reed orchid and allow it to fill the pot until it looks as if the pot will burst. Set container on a deck, poolside, or in a bed of canna and ginger. Or, grow lavender-flowered reed orchid next to lavender-leaved *Echeveria* 'Afterglow'. Where temperatures dip below 30 degrees F, move reed orchid indoors to a sunny window in winter.

### Try This
The best place to find reed orchids is in a friend's garden. Break off a keiki and pot it up. For more selection, attend a meeting of your local orchid society. Hobby growers often bring extra plants to sell or swap. At orchid shows throughout California, growers often sell keikis for a few dollars each. Though there are dozens, if not hundreds, of reed orchid hybrids, the best way to get started is to find one whose flower color you like and enjoy!

# Rock Purslane
## *Calandrinia grandiflora*

## When, Where, and How to Plant

Plant rock purslane from fall through spring and into a spot with full sun or bright shade. Rock purslane prefers well-draining soil but will tolerate heavier soils if grown dry. To grow in a container, use a cactus and succulent potting mix. Water well after planting, and mulch (see "Tips and Techniques" for more on planting).

## Growing Tips

Plants can survive on rainfall alone but appreciate occasional deep water in spring and fall. Water once or twice each month when plants slow their growth in the heat of summer. No fertilizer is needed.

## Care

Rock purslane can be trimmed if it spreads too far. To propagate, cut trimmings into 5- to 6-inch lengths of a *non-flowering* stem. Remove lower leaves, leaving only a few leaves towards the top of each stem. Bury bare stems (leaves should be above ground) in well-draining soil or in a pot of cactus and succulent mix. Mulch well. Keep soil moist (not wet) until stems develop roots, which may take several weeks especially in cooler weather. If a plant gets raggedy after a few years, simply cut it back to a few inches tall. It will quickly regenerate. No significant pests.

## Companion Planting and Design

Grow rock purslane as a low-water ground cover in a succulent garden or in a drought tolerant perennial bed. Tuck stems in cracks to grow over boulders in a rock garden or dry streambed. Use rock purslane in parking strips, on slopes, and other out-of-the-way spots that need dressing up but get little care. Plant rock purslane at the outer edge of a large container so its branches cascade down the sides. Add a purple-leaved New Zealand flax or bronze-leaved giant dracaena in the center and surround with succulent paddle plant (kalanchoe) or violet-leaved echeveria for a fantastic combination of texture and color that requires minimal water and attention.

## Try This

'Jazz Time' is one of the few (maybe the only) named varieties of rock purslane. It forms 1-foot × 3-foot mounds, 2- to 3-foot-tall flower wands, and 2-inch diameter flowers.

Rock purslane is a most unexpected succulent. It makes a low, wide mat of fleshy ice-green or blue-green leaves. In spring and summer, rock purslane sends up 3-foot-tall flower stems, each topped with several poppy-like flowers in glowing lavender/magenta. The flowers appear to float on wands above the foliage. Each has five-petals that form a flower 3 inches across with a center fringe of yellow-tipped stamens. Native to Chile (also a Mediterranean climate), rock purslane's very non-succulent-like flowers put on a dazzling show, especially in contrast to their pale leaves. The combination brightens any low-water garden. It also looks fantastic cascading over the side of a large container planted in mixed succulents. Rock purslane is also sold as Cistanthe grandiflora.

**Bloom Period and Seasonal Color**
Glowing lavender/magenta flowers in spring and summer.

**Mature Height × Spread**
1 ft. × 4 ft. or wider.

Hardy to 8B

Min. Temp. 15° F

# Stonecrop
## *Sedum* spp.

Stonecrop is a group of 400 or more succulent plants, some with tiny bean-shaped leaves, some with tiny rounded leaves, some that grow as horizontal ground covers, and some that have upright stems. Some of the nicest, taller, upright stonecrops are cultivars of Sedum spectabile. These deciduous perennials grow 9 to 24 inches tall with flat succulent leaves that fit one inside the other along the stem, like a child's stacking toy. In summer, branches are topped in clouds of tiny star-shaped flowers in shades of cream, pale green, or rose pink, depending on the cultivar. In late fall, the stems die back and the plant goes dormant.

### Bloom Period and Seasonal Color
Green and cream variegated leaves, mauve-plum colored leaves with cream, pale green, or pink flowers in summer and/or fall.

### Mature Height × Spread
9 to 12 in. × 12 to 24 in.

**Hardy to 4A**

**Min. Temp. -30° F**

### When, Where, and How to Plant
Plant from fall through spring. Stonecrops prefer well-draining soil or potting mix and full to part sun. After planting, water well and mulch. It is best to mulch container plants with gravel or small pebbles and in-ground plants with organic mulch.

### Growing Tips
These are extremely easy plants to grow. Water deeply and frequently (every week or so) through the first spring and summer. Stonecrop needs only minimal water in subsequent years and no water when winter rains arrive and plants are dormant. Fertilize with organic cactus and succulent food in early spring before new growth starts.

### Care
Pinch growing branch tips to make plants bushier. Once stonecrop foliage starts to look ratty at the end of fall, cut it back to the ground or simply wait until foliage dies back and remove dead parts. Within a short time, fast growing new sprouts will poke out of the ground to replace the old ones. Clumps can be divided every few years in early spring (see how to divide rhizomes in "Tips and Techniques"). No significant pests bother stonecrop.

### Companion Planting and Design
Stonecrop adds great texture to perennial beds. Plant them as specimens in blue or purple glazed pots or combine with other succulent or non-succulent perennials in a mixed container planting.

### Try These
Some stonecrops were recently reclassified under the genus name *Hylotelephium*. It will take some time for gardeners and nurseries to make that change. In the meantime, shop for them under both *Sedum* and *Hylotelephium*. Look for 'Autumn Joy' that has large flat bright green leaves on upright stems. Flowers are pink aging to copper red flowers in late summer and fall. 'Vera Jameson' has deep mauve or plum leaves tinged with rose and bright pink flowers. 'Brilliant' has blue-green leaves with rose red flowers. 'Frosty Morn' has pale pink flowers and green leaves edged in creamy white. Similar, but larger and more robust looking, is matrona stonecrop (*Hylotelephium telephium* 'Matrona') that has bronze-green leaves, burgundy stems, and pale pink flowers.

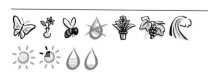

## When, Where, and How to Plant

Plant fall through spring in full sun or light shade (especially in hot inland valleys and deserts). African bulbine prefers well-drained soils but tolerates heavier soils. Water well after planting, and mulch. To grow in a container, use a cactus and succulent potting mix. Saturate the pot after planting and mulch with gravel.

## Growing Tips

Water regularly from the first spring through fall. When blooming slows down in the heat of summer, cut watering back to once a month. No irrigation is needed in winter when it rains. Below 20 degrees F, plants may die back to the ground but will resprout in spring. Fertilizer is not necessary but makes for faster growth (and faster spread). Use an organic cactus and succulent formulation.

## Care

Remove spent flower stems regularly. Because plants spread by rhizomes, what starts out as a small clump can quickly spread to several feet. Don't worry though, the unwanted new growth is easy to thin out. Divide and replant clumps every few years or when plants outgrow their space. Discard any plants whose lower stems have turned brown. No significant pests bother this plant.

## Companion Planting and Design

Plant along the front edge of a low-water garden bed, beneath low-water trees such as palo verde and shoestring acacia, mixed with aloes, or with low-water flowering shrubs such grevillea, rockrose, and shrubby melaleuca. Tuck yellow African bulbine into cracks between rocks or pavers or use in parking strips.

## Try These

A more compact form of yellow African bulbine is orange-flowered *Bulbine frutescens* 'Hallmark'. Even smaller is *Bulbine frutescens* 'Tiny Tangerine' (12 inches × 18 inches) that has orange flowers and dark green foliage. *Bulbine latifolia* is a muscular member of this species. This succulent bulbine has 1- to 2-inch-wide triangular leaves that form a flat rosette. Flower stems rise from the center with flowers much like yellow African bulbine, but bulkier and very striking. It looks great in a brightly colored ceramic pot.

*The leaves of yellow African bulbine look like day-glo green chives—a foot tall, slender, cylindrical, and growing in clusters. Starting in spring, African bulbine is topped in poker-like clusters of bright yellow, star-shaped flowers. Along the coast, plants bloom continuously from spring through fall. In warmer areas, they take a break during the hot months of summer. This evergreen succulent comes from the southern part of Africa. It spreads by rhizomes, eventually making mats that cover 2 or 3 feet in all directions. These are tough plants that look good with minimal water. I once inherited a clump that had been dug up and left sitting in a shopping bag for a month. When I planted them, they took right away.*

**Bloom Period and Seasonal Color**
Yellow flowers in fall through spring. Summer blooms only in milder coastal areas.

**Mature Height × Spread**
1 to 2 ft. × 2 to 3 ft.

Hardy to 8A

Min. Temp. 10° F

# Trees *for California*

A magnificent New Zealand Christmas Tree on Alcatraz Island

Trees are your garden's upright supports and main beams. They are the major structural elements around and beneath which all other plants are arranged.

There are so many ways to use trees: as a main focal point, as a grove, as a dividing line, and as a visual screen. Trees set a mood as well. Think about how it feels to sit in an open field. Then think about how it feels to sit beneath the leafy branches of a tall tree. Beneath the tree, it feels inviting, even cozy and safe as compared to a wide-open space.

This chapter will help you avoid the beginner's mistake of planting your garden with pretty annuals, perennials, and shrubs, before planting the trees. Just as you build a house by first constructing the walls and roof, build your garden by first planting trees. Most listed in this chapter are of a scale that fits today's smaller urban and suburban properties, though there are a few appropriate for larger properties as well. I have included a range of flowering trees, evergreen trees, deciduous trees, native trees, trees from other Mediterranean climates, and palms.

## California Dreaming

Every newcomer to California dreams of growing palms, as if California were a tropical paradise. Truth is, only the Washington fan palm (*Washingtonia filifera*) is native to this side of the Mexican border. Nearly all other garden palms come from Baja or more tropical regions around the globe. Gardeners from Santa

Barbara south can grow hundreds of kinds of palms. Those north of Santa Barbara must choose from a smaller palette of cold tolerant palms. In these pages I've included palms that are adaptable to all regions of California except the highest mountains and deserts. Another palm I've included is a bit more frost tender, but if sited carefully it does great in many regions throughout the state.

Flowering trees are the darlings of trees and for good reason. Crape myrtle, jacaranda, purple orchid trees, and the amazing floriferous floss silk trees bring tremendous color and beauty to the garden throughout the year. Some of those flowering trees are from subtropical regions while others, including granite honey myrtle, New Zealand Christmas tree, chaste tree, and others, are from Mediterranean climates.

If you want to introduce more seasons into your garden, plant deciduous trees. Nothing shouts "Autumn!" like the golden and crimson leaves of fall, or the bare skeletons of branches in winter. Deciduous trees have another value as well. Placed strategically on a southern or western exposure, they cool a home in summer and let the warm rays of the winter sun pass through. Think of them as free heating and air conditioning systems.

Then there are the natives. Can one ever sufficiently praise a majestic oak, a stately sycamore, a flowery desert willow, or a leafy madrone? They are wonderful and they represent a wide world of garden worthy native trees.

There are many more climate-appropriate trees offered in your local nursery than there is room to fit on these pages. Don't limit yourself to the trees in this chapter. Use them as a starting point and explore the options. Whatever you do, be sure you have room for a tree's ultimate size before you decide to plant it.

## Planting Trees from Nursery Containers

Water the tree in its container the day before planting. Dig a hole a bit deeper than, and $1^1/2$ to 2 times as wide as the

California buckeye in bloom

Coral tree dots a corner with red

pot. Fill the hole with water and allow it to drain completely. If it takes more than a few hours to drain, build a mound of well-draining soil and plant into the mound. Most of these trees are best planted into unamended soils. For those that require amended soils, mix amendments into the soil you dug out of the hole.

Fill the bottom of the hole with enough soil so the plant will sit just an inch higher than it was in the pot (it will settle to the right level). Step on the soil to compact it and then toss in several handfuls of worm castings. Lay the container on its side and squeeze the sides gently to loosen the soil from the container. Grab the tree at the base of the trunk and carefully pull it from the container.

Check the roots. If they circle the rootball tightly, then gently loosen them. Cut off any broken roots. Set the tree in the hole (remember to keep it an inch higher than the surrounding soil). Refill with soil, tamping it down as you go to eliminate air pockets.

If you must stake the tree, then add a pair of stakes placed on opposite sides of the hole (see "Tips and Techniques"). As the soil is filled to near the top of the hole, water well to settle soil around the roots. Make a four-inch tall berm around the outer edge of the hole to make sure water saturates the entire root mass. Then, add soil to completely fill the hole. Slowly fill the hole with water and allow it seep down into the soil. Use the moat for watering until the tree is established.

Mulch the area between the trunk and the moat, keeping mulch several inches away from the trunk. Mulch around the outer perimeter of the moat as well.

## Trees and Lawns

Gardeners often ask about planting trees in lawns. That may work fine where year-round rain is plentiful, but it is really tricky here in the Mediterranean west. Trees have roots that grow many feet deep, and lawn grasses' roots are far shorter. The tendency for most gardeners is to put them both on the same irrigation zone and then water only enough to keep the grass green but not nearly long enough to wet the root zone down to the deeper tree roots. The grass competes for what little water may be available to the tree. Meanwhile the tree develops surface roots that interfere with the lawn, while the tree's leafy canopy shades out the grass.

In addition, lawn mowers and string trimmers often damage tree trunks to the point that trees are stunted or simply die. The combination of trees and lawn has other problems as well; the bottom line is that you will have greater success if you grow lawns and trees in different parts of the garden.

Palms standing tall

www.digplantgrow.com

# Arbutus
## *Arbutus* spp.

*Arbutus are stunning evergreen trees and shrubs with rusty cinnamon or mahogany brown bark and a dense canopy of deep green leathery leaves. These small trees look like the big brothers to their shrubby cousins, the manzanita. In fall they are covered in hanging clusters of small, pale pink, pitcher-shaped flowers with a sweet scent. Flowers are followed by marble sized yellow, red, or orange berries, much beloved by birds. The arbutus grown in California gardens includes native madrone, native strawberry tree, and a hybrid called* Arbutus 'Marina'. *Of the three, 'Marina' has the largest leaves and showiest pink flowers. Strawberry tree tolerates the widest variety of soils and climates. Madrone is the trickiest in a garden, but when it takes, it is magnificent.*

### Bloom Period and Seasonal Color
Pale pink spring or fall flowers followed by yellow, orange, or red berries.

### Mature Height × Spread
20 to 50 ft. × 40 to 50 ft.

Hardy to 8A

Min. Temp. 10 to 15° F

### When, Where, and How to Plant
Plant arbutus in the fall or winter rainy season. To grow madrone, start with a 1-gallon plant and site it in a shady spot with well-draining soil. *Arbutus* 'Marina' prefers full sun and can be planted from a 5-gallon can or larger, as can strawberry tree, which tolerates some shade. See tree planting directions in the chapter troduction. Water well after planting and mulch.

### Growing Tips
Keep roots moist (not wet) through their first year. Deep watering encourages deep healthy roots. Once plants are established, they need only occasional deep summer water. No fertilizer is needed.

### Care
Prune to remove dead or diseased wood and discard (do not compost) the wood. See "Tips and Techniques" directions on pruning and on disinfecting tools after pruning—a crucial step to prevent the spread of disease. Control ants to control aphids and black sooty mold (see "Tips and Techniques"). Prevent deadly root rot by maintaining well-drained soils and allowing the soil to dry out between waterings.

### Companion Planting and Design
Arbutus are usually available as standards (single trunk) or multi-trunk specimens. Standards look more formal, while the multi-trunks look more informal. Mass multi-trunk trees for an evergreen screen. Mix with other native or Mediterranean climate shrubs. Underplant with flowers in shades of yellow and orange, especially orange-colored Peruvian lily.

### Try These
Madrone (*Arbutus menziesii*) grows 20 to 40 feet and nearly as wide, with smooth mahogany bark that peels away to reveal pale green beneath. Sweet smelling spring flowers are white. Provide it with bright shade near water or plant it on an eastern slope near a creek. Hardy to 10 degrees F. Sun-loving *Arbutus* 'Marina' (25 to 50 feet tall and nearly as wide) has pink-blush white flowers in spring and fall. Provide an occasional deep watering in summer. Dwarf 'Compacta' is only 6 to 8 feet. × 5 to 6 feet and is hardy to 10 degrees F. Strawberry tree (*Arbutus unedo*) grows 20 to 30 feet × 15 to 40 feet. Fall flowers are pink or white.

# Australian Willow
## *Geijera parviflora*

### When, Where, and How to Plant

Plant Australian willow fall through spring in frost-free gardens and in spring in colder areas. Provide full sun or light shade. Soils can be poor or well amended, or moist, as long as they drain well. Follow tree planting directions in the chapter introduction. Water deeply after planting, and mulch.

### Growing Tips

Water deeply once a week for the first two to three weeks and then once a month until winter rains arrive. In subsequent years, start irrigating when soil dries in late spring. Water deeply once a month until winter rains and until trees are mature. Spray periodically to rinse dust off leaves. Since these trees come from areas where soils have even fewer nutrients than ours, they don't need fertilizer. If leaves yellow, sprinkle the soil beneath the branches with iron sulfate or powdered sulfur and iron chelate (follow directions on the label). Water deeply and wait. Leaves green up over several months.

### Care

These are extremely low maintenance trees. If planted along a walkway, street, or driveway they may need trimming to keep branches from interfering with traffic. Watch for occasional aphid infestation (see "Tips and Techniques").

### Companion Planting and Design

Plant where you want light shade or an airy screen. Australian willow generates minimal litter, so it can be planted near a deck or patio. Deep roots don't damage sidewalks or structures. Grow it a bit back from the salt spray zone at the beach.

### Try This

If you covet a true willow, try curly (or corkscrew) willow (*Salix matsudana* 'Tortuosa'). This is the source of the twisted branches used in flower arrangements. Curly willow is best grown in a pot since it is a water hog and prone to many pests and diseases. Buy one in the nursery or pluck a branch from an arrangement; it will root in a vase of water. Start cuttings in a small pot. As the cuttings grow (they grow very quickly), repot into larger and larger containers. Meanwhile cut branches and use them in your own arrangements, or root them to share with friends.

*Weeping willow is not the best choice for California's dry Mediterranean climate, but that doesn't mean that we don't have weeping trees in our plant palette. Australian willow is the perfect weeper, especially for today's smaller garden spaces. Despite its common name, this is not a true willow. True willows belong to the genus Salix. Australian willow is in the genus Geijera, which is a cousin to citrus. Australian willow doesn't make edible fruits like citrus, but it does make tiny, cream to white flowers in spring. This medium-sized evergreen desert native grows quickly, forming an oval or round weeping canopy of long (3- to 6-inch), narrow, deep-green leaves that hang from the branches. Birds and other critters favor the dry, green summer and fall fruits.*

**Other Common Name**
Wilga

**Bloom Period and Seasonal Color**
Creamy white flowers spring and fall.

**Mature Height × Spread**
20 to 40 ft. × 20 to 25 ft.

Hardy to 8A

Min. Temp. 10° F

# California Buckeye

*Aesculus californica*

California buckeye is a slow growing native with all the right features: large attractive green leaves; huge fragrant flower clusters; and smooth pale bark on fantastically distorted branches. Leaves up to 16-inches across have five to seven ruffled green leaflets joined in the center like a palm. Hundreds of creamy white flowers (some with pink throats) and bright yellow stamens form long conical flower clusters. Against the dark green background, the flowers look like fireworks frozen in space. In summer the trees drop their flowers and leaves to go dormant—a common Mediterranean strategy for surviving the hottest and driest months of the year. Round 3-inch brown fruits remain hanging from the pale skeleton of branches.

**Other Common Name**
California Horse Chestnut

**Bloom Period and Seasonal Color**
Creamy white or pale pink flowers with prominent yellow stamens in late spring or early summer.

**Mature Height × Spread**
12 to 30 ft. × 30 ft. or wider

Hardy to 7A

Min. Temp. 0° F

### When, Where, and How to Plant

Buckeye is best planted from fall through spring while the tree is in leaf. In mild coastal and mountain gardens, plant in full sun. In hot valley gardens, provide some afternoon shade, especially for the first few summers. See planting directions in the chapter introduction. Buckeyes are adaptable to many kinds of soils but prefer those that drain well. Water deeply after planting, and mulch.

### Growing Tips

From planting until the first summer dormancy, keep soil around young trees moist, especially in those occasional hot dry spells of winter. Water occasionally that first summer as well. Once established, California buckeye is very drought tolerant. In coastal areas and the central valley established trees need little or no supplemental irrigation, though irrigation hastens growth and delays summer dormancy. Buckeyes in hot southern valleys survive with occasional deep water, but thrive with more. No fertilizer is needed. **Note:** All parts of this plant are poisonous if ingested.

### Care

Prune to remove dead, diseased, or damaged wood. Pruning out smaller branches to shape the tree and reveal its fantastic skeleton. Pests aren't a problem but overwatering, especially in summer makes buckeyes susceptible to fungal diseases.

### Companion Planting and Design

Don't let the buckeye's summer dormancy scare you away. It has a special beauty both when in leaf and when bare—especially when planted against a deep green background of evergreen shrubs such as toyon or California lilac. Site one at the entry of a garden room or next to a walkway and then prune it to arch overhead. Or leave it unpruned to make a massive hedge.

### Try This

Another drought tolerant native is the pinyon pine (*Pinus edulis*). This evergreen pine has dark green needles and 2-inch-round cones with edible pine nuts. Because of its compact size (10 to 20 feet × 5 to 15 feet), pinyon pine is well suited to gardens and even to containers. Water deeply though infrequently to establish; then cut back to an occasional drink. Birds love this pine. Hardy to 15 degrees F.

# Chaste Tree
## *Vitex agnus-castus*

### When, Where, and How to Plant

Plant from fall through spring in mild winter gardens and in spring in colder gardens. Full sun or light shade are both good. Choose a spot where chaste tree can reach its ultimate size without any (or much) pruning. Soil can be well amended, poor, dry, or moist as long as it drains well. Follow planting directions in the chapter introduction. Water deeply after planting and apply a thick layer of organic mulch. Chaste tree can be grown in large containers as well.

### Growing Tips

Water regularly and deeply the first year to help chaste tree become established. After that, water deeply but only occasionally from late spring to early fall. Fertilizer is not necessary, but a spring application of all-purpose organic fertilizer hastens growth.

### Care

To grow as a tree (rather than as a large shrub), start training it when the plant is young. First reduce the number of upright trunks to three. Then prune off lower branches to reveal the trunks. When flowering is finished, prune the branch tips back to encourage new wood for next year's flowers. You might get a second round of blooms. This is also time to continue shaping the plant, especially if you are trying to keep it smaller than it wants to be. Keep soil surface dry between waterings to prevent deadly root rot.

### Companion Planting and Design

Chaste tree is a classic Mediterranean garden plant. Plant it as the centerpiece of a garden bed pruned as a tree and surrounded by iris, geraniums, lavender, sages, daylilies, bugle lilies, and tall ornamental grasses. Chaste tree is a good plant for a beachside garden as long as it is out of direct salt spray. When grown as a shrub, use it as a screen or as part of an evergreen shrub border.

### Try These

'Silver Spire' has white flowers and gray-green or blue-green leaves above with silvery below. 'Alba' has white flowers and gray-green or blue-green leaves above and silvery below. 'Rosea' has soft pink flowers.

*According to legend, an ancient Greek physicians recommended a drink of peppery chaste tree seeds to the wives of soldiers whose husbands were away at war. The drink, of course, was to dampen their libidos. Chastity aside, chaste tree is a large shrub or small tree from the Mediterranean. At first glance, it looks like a giant sage (to which it is related) or a graceful butterfly bush. A closer look reveals palmate leaves with narrow leaflets, much like dark-green hemp leaves with hairy, silvery undersides. Spires of two-lipped tubular flowers in violet or deep lavender-blue appear in spring and summer. While the leaves have a sagey fragrance, flowers smell sweet. Small fleshy fruits that follow the flowers have those peppery seeds of chastity.*

### Other Common Name

Hemp Tree

### Bloom Period and Seasonal Color

Spring through summer flowers in violet or deep lavender.

### Mature Height × Spread

20 to 25 ft. 20 to 25 ft.

Hardy to 6B

Min. Temp. 5° F

# Chinese Pistache
*Pistacia chinensis*

*California gardeners place such a huge emphasis on evergreens that we often ignore plants that change with the seasons. Where are the vermilions, scarlets, oranges, and golds of autumn? They are on deciduous trees, few of which are quite as striking as the Chinese pistache. Chinese pistache has rough multicolored bark on trunks that reach 50 feet tall and form umbrella-shaped canopies. These trees grow at a moderate rate and tolerate a wide range of conditions from desert heat to temperatures below freezing and require little water once established. From spring through summer, Chinese pistache are covered in fragrant green leaves divided into lacy leaflets. Once the days grow short, leaves undergo the seasonal changes that bring about a spectacular autumn show.*

**Bloom Period and Seasonal Color**
Green leaves in spring and summer turn scarlet, orange, and gold in fall.

**Mature Height × Spread**
30 to 60 ft. × 30 to 60 ft.

Hardy to 6A

Min. Temp. -10° F

## When, Where, and How to Plant
Chinese pistache prefers full sun and well-drained soil but tolerates heavier soil as long as trees are not overwatered. These trees tolerate the temperature extremes of deserts and mountains. Plants can be set in the ground late in winter while bare or after they leaf out in spring. See tree planting directions in the chapter introduction. Water deeply and mulch after planting.

## Growing Tips
Start pruning young trees when dormant. It may take several years of pruning to create a high, umbrella-shaped canopy. Overwatered plants risk developing verticillium wilt, so water established trees infrequently, especially if they are planted in soils that don't drain well.

## Companion Planting and Design
These large deciduous trees make wonderful specimen trees. Their fall display is stunning when many pistache trees are planted to line one or both sides of a long drive. They make good street trees, but not beneath power lines. Planting Chinese pistache or any large deciduous tree on the southern or western side of your home shades it in hot summer months but allows the warming sun through in the winter. In a Mediterranean garden, combine Chinese pistache with white flowered rockrose, evergreen oak, rosemary, bay, species gladiolus, evergreen mastic tree, and yellow-flowered Jerusalem sage.

## Try This
Mastic tree (*Pistache lentiscus*) is a smaller profile, evergreen cousin to Chinese pistache. At 15 to 25 feet tall and wide, mastic tree is a small tree or large shrub with leathery green leaves. It is equally drought tolerant, though not quite as frost tolerant, as Chinese pistache. Plant it next to a patio, around a pool, or use it as an evergreen hedge. The sap of mastic tree is the source of mastic first used by the Greeks for perfumes, flavorings, chewing gums, varnishes, and medicines.

## When, Where, and How to Plant

Plant in full sun and in well-drained soil, year-round in mild winter climates and in spring through fall in colder areas. Protect from wind. See tree planting directions in the chapter introduction. Water deeply and mulch.

## Growing Tips

In the first year, water deeply once soil dries in spring. Continue until first winter rains. Water deeply during hot dry spells in winter. Once established, coral trees are drought tolerant but appreciate occasional deep summer water. Only fertilize coral trees that you grow in containers. **Note:** All plant parts are poisonous if ingested.

## Care

These vigorous trees can grow 2 to 3 feet each year. Brittle branches require regular pruning to remove dead or weak wood, to control shape, and to promote flowering. Prune after bloom. You will need to control aphids. Pruning directions and pest control information are provided in "Tips and Techniques."

## Companion Planting and Design

Don't try to fit too large a coral tree (or any other plant) into too small a space and then prune it to a nub. Plant large corals in large gardens away from structures and sidewalks that can be damaged by their shallow surface roots. Roots of smaller corals are seldom problematic when grown in the ground or as potted plants.

## Try These

Naked coral tree (*Erythrina coralloides*) makes bright red spring flowers in spirals around tips of bare branches (30 feet × 30 feet); hardy to 24 degrees F. Cockspur Coral Tree (*Erythrina crista-galli*) is a thorny small tree or large shrub (15 to 20 feet × 15 to 20 feet) with cascading clusters of fragrant pink to scarlet-red flowers in spring and summer; hardy to 15 degrees F. *Erythrina* × *bidwillii* makes 2-foot-long clusters of red flowers in summer. Slow growing (8 to 12 feet × 10 to 15 feet). *Erythrina humeana* 'Raja' (18 to 20 feet × 18 to 20 feet) has deep red flowers and arrow shaped leaves; hardy to 15 degrees F.

*Coral trees are a diverse group of trees with spectacular flowers in shades of blood red, deep orange, soft salmon, or palest green. Whorls of flowers surround tips of gold or silver barked branches; individual flowers are shaped like a bird's beak or a half-moon. Trunks are often covered in stout (but not threatening) thorns. Coral tree has bright green leaves that are divided in three sections. Leaves drop briefly in winter, during which time some species put on an amazing show of colorful flowers on naked branches. Others wait until after leafing to bloom. Corals are vigorous, fast growing trees. The key to success is in selecting one whose natural size that fits the space in your garden.*

### Bloom Period and Seasonal Color

Blood red, deep orange, soft salmon, or pale green flowers. Bloom time depends on species.

### Mature Height × Spread

8 to 40 ft. × 10 to 30 ft., depending on species

Hardy to 9B

Min. Temp. 25° F

# Crape Myrtle
*Lagerstroemia indica*

One of the ways I mark the change of seasons is by noting when particular plants bloom, especially crape myrtle trees. Crape myrtles are widely planted as street trees, landscape trees on school grounds, and alongside freeways throughout warmer regions of California. They all seem to bloom at once right in the heat of summer. Cranberry-colored buds open to magnificent sprays of crinkly petaled, raspberry-red, deep lilac, pale pink, fiery red, or bright white flowers. Clusters of green fruits follow the flowers in early fall. By winter, their leathery green leaves turn gold, orange, and copper before they drop. At that point, the focus shifts to the tree's fantastic mottled and peeling bark in shades of pink, pale green, red, and soft brown.

### Bloom Period and Seasonal Color
Summer flowers raspberry-red, deep lilac, pale pink, fiery red, or bright white. Fall-colored leaves.

### Mature Height × Spread
25 ft. × 25 ft.

**Hardy to 7A**

**Min. Temp. 0° F**

### When, Where, and How to Plant
Plant crape myrtle from fall to spring in frost-free gardens and in spring in colder winter gardens. Follow basic tree planting techniques in the chapter Introduction. Grow in almost any California climate, though tops may die back in winter cold at high elevation mountains and deserts. Grow for fall foliage in cool damp coastal gardens where trees may not flower well. Crape myrtle is adaptable to clay, sand, or loam soils. Site in full sun. Water deeply and mulch. Dwarf varieties are wonderful container plants.

### Growing Tips
Water deeply the first spring through late fall. Starting the second spring, this drought tolerant tree needs only occasional deep watering, though it tolerates more. Fertilize with all-purpose organic fertilizer in early spring before new growth begins. Mulch with compost.

### Care
If you'd like, reduce young trees to one or three trunks. After that, deadhead or shear after bloom, or allow the tree to develop its natural form without pruning. Choose mildew resistant varieties or spray dormant trees with copper fungicide. Watch for aphids, scale, and sooty mold (see "Tips and Techniques" for treatments).

### Companion Planting and Design
Since crape myrtle is upright or vase shaped, it doesn't make the best shade tree. It works better in the background as part of a screen of evergreens including bay, arbutus, chaste tree, or pineapple guava. In a beachside garden, plant crape myrtle a bit away from the spray zone. Since its roots don't damage sidewalks or structures, crape myrtle can be grown near walkways and foundations. It can even be trained as bonsai.

### Try These
'Catawba' (15 feet × 14 feet) has deep purple flowers and is mildew resistant. 'Dynamite' has fiery red flowers. 'Glendora White' (25 feet × 20 feet) has white flowers. 'Muskogee' has lavender flowers and is mildew resistant. 'Seminole' (6 to 12 feet × 6 to 12 feet) has bright pink flowers and is mildew resistant. Shrubby dwarf crape myrtle 'Chica' (3 feet × 4 feet) has cranberry-red flowers.

# Desert Willow

## Chilopsis linearis

### When, Where, and How to Plant

This desert native thrives in full sun with little to no water (once established), in all but the hottest desert gardens where it benefits from more regular water. Plant into well-draining soil from fall through spring in mild climates and in spring in colder climates. See the chapter introduction for basic tree planting instructions. Water deeply after planting and mulch.

### Growing Tips

In the first year, water deeply and regularly from the time the soil dries in the first spring until weather cools in fall. Then water deeply occasionally in summer only. Avoid overwatering as it can cause root rot. Fertilize if desired before new growth in spring. Use an all-purpose organic formulation.

### Care

These charming plants are naturally multi-trunked but can be pruned to be a one trunk. Prune when tree is dormant. Remove dead, diseased, or damaged wood. Pests aren't a problem.

### Companion Planting and Design

Hanging seedpods enhance the tree's weeping profile. Its small size makes desert willow good for patios or to use along pathways and walkways. Desert willow makes a beautiful centerpiece to a dry garden filled with century plant or other blue-green leaved agave, barrel cactus, Texas ranger, bush anemone, and native penstemons.

### Try These

'Burgundy' (15 to 20 feet × 15 to 20 feet) has burgundy flowers. 'Monhews' (Timeless Beauty™) (15 to 20 feet × 15 to 20 feet) has two-toned flowers with lavender above, burgundy below, and a yellow throat. 'Warren Jones'™ (25 to 30 feet × 25 to 30 feet) has light pink flowers and is only briefly deciduous in milder winter gardens. 'Lucretia Hamilton' (18 to 20 feet × 18 to 20 feet) has intense pink/burgundy flowers. 'Art's Seedless' (25 feet × 25 feet) has deep burgundy and pink flowers but no seedpods. Also look for Chitalpa (*Chitalpas tashkentensis*), a cross between desert willow and southern catalpa (*Catalpa bignonioides*), a southeastern native. Chitalpa has pale pink, desert willow-like flowers and leaves slightly wider and longer than desert willow.

On an early summer visit to Rancho Santa Ana Botanic Garden, I fell in love with a most surprising desert tree, the desert willow. Who could imagine a desert tree with such gorgeous flowers? At the tips of each branch are large clusters of 3- to 4-inch-wide, trumpet-shaped flowers. On the day of my visit, there were desert willow flowering in orchid pink with garnet markings and some flowering in pale rose-pink with tiny burgundy dots. Two-toned cultivars had orchid pink upper petals while the lower petals were garnet. Every flower had a golden yellow streak in its throat. Desert willow is a small but fast-growing deciduous tree with long narrow leaves, which together with the previous year's narrow hanging seedpods, gives the tree a weeping profile.

**Other Common Name**
Desert Catalpa

**Bloom Period and Seasonal Color**
Spring through summer blooms in blush pink, orchid pink, burgundy and/or garnet with contrasting markings and yellow throats.

Hardy to 7A

Min. Temp. 0° F

**Mature Height × Spread**
12 to 30 ft. × 12 to 30 ft.

# Dragon Tree
## *Dracaena draco*

Dragon trees have a long history of myth and legend inspired by their multi-branching structure, medusa-like foliage, and red resinous sap. Medieval Europeans called the sap "blood of dragons" and assigned it magical and medicinal qualities. Ancient Greeks believed the trees first sprouted from the blood of a dragon killed by Hercules. Indigenous peoples used a sap extract for mummification. More recently it has been an ingredient of incense, wood polishes, and stains. These agave relatives gain only 2 to 3 feet of height in ten to fifteen years but have magnificent silhouettes. Stout gray trunks are ringed with scars of past leaves (not past lives!) and topped with 2- to 4-foot-long, strappy, blue-green leaves. They flower every fifteen years or so and then branch, eventually forming an umbrella like canopy.

### Bloom Period and Seasonal Color
Occasional summer sprays of fragrant, creamy white flowers, followed by pea-sized coral-colored fruits.

### Mature Height × Spread
15 to 25 ft. × 15 to 25 ft.

**Hardy to 9A**

**Min. Temp. 20 to 25° F**

### When, Where, and How to Plant
Plant fall through spring in frost-free gardens and in spring in colder winter areas. Provide excellent drainage and full or part sun. Follow basic tree planting directions in the chapter introduction. Water deeply and mulch. Dragon tree will grow in a container (indoors or out) for many years but reaches significant size and branches only in the ground. Use a well-draining potting mix such as cactus mix and high-quality potting soil combined one to one. Mulch the pot with gravel.

### Growing Tips
These natives of arid rocky mountains in the Canary Islands are extremely drought tolerant. Water deeply and regularly the first year to establish and then water rarely but deeply in summers after that. Do not overwater. Feed with an all-purpose organic fertilizer in early spring if desired.

### Care
Prune only to remove damaged branches. Watch plants for scale, mealybugs, spider mites, and thrips. See treatment methods in "Tips and Techniques."

### Companion Planting and Design
Dragon tree's incredibly dramatic garden silhouette enhances any succulent or low water Mediterranean garden. Dragon trees decorate the Canary Island garden at Quail Botanical Gardens in Encinitas where they add structure and height to the plantings. Or visit Lotusland in Santa Barbara and stroll through a spectacular ancient grove of dragon trees with their enormous multibranched umbrellas almost 30 feet overhead.

### Try This
A small slender dragon tree relative, dracaena (*Dracaena marginata*) is an easy-to-grow potted plant for indoors or out. Its narrow, upright, ringed stems can reach 12 feet tall. Each stem is topped in clusters of 4- to 12-inch narrow strappy leaves that are deep glossy green, striped green and red, or green, gold, and red. To keep these slower growing plants small, simply use a small pot or snip a too-tall branch at the height where you want new branches to form. The cut piece will root in potting soil, and the cut branch will sprout at least two new branches. The more you cut, the more branches will sprout. It tolerates low light and low water.

## When, Where, and How to Plant

Floss silk trees thrive along the entire coast and in southern valleys and low deserts. In other regions plant floss silk in the hottest area of the garden and protect from frost when young. Plant any time of year in frost-free gardens and in spring through fall in colder areas. For maximum flowering, site in full sun and well-draining soil. See chapter introduction for tree planting directions. Young trees can be grown in pots for a while, but eventually must be planted in the ground. Water deeply after planting, and mulch.

## Growing Tips

Water deeply and frequently through the first spring to fall. In the second year, water deeply but infrequently spring to fall. Starting in the third year, in all but desert areas the trees should require only occasional deep summer water. In all areas, letting the soil go dry in fall promotes a larger winter bloom.

## Care

Floss silk trees grow relatively quickly when young and then slow as they mature. These trees are not known for having a handsome branching structure. In fact the branch pattern can be a bit awkward, like a tree from a Fred Flintstone cartoon. Either allow them to develop freeform or start pruning when young to create a pleasing shape. Pests are not a problem.

## Companion Planting and Design

Floss silk makes a magnificent fall-flowering shade tree that is best used as a specimen or as the tall element in a shrub border. The wide conical trunks of these stunning trees are often lined with stout spines, so plant them a distance from play areas, walkways, or other areas where people might accidentally brush up against them. Or look for a smooth trunked tree.

## Try These

Floss silk 'Los Angeles Beautiful' has burgundy flowers. Flowers of 'Monsa' are more pink than magenta. White floss silk tree (*Chorisia insignis*) is very similar to its pink cousin, but its flowers are white to pale yellow.

*One of California's little-known botanical treasures is a residential block of Yanonali Street in Santa Barbara, quite close to the beach. It is a street of gracious old homes and duplexes in Spanish Revival style, the city's vernacular architecture that arose following the earthquake of 1925. In fall and early winter, however, it is the street trees that put on the greatest show. Block-long canopies of huge star-shaped magenta flowers line the green branches that arch over the street, nearly touching in the center. Bright green leaves emerge as petals start to drop, carpeting the street in pink and leaving behind hanging green seedpods. Eventually the pods split to release long silky white strands of floss for which the tree is named.*

**Other Common Name**
Kapok

**Bloom Period and Seasonal Color**
Magenta pink flowers in fall and winter, huge green seedpods in winter and spring split to reveal silky white strands of floss.

**Mature Height × Spread**
40 to 65 ft. × 20 to 40 ft.

Hardy to
9A

Min.
Temp.
20 to 30° F

# Granite Honey Myrtle
## *Melaleuca elliptica*

*When a gardener I know purchased the ranch house of a long ago subdivided avocado grove, he inherited a hillside stand of elderly avocado trees. As the avocados declined, he replaced them with a lovely sloping meadow of yarrow spiked with harlequin flower, daffodil, and other spring flowering bulbs. Around this beautiful meadow, the gardener planted a border of rockrose, ornamental grasses, and a lovely small tree with blue-green leaves the size and shape of my pinky nail. When I visited in spring, the tree's oval canopy included raspberry colored, bottlebrush-type flowers along branches covered in papery bark. This was my introduction to granite honey myrtle, an evergreen Australian melaleuca that performs spectacularly in both large and small gardens in our Mediterranean climate.*

**Other Common Name**
Crimson Melaleuca

**Bloom Period and Seasonal Color**
Watermelon red flowers, spring through fall.

**Mature Height × Spread**
15 to 20 ft. × 15 ft.

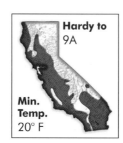

Hardy to
9A

Min.
Temp.
20° F

### When, Where, and How to Plant
Plant fall through spring in frost-free gardens and in spring in colder winter gardens. Granite honey myrtle prefers full sun but will tolerate light shade. Poor soils are fine if they drain well. Follow planting directions in the chapter introduction. Water well and mulch. To grow in a container, start a small tree in a small container. Move it to larger and larger containers as it gains height and width. Ultimately granite honey myrtle can fill a very large pot.

### Growing Tips
In year one, water deeply once a week for the first two or three weeks and then water deeply once a month until winter rains begin. In year two, water deeply each month from the time soil dries in spring until winter rains. After that water deeply just a few times through summer. Spray periodically to rinse dust off leaves. Since most Australian plants come from areas where soils have even fewer nutrients than ours, they don't need fertilizer. If leaves yellow, sprinkle the soil beneath the branches with iron sulfate or powdered sulfur and iron chelate (follow directions on the label). Water it in and wait for leaves to green up over several months.

### Care
Pests aren't a problem. Avoid overwatering to prevent root rot and deadly soil fungi. Pruning is not necessary, but if you want to shape the tree, prune right after flowering.

### Companion Planting and Design
Grow these small trees as the center of a Mediterranean theme garden with rockrose, sedge, bugle lilies, blazing star, and bush anemone. You can grow them as patio trees or near walkways since roots do little damage.

### Try These
Totem pole (*Melaleuca decussata*) is a large shrub or small tree (6 to 16 feet × 10 to 20 feet) with branches covered in small gray-green leaves, shreddy bark, and lilac flowers in spring or summer. Dotted Melaleuca (*Melaleuca diosmifolia*) has curving branches covered in bright green, scale-like leaves (5 to 12 feet × 12 feet) and has yellow-green, bottle-brush flowers from spring to summer.

# Guadalupe Palm

*Brahea edulis*

## When, Where, and How to Plant

Plant in late summer or early fall in full sun. Well-draining soil is key. If soil drains poorly, amend it, create a planting mound of well-draining soil, or grow the tree in a container. Follow tree planting directions in the chapter introduction. Water deeply after planting, and mulch, leaving the first six inches encircling the trunk bare.

## Growing Tips

Keep soil moist (not wet) the first two growing seasons. After the second summer, this palm should survive on rainfall in the wetter northern part of the state, with occasional deep summer watering in the south. Wait several weeks after planting and then fertilize four times between March and October and any time that fronds look yellow (not brown). Wait at least a month between applications. Use an organic palm fertilizer, fish emulsion and kelp extract, or any 3:1:3 fertilizer with micronutrients (water soil before applying fertilizer).

## Care

Old fronds slough off on their own (that is what makes them "self cleaning"). Prune any fronds that are damaged or ragged. Watch for scale, aphids, and mealybugs (see treatments in "Tips and Techniques"). Prevent fungus by not overwatering, practicing good garden sanitation, and disinfecting tools before and after pruning (also in "Tips and Techniques"). Pick fruit to eat fresh or cook to make jam.

## Companion Planting and Design

If you plant a combination of palms, site taller ones where they won't shade out lower growing sun lovers like Guadalupe Island palm. Plant as a specimen or focal point. Arrange geometrically in a formal garden. It is suitable for planting as a street tree providing there are no overhead wires. For a dry tropic look, combine with reed orchids, succulent flapjack plants, pink-flowering floss silk tree, and yellow-blooming winter cassia.

## Try These

Mexican Blue Fan Palm (*Brahea armata*) (20 to 40 feet × 25 feet) has 4- to 8-foot silvery-blue leaves and a 2-foot diameter trunk; hardy to 15 degrees F. San Jose Hesper Palm (*Brahea brandegeei*) (40 feet × 15 feet.) has 3- to 4-foot light gray leaves and is hardy to 25 degrees F.

*Have you ever noticed that some palm tree trunks look just like elephant legs? One is Guadalupe palm, a short, dry-growing palm with a gray ringed trunk that resembles elephant hide. Guadalupe palm originally comes from Cedros Island, off the coast of Baja where it is now endangered. Most Guadalupe palms offered by nurseries, however, are seed raised rather than wild harvested. Guadalupe palm's green, palmate fronds are 3 to 6 feet long or longer and 3 to 4 feet wide and self-cleaning. "Edulis" means edible and refers to the black date-like fruits that appear in spring and summer. Guadalupe palm grows well throughout California, tolerating salt spray, cold winters, and hot summers. This palm has grown in the gardens at Stanford University since 1900.*

### Bloom Period and Seasonal Color

Large, arching sprays of hanging, cream-colored flowers in spring and summer; black fruits.

### Mature Height × Spread

20 to 35 ft. × 10 to 20 ft.

Hardy to 8B

Min. Temp. 18° F

# Jacaranda
## *Jacaranda mimosifolia*

*It happens on a particular day in spring. It is the day when all the jacarandas bloom, seemingly in synchrony. I sometimes imagine an annual wintertime jacaranda convention when all the jacarandas gather and decide on that year's spring bloom date. They then return to their spots lining city blocks, shading gardens, and standing guard over playgrounds. The trees wait, naked and silent, for the day to arrive. When it does, they erupt, forming dense canopies of tubular flowers in the most amazing shade of periwinkle/lavender. The display lasts for weeks, during which time ferny green leaves appear. Soon the flowers fall in a purple rain so beautiful that, rather than mind the litter, we focus on the indelible memory of the spectacular bloom.*

**Bloom Period and Seasonal Color**
Spring flowers periwinkle or lavender.

**Mature Height × Spread**
25 to 50 ft. × 15 to 30 ft.

**Hardy to** 9B

**Min. Temp.** 25 to 30° F

### When, Where, and How to Plant
Plant in spring, following directions in the chapter introduction. These natives of Brazil, Bolivia, and Argentina are heat-loving trees that prefer winter nighttime temperatures that seldom dip below freezing. As with most trees, younger ones are most susceptible to cold. Jacaranda does well in all southern climates and in coastal valleys up and down the state. Provide full sun and well-draining soil. Sandy soil is optimal. Amend poor-draining soils or build a planting mound. The hottest part of the garden will promote the best bloom. Jacaranda lovers in colder winter areas can grow the trees in portable containers and move them indoors or into a greenhouse in winter.

### Growing Tips
Young trees need frequent deep water to keep the rootball moist but not wet through the first several summers. Deep watering encourages deep roots so the tree needs less water as it matures. Eventually jacaranda needs only occasional deep summer irrigation (more in deserts). Overwatered trees can develop root rot, so err on the dry side, especially with established trees. Fertilize once in early spring with an all-purpose organic fertilizer.

### Care
Jacaranda trees are naturally multi-trunked and vase shaped. If you'd like, prune to a single trunk for an umbrella canopy. Prune to remove dead or diseased limbs and those that sprout at an awkward angle. Watch for aphids (see treatments in "Tips and Techniques").

### Companion Planting and Design
Jacaranda are spectacular shade and street trees (but avoid power lines). They soften any style garden, especially a tropical garden. Create a multi-level screen by planting jacaranda with pineapple guava (pink spring flowers and green fall fruit) and winter cassia (yellow flowers in winter). Underplant with felty-leaved peppermint geranium. Jacaranda will tolerate beach conditions as long as the tree doesn't get direct salt spray. Flower arrangers covet Jacaranda's very round, flat, and shiny brown seed pods.

### Try This
*Jacaranda mimosifolia* 'Alba' has white flowers and lusher foliage.

# Japanese Maple
## *Acer palmatum*

## When, Where, and How to Plant
Plant into well-draining soil when the ground is workable. To grow Japanese maple in the ground, start with a 15-gallon tree or larger. In areas with hard (alkaline) water, backfill with 1/3 soil, 1/3 azalea mix, and 1/3 peat. Follow planting directions in the chapter introduction. In coastal gardens, Japanese maples can handle full sun. In hotter areas, they prefer shade and/or northern or eastern exposure. Protect from wind and salt spray. Because young Japanese maples grow slowly, they make great container plants.

## Growing Tips
Keep the rootball moist, not saturated. Water regularly, slowly, and deeply. Allow soil to drain between waterings. Do not let water stand in saucers beneath potted Japanese maples. Use a slow-release fertilizer for pots. In-ground trees need little or no fertilizer. If you have hard water, leach soil (in the ground or pots) monthly in summer to wash away salts that cause leaf burn (see "Tips and Techniques"). Sprinkle the soil with powdered sulfur to counter the alkalinity. To avoid additional salt accumulation, use *organic* fertilizers, not synthetic ones. Apply at the lowest rate indicated on the label.

## Care
Prune only dead, diseased, or crossing branches for the first five years while the tree finds its shape. Watch for aphids (see "Tips and Techniques").

## Companion Planting and Design
Create a shady foliage garden of Japanese maple, bamboos, Japanese sweet flag, camellias, and hellebore. To provide critical humidity in dry climates, plant near a streambed, pond, or swimming pool.

## Try These
'Atropurpureum' (20 feet × 20 feet) has deep purple-bronze leaves. The green leaves of coral bark Japanese maple 'Sango Kaku' (15 to 20 feet × 15 to 20 feet) turn gold in fall then drop, revealing bright coral branches. 'Emperor One' (11 to 15 feet × 11 to 15 feet) has blood red leaves and is a good choice for beginners. Leaves of 'Kamagata' (6 to 10 feet × 6 to 10 feet) are finely textured red-blushed-green turning vermillion red, yellow, and gold in fall. 'Fireglow' (6 to 10 feet × 6 to 10 feet) is upright with deep red leaves.

Among the maples, Japanese maples are royalty. Gardeners admire them, honor them, and covet them. What makes these trees so appealing? It could be their lacy palmate leaves. Or perhaps their airy graceful forms. Then again it could be their multicolored foliage. All of these features and more make these deciduous beauties so attractive. Japanese maples can be finicky in the garden, depending on where in the state you live. In moderate coastal, northern, and high elevation gardens, they do well. In gardens where the climate is dry and water is alkaline, they need special care. But in the right spot and given proper garden conditions, Japanese maple will make your heart skip a beat every time you see it.

**Bloom Period and Seasonal Color**
Fantastic red, green, gold, and multicolored leaves spring through fall.

**Mature Height × Spread**
6 to 20 ft. × 6 to 20 ft.

Hardy to 5A

Min. Temp. -20 to 10° F

# Jelly Palm
## *Butia capitata*

*When my children were small, they asked to pick the golden "dates" that hung from palms we often saw in parking lots. I hesitated. I knew the palm trunks were too short and their leaves too blue to be date palms. What were they? And were their fruits edible? After a bit of sleuthing, I learned that they were jelly palms, that their fruits are indeed edible, and that while there are only a few areas in California warm enough for date palms to fruit, jelly palms fruit quite readily through most of the state. These handsome, drought tolerant palms tolerate cold, wind, and salt spray. Their fruit, we discovered, tastes like a mixture of banana, pineapple, and apricot.*

**Other Common Name**
Pindo Palm

**Bloom Period and Seasonal Color**
Creamy yellow to coppery flowers in spring; golden orange fruit in summer.

**Mature Height × Spread**
15 to 20 ft. × 15 to 20 ft.

Hardy to 8B

Min. Temp. 15° F

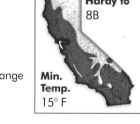

### When, Where, and How to Plant

Plant in late summer or early fall. Full sun is best, but light shade is okay. If soil drains poorly, create a planting mound (see "Tips and Techniques"). For planting directions, see the chapter introduction. Water deeply after planting, and mulch, leaving the 6 inches closet to the trunk bare. You can also plant these slow-growing compact palms into containers.

### Growing Tips

Keep soil moist (not wet) the first two growing seasons. Once established (after the second summer), these dry region, South American natives do fine on rainfall in the wetter northern part of the state, with occasional deep summer watering in the south. Wait several weeks after planting, then fertilize and repeat three more times between March and October or fertilize any time fronds look yellow (not brown). Wait at least a month between applications. Use an organic palm fertilizer, fish emulsion and kelp extract, or any 3:1:3 fertilizer with micronutrients. (Water the soil before applying fertilizer).

### Care and Harvest

Watch for scale. Avoid overwatering, practice good garden sanitation, and disinfect tools before and after you prune (tool cleaning and pest control information is in "Tips and Techniques"). Cut fruit by the bunch to make jelly or wine. Hire a professional to remove dead, damaged, or ragged leaves.

### Companion Planting and Design

Use jelly palms as specimen plants, street trees (not under utility lines), in small groves, or in containers. Keep away from sidewalks and patios as dropping fruits can make a mess in summer (or cut fruiting stalks before fruits ripen).

### Try This

Chilean wine palm (*Jubaea chilensis*) also makes edible fruit. The trunk of this palm grows slowly to 80 feet × 5 feet (!) topped with gray-green pinnate fronds. It is native to Chilean habitats similar to California's dry chaparral, making it both drought and cold tolerant (to 15 degrees F). Golden fruits taste like juicy coconuts, but Chilean wine palm gets its name from the sap that Spaniards fermented for wine in the 1500s. Today's palm honey is made from the same sap.

# King Palm
## *Archontophoenix cunninghamiana*

### When, Where, and How to Plant
Plant in late summer or early fall so roots are established and ready to grow in spring. Provide full sun or light shade. The key to success is well-draining soil. If soil is heavy, build a large planting mound of well-draining soil or grow it in a container. Follow directions in the chapter introduction, adding a handful of aged manure to the planting hole. Minimize root disturbance while planting. King palm is not for desert gardens.

### Growing Tips
Water regularly to keep soil moist, not wet. Fertilize several weeks after planting. Repeat three more times between March and October or fertilize any time that fronds look yellow (not brown). Use a palm fertilizer, fish emulsion and kelp extract, or any 3:1:3 fertilizer with micronutrients (water soil first). Wait at least a month between applications.

### Care
Young king palms are sensitive to salt spray, cold, and wind so buy the largest king you can afford. Young kings won't necessarily succumb under adverse conditions, but it may take a few years until they look good. Since old leaves slough off, prune only to remove damaged or ragged leaves. To avoid fungal diseases, practice good garden sanitation, and disinfect tools before and after you prune (see "Tips and Techniques"). Watch for scale, aphids, and whitefly (treatments also in "Tips and Techniques"). Avoid digging or cultivating beneath an established palm.

### Companion Planting and Design
Plant king palms as specimen plants or in small groves. Three or five young king palms planted in a single hole create the impression of a clump. King palms are good street trees (but not under utility wires), courtyard trees, and container specimens. These thirsty palms will grow in a lawn as long as the soil drains well.

### Try These
Cold-hardy king palm include: Illawarra King Palm (*Archontophoenix cunninghamiana* 'Illawara') and Mount Lewis King Palm (*Archontophoenix purpurea*), which develops a red/purple-tinged crownshaft. At 80 feet tall, Walsh River Palm (*Archontophoenix maxima*) is the largest king palm.

*Palms, especially those with green pinnate (feather-shaped) fronds, are the defining plants of tropical gardens. One of the most attractive is the king palm, which has a tall sleek profile and long arching leaves. These fast growing, thirsty palms are native to the rain-forests of eastern Australia. They have single smooth trunks, a foot or so across, topping out at 65 feet under the best conditions. Their graceful fronds slough off as they age, leaving a slender crownshaft (where the bases of the leaves wrap around the trunk). They produce long hanging strands of small purplish flowers that become red fruits. King palms do best in gardens where temperatures seldom dip below freezing, but more cold hardy varieties are suitable for northern coastal gardens.*

**Bloom Period and Seasonal Color**
Cream colored flower strands with purplish flowers in fall, followed by red fruits.

**Mature Height × Spread**
40 to 65 ft. × 10 to 15 ft.

**Hardy to 9B**

**Min. Temp. 28° F**

# New Zealand Christmas Tree
## *Metrosideros excelsa*

*The most magnificent New Zealand Christmas trees I have ever seen grew in a most unexpected location—on a windy hillside of Alcatraz, the former prison island in San Francisco bay. Planted in the early 1940s, these trees stand at least 40 feet tall and 30 feet wide. I last visited on a foggy day in June when the trees were in full glorious bloom; silvery green buds and crimson red flowers of fringy stamens blanketed the canopy of shiny, deep green, leathery leaves, whose undersides were silvery with fine hairs. Alcatraz's seaside exposure is similar to the trees' native coastal New Zealand: well-draining soil, constant winds, some salt spray, and cool fog. Fortunately, they do nearly as well in gardens far from the coast.*

**Other Common Name**
Pohutukawa

**Bloom Period and Seasonal Color**
Silvery green buds and deep red fringy flowers in summer.

**Mature Height × Spread**
20 to 40 ft. × 10 to 30 ft.

Hardy to 9B

Min. Temp. 25° F

### When, Where, and How to Plant
New Zealand Christmas tree thrives in coastal regions statewide and in southern inland valleys. In other climates, site in the garden's warmest exposure. Trees are extremely drought tolerant but tolerate moist, well-draining soils. Plant fall through spring into frost-free gardens and in spring in cooler gardens. It flowers best in full sun, though plants tolerate part sun or part shade. See the chapter introduction for tree planting directions. Water deeply and mulch well after planting.

### Growing Tips
Water young trees regularly from spring to early fall. In year two, soak monthly from late spring until temperatures cool in fall. By the third year, water only occasionally in summer. Mature trees need little to no water. Water all container-grown plants regularly and deeply. Fertilize in early spring with a balanced organic fertilizer. If leaves pale or yellow, treat with iron sulfate or powdered sulfur and iron chelate (follow label directions). Water deeply. Leaves green up over several months.

### Care
Young trees are more shrub-shaped, single or multitrunked, and low branched, but with age they become tree shaped (more so with judicious pruning). Avoid overwatering, which can cause root rot and encourage fungi. No pests bother this tree.

### Companion Planting and Design
Use as a specimen tree, evergreen hedge, garden background, or screen. These smog tolerant trees make good street trees (but not under power lines). Their salt and wind tolerance makes them excellent trees for beachside gardens. Both tree-like and dwarf (see below) varieties do well in containers. I am particularly fond of a pair of trees in enormous terracotta pots that flank a parking lot entrance in Del Mar, California.

### Try These
Leaves of 'Midas' (20 feet × 8 feet) are deep green edged in yellow. 'Aurea' has green leaves and golden yellow flowers. *Metrosideros collina* 'Spring Fire' (8 to 12 feet × 4 to 6 feet) blooms orange-red in spring. Shrubby *Metrosideros excelsa* 'Gala' (6 feet × 6 feet) has variegated leaves, green with creamy yellow centers.

# Oak

*Quercus* spp.

## When, Where, and How to Plant

In snow-free gardens, plant fall through spring. In snowy winter areas, wait until spring. See chapter introduction for planting directions. Full sun and well-draining soils are best, though soil needs can differ by species. Water deeply after planting, and mulch.

## Growing Tips

Mature oaks want little to no water once mature. Young trees, however, need deep irrigation to become established. To garden beneath oaks, select plants that grow naturally in oak's dry shade, and plant at the same time as the oak so they can become established together. Keep all plants at least 6 feet from the tree trunk. Don't plant under the canopy of an already established oak. The water needed to establish those plants can weaken the tree and encourage deadly fungi. No fertilizer.

## Care

Prune to remove dead or damaged branches. Do not dig, pave, or plant beneath the canopy of an established oak. Healthy oaks resist most pests and diseases. Watch for scale (see treatment in "Tips and Techniques"). Sudden oak death can infect forest grown oaks but is seldom a problem in a cultivated garden.

## Companion Planting and Design

Use oaks in low water native and wildlife gardens. Combine newly planted oaks with bush anemone, California fescue, monkey flowers, iris, and currants.

## Try These

Coast live oak (*Quercus agrifolia*) has a dome-shaped crown of holly-like leaves (40 feet × 40 feet) and is hardy to 10 degrees F. Scrub oak (*Quercus berberdifolia*) has glossy-green toothed leaves (10 to 20 feet × 10 to 20 feet) and is hardy to -10 degrees F. Shrubby California scrub oak (*Quercus dumosa*) has a round crown (3 to 10 feet × 15 feet) and is hardy to 15 degrees F. Island oak (*Quercus tomentella*) has a rounded crown of large, leathery, glossy green leaves with sharp teeth (40 to 60 feet × 20 to 30 feet) and is hardy to 20 degrees F. Deciduous valley oak (*Quercus lobata*) has lobed soft green leaves, fantastic gnarled, twisted branches, and is suited for high mountain gardens (40 to 60 feet × 40 to 60 feet). It is hardy to -15 degrees F.

*Legend has it that when Spaniards first arrived in California, our coasts, valleys, and foothills were covered in oak trees so thick that the conquistadors could ride their horses an entire day without seeing the sun. Oaks' common names reveal their expanse and variety: coast live oak, valley oak, California scrub oak, island oak, and so on. Their small, dark green, leathery leaves complement the gnarled trunks and branches. Many are tall with broad, beautiful canopies and some are smaller and more shrub-like. Garden-worthy oaks come from other Mediterranean regions as well. One of the best is cork oak (Quercus suber). In its native Spain and Portugal, cork oak trees are harvested—peeled actually—every ten years to make wine corks, corkboards, and other products.*

**Mature Height × Spread**
10 to 60 ft. × 40 ft.

**Minimum Temperature**
Depends on species.

Hardy to 5A

Min. Temp. -15 to 20° F

# Palo Verde

*Parkinsonia* spp.

*Among the dazzling mosaic of springtime desert blooms are wispy green-barked trees covered in brilliant yellow flowers. These are palo verde "green stick" trees and they are great trees for low-water gardens. Palo verde has a small stature with spreading and sometimes weeping canopies that top multiple trunks (prune for a single trunk). Palo verde is very drought tolerant, heat resistant, and tolerant of poor soils. Some palo verde are spiny and most are fast growing. While most plants photosynthesize with green pigments in their leaves, the leaves of palo verde are so small and short-lived that the tree has green bark that photosynthesizes like a giant leaf. These trees are best suited for hot inland valleys, deserts, and most of Southern California.*

**Other Common Name**
Jerusalem Thorn

**Bloom Period and Seasonal Color**
Golden yellow flowers peak in spring, bloom sporadically through summer.

**Mature Height × Spread**
25 ft. 25 ft. or wider

**Minimum Temperature**
Depends on species.

Hardy to 8B

Min. Temp. 15 to 20° F

## When, Where, and How to Plant
Plant any time of year into full sun and in the warmest part of the garden. These trees are adaptable to any kind of soil but prefer soil that is well draining. See chapter introduction for tree planting instructions. Water deeply after planting, and mulch.

## Growing Tips
Since palo verde are native to areas with less than 10 inches of rainfall per year, they are extremely drought tolerant once established. Water deeply but infrequently through the first summer. Starting in the second year, water deeply once or twice in summer and not at all the rest of the year. When in doubt, don't water. Too much water makes palo verde grow too fast and become too top heavy. No need to fertilize.

## Care
Prune regularly to shape, starting when trees are young. Multitrunked trees can be reduced to a single trunk if you prefer that style. Along the coast, leaves can be afflicted with powdery mildew, but leaves are so short-lived the problem soon disappears.

## Companion Planting and Design
These small trees are perfect for shading patios, courtyards, and small gardens, especially in hot valleys and desert areas. Site palo verde against a terracotta or deep purple colored wall for a beautiful silhouette. Plant as an open canopy over a colorful succulent garden or mix with drought tolerant flowering perennials and shrubs such as California poppies, Mexican tulip poppies, low water sages, grevillea, and Texas ranger. Palo verde even make good parking lot and street median trees. One caution however: If your palo verde is a spiny species, plant it well away from pathways and play areas.

## Try This
My favorite palo verde is the hybrid, *Parkinsonia* 'Desert Museum' that does well in milder areas, especially near the coast. 'Desert Museum' has the largest flowers of all palo verde. Its upright form, small amount of litter, and smooth, spineless green branches makes it a good garden, street, or sidewalk tree.

# Peppermint Tree
## *Agonis flexuosa*

### When, Where, and How to Plant

Plant from fall through spring in frost-free gardens and in spring in colder winter gardens. Provide full sun along the coast. Trees tolerate extreme heat, but protect young trees from scorching sun in hot inland gardens. Soil can be rich, poor, moist, or dry, but must drain well. Follow planting directions in the chapter introduction. Water well after planting, and mulch.

### Growing Tips

Deep water once a week for the first two or three weeks, then once a month until winter rains. In year two, start watering when soil dries in late spring. Water deeply once a month until winter rains. After that trees in hottest gardens appreciate a few deep summer waterings. Along the coast they may need no irrigation at all. Most Australian plants come from soils even poorer than ours, so they don't need fertilizer. If leaves yellow, sprinkle iron sulfate or powdered sulfur and iron chelate on soil beneath the branches (follow label directions). Water deeply. Leaves will green up over time.

### Care

Where winter temperatures hover in the low 20s, branches may freeze back but recover. Allow damaged branches to protect interior foliage until after the last spring frost. Pruning is not necessary and pests are not a problem. Watering too frequently can cause root rot and deadly soil fungi.

### Companion Planting and Design

Peppermint tree can be single or multitrunked. Both styles make dramatic container specimens, patio trees, courtyard trees, and even evergreen privacy screens. Peppermint tree suits almost any style garden, from Asian to English cottage and from tropical to Mediterranean. Site far enough from foundations and sidewalks so that larger roots will not cause problems.

### Try These

Purple Peppermint Tree (*Agonis flexuosa* 'After Dark' also 'Jervis Bay After Dark') is grown for its amazing foliage that emerges garnet-red in spring and deepens to dark burgundy and almost-black by summer. White flowers appear against this dark background. It grows 18 feet × 10 to 15 feet. Juniper myrtle (*Agonis juniperina*) has narrow, almost needle-like, bright green leaves.

Peppermint tree is an evergreen tree popular for its attractive weeping silhouette, its adaptability, and its easy growing nature. The trunk and larger branches of this western Australia native are covered in deeply furrowed, almost shreddy, brown bark. Slim silvery branches hang pendulously from the main branches, forming a low weeping canopy. Narrow, deep green leaves clothe the branches. Pick a leaf and crush it to release a mild peppermint fragrance. Though these trees are grown primarily for their wonderful form, they are even more beautiful in late spring or early summer when the end of each branch is covered in tiny, rounded white flowers. Though not among the fastest growing trees, peppermint tree is one of my favorites for both residential and commercial plantings.

### Other Common Name
Willow Myrtle

### Bloom Period and Seasonal Color
White flowers with maroon centers in spring and summer.

### Mature Height × Spread
25 to 40 ft. × 15 to 20 ft.

Hardy to 9B

Min. Temp. 25° F

# Purple Orchid Tree

*Bauhinia purpurea*

*Few trees are more exotic or tropical looking than the lovely purple orchid tree. These trees are native to India, Nepal, Sri Lanka, Thailand, and neighboring areas—and they look the part. Their graceful slender trunks lead to smooth branches that form a vase shape when the trees are young. As the purple orchid trees mature, their branches create rounded canopies that cast just the right amount of shade. Voluptuous, fist-sized leaves are bright green and two-lobed, making them the perfect foil for sprays of 2- to 3-inch large flowers. Each orchid shaped flower has five narrow petals in magenta or purple with white markings and long curved stamens. Sometimes sold as Bauhinia variegata.*

## Other Common Name
Butterfly Orchid Tree

## Bloom Period and Seasonal Color
Trees bloom from late summer into fall with magenta to purple flowers in fall and winter. Long, flat, green bean-like seedpods follow.

**Hardy to**
9A

**Min. Temp.**
20° F

## Mature Height × Spread
20 to 35 ft. × 25 ft.

## When, Where, and How to Plant
Plant fall through spring in frost-free gardens and in spring in colder winter environments. These trees prefer well-draining soil and either loam or sand. They bloom best in warmer climates of Southern California and bloom less in the Central Valley and farther north but can be grown there more as a shade tree. Follow planting directions in the chapter introduction.

## Growing Tips
Water deeply and frequently through the first year and in the second summer. Established trees typically need far less water than young trees. Eventually they should need watering just a few times through the summer except in the hottest regions. Fertilize with all-purpose organic fertilizer in early spring as new growth begins.

## Care
Prune to remove damaged or diseased branches, or to shape. Watch for aphids (see "Tips and Techniques").

## Companion Planting and Design
Purple orchid trees are spectacular specimen trees that look lovely alongside a patio, planted as a street tree (not under power lines), or shading the hot side of your home in summer. Set your summer outdoor dining table beneath the shade of an orchid tree.

## Try These
*Bauhinia variegata* 'Candida' has white flowers. Hong Kong orchid tree (*Bauhinia × blakeana*) (20 feet × 20 feet) has 5 1/2- to 6-inch, long-lasting flowers, starting in fall and persisting through winter. They are rose-pink, purple, deep burgundy, or fuchsia-pink with white markings. This is Hong Kong's official flower. Anacacho orchid tree (*Bauhinia lunarioides or Bauhinia congesta*) is 12 feet × 10 feet, forming a petite multi-trunk tree or large shrub with pale pink or white flowers from spring through summer. It is deciduous with small, gray-green leaves, needs little water, does well in the desert, and is hardy to 15 degrees F.

# Purple Smoke Tree
### *Cotinus coggygria purpureus*

## When, Where, and How to Plant
Plant fall through spring, following directions in the chapter introduction. Foliage shows best when planted in full sun, but trees do fine in part shade as well. Smoke trees prefer well-draining soil but tolerate moist soils. Water deeply after planting, and mulch. If planting in a beachside garden, keep it out of the salt spray.

## Growing Tips
Water well the first year once the soil dries in spring, through summer and fall until winter rains begin. In the second year, water occasionally spring to fall. Once established, water only occasionally in summer. Apply a balanced organic fertilizer before new leaves appear in spring. **Note:** Leaves are poisonous if ingested.

## Care
This tree is an open grower that is beautiful left unpruned. To shape, start when the plant is young, pruning in winter when plants are dormant. Root rot and wilt can be problematic for these trees if overwatered. Once they are established, err on the dry side.

## Companion Planting and Design
Plant smoke trees where their leaves are backlit. Combine purple smoke tree with gray-green, chartreuse, or olive-green leaved plants. Planted next to shrubby dune sage (*Salvia africana-lutea*), smoke tree brings out the red-bronze tones of the sage's calyx and complements its apricot-colored flowers. Underplant with fuzzy gray-green ornamental oregano 'Dittany of Crete' and add the similar colored, but contrasting leaf texture, of wine-colored 'Shirazz' New Zealand flax.

## Try These
'Royal Purple' has the darkest smoke tree leaves—wine red turning plum colored by the end of summer and then purple-red before they drop in fall. The leaves of 'Velvet Cloak' are round and a deep wine red that's almost black. Flower clusters are mauve (8 to12 feet × 8 to 12 feet). 'Ancot' (Golden Spirit) is an unusual smoke tree with shocking lime green leaves that age to gold before turning red, orange, and coral in fall. Clouds of pink flowers develop at branch tips in summer. It likes part sun to bright shade (8 feet × 6 feet).

*Smoke tree is a stunning large shrub or small tree grown for foliage, unusual summer flowers, and fantastic fall color. This deciduous plant has large, round (sometimes oblong) leaves, 3 inches across, that emerge deep plum. Leaves on younger wood stay plum colored, but those on older wood turn blue-green through summer. Once fall arrives, leaves turn red, orange, and copper for a stunning fall show, especially when plants are sited so that leaves are backlit. The "smoke" of smoke trees is actually flowers. Clusters of tiny greenish or cream flowers appear at branch tips in late spring or early summer. As they fade, they develop fuzzy purplish hairs that suggest rose pink, feathery down or hazy plumes of smoke.*

**Bloom Period and Seasonal Color**
Purple leaves spring through fall; airy rose pink flowers in summer.

**Mature Height × Spread**
12 to 25 ft. × 12 to 25 ft.

Hardy to 4B

Min. Temp. -25° F

# Shoestring Acacia

*Acacia stenophylla*

*Gardeners often wish for the impossible: a beautiful, tall, evergreen tree that requires little water and takes up little space in the garden. It should also be clean enough that dropping leaves don't make a mess, and it should require minimal pruning and no fertilizer. One of the few trees that can fulfill that wish list is shoestring acacia. Shoestring acacia is a graceful, single-trunk tree with weeping blue-green leaves. This fast growing Australian native has an open canopy. The wispy 16-inch-long leaves cast a gentle shade, making it compatible with sun-loving shrubs, perennials, and annuals. While some acacias bloom brilliantly, shoestring acacia's ivory-colored flowers are its most subtle feature. Young trunks feature beautiful mottled bark of lavender purple and pink shaded with pastel green.*

## Bloom Period and Seasonal Color
Ivory colored flowers in fall, winter, or spring; lavender purple and pink bark with a green blush.

## Mature Height × Spread
30 ft. × 20 ft.

**Hardy to 9A**

**Min. Temp. 20° F**

## When, Where, and How to Plant
Plant from fall through spring in frost-free gardens and in spring in colder winter gardens. Follow directions in the chapter introduction. Shoestring acacia tolerates a range of soils but prefers those that drain well. Water well and mulch. To grow in a container, start a small plant in a small container. Move the plant to larger and larger containers as it gains height and width. Ultimately this tree can fill a very large pot.

## Growing Tips
Deep water once a week for the first two or three weeks and then once a month until winter rains. In year two, start watering when soil dries in late spring. Water deeply once a month until winter rains begin. After that, the roots are likely to be deep enough to require just a few deep waterings in summer. Since most Australian plants such as this one come from areas where soils have even fewer nutrients than ours, they don't need fertilizer.

## Care
As trunks grow taller, prune off straggly lower branches. These trees make almost no leaf litter and have no pests.

## Companion Planting and Design
Shoestring acacia's wonderful silhouette shows off well against a deep-colored wall. Plant it as a specimen in a small garden. In a larger garden, plant 3 or 5 trees in a triangle for a graceful "grove." Underplant with agave, aloe, Indian mallow, Texas ranger, desert mallow, woolly butterfly bush, and different kinds of grasses. Good companions also include succulent blue chalk sticks and fragrant-leaved sages, as well as California natives like toyon, California lilac, and penstemon.

## Try This
There are many great smaller acacia trees such as knife-leaf acacia (*Acacia cultriformis*). This multi-trunked tree (or tall shrub when left unpruned) has a rounded canopy. Its young stems and smaller branches are lined in rows of ice green triangular leaves the size of your pinky nail and reminiscent of the scales on the back of a stegosaurus. In early spring, it produces bright yellow, fragrant, pea-sized flowers. It is adaptable to both medium and low water gardens (15 feet × 15 feet).

# Sycamore
## *Platanus racemosa*

### When, Where, and How to Plant
Sycamores are native to creekbeds and riverbanks from the Sacramento Valley and the Sierra foothills south to Baja. They are extremely adaptable to all regions of the state. In snow-free gardens, plant fall through spring. In snowy winter areas, wait until spring. Plant in full sun and in well-draining soils (see chapter introduction for planting details). Because sycamores grow quickly (up to several feet each year) there is no reason to invest in a large tree.

### Growing Tips
Provide regular deep waterings (once a week or so) through the first spring through late fall to keep soil moist and encourage deep rooting. In the second year, cut watering by half. After that, trees growing along the coast, near a stream, or where the water table is high can survive on rainfall. In all other areas, water deeply and occasionally through the hot, dry months (more in deserts).

### Care
Prune to remove damaged, dead, or diseased wood. Allow sycamore to find its own shape; its fascinating branch arrangement is one of its major attractions. Pests and diseases include anthracnose fungi ("sycamore blight"). Twigs and young leaves drop, but new ones soon sprout. Avoid getting water on leaves, prune to increase air circulation (cover yourself well to protect your skin from the leaves' irritating hairs), and then stop worrying since there are few assaults that will kill this tree.

### Companion Planting and Design
Sycamore is a large tree for a large space. Plant it in an informal or naturalistic garden where its abundance of leaves can be left in place as mulch. Underplant with larger shade and moisture tolerant natives such as toyon, manzanita, and currant. Sycamores grow well along the edge of irrigated lawns, but keep away from sewer lines, water lines, and septic systems that offer an easy drink to thirsty, invasive roots.

### Try This
'Roberts' is a variety that has larger and more sculptural leaves than the species. It also has patchy white bark and is resistant to anthracnose (50 feet × 40 feet), and is hardy to 0 degrees F.

*One of California's most magnificent trees is the sycamore. Sycamore has huge gnarled and twisting branches covered in peeling mottled bark in shades of silvery cream, brown, tan, and pale green. Huge maple-like leaves are green when young, aging to fuzzy gold and then paper bag brown before dropping in autumn. Sycamore's minute spring flowers are followed by skeins of spiny 1/2- to 1 1/2-inch burgundy fruits that mature to green. A sycamore in your garden turns it into a virtual wildlife hotel and restaurant. Native butterfly caterpillars eat sycamore leaves, eagles and hawks sit in high branches watching for rodents, woodpeckers and songbirds eat borers that tunnel through sycamore wood (but won't kill the trees), and lizards will live among the fallen leaves.*

**Other Common Name**
Western Sycamore

**Bloom Period and Seasonal Color**
Leaves turn yellow then paper bag brown in fall.

**Mature Height × Spread**
30 to 40 ft. × 30 to 40 ft.

Hardy to 8A

Min. Temp. 10° F

# Triangle Palm
*Dypsis decaryi*

*One of my favorite homes is done in Mediterranean style with an ochre-colored stucco privacy wall separating the streetside planting from the entry garden. White and yellow roses tumble over the top of the wall. In front are white flowering rockrose, gray-leaved sweet lavenders, and blue fescue that surround a 20-foot-tall triangle palm. The palm is spectacular. Its trunk is gray and ringed from the ground up eight feet. Above that a spray of tall blue-green leaves form gentle arches. The leafbases form an amazing three-dimensional triangle where they wrap around the upper 4 or 5 feet of trunk. Triangle palms come from arid regions of Madagascar and thrive in hot dry gardens. Still, gardeners in San Francisco's "banana belt" microclimates grow them successfully.*

**Mature Height × Spread**
18 to 30 ft. × 12 to 15 ft.

Hardy to
9B

Min.
Temp.
28° F

## When, Where, and How to Plant

Plant in late summer or early fall and into full sun and well-draining soil. Follow planting directions in the chapter Introduction. If soil drains poorly, build a planting mound of well-draining soil (see "Tips and Techniques). Add a handful of compost or composted manure to the planting hole. Water deeply after planting and mulch, leaving bare dirt for the 6 inches closet to the trunk. Triangle palms are great in desert gardens.

## Growing Tips

Keep soil moist (not wet) the first two growing seasons. Once established, water deeply but infrequently from spring to fall. Let soil dry in winter. Fertilize four times between March and October or any time that fronds look yellow (not brown). Use an organic palm fertilizer, fish emulsion and kelp extract, or any 3:1:3 fertilizer with micronutrients (water soil before fertilizing). Wait at least a month between applications.

## Care

Dead leaves eventually release from the trunk and can be pulled off by hand (wear gloves). If you cut leaves, cut the entire stem and do not leave a stump. Young trees are more susceptible to diseases, so buy the largest one you can afford. Watch for scale, aphids, and mealybugs (see "Tips and Techniques"). To prevent fungus, don't overwater, practice good garden sanitation, and disinfect tools before and after pruning (see "Tips and Techniques).

## Companion Planting and Design

Plant a blue foliage garden using triangle palm as the focal point, surrounded with blue chalk sticks, African daisy, blue fescue, gray-leaved aloes, and an enormous century plant. Add a deep burgundy New Zealand flax like 'Shirazz' or red giant dracaena plant as a colorful accent.

## Try This

Manambe palm (*Dypsis decipiens*) is another palm from Madagascar. It is shorter (10 to 15 feet tall), hardier (to 18 degrees F), and thirstier than triangle palm. Manambe palm's broad gray trunks can be single or form a small cluster. Each trunk is topped with long pinnate leaves that emerge reddish and mature blue-green. Young manabe palms grow slowly, and older ones grow faster.

# Western Redbud

*Cercis occidentalis*

## When, Where, and How to Plant

Plant in fall through early spring as long as the ground is workable. These trees thrive in sun or part sun and even tolerate dry shade. Redbuds are tolerant of many soils types and nearly all climates, including the extreme cold and heat of high desert gardens. Flowering seems to be more intense in cold winter gardens. Follow planting directions in the chapter introduction. Water well after planting, and mulch.

## Growing Tips

Water deeply and regularly from spring until the weather cools the first fall. After that, water deeply and occasionally in summer. Trees survive on rainfall in northern gardens but appreciate occasional deep water in southern gardens. While drought tolerant, redbuds grow faster with some summer water. Avoid overwatering. No fertilizer is needed.

## Care

These fast growers take well to pruning that reveals their handsome structure. To encourage vigorous growth, thin out the oldest trunks each year. To rejuvenate a redbud, cut it to the ground. It will resprout from the base. For a tree shape, limit redbud to three upright trunks (for multitrunk) or one trunk (for a standard). No pests bother redbud.

## Companion Planting and Design

Plant this native in formal or informal gardens, as a single specimen plant or combined with mounding shrubs for a background or screen. Plant with other natives such as California lilac, flannel bush, and fragrant California buckeye, all of which bloom around the same time.

## Try These

Forest pansy redbud (*Cercis canadensis* 'Forest Pansy') has plum colored flowers that turn greenish then yellow before they drop in fall. Flowers are rose-pink and it is hardy to -20 degrees F (20 feet × 25 feet). 'Hearts of Gold' has fantastic gold colored leaves and lavender blooms (15 feet × 18 feet), hardy to -20 degrees F. Mediterranean redbud (*Cercis siliquastrum*) has magenta pink flowers with purplish leaves that mature dark green (15 to 25 feet × 15 to 25 feet) and is hardy to -10 degrees F. Mexican redbud (*Cercis mexicana*) has purple flowers and blue-green leaves, likes full sun (12 to 15 feet × 7 feet) and is hardy to 20 degrees F.

*Hike through the Sierra foothills in early spring and you'll notice small trees blooming rosy pink on the hillsides. Those beauties are western redbuds, and the pink spots are tiny pea-like flowers that line bare silvery, branches in spring. This phenomenon of bloom before leaf is typical of deciduous plants. It also draws our attention, especially when the bloom color is so vivid. As redbud flowers fade, they become long, flat seedpods that start out bright green and turn purple. Soon soft, light green, heart-shaped leaves cover the branches and turn leathery blue-green as they age. In cold winter gardens redbuds flower more prolifically. In the coldest gardens, foliage turns yellow and red before leaves fall in autumn, revealing handsome bare branches.*

**Bloom Period and Seasonal Color**
Early spring flowers are pink to rosy red.

**Mature Height × Spread**
15 to 20 ft. × 15 to 20 ft.

Hardy to 8B

Min. Temp. 15° F

# Vines *for California*

Vines are the garden's hanging drapes and curtains. Their vining, climbing stems separate spaces, obscure views, provide shade from the sun, or frame views. Fragrant vines adjacent to a patio perfume your outdoor lounge; those growing near an open window can perfume the indoors as well. A few vines reward gardeners with sweet fruits.

This chapter includes featured vines from Brazilian bougainvillea to a burgundy-leaved native California grape vine; from bright flowering subtropicals from Baja and central America to the hardy native clematis whose feathery seedpods are as beautiful as their multi-petaled flowers.

Some of these vines have large flowers, others teem with tiny, bright-colored flowers; some are evergreen, others deciduous; some have narrow, pliable green stems with clasping tendrils to embrace their supports, others have thick, woody stems that scramble rather than climb. It falls to us gardeners to direct those woody stems upward and attach them to supporting structures.

Snail vine

Support is key to success with vines. Before you put a vine into the ground, have a strong support structure already in place. The woodier and heavier the vine, the stronger the support. Don't bother with those pretty little white or redwood trellises, not even for narrow-stemmed twining vines. Their stems may be slender, but they will grow too large and, more importantly, too heavy for those lightweight trellises after a year or two. Instead, invest in a sturdy arbor, plant your vine against a wooden or chain link fence, train it over a patio overhang, or build a trellis custom-made to your site.

Avoid the mistake of planting a vine into a too-small cutout in a cement sidewalk or patio. One square foot simply does not provide enough soil space for a vine to grow to a significant size. Vines, like

Mexican flame vine

all other plants, need space for roots to expand and for air and water to reach the roots. A tiny space can't provide that.

While most people think of vines as plants that climb skyward, many can also be grown as sprawling, horizontal ground covers. Bougainvillea, grapevines, and coral vine in particular fall into this category.

Some more novel ways to use vines:

- Grow deciduous vines on a south- or west-facing wall so their lush leaves can shade the wall to cool it in the heat of summer. When leaves drop, the wall will act as a solar collector, accumulating the heat from the rays of the winter sun and transmitting it indoors.

- Plant an evergreen vine at the base of a deciduous tree and train the vine up into the branches. When the tree is in leaf, the vine will enhance its texture and color. When branches are bare, the vine will take center stage.

- Plant a vine at the base of a low wall so the branches can spill over the edge. This is a particularly good way to soften the hard angles of a block wall.

- Clematis and other fine-textured vines, can be planted to scramble up and over leafy shrubs.

At that height, the vines are more easily seen and appreciated. The beautiful flowers will be enhanced by the dense, green, leafy background as well. Take care, though, not to let the vine grow so dense that it shades out the shrub.

Plant vines as you would any tree or shrub (see "Tips and Techniques" for details). Pay attention to shaping your vine and establishing its basic structure, especially in the early years. If your

A bougainvillea trained to a single trunk spills over a wall

intent is to train it up an arbor to sprawl across the top, limit the vine to a single main upright. Allow it to develop horizontal branches only once it reaches the top. If your goal is to create a green screen or cover a fence, encourage as many upright and horizontal branches as you can, directing them or weaving them between uprights until the vine covers the entire surface in all directions.

# Bougainvillea
## *Bougainvillea* spp.

Bougainvillea are the jewels of California gardens. Though native to Brazil, these woody vines are ubiquitous throughout our coastal and valley landscapes. From summer through fall, they are covered in cascades of flowers that are not truly flowers at all but rather colorful, papery bracts that frame tiny, cream-colored, tube shaped flowers. Hybridizers have gone wild creating bougainvillea in every shade from vibrant red to palest pink, raspberry, golden orange, white, and apricot. Most have heart-shaped green leaves, but some have variegated leaves, yellow and green or cream and green. Bougainvillea are extremely tough plants which, once established, thrive on neglect. While their colors light up the garden, they are very thorny and quite messy, so place them well away from play areas, walkways, and swimming pools.

### Bloom Period and Seasonal Color
Summer through fall blooms in vibrant red to palest pink, raspberry, golden orange, white, and apricot, some multicolored.

**Hardy to 10A**

**Min. Temp. See below**

### Mature Length × Width
Mounds: 1½ ft. to 3 ft. × 5 to 8 ft.
Vines: 20 to 30 ft. × up to 8 ft.

### Minimum Temperature
Evergreen to about 30 degrees F.

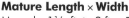

### When, Where, and How to Plant
Plant once soil warms in spring. Choose a spot in full sun in the warmest part of the garden. In desert gardens, provide afternoon shade. Well-draining soils are best, but poor soils are fine. These heavy vigorous vines need a strong structure in place before planting. Since bougainvillea doesn't attach to supports on its own, tie or wire branches into place. The key to successful transplanting is to disturb the rootball as little as possible (see "Tips and Techniques"). To grow in a container, choose a pot that is at least 20 inches in diameter.

### Growing Tips
Water deeply through the first summer. After that, bougainvillea are quite drought tolerant. Allow soil to dry several inches down between waterings (this applies to bougainvillea in pots as well). Fertilizer isn't necessary, but to encourage growth apply organic fertilizer once in early spring. Bougainvillea thrives on neglect. If yours doesn't bloom, cut back on water and/or fertilizer. If it still doesn't bloom, move the plant to a warmer spot.

### Care
To train on an arbor or espalier, start directing branches immediately after planting. Prune to shape and control overly exuberant growth. Watch for whitefly (see 'Tips and Techniques").

### Companion Planting and Design
While bougainvillea brightens tropical theme gardens, it is also a mainstay of Mediterranean style gardens. A common approach is to train bougainvillea over an arbor. Use them to cover a slope, scale a tree, or be espaliered against a wall. Dwarf varieties are perfect for containers, hanging baskets, spilling over low walls, and as ground covers for small spaces.

### Try These
Dwarf 'Raspberry Ice' (2 to 3 feet × 5 to 6 feet) has raspberry-pink bracts, green and cream variegated leaves. 'Purple Queen' (1½ feet × 6 to 8 feet) has deep purple bracts. 'La Jolla' (4 to 5 feet tall) has bright red bracts. For long, vining varieties, try 'California Gold' (20 to 30 feet) with gold bracts, 'San Diego Red' (15 to 25 feet) with deep red bracts.

# Butterfly Vine
*Dalechampia dioscoreifolia*

## When, Where, and How to Plant
Plant butterfly vine in fall through spring in mild winter climates and in spring in climates that get much below freezing in winter. These vines prefer well-amended and well-draining soils in full sun along the coast. They tolerate part sun to part shade inland. In cold winter gardens, plant in the warmest south- or west-facing exposure. Have a good support system in place before planting. See the Perennials introduction for planting directions. Water well after planting, and mulch to insulate roots. **Note:** This plant is poisonous if ingested.

## Growing Tips
Butterfly vine prefers regular water through the growing season and less in the winter, especially in cooler winter gardens. These vines can be grown drier but may not flower as prolifically. No fertilizer is necessary if you maintain a layer of organic mulch.

## Care
Butterfly vine is a vigorous grower. You might find a stray branch or two creeping into your bedroom window or around the base of a nearby pot. Rather than prune, redirect branches in the direction you'd like them to grow. Whiteflies are a problem on occasion but seldom seriously enough to kill the plant. For whitefly control, see "Tips and Techniques."

## Companion Planting and Design
Butterfly vine has twining tendrils that climb a fence, arbor, or other structure. Plant for a fast evergreen screen, to shade a too-hot patio, or simply to adorn an otherwise blank wall. In my garden, the butterfly vine climbed the cable that delivers digital television and Internet to the house. The foliage does a great job of hiding a less-than-attractive cable, all the way up to the eaves. This beauty would also be wonderful grown as a green wall to enclose an outdoor room. Combine with bright chartreuse flowering spurges and billowy fountain grass for a Mediterranean look, sweet gingers, canna, and banana for a tropical look.

## Try These
Though butterfly vine doesn't attract or provide shelter for butterflies, vines that *do* support butterflies and their caterpillar larvae include passion vines (*Passiflora* spp.), bougainvillea, and native Dutchman's pipe (*Aristolochia californica*).

*Butterfly vine is not a vine that attracts butterflies. Instead its flowers look like butterflies. This vigorous evergreen vine's orchid-purple "butterflies" appear to perch above the deep green, heart-shaped leaves. Like poinsettias and bougainvillea, the colorful petals are actually bracts. Each pair of pointed horizontal bracts has the texture of crepe paper and flutters like butterfly wings in the slightest breeze. Connecting the bracts is a sort of bud that looks like a red cranberry. It opens to reveal minute red and creamy yellow flower parts. Butterfly vine comes from South America and stays evergreen unless nighttime temperatures dip below freezing. Leaves drop in cooler regions, but vines recover as long as the air remains above 25 degrees F.*

**Other Common Name**
Winged Beauty Vine

**Bloom Period and Seasonal Color**
Orchid purple flowers much of the year, peak in summer/fall.

**Mature Length × Width**
20 ft. × 4 to 6 ft. or wider

Hardy to 9B

Min. Temp. 25° F

# Chocolate Vine
## *Akebia quinata*

Do you have a spot that needs a delicate vine or a vine that doesn't have huge leaves and bold flowers? Consider evergreen chocolate vine. No, this vine doesn't grow chocolate (chocolate grows on Theobroma cacao, a South American tree), it makes flowers that smell like chocolate. Chocolate vine has narrow woody stems that twine around and around their support. Each dark-green leaf has five finger-like lobes that are an inch or two long with a notch at the tip. Hanging clusters of tight round green or pink-blush buds open to raspberry-chocolate, inch-long flowers with three cupped petals each. There are two types of flowers, tiny male flowers and slightly larger female flowers. Vines sometimes produce 2- to 4-inch-long oval fruits with purple tinged skin and edible pulp.

**Other Common Name**
Fiveleaf Akebia

**Bloom Period and Seasonal Color**
Raspberry-chocolate colored flowers in spring.

**Mature Length × Width**
20 to 30 ft. × 6 to 9 ft.

Hardy to
5A

Min.
Temp.
-20° F

## When, Where, and How to Plant
Plant into well-drained and well-amended soil in a spot with full sun to part shade. Plant in fall in mild winter areas and in spring in gardens with winter freeze. Have a strong support structure in place before planting. Follow perennial planting directions. If your goal is to produce fruit, plant two or more vines for cross-pollination. Water deeply after planting and cover the soil with a thick layer of mulch. Keep mulch away from touching the stems.

## Growing Tips
Water regularly and deeply through the first year. You can cut back on watering in the second and subsequent years, but these plants still like the soil to be moist. Thick mulch is key to maintaining that moisture. Feed annually in early spring with a balanced organic fertilizer.

## Care
Direct stems in the early years so chocolate vine will grow in the direction you want. Keep in mind that flowers form on older wood. So, to prune without sacrificing flowers, prune after flowers fade. If stems grow chaotic and out of control, cut chocolate vine back to the ground and allow them it to regenerate. Watch for scale (see "Tips and Techniques" for treatment).

## Companion Planting and Design
Plant chocolate vine where you can get close enough to appreciate its diminutive flowers, delicate fragrance, and attractive leaves. As with other vines, this one needs a strong support structure. Direct it up a bamboo screen in an Asian theme garden. Use in the background of a garden bed to cover a wall or fence. Plant to grow up a trellis or shade an arbor. When controlled, chocolate vine can be trained as an espalier. Alternatively, allow it to sprawl over the ground as a ground cover for a shady spot.

## Try These
*Akebia quinata* 'Shirobana' and 'Alba' are white-flowered. 'Purple Bouquet' flowers are more mauve than raspberry. 'Rosea' has pink flowers. Threeleaf akebia (*Akebia trifoliata*) is much like chocolate vine, but its leaves have three leaflets instead of five.

## When, Where, and How to Plant

Plant clematis in spring. Site them so their leaves are in the sun and roots are in the shade. Choose a spot with well-draining, well-amended soil and five to six hours of sun each day. Set the rootball 3 to 5 inches *below* the soil surface. New roots will form at nodes along the buried parts of stems. Soak deeply after planting. Mulch with rocks or compost, or use neighboring plants to cool roots. To grow in container, choose one 24 inches × 24 inches or larger. Add a sturdy trellis. Use a well-draining potting mix. Set the plant 3 to 5 inches below the soil, just as if it were in the ground. Water well and mulch.

## Growing Tips

Water clematis regularly and deeply all year, especially in summer. Feed in March with 3-12-12 fertilizer and five weeks later with 5-3-1 fertilizer. Wait five weeks, then repeat the cycle and continue until late October.

## Care

Once clematis has at least six vertical branches, prune to stimulate flowering. In November, cut half of the branches to a bud 18 inches above the ground. Prune remaining branches back by a third. Disinfect pruning shears between each cut to avoid clematis wilt (see "Tips and Techniques" for disinfecting pruning tools). If a vine gets wilt, remove and dispose of infected branches (don't compost!). Protect clematis from earwigs, slugs, and snails (see "Tips and Techniques").

## Companion Planting and Design

My favorite use of clematis is as a collection grown in pots about 3 feet tall and wide and scattered through a shady foliage garden. Plants will clamber over fences, nearby trees, and shrubs

## Try These

Hybrids 'Duchess of Edinburgh' (6 to 8 feet) has creamy-white double rosettes. 'Proteus' (6 to 8 feet) has lilac pink blooms. 'Victoria' (8 to 15 feet) has rosy purple blooms. 'Huldine' (8 to 15 feet) has white flowers with mauve pink undersides. 'Star of India' (12 to 20 feet) has reddish plum flowers. Native to California streamsides are western white clematis (*Clematis ligusticifolia*) (30 feet) and *Clematis lasiantha* (20 feet). Both have small white flowers.

*Vining clematis are known for their beautiful fringed, flat flowers in shades of white to pink, red to deep burgundy, purple, and even yellow. Some have four petals, some five, some six or more. A cluster of golden yellow stamens is at the center of most flowers. While there are native clematis, the more widely known hybrids are divided into two basic categories: those with unscented flowers on vines that top out at about 8 feet and those with smaller fragrant flowers on 12-foot vines. Blooms are followed by swirled feathery seedpods. Remove them and the vine will bloom again. On the other hand, the large seedpods are so beautiful you might want to leave them to enjoy on the vine.*

**Bloom Period and Seasonal Color**
April through November blooms in white to pink, red to deep burgundy, purple, and yellow.

**Mature Length × Width**
8 to 12 ft., vining

**Minimum Temperature**
Depends on species and variety.

# Climbing Bauhinia
*Bauhinia corymbosa*

*A deep green background can bring a garden to life. When that background also has delicate, pink, orchid-like flowers, it becomes an even stronger element in the garden. Such is the effect of Bauhinia Corymbosa. Like its cousin, the Hong Kong orchid tree, pink orchid vine has deep green, almost blue-green, leaves split down the middle into two oval lobes. Where the tree leaves are tennis ball sized, the vine has petite grape-sized leaves. These vigorous vines have curling tendrils and narrow stems with new brick-red growth maturing to deep green. Spring through fall, the vine is adorned with pale pink flowers, 2 to 3 inches across with five petals, three of them veined in bright fuchsia with a long curling pink stamen and pistil.*

**Other Common Name**
Phanera

**Bloom Period and Seasonal Color**
Spring through fall pink flowers veined in bright fuchsia.

**Mature Length × Width**
25 ft., vining

**Hardy to 9A**

**Min. Temp.**
20 to 25° F

## When, Where, and How to Plant
Plant climbing bauhinia fall through spring in frost-free gardens and in spring in colder winter gardens. Site in full or part sun with amended well-draining soil. See the Perennials introduction for planting directions. Water deeply and mulch after planting. You can also grow climbing bauhinia in a large pot. In a pot or in the ground, be sure to have a strong support in place first.

## Growing Tips
Water regularly through the first summer and early fall. Once rains arrive, let Mother Nature take over unless there is a long dry period in winter. Once established, climbing bauhinia can get by on occasional deep summer water, especially along the coast and in the north. With more frequent watering, vines are more vigorous and lusher. Climbing bauhinia is a member of the pea family, so it fixes its own nitrogen. Therefore, fertilize with low nitrogen fertilizer in very early spring, or simply mulch with good compost.

## Care
Established vining bauhinia is fairly frost tolerant though leaves sometimes drop in the cold of winter. If vines and foliage are damaged by frost, wait until spring to prune; outer leaves will protect the inner leaves from the cold. Direct new vines as they develop. No major pests bother this plant.

## Companion Planting and Design
Climbing bauhinia planted on a fence behind a rose garden fills in the visual spaces between the roses and gives the garden the year-round green that roses simply can't provide. It also makes a terrific green screen—whether covering a fence or trellis to make a vertical wall, or trailing over a pergola, arbor, or patio covering to make a ceiling. Occasional seedlings can be moved or potted up to share with others.

## Try This
Red orchid bush (*Bauhinia galpinii*) grows 10 feet × 10 to 15 feet. This scrambling African shrub can be trained on a fence, over a wall, or up pergola. Typical five-petal flowers bloom in intense coral-red to deep orange with a touch of yellow right in the center. It is drought tolerant and hardy to 20 degrees F.

# Coral Vine
## *Antigonon leptopus*

### When, Where, and How to Plant
Plant coral vine in spring or fall. Along the coast, plant in the hottest and sunniest part of the garden, such as a south- or west-facing wall. In hot valley and desert gardens, coral vine tolerates light shade but may not bloom as prolifically. Make sure that you have a sturdy support in place before planting. See Perennials introduction for planting directions. Coral vine tolerates poor soils, rocky soils, and sand, as well as well-amended garden soils. Water well after planting, and mulch. To cover a large expanse, space plants 3 to 5 feet apart.

### Growing Tips
Water deeply and regularly through the first summer to get coral vines established. After that, water deeply but only occasionally in summer. As little as one deep watering a week in desert areas keeps the vine going. More water makes for faster growth and lusher foliage. Fertilize lightly (half dose) with an organic fertilizer when new growth appears in spring.

### Care
When coral vine starts its rapid summer growth, direct branches where you want them to go. Each year, coral vine's tuberous underground root will send up more stems than it did the previous year. If stems become too dense, prune selectively to open the vine and increase air circulation. In frost-free areas where vine does not die back, prune to the ground in winter. No pests are a problem.

### Companion Planting and Design
Coral vine is the perfect choice for a fast screen and quick summer shade or to hide an unattractive chain link fence. Left unsupported, coral vine makes a good summertime ground cover. Or grow it cascading over a wall or down a slope. In a dry garden or Mediterranean theme garden, combine with purple-flowering penstemon and gold-flowered Mexican tarragon. In a native garden, mix with deep-green-leaved California lilac and yellow-flowered Mexican tulip poppy.

### Try These
Flowers of coral vine 'Baja Red' have the deepest rose color; 'Album' (also sold as 'Alba') has white flowers but is not as cold hardy as the pink varieties.

*Coral vine is a graceful ethereal vine with long dense sprays of petite coral pink or rose pink (sometimes white) flowers that make a beautiful contrast against frilly, green, heart-shaped leaves. This easy and fast growing perennial vine comes from forested areas, from Baja down into Central America where it climbs trees and shrubs. In our gardens, coral vine's curling tendrils need a strong support structure, be it fence, wall, sturdy trellis, or tree. Grow coral vine up a south- or west-facing wall or over a patio arbor so its shade can cool your home in summer. With the first frost, coral vine dies to the ground, allowing the sun's warm rays through. Come the next spring, coral vine resprouts from underground tubers.*

**Other Common Name**
Queen's Wreath Vine

**Bloom Period and Seasonal Color**
Rose or coral pink (sometimes white) flowers summer through early fall.

**Mature Length × Width**
20 to 40 ft., vining

**Minimum Temperature**
Root hardy above 20 degrees F.

Hardy to 9A

Min. Temp. See below

# Cup of Gold Vine

*Solandra maxima*

In the old neighborhoods of Los Angeles stand charming courtyard bungalows from Hollywood's Golden Age. In these little enclaves, single story one- or two-bedroom units face a center courtyard that serves as the residents' frontyard/backyard/garden. Historically these common areas included a square of lawn surrounded by beds of bird of paradise, yucca, bougainvillea, and my favorite cup of gold vine. Cup of gold is large woody vine (technically a liana) with golden dinner plate-sized flowers. Five petals fuse to make a primitive bowl-shaped bloom enhanced by a burgundy-brown stripe down each petal and forming a star in the throat. Flowers are set against large, lush, shiny green leaves that enhance the vine's tropical appearance. At night, cup of gold flowers perfume the air. It is sometimes sold as Solandra guttata.

**Other Common Name**
Chalice Vine

**Bloom Period and Seasonal Color**
Spring flowers in deep mustard gold to pale creamy yellow with a burgundy/brown star in the throat.

Hardy to 9B

Min. Temp. 25° F

**Mature Length × Width**
40 ft. × 4 to 6 ft.

## When, Where, and How to Plant

Plant fall through spring in frost-free gardens and in spring in cooler gardens. Place in full sun (or light shade in valleys) and in well-draining soil. In a garden where temperatures drop below freezing, plant in the hottest exposure, against a south- or west-facing wall. This is a very heavy vine that absolutely needs a strong support in place before planting. See the Perennials introduction for planting directions. Water deeply and mulch heavily. In cooler winter areas of California, grow in a container on wheels and with a good support structure. Move to a greenhouse or indoors in a brightly lit window for winter.

## Growing Tips

Water well through the first two years to establish, then reduce water frequency in summer to encourage flowering. High phosphorus (P) organic fertilizer in spring also promotes flowering. **Note:** This plant is poisonous if ingested.

## Care

In early spring, pinch back branch tips, cut back long canes, and prune wayward branches—all of which promote new growth that translates to new flowers. Direct branches by attaching them to a supporting structure. If temperatures fall low enough to damage the foliage, don't prune off damaged parts right away. Leave them to protect the rest of the plant until after winter's last frost, then prune. Watch for scale insects.

## Companion Planting and Design

Like bougainvillea, this vine needs a sturdy support and guidance as it climbs upward then scrambles and spills over the edges of a pergola, arbor, etc. Train over a low fence for a flowering hedge. For fun, pluck a full, round bud and float it in a bowl of water to watch it open.

## Try These

Cup of gold vine is in the same family as tomato, pepper, and eggplant. Other relatives include angel trumpet (*Brugmansia*), which also has huge fragrant flowers, and the vine *Solandra grandiflora* that is similar to cup of gold but has smaller leaves and smaller, more tubular flowers. The leaves of variegated cup of gold vine (*Solandra maxima* 'Variegata') are blush purple when young, fading to soft green and cream.

# Dutchman's Pipe
## *Aristolochia littoralis*

### When, Where, and How to Plant
Plant in well-draining soils and in full sun along the coast or in afternoon shade in hot interior gardens. Plant fall to spring in frost-free gardens and in spring in colder gardens. In colder gardens, site in the warmest areas with a southern or western exposure or against a masonry wall that absorbs the heat in winter. See Perennials introduction for planting directions. Established plants may freeze back to the ground, but they will sprout again in spring. Have a good support in place before you plant. Water well after planting, and mulch.

### Growing Tips
Water deeply and regularly, allowing the soil to dry several inches deep between waterings. Apply a thick layer of mulch to reduce the need to water. In spring, apply an organic fertilizer high in phosphorus (P) to promote flowering. **Note:** This plant is poisonous if ingested.

### Care
Dutchman's pipe blooms on new growth each spring, so for the greatest bloom, pinch back or prune stems in early spring before new growth starts. Watch for whiteflies and mealybugs (see "Tips and Techniques" for treatments).

### Companion Planting and Design
Dutchman's pipe has dense foliage that makes a good screen when planted on a trellis, along a fence, or up a wall. Plant in a garden bed where the vines can scramble amidst shrub and tree trunks. Site the plant in a spot where flowers are at eye-level so they can be best appreciated.

### Try These
Dutchman's pipe is also sold as *Aristolochia elegans*. Native California Dutchman's pipe (*Aristolochia californica*) is a 6- to 12-foot deciduous vine with dangling 1- to 2-inch pipe-shaped flowers. Early spring flowers are pale green with pink veins. They bloom before the large fuzzy leaves that are host to the caterpillar stage of the pipeline swallowtail butterfly (hardy to 10 degrees F). Giant Dutchman's pipe (*Aristolochia gigantea*) reaches 20 feet with long green leaves and 12- × 6-inch vaguely erotic flowers that look like a deflated balloon. Flowers are deep burgundy netted in cream with velvet burgundy throats (hardy to 30 degrees F).

*Ever wonder how plants get common names? Sometimes the name describes a part of the plant—its leaves, trunk, or in the case of Dutchman's pipe, the shape of its flowers. Dutchman's pipe is a vigorous evergreen vine with shiny green, heart-shaped leaves. In a sideview, dangling tubular flowers look like old-fashioned tobacco pipes. From the front, these flowers have a 4-inch-broad "collar" in deep maroon and ivory, mottled like a calico print. The flower's throat is velvety maroon with a golden yellow center. According to the experts, the flower pattern looks like rotting meat to its insect pollinators. Fortunately Dutchman's pipe is not foul scented like other flowers that use that same approach to attract pollinators. This plant is also sold as* Aristolochia elegans.

**Other Common Name**
Calico Flower

**Bloom Period and Seasonal Color**
Maroon and ivory colored blooms through year, peaking in spring.

**Mature Length × Width**
10 ft., vining or longer

Hardy to 9B

Min. Temp. 25° F

# Flame Vine
## *Pyrostegia venusta*

*Is it any wonder that this vine's botanical name comes from the root for fire? And its species name means "handsome or charming." Indeed, when in bloom this handsome vine looks like it is fully on fire. Flame vine is a South American evergreen with bright orange flowers appearing in late winter when almost nothing else is blooming—which may be a strategy for keeping our attention all to itself. This vigorous vine climbs by curling tendrils 20 or 30 feet tall, reaching a second story balcony or higher in short order. At the tip of each branch, clusters of twenty or more 3-inch tubular orange flowers each curl back at the mouth, framing long thin reproductive parts that look like many pale orange tongues.*

**Other Common Name**
Flaming Trumpet

**Bloom Period and Seasonal Color**
Clusters of bright orange flowers through the year in mild climates, peaking in fall and winter.

**Hardy to** 9B

**Min. Temp.** 25° F

**Mature Length × Width**
80 ft., vining

### When, Where, and How to Plant
Flame vine grows well in coastal gardens, coastal valleys, and in inland deserts. Along the coast, plant in your warmest location (south and west exposures are good) with well-draining soil. If your soil drains poorly, build a raised mound. In frost-free gardens, plant fall through spring. In cold winter gardens, plant in spring. See Perennials introduction for planting directions. Have a sturdy support in place before you plant. Though a single vine will cover a fence or wall, to cover a long expanse set vines at least 5 feet apart. Water deeply after planting, and mulch.

### Growing Tips
This vigorous vine grows fast with regular water but is fairly drought tolerant once established. Keep soil moist several inches down through the first summer. In subsequent summers, water deeply when the soil is dry more than three inches down. A thick layer of organic mulch keeps the soil moist and weeds down. Fertilize in early spring with organic low nitrogen fertilizer.

### Care
Direct the branches of young vines. Cut branch tips back after flowers fade each year to encourage new, flowering, side branches. Watch for scale (see "Tips and Techniques" for treatment).

### Companion Planting and Design
Flame vine looks at home in both dry tropical and Mediterranean landscapes. It is spectacular climbing a column in a sunny courtyard, especially in a Monterrey style home. This vine is adaptable to espalier, spilling over the top of an arbor, cascading over a wall, and for screening out an unwanted view. For a flowering companion, try winter cassia whose yellow flowers blooming about the same time.

### Try These
Flame vine (also sold as *Pyrostegia ignea*) is one of many plants in the trumpet vine family, whose 60-foot stems are covered in shiny dark-green leaves and orange-red springtime flowers with a yellow mouth (hardy to 0 degrees F or lower). Also related is cat's claw (*Macfadyena unguis-cati*) that reaches 25 feet with bright yellow trumpets in early spring, creating a big luscious tropical look for a drought tolerant vine (hardy to 15 degrees F).

# Mexican Flame Vine
## *Senecio confusus*

### When, Where, and How to Plant

Plant in spring in gardens that freeze in winter. In frost-free gardens, plant fall through spring. This vine has been known to thrive in desert climates as well. Pick a spot in full sun. Plants tolerate light shade but bloom better in sun. If soil drains poorly, build a mound of good soil and then follow perennial planting directions. To cover a long expanse, space vines 5 to 6 feet apart.

### Growing Tips

Water deeply and frequently through the first summer to help Mexican flame vine become established. After that, summer watering should be deep but infrequent. Water when soil is dry several inches down. Mulch thickly to conserve moisture. Winter rains should suffice, but you may need to water during long dry spells. Water occasionally in spring and fall. Fertilize with an all-purpose organic fertilizer in early spring.

### Care

Old flowers and those going to seed can look ratty, so prune as they start to fade. Left undirected, this vine tends to grow up its support, and when it runs out of support, it forms a topknot. It isn't a bad look, but if you prefer more control, start directing its upright stems when the vine is young. Once it has a structure, then prune out the strays. Mexican flame vine often roots where it touches the ground. Where winter temperatures dip far below freezing, the vine may die back to the ground but resprout in spring. Mexican flame vine has no significant pests.

### Companion Planting and Design

Since this vine is relatively short, use it where you need a shot of color to cover an arch, to climb stanchions on either side of a gate, or to climb a column or mailbox post. Mexican flame vine looks wonderful cascading over a low wall or over the edge of a hanging basket. For something completely different, grow Mexican flame vine as a sprawling ground cover.

### Try This

The leaves of Mexican flame vine 'Sao Paolo' have a bronze tinge. Large flowers are almost brick red.

With its shocking color and fantastic contrast of deep green and crayon orange, Mexican flame vine brightens even the most boring spot in the garden. This member of the daisy family is native to Mexico and points farther south. Though many plants in the genus Senecio are succulents (see blue chalk sticks in Succulents), Senecio includes trees, annuals, shrubs, and the twining Mexican flame vine. All have daisy-shaped flowers with many long petals encircling a center disc of tiny tubular flowers. As flowers age, their velvety petals turn even deeper orange, verging on red. The tiny center flowers start out gold and fade to orange as they mature as well. Branches are covered with fleshy, deep green leaves, each with slightly pointed scallops.

**Bloom Period and Seasonal Color**
Bright carrot-orange flowers much of the year, peaking spring to fall.

**Mature Length × Width**
10 ft., vining

**Minimum Temperature**
Grown as an annual in cooler climates.

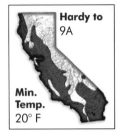

Hardy to 9A

Min. Temp. 20° F

# Passion Vine

## *Passiflora* spp.

Passion vines have fantastic flowers and heavenly fragrance. They make delicious fruit, and gulf fritillary butterflies favor their shiny green leaves. Passion vines climb to the tops of tree canopies in their native rainforests of Central and South America. In our gardens, these vigorous evergreens can smother a chain-link fence or cover an arbor in a year or two. Passion vines' amazing and complex flowers are 2 to 6 inches across with five sepals, topped by five petals, and topped by a fringed crown of colorful rays. Large, creamy yellow reproductive parts perch high above the rays. The common name comes from early Christian missionaries who saw the flower parts as symbolic of the passion of Christ: the crown of thorns and the ten apostles.

**Bloom Period and Seasonal Color**

Spring through fall flowers in multilayered combinations of purple, lavender, white, red, yellow, coral, rose, orange, or pink.

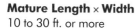
Hardy to 9B

Min. Temp. See below

**Mature Length × Width**
10 to 30 ft. or more

**Minimum Temperature**
Mostly evergreen down to 25 degrees F. Deciduous or semi-deciduous down to 10 degrees F, depending on species.

### When, Where, and How to Plant

Plant spring through fall into full sun or light shade. Well-drained soils are best, but vines adapt to heavier soils (though they may suffer in clay). See Perennials introduction for planting directions. Alternatively, grow passion vines in a large container (at least 24 inches across for smaller vines and wider for larger vines). Water all passion vines (in the ground and in containers) deeply after planting and apply a thick layer of mulch.

### Growing Tips

Water deeply each time you water. Let soil dry out a few inches down before watering again. To prevent premature fruit drop, water more frequently during fruiting season. In early spring, apply an organic low-nitrogen fertilizer. If vines have lush leaves but few flowers, cut back on fertilizer.

### Care

If passion vine leaves get eaten to nubs in the summer, don't reach for insecticide. The nubs signify that hungry gulf fritillary caterpillars have been satisfied. Once caterpillars complete their metamorphosis to orange, white, and black butterflies, the vine will quickly recover. If you want, cut the vine back by a third after caterpillars are gone and you have harvested all the fruit. Passion fruits drop when they are ready to ripen. Collect fallen fruit and leave at room temperature until they are dark colored, wrinkled, and fragrant. Cut off the top and scoop out the juice and seeds with a spoon. Caution: Unripe passion fruit is a tart mouthful!

### Companion Planting and Design

Grow passion vines as a beautiful flowering screen, for overhead shade, to cover an unsightly fence, cover an arbor, or as a patio cover. Place container-grown passion vine at the base of a stanchion for support or set a trellis in the pot.

### Try These

Passion vines grow throughout the state and include 'Coral Glow' that blooms coral pink from spring through fall (evergreen to 20 degrees F). 'Incense' has extremely fragrant purple flowers with frilly white rays and yellowish fruit. *Passiflora edulis* 'Frederick' is the opposite (purple petals, white rays) with some of the best fruit. Both die to the ground at 0 degrees F but resprout from roots.

# Snail Vine

*Vigna caracalla*

## When, Where, and How to Plant

Plant fall through spring in frost-free gardens and in early spring in colder winter gardens. Site in full sun and in well-amended soil. Follow perennial planting directions. To cover a long space, plant vines 6 to 8 feet apart. Water deeply and mulch to keep soil moist. Snail vine can be grown in a container as well.

## Growing Tips

Snail vine makes its own nitrogen. Fertilize with low-nitrogen fertilizer before growth starts in early spring. If vines have lush leaves but few flowers, cut back on fertilizer. Water deeply and regularly from late spring through early fall. When the weather cools in fall, water less often and not at all if winter rains are regular. Water during winter's occasional long dry spells.

## Care

Snail vine foliage can be damaged or killed altogether when temperatures fall much below freezing. Leave frost-damaged leaves to protect inner leaves until after the last frost date. If damage is extensive, cut the vine to the ground in spring. If temperatures remain in the 20s and the vines die back completely to the ground, they should sprout back when the soil warms in spring. Aphids often hide in the crevices of these flowers (see "Tips and Techniques" for treatment).

## Companion Planting and Design

Like other flowering subtropical vines, this fast grower attaches itself by curling tendrils and covers a trellis, arbor, or pergola in a short time. Snail vine is especially good planted to cover a chain-link fence. When covering a long expanse, you might consider planting several species of flowering vines that bloom at different times of year, that have various shaped or colored flowers, or that have different frost tolerances.

## Try These

Combine snail vine with these passion vines: 'Lavender Lady' has short purple rays atop lavender petals (evergreen to 20 degrees F). Large fragrant flowers of *Passiflora alata* 'Ruby Glow' are red with purple and white-banded rays (evergreen to 30 degrees F). *Passiflora mollissima* has bright pink flowers and yellow fruit (evergreen to 25 degrees F).

Snail vine is a twining evergreen pea vine native to South America. It has bright green leaves and fragrant pale to deep lavender blooms that are a twist (literally) on pea flower shape. The upper petal is oval, but the lower petal twists into a curl, much like a nautilus shell. Long grown in Spain, snail vine came to the attention of Thomas Jefferson in a hothouse in England. In 1792, he wrote to a colleague of his longing to add snail vine to the gardens of Monticello, his plantation in Virginia. "The most beautiful bean in the world," he wrote, "is the Caracalla bean." Though snail vine remained elusive to Jefferson, modern day caretakers of Monticello grow it in homage to his long ago desire.

**Other Common Name**
Caracalla Bean

**Bloom Period and Seasonal Color**
Summer flowers white to lavender, sometimes accented in custard yellow.

**Mature Length × Width**
20 ft., vining

**Minimum Temperature**
Foliage dies back at 25 degrees F but resprouts from roots.

**Hardy to**
9B

**Min. Temp.**
See below

# Roger's Red California Grape

*Vitis californica* 'Rogers Red'

*If you crave the deep reds of autumn, plant native California grapes, especially a variety known as 'Roger's Red'. As the story goes, a horticulturist named Roger was driving through Sonoma County one fall and noticed a grape with especially brilliant red foliage. He stopped to check it out, and the rest is history. From spring through late summer, 'Roger's Red' is covered in large green leaves. Clusters of small grapes that are deep purple follow fragrant, green spring flowers. The grapes are sweet, but the pleasure of eating them pales in comparison to the pleasure of watching birds enjoy them. With the short days of fall, leaves turn gold and then an amazing scarlet. They eventually drop, and the vine remains naked through the winter.*

**Mature Length × Width**
25 to 40 ft.

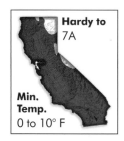

Hardy to
7A

Min.
Temp.
0 to 10° F

## When, Where, and How to Plant

Plant in full sun or in light shade and in sand or clay. This plant is drought tolerant and tolerant of periodic flooding. Plant from bare root in winter or from nursery cans in spring and fall. See the Perennial introduction for planting directions. Be sure to have a structure in place to support the vine. If planting into a natural area, site it next to a tree or shrub for the grape to climb. With no support, it will grow as a ground cover. Mulch well, water deeply.

## Growing Tips

Grapevines are extremely drought tolerant once established. Water deeply and regularly through the first spring and summer. From spring through fall, cut back to deep monthly watering along the coast and in the north, and cut back to weekly watering in hot inland valleys and deserts. Let Mother Nature water in winter. No fertilizer is needed.

## Care

The less you prune, the longer the vines and the bigger the fall show. Start directing growth early to create the plant's structure. Prune errant branches any time, but for major pruning, wait until the vine is dormant in winter. Plant the cuttings to start more grapes. No significant pests.

## Companion Planting and Design

Tree of Life native plant nursery in San Juan Capistrano has a glorious display of 'Roger's Red' growing along vigas to shades their "roundhouse" in summer. If you don't have vigas, grow the vine up an arbor, a pergola, or a trellis, especially on a southern exposure for protection from hot summer sun and to add warmth and light in winter when vines are naked. In a naturalistic garden, let grapevines scramble up trees (dead or alive), native toyon, or other native shrubs.

## Try These

Bring birds to a small garden with 'Walkers Ridge', a native grape that tops out at 10 to 15 feet and is hardy to -10 degrees F. Desert wild grape (*Vitis girdiana*) is another native but with smaller pale green leaves covered in fine hairs. Native to sage scrub, creeks, and oak woodlands from Inyo County west to the coast and south into Baja, it grows to 10 feet and is hardy to 0 degrees F.

## When, Where, and How to Plant
Plant this Baja native in the hottest part of the garden (western or southern exposure) in full sun. Best planted from fall through late spring in frost-free gardens and in spring in colder winter gardens. Adaptable to most soils, hot valleys, and even desert gardens, this plant does well along the coast as well. See Perennials introduction for planting directions. Be sure to have a solid support structure (trellis, arbor, etc.) in place before planting. Water well after planting, and mulch.

## Growing Tips
Water this drought tolerant vine deeply and regularly through its first two summers to get it established. After that, it will survive on only occasional deep irrigation but will be lusher if watered deeply twice each month or so in summer. Fertilizer is not necessary.

## Care
Prune or redirect errant branches onto the support structure. To grow as a mounding shrub or sprawling ground cover, leave the plant unsupported and prune to shape. Pests are not a problem.

## Companion Planting and Design
Plant yellow orchid vine to climb a wall or trellis or to cover a chain link fence. This vine is a good choice for poolside and for those remote spots in the garden where thirstier vines simply fail. Yellow orchid vine makes a good informal screen or background for a low water plant composition that includes purple flowered sages, orange and yellow red-hot poker, knife-leaf acacia, and coral colored cape fuchsia. Orchid vine's shiny green leaves fit right into a tropical garden setting to complement palms, angel trumpet, and bromeliads. Cut branches of orchid vine fruits to use in flower arrangements.

## Try This
*Callaeum lilacina*, purple mascagnia, is the purple cousin of the yellow orchid vine. It has clusters of purple flowers with yellow centers. This vine is a bit more cold hardy and somewhat shorter than yellow orchid vine. Flowers appear in summer, and plants can tolerate some more shade. Like yellow orchid vine, this desert native requires very little water.

*Before it blooms, the long, shiny, dark green leaves of yellow orchid vine make it look a bit like twining honeysuckle. Once the flowers appear, however, it is clearly a different plant. Clusters of yellow flowers are about an inch across. Each flower has five petals with crenulated edges and resemble a miniature orchid. Flowers fade to bright chartreuse and then form tan papery fruits reminiscent of a butterfly. I like the flowers, but some people think the fruits are more attractive. Yellow orchid vine is a fast growing, heat loving, evergreen vine (briefly deciduous in the coldest climates) that grows 30 feet tall and attaches itself to a fence or trellis. Leave unsupported to sprawl as a ground cover or mound as a shrub. Also sold as Callaeum macroptera.*

**Other Common Name**
Butterfly Vine

**Bloom Period and Seasonal Color**
Yellow flowers in spring and summer, sometimes again in fall.

**Mature Length × Width**
12 to 30 ft. × 6 to 12 ft.

Hardy to 9B

Min. Temp. 25° F

# Tips & Techniques
## for California Gardening

## Cold Hardiness

### How to interpret cold hardiness

Cold hardiness is a term that describes the minimum temperature that a plant is likely to survive. Keep in mind that cold hardiness temperatures are estimates, rather than hard and fast rules, and that there is tremendous variability. After a few hours at its coldest temperature, a plant may sustain some leaf or stem damage, or it may die back to the ground altogether, yet it will still resprout in spring. After many hours at its coldest temperature or several nights at the coldest temperature, the same plant may die completely.

Should you try a plant if your garden gets colder than the plant's minimum temperature rating? If there is a big difference, say 10 degrees or more, chances are the plant won't survive winter in the ground, though it may survive in a pot if you move the pot indoors or otherwise protect it. But if a plant is rated to 28 degrees F and your garden gets to 25 degrees or 22 degrees F, find the warmest spot and try it. The worst outcome is the plant dies and you get to try something different in its place.

### How to treat frost damaged plants

When a plant suffers frost damage to leaves, stems, or trunk, *do not prune immediately*. Wait to prune until after the last frost date in your community (check with Master Gardeners for local frost dates). In the meantime, those outer damaged branches will protect the still living core from additional freezes that may happen before spring. Some plants can resprout from the roots even after the entire above-ground portion of the plant dies.

Once the weather warms, wait until you see new growth so you know how far back to prune. You can also do the "scratch test." Start at the part of a branch farthest from the trunk. With your fingernail, scratch at the outer layer of bark. If you see green beneath, that part of the branch is still alive and you simply need to wait for the plant to recover. If it is brown beneath the surface, the branch is probably dead. Continue doing scratch tests, working your way towards the trunk and then down the trunk towards the base. You'll quickly realize how far back the plant has died. Once you know how far back to prune, follow pruning directions in this section. Be patient and observe. If the rest of your garden has recovered and the plant has yet to resprout, chances are it is truly dead and you can remove it.

# Soil Drainage

Before you plant, test your soil drainage. Soil drainage is important because it determines how much critical water and oxygen are available to plant roots. There are several reasons that soil might drain poorly, and exploring them all would take an entire book. At the most basic level, however, the type of soil in your garden determines its drainage.

Heavy clay soils have very small, flat particles that fit closely together, leaving only small pores in between. When water fills the pores, it stays there for a long time, excluding critical oxygen. When heavy clay soils are watered too frequently, plant roots can become waterlogged. Roots turn dark brown or black and quite literally drown. Eventually, the soil starts to smell like rotten eggs from the accumulation of anaerobic bacteria—a sure sign of oversaturated soil.

Sandy soils, on the other hand, consist of relatively large, irregularly shaped particles that leave large pores through which water flows more freely, leaving room for oxygen to penetrate the soil. With these well draining soils, the challenge is watering often enough to keep the roots moist.

Loamy soils are those with a balance of sand, clay, and silt whose particle size is between those of clay and sand. Loamy soils hold enough water to keep roots moist yet drain fast enough to allow oxygen to penetrate and keep roots aerated.

### How to test soil drainage

Pick a spot in the garden. Dig a hole large enough to accommodate a 5-gallon nursery container. Fill the hole with water and let it drain completely. Fill with water again and note how long it takes to drain. Well draining soils drain within an hour or two. Heavier soils take longer, sometimes as long as several days.

### How to deal with heavy, poorly draining soil

One way to deal with heavy soils is to incorporate generous amounts of organic matter, repeatedly, over a long period of time.

My favorite solution, however, is to build raised beds or mounds out of well-amended, well-draining soil. I am not talking about a series of little molehills each a foot or so across, but rather bed-sized mounds that are many feet long, a foot or two tall, and sculpted with peaks and curves.

This well-draining soil gives plants the opportunity to become established into good soil. The sculpting creates nooks and crannies, each of which presents an opportunity for placing a plant at a slightly different height or angle. Once you start working with raised, contoured garden beds, you'll soon realize not just how well they work for plants, but also how much more interesting they are than flat beds.

Be sure to use a high quality, well-draining soil. This kind of soil can be purchased by the yard or even by the truckload from local suppliers. Ask local gardening friends for recommendations of reputable suppliers. When you talk with the supplier, be sure to emphasize that you need a mixture that drains well and includes plenty of composted organic matter.

### To amend or not to amend soil

Research and experience suggest that plants adapt better over time when there is little difference between the soil used to backfill the planting hole and the soil surrounding the hole. Some gardeners like to mix in copious amounts of organic amendments and fertilizers into the planting hole. I suggest avoiding that route. The majority of plants in this book require minimal soil amendment (none if you are planting into raised mounds).

I do, however, add a small amount of worm castings to planting holes. Worm castings (a genteel term for worm poop) are rich in nutrients and microorganisms, which, over time, colonize the surrounding soils and form beneficial associations with plant roots.

# Planting

### How to plant with minimal root disturbance

When it comes to planting bougainvillea, Matilija poppies, and some other plants, if you disturb the roots too much, poof! They are goners. For these plants start with a small plant. One-gallon plants are ideal.

- Dig and prepare the hole. Dig the hole just as deep as the depth of the rootball and $1^1/_2$ times as wide as the pot. Amend the hole as described above.
- Lay the plant on its side. Use a sharp knife to cut out the entire bottom of the plastic nursery container. Don't let the plant slip out of the container. Instead, place your hand over the cut end to support the exposed rootball. Carefully lift and set the container (with the plant inside) into the hole.
- Remove your hand and adjust the plant's position. Use your knife to slit up the sides of the container in two or three places. Then holding the plant in place with one hand, gently pull the pieces of the can away from the rootball. Carefully backfill the hole with native dirt.
- Water deeply to settle the roots, then build a watering basin and complete the process the same as for any other plant.

### How to create container plantings

Container planting is an art form in and of itself. Don't let that put you off, however, as containers offer a huge range of design options.

You can create container plantings using a single large specimen or by planting combinations: annuals with perennials, shrubs, grasses, and so on. The most beautiful combinations include plants of different shapes, textures, and sizes—tall narrow spikes or sword-shaped leaves surrounded by broad leaves and a ground cover or trailing plant to spill over the edges. Plan your flower and leaf color combinations as well.

### How to match plants with pots

Whether you choose the container first or the plants first, look for complementary colors, shapes, and sizes. Gray-green leaves, for example, look stunning in a terracotta pot, one with a burgundy glaze, or even a deep green glaze. But put that same plant into a pot with a light green glaze and chances are it will look quite sickly.

Choose a pot that is large enough for the ultimate size of the plant and the root mass. If you must err, err on the slightly larger side rather than the smaller side. In terms of sizes, place a tall plant into a tall pot that balances its proportions and accommodates its roots. Tiny plants are lost in a large pot but look very much in proportion if placed in a small pot.

Choose unglazed pots for plants that prefer to grow on the dry side. Without the glaze, the pot surface "breathes," that is, it allows for water to evaporate readily from the surface. Plants that prefer moist conditions are best in glazed ceramic or plastic pots, which hold moisture longer.

### Drainage holes

Be sure the pot has several $^1/_2$-inch or larger drainage holes in the bottom. If there are no holes, drill some. Many pottery stores drill holes for a small charge. Cover any holes in the bottom of the pot with a small square of fiberglass window screen. The screen lets water flow freely but keeps soil from flowing out the hole and critters from crawling in.

### Potting mixes

When it comes to potting mixes, you truly do get what you pay for. Cheap ones are not worth the money. For most plants, all-purpose potting mix is fine, but there are special well-draining mixes for plants such as cactus and succulents. Orchids, epidendrum, and epiphyllum do best in mixtures that include small chunks of bark.

Choose a good granular fertilizer (preferably organic) to mix into the potting soil while planting. Some gardeners also add biodegradable water-absorbing granules that swell when wet and release water slowly as the roots need them. I like to add worm castings too.

## How to Pot Plants

Here is my favorite way to pot plants:

- Spread a tarp on the ground as a working surface. Place a plastic cement mixing tray (available at the hardware store) onto the tarp to use as a workspace.
- Put the pot into one corner of the cement-mixing tray.
- Place the screen over the holes in the pot.
- Remove all pants from their nursery containers and lay onto the tarp.
- Estimate how much potting mix will fill the pot and pour that amount into the mixing tray. Add fertilizer and worm castings. If the potting mix is very dry, moisten it and mix well.
- Check the size of the largest rootball. Fill the pot with potting mix up to the level that allows the surface of that plant to sit just below the lip of the pot. Place the plant into the container.
- Place the rest of your plants (for a mixed container). When you are done, fill the remaining space so potting mix is an inch or two below the rim. The plants may look like they sit unusually high in the pot, but don't worry, after it is watered a few times the soil will settle a few inches.
- Remove the pot from the cement-mixing tray. If it is large, place it in its permanent location before watering. Water thoroughly and gently so you don't wash the potting mix over the side. Stick your finger down into the potting mix to determine when the water has penetrated completely.
- Top the surface with an inch or two of rounded gravel for mulch. It will retard water loss, keep weeds from invading the pot, minimize soil from splashing out when you water, and deter cats from using the pot as a litter box. It also gives the pot a finished look.
- Remember, a very large pot may need to be placed before being filled (becoming heavy).

Remember that no potted plant is permanent. After a year or two, some plants will have pooped out, some will have overgrown their neighboring plants, and some will outgrow their pots and need to be planted into the ground. Potting mix needs to be replenished or replaced every few years as well.

# Starting Plants from Seeds

Seed packets offer an amazing amount of important information. Most have the usual info: how much sun, water, and the type of soil each kind of seed needs, along with the season in which it fruits or flowers. The better seed companies also include detailed information on how to space the seeds, how far apart to thin seedlings, plant size estimates, the time from planting to germination, and days-to-maturity (how long from planting to flowering or fruiting). Keep in mind that days-to-maturity is not a hard and fast rule. In fact, it is based on results from test farms that may be hundreds, if not thousands, of miles from your garden and in a place where the climate is completely different. While our daytime temperatures may be high, the nights cool significantly, especially in coastal gardens. The temperature differential has little effect on sprouting rates, but often spring- and summer-grown plants take far longer than the label says to reach maturity. That translates to longer ripening times for summer vegetables as well.

## How to start seeds directly into the ground

- Prepare a seedbed by raking the soil smooth. It doesn't need to be uniformly even. If the soil is dry, soak it one or two days before you plant.
- Start with twice the number of seeds you think you need. Birds or rodents will eat some, some will wash away, and others will simply disappear.
- Small seeds like the poppy seeds are difficult to distribute evenly over a large area. For best results, mix one-part seeds with three or four parts dry construction sand or dried coffee grounds. These materials act as fillers so disperse seeds more evenly.
- Broadcast seed over the seedbed by hand, then rake gently. Tiny seeds need very little soil to cover them—a thin dusting will do.
- With larger seeds such as sweet pea seeds, place the seeds in rows or scatter into a seedbed. Cover larger seeds with a layer of soil about three times the thickness of the seeds.
- Water the seedbed every few days to keep it moist until seeds sprout. A gentle spray shouldn't

wash seeds away. If it rains enough to keep the soil moist, there is no need to water.

- The seed packet will suggest a germination time—how long from the time you plant until seeds sprout. Once they sprout, thin seedlings according to the directions on the packet. After seedlings are several inches tall, spread a fine mulch to keep the seedbed moist and to minimize weeds.
- Keep foot traffic out of seedbeds. Seeds can stick to the soles of shoes and literally walk out of the garden. Stepping on a seedling typically ends its short life.

## How to start seeds in containers

- Large seeds are often better started in a flat or pot than in the ground. Use clean disinfected pots (see "How to disinfect pots"). Check the seed packet to find out the best time of year to start each type of seed. Prepare labels before you begin. Use a pencil (lead is waterproof) on a piece of plastic or a recycled plant label. Or write onto the pot with a china marker. Be sure to include the name of the plant, its variety, and date planted.
- Fill pots with dampened seed starting mix (a special fine textured potting mix). Poke holes in the mix and place seeds, then cover with a layer of potting mix three times as thick as the seed is. Leave a quarter inch between the mix and the top edge of the pot.
- Put a label into each pot.
- Set the pots into a container with a few inches of water. Let them sit until water wicks up to the surface of the pot—usually several hours. Remove the pots and allow to drain for an hour or so.
- Top off the pot with a layer of construction sand, perlite, or #10 granite grit (fine ground granite). These materials keep the surface dry and prevent the onset of "damping off," a fungal disease that causes the stems of seedlings to wilt.
- Some gardeners cover their pots with a light sheet of plastic, like a dry cleaning bag, to keep moisture while seeds are germinating. If you do that, place chopsticks strategically in pots to keep the plastic from touching the surface of the pots.
- Place pots in a sheltered location with good air circulation. Once seeds sprout, remove the plastic.

## How to disinfect pots and containers before starting seeds

I reuse small plastic nursery pots for starting seeds and cuttings. Before I reuse the pots, I disinfect them to kill any leftover soil fungi or other plant diseases. First rinse empty pots and scrub off the remnants of past lives. Submerge pots in a diluted bleach solution, typically 1 part bleach to 10 parts water (wear old clothes and do this in a sink or outside). Soak for an hour or so, then rinse pots and let them dry completely before using. Terracotta pots can be treated this way as well. I usually disinfect a bucketful of pots all at once and store them until I need them.

## How to pre-sprout seeds

Larger seeds—like peas, corn, and beans—can be pre-sprouted before planting in the ground or container.

- For each type of seed, use four layers of paper towels and a Ziplock bag or lightweight plastic bag from the vegetable section of the supermarket.
- Write a label for each type of seed. Use a small piece of paper and pencil (pencil stands up to water). Include the type of seed, variety, and date started. Place the label in the plastic bag.
- Separate the paper towels into two sets, each with a double layer.
- Spritz one set of paper towels with water to dampen.
- Place seeds onto the damp paper towels, leaving plenty of space around each one.
- Set the second set of paper towels on top of the seeds and press to make a sealed seed "sandwich."
- Lay the seed sandwich carefully into the plastic bag and close gently, leaving a corner open for air circulation.
- Set the seed packet onto top of a refrigerator or in another brightly lit but protected location.
- Check daily as seeds take only a few days to sprout. Newly sprouted, carefully cut the seeds apart, leaving each intact with its surrounding paper towel, just sprouted roots and shoot. Each seed will be a little packet all its own. Plant it just like that. The paper towel will eventually rot away.
- Don't leave sprouted seeds too long as they quickly mold.

### How to transplant annual flower and vegetable seedlings

- Dig a hole $1^1/2$ times as wide and just as deep as the size of the nursery container (or 6-pack). If you want to add fertilizer, mix it into the soil that you will use to backfill the hole.
- Toss a small handful of worm castings into the planting hole (no need to mix it).
- Set seedling at the same height it was in the nursery container.
- Refill the hole, gently tamping down the soil around the roots.
- Drip water onto the soil so the rootball is fully saturated. This also ensures that the soil washes in to fill any air pockets.
- Mulch with a thick layer of organic matter. Mulch should not touch any part of the plant.

## Working with Perennials

Purchase perennials as 4-inch, 1-quart, or 1-gallon plants. Some are available in 5-gallon containers, but smaller ones adapt more quickly to being transplanted.

### How to plant perennials

- Dig a hole just as deep as the rootball and $1^1/2$ to 2 times as wide as the nursery container.
- Saturate both the plant in the container *and the planting hole* before planting so everything is nice and moist at planting.
- The majority of perennials in this book require minimal soil amendment (none if you are planting into raised mounds). Some gardeners like to mix fertilizer into the planting hole, but I find that plants adapt better to unamended or only lightly amended soils.
- Add a small amount of worm castings to the planting hole.
- Place the plant in the hole so that it will sit at the same level it was in the pot.
- Refill the hole, gently tamping down the soil around the roots.
- Drip water onto the soil so the rootball is fully saturated and soil washes in to fill any air pockets.
- Mulch with a 3-inch layer of organic matter. Mulch should not touch any part of the plant.

## Working with Trees, Vines, and Shrubs

### How to plant bare-root trees, vines, and shrubs

- If your bare-root plants arrive before you can plant them, set the roots in a container of dampened sawdust or construction sand and place in a shaded location.
- When you're ready to plant, soak rootball for several hours.
- Dig a hole twice as wide and half again as deep as the size of the rootball. Fill the hole with water and allow it to drain completely. If it takes more than a few hours to drain, build a planting mound or raised bed of well-draining soil. Dig a hole in the mound and fill the hole with water as described above.
- If fertilizer is specified, add a balanced, organic fertilizer to the backfill soil and incorporate thoroughly. It is important that concentrations of fertilizer don't touch plant roots. Check the label for instructions on how much fertilizer to use.
- Whether or not fertilizer is called for, throw in a few handfuls of worm castings.
- Set the plant in the hole so the roots can spread out. If you have to twist or crush roots to fit the hole, the hole is not wide enough.
- Check the trunk of the tree/shrub for the dirt line. The line shows you how deep the plant was buried before it was dug up and the soil washed from the roots. Make sure that your hole is deep enough so that the tree will sit an inch or so above the dirt line once the hole is refilled.
- Set the plant in the hole. Gently scoop soil back into the hole, directing it and tamping it down around the roots. Wet the soil as you go if you'd like. Once the soil is level with the ground, build a watering basin (see below) and water deeply.
- Apply 3 or 4 inches of mulch to the soil surface, making sure that the mulch covers the entire rootball area. Make sure no mulch touches the trunk, so stop the mulch at least 3 inches away from the trunk.

## How to plant trees, vines, and shrubs from nursery containers

- Water the plant in its pot thoroughly the day before you intend to plant. Dig a hole just as deep as the pot is tall and $1^1/_2$ to 2 times as wide as the pot.
- Fill the hole with water and allow it to drain completely. (See directions above.)
- Most of the plants in this book are planted best into native, unamended soils. For those that require amended soils, mix amendments into the soil that came out of the hole.
- Add a few handfuls of worm castings to the bottom of the hole.
- Refill the bottom of the hole with enough soil so the plant will sit at the same level it was in the pot. When planting natives, set plants an inch higher than they were in their pots.
- Step on the soil in the bottom of the hole to pack it down.
- Lay the pot on its side and squeeze the sides gently to loosen the plant from the pot.
- Grab the plant at the base of the trunk and carefully pull it from the pot.
- Check the roots. If they circle the rootball, gently loosen them unless they require minimum root disturbance. Remove any roots that are broken or dead.
- Set the plant into the hole. Refill with soil, tamping it as you go to eliminate air pockets. Before you reach the top, water the soil to settle it, then continue adding soil.
- Make a watering basin (see directions below).
- Apply 3 or 4 inches of mulch to the soil surface, making sure that the mulch covers the entire rootball area. Make sure no mulch touches the trunk, so stop the mulch at least 3 inches away from the trunk.

## How to prepare for plants that have invasive roots

Before you plant a running bamboo or other plant with invasive roots, be sure to have a good, solid root barrier in place. Plastic or concrete root barriers are about the only way to control these kinds of roots.

- Dig a trench, angled outward, and at least 3 feet deep around the perimeter of the planting hole.
- Line the hole with a 3-inch thick layer of concrete. Or apply HDPE (high-density polyethylene) root barrier (40 ml.), lining a trench that is at least 30 inches deep. This material can be ordered online or purchased through a bamboo supplier.
- Leave 2 to 3 inches of root barrier or concrete above ground level so you can see the roots that climb over the top of their enclosure, and trim them before they escape.
- Plant inside the root barrier (see how to plant trees and shrubs).
- Monitor the plant every few months so you can catch and remove any escapee roots.

## How to stake a tree

Trees in forests are never staked, yet they grow tall and strong. Still gardeners assume that trees in the garden need to be staked. That may be true for trees that are somehow unstable or in windy areas or spots where they can be knocked over. Otherwise, staking is purely optional.

If you must stake a tree, avoid the common mistake of binding the trunk tightly to a single stake. To develop strong wood, a tree needs to be able to flex and move—both of which are prevented by the single stake method. Instead, use two tall sturdy stakes.

- Once the plant is in its hole but before you fill it with soil, set stakes opposite each other against the outer edges of the planting hole.
- Orient the stakes to form a plane with the tree trunk, perpendicular to the direction of the wind.
- Use rubber tree ties to tie the tree *loosely* between the two stakes. Do not use wire. As the tree grows taller, add ties if necessary. Check the ties periodically to make sure that they are not cutting into the trunk.

Remember that the stakes are temporary. After a year or two (or once the trunk is thicker than the diameter of the stakes), remove the stakes altogether. Don't forget this important step!

## How to make a watering basin around trees, vines, and shrubs

A temporary watering basin is a moat that surrounds a plant's trunk, but sits several inches away from the trunk itself. The idea is to make a reservoir of water that slowly seeps down to saturate the roots.

After you finish planting, use any extra soil to build the basin around the outer edges of the planting hole. The basin can be 4 to 8 inches wider than the rootball and planting hole and rimmed in soil 3 or 4 inches high.

Use a hose to fill the basin with water and allow it to drain completely, every time you water. Refill as many times as is necessary to ensure that the water penetrates down past the rootball. Whichever watering method you do use, be sure that water penetrates deeply enough to wet the entire rootball mass. Poke the soil with a metal probe or an unwound wire hanger to see how deep the soil is saturated.

When you fertilize, wet the basin, sprinkle in fertilizer, and then fill with water so the fertilizer can begin to penetrate the soil.

## Working with Succulents

Plant large succulents just as you would any other tree or shrub. Plant small succulents as you would any perennial, but with one critical difference: succulents require very well draining soils. If your soil does not drain well, you have two choices: grow your succulents in pots filled with high quality cactus and succulent mix or build large planting mounds of imported, well-draining soil.

## Mulch

While real estate is about "location, location, location," gardening is about "mulch, mulch, mulch." No matter how good or bad your soil or how well or poorly it drains, your garden will benefit from mulch, especially composted organic mulch.

At its most basic, mulch is any kind of material spread over the soil in a 2- to 3-inch thick layer. Beginners often think that the purpose of mulch is to make the garden look tidy, which certainly is one result.

Organic mulches, such as compost, aged wood chips, aged sawdust, straw (be sure to ask for "seed free" straw), and garden compost offer greater benefits when layered on thickly. They seal in the soil moisture so plants need less frequent irrigation. They buffer roots from changes in temperature and keep weed seeds in the dark so they don't germinate. Weeds that do blow in on the wind or are carried in by birds (a nice way to say that birds poop the seeds into the garden) pull easily from a thick layer of mulch. Perhaps the most important function, though, is that as organic mulches break down, they blend into the soil, improving its texture, increasing drainage, and creating habitat for earthworms, beneficial fungi, and other microorganisms that help plants grow.

Succulent plants are the only exception to using organic mulches. Succulents still benefit greatly from being mulched, but they often do better with a mulch of gravel, pebbles, tumbled glass, etc. Even children's marbles make good mulches for succulents!

Don't be stingy with your mulch. Buy it by the truckload from your local greenwaste facility or from a garden supplier. Spread it generously—a 3-inch thick layer is optimal. When you are done spreading mulch, there should be no bare dirt anywhere in the garden, with one important exception—immediately around the base of each plant. *Mulch should never touch any part of a living plant.* Mulch against stems, trunks, and leaves will hold moisture and that can lead to problems with harmful fungi and rot.

Renew organic mulch twice yearly or as needed.

## Managing Pests

### Ants

Oh the cursed Argentine ant! In addition to being a pain-in-the-rump household pest, ants also cause a number of garden problems. Rumor has it that California is one big anthill, from north to south and from east to west. It certainly seems like that in my garden.

Ants literally transport aphids, scale, whiteflies, mealybugs, and other insects around the garden. Why? Ants place these sucking insects onto fleshy leaves where they go to work, sucking plant juices and exuding a sweet honeydew that the ants "harvest" and take back to their anthills. Some of the honeydew inevitably falls onto surrounding leaves, where its sugars attract a black fungus that covers the leaves in what looks like soot. It is most appropriately called "sooty mold."

If only ants were easy to control! It helps to keep your garden clean and the ripe fruit picked, rather than leaving it on the tree or, even worse, decomposing on the ground.

One way to treat the trunks of fruit trees and other woody plants is to apply ant barriers. Ant barriers have the texture of the thickest, gooiest petroleum jelly imaginable. Ants walk onto it and get stuck (and you'll have equal trouble getting it off your fingers). Manufacturers suggest applying a wide band of duct tape around the trunk of the afflicted plant and applying the ant barrier onto that, but I just smear it right onto the trunk with a plastic knife. Wear disposable gloves—they will be coated by time you are done. Replace the sticky stuff every few weeks as it loses its stickiness to a coat of dust and dirt or to a layer of dead ants that form a bridge across the barrier for their brethren.

There are numerous ant baits on the market. Some are pesticide based, and others are made of a sweetener to attract the ants to the boric acid to kill them. The boric acid baits don't work for me, but other people swear by them. Give it a try and see if it works for you—it can't hurt!

## Aphids

Wash aphids off your plants with a sharp spray of water, rub them off with your fingers, or spray with insecticidal soap. Insecticidal soaps are not toxic to humans and animals (except perhaps aquatic invertebrates). Thoroughly coat the leaves, both the upper and undersides, the joints between leaves and stems where pests tend to collect, and the tender new growth at the tip of each branch. Follow label directions. Repeat as needed.

## Black sooty mold

Black sooty mold is a catchall term that describes black fungi that grow in the sweet, honeydew-like excrement of scale, mealybugs, whiteflies, and other insects that suck plant juices. Black sooty mold looks like a thin layer of soot that primarily covers the surface of plant leaves. The best way to control black sooty mold is to control the insects. If you have the mold, first get rid of the insects. With the insects gone, the black sooty mold will eventually disappear. If the mold is especially bad or unsightly, you can also wash the plant with a solution of warm water and mild soap. Coat all leaf and stem surfaces thoroughly.

## Gophers

If your garden seems like gopherville (and many of ours do), try planting your most prized plants into gopher cages. Contrary to their name, gopher cages *exclude* gophers, rather than contain them. These wire mesh baskets are an easy way to protect plant roots without resorting to traps or poisons.

Purchase pre-made cages at independent nurseries, or online. Or, make your own using 1/2-inch hardware cloth mesh. *Do not* use chicken wire as it quickly falls apart when exposed to the elements.

Wear protective gloves and long sleeves so you don't get scratched. Unroll a length of hardware cloth and set your plant in its pot into the center. Wrap the hardware cloth up the sides to estimate the amount you need—then add a few inches. Cut with tin snips.

Line the planting hole with hardware cloth, folding the sides up and overlapping the edges. Zip ties can help secure the overlapping edges. Allow the hardware cloth to stick up a few inches above the ground so gophers can't dive over the side—fold down the cut ends to protect your hands. Set the rootball directly into the cage and then continue planting as usual. Eventually, roots will grow through the cage, but the critical mass of the rootball will be protected from those pesky critters.

## Powdery mildew

Powdery mildew is a fungus that develops on leaf surfaces. Breeders have created mildew resistant varieties of many plants such as crape myrtle whose mildew susceptibility is well known. Avoid wetting leaves when you irrigate (another reason to use drip irrigation) and water early in the day so the leaves dry out completely before the cool of evening. Dust grapes and other susceptible plants with powdered sulfur as a preventative. Once a plant has powdery mildew, it can be treated with minimally toxic sprays such as horticultural oil or a baking soda solution. For more information, contact your local Master Gardeners.

## Scale and mealybugs

Scale look like tiny, oval-shaped, brown scabs on a plant leaves and stems. Mealybugs are about the same size as scale, but are covered in what looks like white down. If you find just a few of either one, scrape them off with your fingernail and then monitor the plant for several weeks—these critters produce tiny babies that hide in the joints between leaves and stems. If you get an extensive infestation, treat with horticultural oil that basically suffocates these insects, rather than poisoning them. Follow the directions on the package. Be sure to coat both the top and bottom of leaves, the joints where leaves attach to stems, and the entire length of the stems. You may need to treat several times.

## Snails and slugs

Control snails and slugs with iron phosphate baits such as *Sluggo*. These baits are not toxic to humans, pets, or wildlife. See the product label for specifics about toxicity and instructions for use. Some counties also permit the use of decollate "carnivorous" snails. These cone-shaped shell snails eat young brown snails. As the decollate snail population grows, your brown snail population diminishes. This is not an instant solution, however. It can take a few years for the decollate snails to dominate, but once they do your brown snail problem will be over (I can vouch for decollate snails from my personal experience).

A note of caution: snail bait poisons decollate snails just as it does brown snails. The critical difference is that brown snails climb to find good things to eat, while decollate snails climb only under duress, like when their only other option is to drown in a puddle of water. So for a "double whammy," place decollate snails at ground level, and put snail bait in a flower pot or saucer raised up off the ground. Either way, the brown snails are doomed.

## Spider Mites

If you notice a plant with a filmy web around the new growth at the tip of a branch, chances are it is infected with spider mites. If the leaves look stippled, chances of spider mite are even greater. The actual mites are almost too tiny to be seen. Look hard with your naked eye and you might notice tiny black (sometimes orange or red) dots on a leaf surface, typically on the underside of the leaf. Drought stressed plants are most susceptible to spider mites, as are those with very dusty leaves. To avoid infection keep your plants adequately hydrated, and rinse off leaves periodically, especially in the dry months of summer. If mites do appear, spray them off with water, insecticidal soap, or oil. Follow directions on the label.

## Thrips

Talk about tiny! Thrips are nearly impossible to see. Adults are less than $1/20$ of an inch long! Still, they can destroy flower buds and new leaves. Leaf surfaces look discolored and almost silvery, much as they do with a spider mite infestation. Woody plants in good health easily survive a thrip infection, and some kinds of thrips have natural predators that will keep them in check. If a plant gets an infestation that needs to be controlled, you have several options. You can cut back on nitrogen fertilizer, use a sharp spray of water to wash the thrips away, prune off infected plant parts (put into a sealed plastic bag and dispose, do not compost), or spray with horticultural soap. Try them one at a time or all at once. It can't hurt.

## Whiteflies

If you bump a plant only to notice a cloud of white rise from the leaves, your plant is infected with whiteflies. These are sucking insects much like aphids and mealybugs. Also like aphids and mealybugs, whiteflies can cause black sooty mold. Whiteflies prefer the undersides of leaves where they feed and lay their white eggs.

If you find a small colony of whiteflies, rub the flies, *their young, and their eggs* off the leaf with your fingers. Larger infestations can be more challenging to control. Set yellow sticky traps into the garden to capture the adults. Treat infected plants with insecticidal soap or with horticultural oil—both will coat the eggs, but the adults will likely fly away and return. Prune off the infected plant parts, seal them in a plastic bag, and dispose (do not compost).

Giant whitefly was a huge problem in the 1990s, but now seems to be under quite good control thanks to natural predators released by the University of California.

# Best Watering Practices

The goal of watering all plants during their first year or two in the ground is to get them to develop deep roots. Roots follow the water, so deep, infrequent irrigation encourages roots to go deep into the soil where they are less subject to desiccation than shallow roots are. Deep roots also do a better job of anchoring larger plants. Once the deep roots are established, most of the plants listed in this book will need watering only when the top several inches of soil are dry.

When you do water, be sure to saturate the ground thoroughly past the deepest roots (especially for annuals, perennials, and smaller shrubs). Drip irrigation is ideal for this deep watering because it applies water slowly and directly to the soil.

## When to water

Poke your "ten little moisture sensors" (your fingers) into the ground to feel the soil and determine how wet or dry it is. Or, use an unwound metal hanger to determine soil moisture. Use the hanger like a dipstick and push the tip into the ground near the base of the plant. When you pull it out, note where along its length the metal is damp. That tells you how deep the water has penetrated. Another option is to invest in a soil moisture probe that pulls a plug of soil out of the ground. Feel the moist soil to see how deep it is.

Water frequency needs to be adjusted with the seasons (better yet, monthly). That may sound demanding, but it is not so hard to understand. Plants, like people, generally need the most water in hot summer months, and the least in cool winter months. Because the sun is at a lower angle in fall and winter than in summer, plants are less active and require less water then too. Spring is an active growth time, but the cooler air keeps water demand lower than in the heat of summer.

## How to water pots

Water pots slowly, using a soft gentle spray. Fill each pot with water up to the brim twice or until water runs out the hole in the bottom. The goal is to saturate the potting soil all the way through the pot.

After years of testing different hose-end sprayers, the only ones I use are the watering "wands" made by a company called Dramm. These hose-end sprayers have flat discs with concentric rings of tiny holes through which water falls like rain. You can skip all of the hose-end pistols and nozzles with multiple settings from fine mist to a sharp stream. They may be great for washing the car, but not for watering plants. Mist settings won't saturate the soil. Sharp sprays damage plants. Besides, the idea is to fill the pot with water, not to shoot the soil out of the pot and onto the patio. Even nozzles with "flood" settings don't work as well as the water wands.

## How often to water pots

Container-grown plants need to be watered far more often than plants grown in the ground. While succulents can dry out completely between waterings, most other plants prefer consistent moisture. Soil should be damp, but not wet.

Watering frequency depends on the season, the kind of plant, and the kind of pot. Plastic pots hold water better than glazed pots, which in turn, hold water better than unglazed pots. Plants that prefer to be on the dry side (succulents for example) do best in unglazed terracotta. Plants that like moisture (like gingers and other tropicals) do better in glazed ceramic or plastic. With some experience, you'll get a feel for matching plants to pots.

Stick your fingers into the potting mix. How deep do you poke before you encounter damp soil? An inch? Three inches? Is it dry as deep as you can feel? If you find moist soil an inch or even five inches beneath the surface, wait to water—unless you are growing a very thirsty plant or the leaves look wilted. If the leaves are slightly wilted at the peak of a hot day but recover as the air cools, your plant is probably fine. Check again first thing the next morning. If leaves are still wilted, water.

When you have a water stressed plant, i.e. one with severely wilted leaves or bone dry potting soil, set the entire pot into a bucket filled with several inches of water. Allow the pot to sit in the water for a few hours. The water will wick up into the potting soil and saturate it completely. Once the soil is saturated, remove the pot from the bucket and allow the excess water to drain away. If the plant perks up by the next day, it will survive.

If you "forget" to water a pot for a long time and notice that the planting mix has pulled away from the sides, repot it right away. Pull the old plant out and set its rootball in a bucket of water for an hour or so. Meanwhile replace the old potting soil with brand new, damp potting soil. Repot the plant and water thoroughly.

A few things to watch out for:

- More potted houseplants die from overwater than underwater. Let the soil dry several inches deep between waterings.
- Black plastic nursery containers (and other dark colored containers) can overheat in full, blazing sun and literally cook plant roots. If you can't repot right away, set the black container inside a lighter colored pot or even into a terracotta pot.
- A layer of gravel mulch over the surface of a pot slows evaporation and allows the plant to go longer between waterings.
- All pots need drainage holes. If the pot you want to use doesn't have at least one good-sized hole ($1/2$ inch or larger), drill one.

## Leaching soil

Leaching soil entails dripping water through the soil over a long period of time to wash through salts that build up in the surface layers. Salt accumulation in the soil can translate to salt accumulation in the leaves, especially in avocado and Japanese maples. Leaf edges and leaf tips turn brown and crunchy, particularly towards the end of summer and into fall. This condition is referred to as "leaf-tip burn."

Leaching soil is very water intensive, so you need to decide whether to grow these more salt-sensitive plants and if you do, whether to "spend the water" to leach them or to simply tolerate the crinkly leaves.

To leach plants in the ground, set up a slow sprinkler and allow it to water for many hours. Watch for surface runoff—a sure sign that the soil is saturated. Stop watering and wait several hours for the soil to drain before continuing.

Potted plants can be leached to remove salt buildup from potting soil too, though it may make more sense to repot the plant into fresh potting mix. Have you ever noticed a white crust on the surface of your pots, particularly terracotta pots? That crust is the accumulation of salts. Brush the crust off with a stiff brush. Repot the plant into fresh potting soil or leach the soil in the pot. Let water drip through the pot for a long time, long past when water runs out the bottom of the pot.

# Pruning

There are different reasons to prune a plant: to stimulate new growth or encourage bushiness, to remove dead or diseased wood and rejuvenate a declining plant, to shape the plant, and to stimulate the production of flowers or fruit.

One of the key concepts in low maintenance gardening is to avoid overplanting the garden. Not all plants need to be pruned, and in fact most of the plants in this book require no pruning at all—as long as they are planted with enough room to accommodate their ultimate sizes. Allowing each plant enough room to attain its ultimate size, saves you from constant pruning to keep plants in bounds.

## How to prune

**Herbaceous annuals and perennials:** Pinch back branch tips when plants are young to encourage side growth and bushiness. Use your fingernails to pinch out the newest softest growth, or use pruning shears to cut back larger branches. Always pinch or cut to just above a branching point. Do not leave any stubs. Once the plant starts to develop flower buds, stop pinching. If you continue, you are likely to pinch off the flower buds and you'll end up with no flowers. As blooms fade, pinch or cut them (deadhead), which often stimulates another round of blooms.

**Shrubs:** Pinch or cut back the branch tips as for annuals and perennials to encourage side growth and bushiness. Always cut at just above a branching point and never leave any stubs. If there is a collar (a slight swelling) around the base of the branch, be sure to leave it rather than cutting it off.

**Trees:** First remove all damaged, dead, and diseased wood. Then remove branches that cross or point towards the center of the tree. After that, prune for shape, paying attention to branch collars (as above) and making sure you prune to just above a branching point. Do not leave any stubs.

When pruning fruit trees, determine where fruit develops along the branch—some fruits develop on old wood, some on new wood, and some on fruiting spurs that look like stubby branches lining the length of the branch.

### How to disinfect pruning tools

Disinfect pruning tools (pruners, saws, etc.) to prevent spreading disease from plant to plant, especially when pruning woody trees and shrubs. Some gardeners disinfect tools after each cut, others disinfect between plants. To disinfect, dip pruning tools into a 10 percent bleach solution (9 parts water, 1 part bleach or approximately 1$^1$/2 tablespoons of bleach in 1 cup of water) or spray with a foaming disinfecting bathroom cleaner. Wipe dry with a soft cloth and oil as needed.

## Caring for Bulbs, Corms, Tubers, and Rhizomes

### Fertilizing

Every bulb grower has his or her own method for fertilizing bulbs, corms, tubers, and rhizomes already in the ground. For true bulbs and corms, some growers top-dress the bulb bed in early spring with bone meal, a low-nitrogen fertilizer, or with specialized organic bulb formulations.

Feed rhizomes and tubers regularly from spring through fall, irises in particular. Organic formulations are inherently slow release and are your best bet for fertilizer. You can top-dress rhizomes and tubers with fresh rabbit manure. Age or compost all other manures before using as a top-dressing.

### Caring for foliage

Cut bulb, corm, tuber, and rhizome foliage back to the ground *only* after the leaves have dried completely. Even after flowers are gone, leaves continue to photosynthesize and store energy for the next year's bloom. If you find the fading foliage to be too unsightly, you can braid it or knot it to make it look a bit tidier. Once foliage fades, cut it (don't pull) and add to your compost.

### How to divide bulbs and corms

Over time, a few bulbs and corms will form a clump that will then form a mass. When a mass outgrows its spot, it is time to divide.

Divide bulbs when they are dormant or in leaf, but not when they are in flower. Carefully dig up the mass of bulbs with a pointed shovel angled beneath the bulb mass. Some masses will fall apart easily in your hands or on the shovel as you dig them out of the ground. Simply separate the mass into several clumps, each with at least three bulbs. Find a new spot for these bulbs and replant them (follow planting directions in the bulb chapter) at the same depth they were before.

If your bulbs make a solid mass that stays intact when you dig it up, gently lift the mass, taking care not to damage bulbs or roots. Once the mass starts to loosen from the ground, you may want to use a wide-tined pitchfork (called a "spade fork" or a "digging fork") to pry up the bulbs. Avoid poking the tines into the bulbs.

Brush away the dirt so you can see the bulbs clearly. Try to pull the bulbs apart with your hands. If that doesn't work, use a sharp knife to carefully cut them apart without cutting up the bulbs. Discard any damaged or dead bulbs. You can dust the remaining bulbs with soil sulfur to ward off fungal infections. Replant bulbs into prepared soil at the same depth they were before. Or share spare bulbs with gardening friends.

Water bulbs thoroughly after planting, and mulch. Bulbs typically skip a year of bloom after division.

### How to divide tubers or rhizomes

Rhizomatous and tuberous plants increase over time, ultimately making sizeable clumps that eventually need dividing. Divide clumps every few years, when flowering declines, or when the center of the plant dies out while the outer edges are still going strong.

Water well the day before dividing so the soil is soft to work in. When dividing plants with evergreen leaves, your job will be easier if you first cut the leaves back to $1/2$ or a $1/3$ of their original length.

Use a sharp-pointed shovel to carefully slice around the perimeter of the mass as you begin separating the rhizomes or tubers from the soil. Angle the point of the shovel inward a bit, beneath the roots. Gently start to lift the root mass from the soil.

Using a wide-tined pitchfork (called a "spade fork" or a "digging fork"), carefully pry up the rhizomes or tubers until they are out of the ground. This can take a bit of work so be patient and persistent.

Examine the mass at the base of the leaves (you may want to wash the soil away first). Rhizomes and tubers often look like pieces of ginger with thick sections connected at narrow "joints."

Using a sharp knife, cut through the joints to create several grapefruit-sized clumps. When dividing evergreen plants, you may need to spread leaf fans apart to find the joints. With dormant (leafless) rhizomes, make sure each rhizome piece has three or four little buds (called "eyes" where the new stalks will emerge. If a knife isn't strong enough to cut through the joints, use the spade or a narrow-tined pitchfork to sever the joints. A knife will give you better control and do less damage.

Remove damaged or dead rhizomes and tubers. Dust with soil sulfur to help prevent fungal infection. Replant into a prepared spot in the ground or into a pot. Set rhizomes and tubers at the same depth they were before. Water well and mulch. Keep soil moist (not wet) for a few months until the plants re-establish their roots.

Rhizomes and tubers typically skip a year of bloom after division.

## Propagation

Many gardeners take great pride in their ability to make many plants from a single plant. Propagation is fun, especially if you have a plant that you especially love and want to share with others.

Bulbs, corms, tubers, and rhizomes are propagated by division as described above. Perennials are propagated by softwood cuttings. Many trees and shrubs are propagated from dormant-wood cuttings.

### Softwood cuttings

Coleus, sages, Jerusalem sage, and many other perennials are easy to propagate from cuttings, especially during active growth in spring.

You will need a healthy plant, cleaned and disinfected pruning shears, cleaned and disinfected 4-inch pots (recycled from other plants is fine), rooting hormone, plant label, pencil, fresh potting soil, perlite, and coarse construction sand or granite grit (also called "chicken grit" and sold by feed stores). Make sure that you are getting the granite grit, not the shell grit. Or look for the smallest sized granite grit sold by a roofing supply house.

Soak pots for an hour or so in a 10 percent bleach solution (1 part bleach in 9 parts water). Dip pruning shears into the mixture as well. Write labels for your pots in pencil (it doesn't wash off). Include the type of plant and date of cutting.

Each gardener has his or her favorite mix for propagating cuttings. One of the easiest is to mix two parts potting mix with one part perlite. Once combined, dampen thoroughly and fill the pots so they are ready for cuttings.

Select several branches that have not yet developed flower buds. Cut 4- to 6-inch-long pieces off the tips of the branches, including at least three "nodes," joints along the stem where leaves are or were attached.

Strip off all but the top set of leaves. Dip the cut end of the cutting into rooting hormone (available at your local garden center) to stimulate root growth. Follow directions on the label.

Poke holes into the center of the potting soil and insert several cuttings into each, making sure that at least two of the nodes sit below the potting mix. Roots will form at the nodes.

Don't hesitate to put a dozen cuttings into a single pot. Cuttings often root better when they are crowded together. Water to settle the potting mix around the stems.

Insert a chopstick into either side of the pot, sticking higher out of the pot than the cuttings. Set a clear plastic newspaper bag or vegetable bag over the top of the chopsticks like a loose tent. The bag keeps

www.digplantgrow.com

the air around the cuttings humid while they root, and the chopsticks keep the bag from touching the cuttings. You can put a rubber band around the bottom bag to hold it in place around the pot, but it is not necessary. Place the pot in a sheltered location with indirect light.

Check the pot regularly to be sure it stays damp (but not wet) while the cuttings develop roots. After several weeks, tug gently at a few of the cuttings to see if you get any resistance, which would tell you that the cuttings have grown roots. Once cuttings root, empty the pot and separate the cuttings carefully so you don't damage the roots. They may be intertwined, so take your time to separate them. Once the cuttings are separated, replant each in its own pot. Place in a spot in full sun. Once the plant puts on some size, it can be planted out into the garden.

## Dormant-wood cuttings

Some woody plants such as figs, pomegranates, grapes, olives, and coral trees start easily from dormant-wood cuttings.

- You'll need the mother plant, potting soil, perlite, the plant label, a pencil, gallon pots (cleaned and disinfected as described above), construction sand or gravel grit, pruning shears, a hand trowel, and rooting hormone.
- Once the shrub or tree has lost all its leaves in winter, cut several "whips" (pieces of bare branch), 8 to 12 inches long.
- Treat the cut end of the whips with a rooting hormone (available at your local garden center) to stimulate root growth. Use according to directions on the label.
- Insert several cuttings into a single-gallon pot filled with damp sand or perlite. Cuttings often root better when they are crowded together. Bury the whips at least 6 inches deep. Water well.
- Insert a chopstick into either side of the pot, sticking higher out of the pot than the cuttings. Set a clear plastic bag or vegetable bag over the top of the chopsticks like a loose tent. The bag keeps the air around the cuttings humid while they root; the chopsticks keep the bag from touching the cuttings. You can put a rubber band around the bottom bag to hold it in place around the pot, but it is not necessary. Place the pot in a sheltered location with indirect light.
- Check the pot regularly to be sure potting soil stays damp (but not wet) while the cuttings develop roots. In spring, tug gently at a few of the cuttings to see if you get any resistance, which would tell you that the cuttings have grown roots. Once cuttings root, empty the pot, and carefully separate the cuttings so you don't damage the roots. They may be intertwined, so take your time to separate them. Once the cuttings are separated, replant each in its own pot. Once the plant puts on some size, it can be planted out into the garden.

## Root divisions

Root divisions are the easiest way to propagate plants and the best method to propagate plants like oregano and thyme that spread by underground roots.

You need the mother plant, 4-inch pots or a nursery flat lined with a thick layer of newspaper, potting mix, the plant labels, a pencil, pruning shears, and a hand trowel.

- Prepare the label with the type of the plant and the date of the division.
- Fill the pots or flat with damp potting mix (no need for perlite with this method).
- Find a non-flowering branch of the plant and gently pull or dig to dislodge it. Cut off a 4- to 6-inch length of stem with roots attached.
- Bury the root end of the division, water to settle the soil, then place in a sheltered location with indirect light. These divisions should take quickly—within a couple of weeks at the most.

# California Gardening Resources

## Gardening Organizations

California is home to countless garden related organizations, from garden clubs to special interest groups for bamboo, palms, cycads, succulents, begonias, orchids, roses, and so on. Below are some general interest organizations and larger special interest groups. Ask about others at your local independent nursery or botanical garden. Even better, ask your gardening friends.

- California Garden Clubs, Inc. www.californiagardenclubs.org. Clubs statewide.
- California Horticultural Society, San Francisco County Fair Building, 9th Avenue & Lincoln Way, San Francisco, CA 94122, (800) 884-0009, http://www.calhortsociety.org/.
- California Native Plant Society, http://www.cnps.org/. Chapters statewide.
- California Rare Fruit Growers, WWW.CRFG.org. Chapters statewide.
- Master Gardeners, University of California Cooperative Extension, One Shields Ave., Davis, CA 95616-8575, (530) 754-6000, www.MasterGardeners.org. Groups in most counties.
- Mediterranean Garden Society, www.mediterraneangardensociety.org. Chapters in Southern, Central, and Northern California.
- San Diego Horticultural Society, PO Box 231869, Encinitas, CA 92023-1869, (760) 295-7089, www.sdhortsoc.org.
- Southern California Horticultural Society, P.O. Box 94476, Pasadena, CA 91109-4476, (818) 567-1496, www.socahort.org.
- The California Garden & Landscape History Society, www.cglhs.org.
- The Garden Conservancy, 1014 Torney Avenue, 1 Tides Center at The Presidio, San Francisco, CA (415) 561-7895, www.gardenconservancy.org.
- Western Horticultural Society, P.O. Box 60507, Palo Alto, CA 94306, (408) 867-9428.

## Public Gardens

Public gardens and arboreta are great places to see plants that grow well in your area and how they look in the ground. Below is a sampling of the many public gardens throughout the state. Many hold annual or twice-annual plant sales.

- Balboa Park. Visitor Center, 1549 El Prado, Suite 1, San Diego, CA 92101-1699, (619) 239-0512. www.balboapark.org. Many gardens throughout the park.
- Descanso Gardens, 1418 Descanso Drive, La Cañada Flintridge, CA 91011, (818) 949-4200, www.descansogardens.org.
- Filoli Center, 86 Cañada Road, Woodside, CA 94062, (650) 364-8300, www.filoli.org.
- Fullerton Arboretum, 1900 Associated Road, Fullerton, CA 92831, (714) 278-3579, www.arboretum.fullerton.edu.
- Humboldt Botanical Gardens Foundation, P.O. Box 6117, Eureka, CA 95502, (707)442-5139.
- Los Angeles County Arboretum & Botanic Garden, 301 N. Baldwin Ave. Arcadia, CA 91007, (626) 821-3222, www.arboretum.org.
- Lotusland. 695 Ashley Road, Santa Barbara, CA 93108, (805) 969-9990, www.Lotulsand.org. Reservations required.
- Mildred E. Matthias Botanical Garden, Department of Biology, Box 951606, University of California, Los Angeles, CA 90095-1606, (310) 825-1260, www.botgard.ucla.edu.
- Quail Gardens, 230 Quail Gardens Drive, Encinitas CA, 92024, (760) 436-3036, www.qbgardens.org.
- Rancho Santa Ana Botanic Garden, 1500 North College Avenue, Claremont, CA 91711-3157, (909) 625-8767, www. rsabg.org.
- Ruth Bancroft Garden, 1500 Bancroft Road in Walnut Creek, CA, 94598, (925) 210-9663, www.ruthbancroftgarden.org.
- San Francisco Botanical Garden at Strybing Arboretum, 9th Avenue at Lincoln Way, San Francisco, CA 94122, (415) 661-1316.
- San Luis Obispo Botanical Garden, Post Office Box 4957, San Luis Obispo, CA 93403, (805) 546-3501, www.slobg.org.
- Santa Barbara Botanic Garden, 1212 Mission Canyon Road, Santa Barbara, CA 93105, (805) 682-4726, www.sbbg.org.

- South Coast Botanic Garden, 26300 Crenshaw Blvd., Palos Verdes Peninsula, CA 90274, (310) 544-6815, http://parks.co.la.ca.us/south_coast_botanic.html.
- The Huntington Library, Art Collections, and Botanical Gardens, 1151 Oxford Road, San Marino, CA 91108, 626-405-2100, www.huntington.org.
- The Living Desert, 47-900 Portola Avenue, Palm Desert, CA 92260, (760) 346-5694, www.livingdesert.org.
- The San Mateo Arboretum Society, San Mateo Central Park, 101 Ninth Avenue, San Mateo, CA 94401, 650-579-0536, www.sanmateoarboretum.org.
- The Water Conservation Garden, 12122 Cuyamaca College Drive West, El Cajon, CA 92019, (619) 660-0614, www.thegarden.org.
- University of California Botanical Garden, 200 Centennial Drive #5045 Berkeley, CA 94720-5045, (510) 643-2755, http://botanicalgarden.berkeley.edu.
- University of California Davis Arboretum, University of California, 1 Shields Avenue, Davis, CA 95616, (530) 752-4880, www.arboretum.ucdavis.edu.
- University of California, Santa Cruz Arboretum, UC Santa Cruz, 1156 High Street, Santa Cruz, CA 95064, (831) 427-2998, www2.ucsd.edu/arboretum.

## Retail Specialty Nurseries
Many specialty nurseries feature demonstration gardens. Several sell by mail order too.

- Annie's Annuals and Perennials: Unusual annuals, bulbs, and perennials. 740 Market Ave, Richmond, CA, (510) 215-1671. www.anniesannuals.com.
- Australian Plant Nursery: 9040 North Ventura Avenue Ventura, CA 93001, (800) 701-6517. www.australianplants.com.
- Azalea Wood Nursery: Japanese maples. Vista, CA. (760) 643-2314.
- Bamboo Giant: 5601 Freedom Blvd., Aptos, CA , 95003 (831) 687-0100, www.bamboogiant.com.
- Bamboo Headquarters: 2498 Majella Road, Vista CA, 92084-1625. (866) 293-2925. www.bambooheadquarters.com.
- California Cactus center: 206 S. Rosemead Blvd., Pasadena, CA 91107. (626) 795-2788, www.californiacactuscenter.com.
- California Flora Nursery: Native and Mediterranean plants. Somers and D Street, CA 95439. (707) 528-8813, www.calfloranursery.com.
- Clausen Nursery: Fruit trees and vines. 3132 Blackwell Dr., Vista, CA 92084, (760) 724-3143, www.clausennursery.com.
- East Bay Wilds Native Plant Nursery: Mile marker 2.45, Cull Canyon Rd., Castro Valley, CA, (510) 409-5858.
- Elkhorn Native Plant Nursery: 1957-B Highway 1, Moss Landing, CA 95039, (831) 763-1207, www.elkhornnursery.com.
- Exotica Nursery Inc.: Rare fruits. 2508-B East Vista Way, Vista, CA 92083, (760) 724-9093.
- Golden Gate Palms and Exotics: 420 South 3rd Street, Point Richmond, CA (925) 325-PALM, www.goldengatepalms.com.
- Jungle Music: Cycads and palms. 450 Ocean View Ave, Encinitas, CA, (619) 291-4605, www.Junglemusic.net.
- Larner Seeds: Native plants and seeds. PO Box 407, Bolinas, CA 94924, (415) 868-9407, www.larnerseeds.com.
- Las Pilitas Nursery: Native plants. (Two locations) 3232 Las Pilitas Rd, Santa Margarita, CA. 93453, (805) 438-5992. Also in Escondido, CA (760) 749-5930. www.Laspilitas.com.
- Living Desert Nursery: Desert adapted plants. 47-900 Portola Ave., Palm Desert, CA 92260, (760) 346-5694, www.livingdesert.org.
- Lone Pine Gardens: Cacti and succulents. 6450 Lone Pine Road, Sebastopol, CA 95472, (707) 823-5024, www.lonepinegardens.com.
- Marca Dickie Nursery: Japanese Maples. PO Box 1270, Boyes Hot Springs, CA 95416, (800) 990-0364.
- Matilija Nursery: Native plants. 8225 Waters Road, Moorpark, CA 93021, (805) 523-8604, www.matilijanursery.com.
- Momiji Nursery: Japanese Maples. 2765 Stony Point Road, Santa Rosa, CA 95407, (707) 528-2917, www.momijinursery.com.
- Mostly Natives Nursery: Native and Mediterranean plants. PO Box 258, 27235 Highway One, Tomales, CA 94971, (707) 878-2009, www.mostlynatives.com.

- Native Revival: Native plants. 2600 Mar Vista Drive, Aptos, CA 95003-3615, (831) 684-1811, www.nativerevival.com
- Neon Palm Nursery: 3525 Stony Point Rd. Santa Rosa, CA, 95407-8037, (707) 585-8100.
- Nuccio's Nursery: Camellias and Azaleas. 3555 Chaney Trail, Altadena, CA 91001, (626) 794-3383, www.nucciosnurseries.com.
- Palm Island Nursery Outlet: 3851 Joslin Lane, Vacaville, CA 95688, (707) 449-6366, www.palmislandnursery.com.
- Pearson's Gardens and Herb Farm: 1150 Beverly Drive, Vista, CA 92085, (760) 726-0717.
- Sierra Azul Nursery and Gardens: Mediterranean plants, 2660 East Lake Avenue, Watsonville, CA 95076, (831) 763-0939, www.sierraazul.com.
- Solana Succulents: 355 North Hwy. 101 in Solana Beach, CA, 92075, (858) 259-4568, www.solanasucculents.com.
- Sonoma Horticultural Nursery: Rhododendrons and azaleas. 3970 Azalea Avenue, Sebastopol CA 95472, (707) 823-6832, http://sonomahort.com.
- Succulent Gardens: 2133 Elkhorn Rd. Castroville, CA, 95012, (831) 632-0482.
- The Dry Garden: Succulents and drought tolerant plants. 6556 Shattuck Avenue, Oakland, CA 94609, (510) 547-3564.
- The Great Petaluma Desert: Succulents. 5010 Bodega Avenue. Petaluma, CA 94952-7604, (707) 778-8278, www.gpdesert.com.
- The Palm Broker/Flora Grubb Gardens. 1634 Jerrold Avenue, San Francisco, CA, (415) 626-7256, www.floragrubb.com.
- The Plant Man: Succulents and oddities. 2615 Congress St, San Diego, CA 92110, (619) 297-0077.
- Theodore Payne Foundation: Native plants. 10459 Tuxford Street, Sun Valley, CA 91352-2116, (818) 768-1802, www.theodorepayne.org.
- Tree of Life Nursery: Native plants. 33201 Ortega Highway, San Juan Capistrano, CA 92693 (949) 728-0685.
- Western Hills Nursery: Rare and unusual plants. 16250 Coleman Valley Rd., Occidental, CA 95465, (707) 874-3731. www.westernhillsnursery.com.
- Yerba Buena Nursery: Native plants. 19500 Skyline Blvd., Woodside, CA 94062, (650) 851-1668. www.yerbabuenanursery.com.

## Mail Order Specialty Nurseries
Some of these nurseries are open by appointment as well. You can find more information online.

- Aloha Tropicals: (760) 631-2880, www.alohatropicals.com.
- Amity Heritage Roses: PO Box 357, Hydesville, CA 95547-0357, (707) 768-2040, www.amityheritageroses.com.
- Bamboo Giant: 5601 Freedom Blvd., Aptos, CA 95003, (831) 687-0100, www.bamboogiant.com.
- Bamboo Sorcery: 666 Wagnon Road, Sebastopol, CA 95472, (707) 823-5866, www.bamboosourcery.com.
- Bill the Bulb Baron: Amaryllis and narcissus. (831) 659-3830, www.billthebulbbaron.com.
- Canyon Creek Nursery: Perennials. 3527 Dry Creek Road, Oroville CA 95965, (530) 533-2166, www.canyoncreeknursery.com.
- Chalk Hill Clematis: Healdsburg. PO Box 1847, Healdsburg, CA 95448, (707) 433-8416, www.chalkhillclematis.com.
- Daniel's Specialty Nursery: Cacti and succulents. www.danielscactus.hypermart.net.
- Digging Dog Nursery: Perennials, grasses, and more. PO Box 471, Albion, CA 95410, (707) 937-1130, www.diggingdog.com.
- Four Winds Growers: Citrus. www.fourwindsgrowers.com.
- Geraniaceae: Geranium, Erodium, and Pelargonium. 122 Hillcrest Ave., Kentfield, CA 94904, (415) 461-4168, www.geraniaceae.com.
- Greenwood Daylily Gardens, Inc.: 8000 Balcom Canyon Road, Somis, CA 93066, (562) 494-8944, www.greenwooddaylily.com.
- Kartuz Greenhouse: Passion vines and exotics. 1408 Sunset Drive, Vista, CA 92081 (760) 941-3613, www.kartuz.com.
- Mountain Valley Growers: Herbs and perennials. 38325 Pepperweed Road, Squaw Valley, CA, 93675, (559) 338-2775, www.mountainvalleygrowers.com.
- Seedhunt: Unusual annuals, natives, perennials, and salvias. PO Box 96, Freedom, CA 95019-0096, www.seedhunt.com.

# Botanical Index

# Meet the Author

*Nan Sterman*

Nan Sterman's earliest memory is wandering through the "forest" of tomato plants that her grandfather grew each spring in the family garden, near the Los Angeles Airport. In the decades since, she's grown tomatoes and countless other plants from Berkeley to San Diego.

More than simply a gardener, Sterman is a gardening expert and award winning communicator who writes, lectures, and is featured on television, radio, and the Internet. In her half-acre garden Sterman grows a wide range of plants.

Sterman specializes in plants and techniques that are appropriate and sustainable in California's Mediterranean climate. She consults on garden design and plant selection. Her articles appear regularly in the *San Diego Union Tribune*, *Los Angeles Times*, *Sunset*, *Organic Gardening*, and other publications. Her writing covers "green" gardening how-to's, specialty nurseries, beautiful and unique gardens, and interesting gardeners. She is a contributor to a number of books, including the 2007 edition of *Sunset Western Garden Book*. *California Gardeners Guide Volume II* is her first solo book.

In addition to her writing, Sterman is co-producer and host of *A Growing Passion*, an award-winning television program that introduces viewers to real gardens created by ordinary people, who happen to be extra-ordinary gardeners. The show explores gardening as a quality of life activity, and demonstrates earth-friendly, sustainable gardening techniques that benefit local communities and the overall environment. Sterman has appeared on several shows for the Do It Yourself Network and is a regular guest on *These Days*, on KPBS 89.5 in San Diego.

Sterman is active in the Garden Writers Association and is chairperson of the annual Encinitas Garden Festival. She is a former board member of the San Diego Horticultural Society and also coordinates a 5,000 square foot school garden. Her education includes a Bachelor's degree in botany from Duke University and a Master's in biology from UC Santa Barbara. She was trained in organic gardening methods and sustainable horticulture at the Integral Urban House of the Farallones Institute in Berkeley, California. Sterman has served as a Master Composter and Master Gardener as well.

Nan Sterman lives with her husband (the garden Sherpa), teenage son and daughter (both budding gardeners) in Olivenhain, a community in the city of Encinitas in northern San Diego County.

We understand that gardening in Santa Barbara is different than in La Jolla or Riverside.

introducing...

GARDENING WHERE YOU LIVE